Essays in
CONTEMPORARY
ECONOMIC
PROBLEMS

Essays in CONTEMPORARY ECONOMIC PROBLEMS Demand, Productivity, and Population

William Fellner, Project Director

American Enterprise Institute
Washington and London

ISBN 0-8447-1341-4 clothbound edition
ISBN 0-8447-1340-6 paperback edition

ISSN 0149-9130

CONTENTS

PART TWO

PRODUCTVITY AND SUPPLY: INTERNATIONAL COMPARISONS

PART THREE

DEMOGRAPHIC PROBLEMS

PREFACE

I believe that the subtitle and the three part titles give a fair description of the content of this volume, which is the sixth in our annual series. My study on gold is the only item that was not prepared specifically for this series but is included here with minor adjustments. As in the previous years, the participants in this project held several meetings during the year, and we all benefited from each others' comments. Controversial value judgments, however, should be attributed to the individual authors alone.

W. F.

Part
One

Demand Restraint
and Statistical Ambiguities
in an Inflationary Era

On the Merits of Gradualism and on a Fall-back Position If It Should Nevertheless Fail: Introductory Remarks

William Fellner

Summary

This brief paper is an elaboration on a theme touched upon in my introductory remarks to the 1980 volume of this series. I do not take a defeatist attitude toward gradualism with perceptible speed—that is, to consistent and gradual disinflation that takes account of what I have suggested calling the "credibility effect"—yet I continue to believe that economists should concern themselves also with the essentials of the process on which it would be advisable to rely if gradualism should fail. In that event full disinflation in one step would be the appropriate policy, and I am raising here the question of the nature of shock-reducers by which such a policy could be supplemented. The analysis distinguishes between three regions which the inflation rates may have reached by the time disinflation receives serious consideration.

In the final section of these remarks the position is taken that within the foreseeable future, no variety of gold-standard systems will be a viable element of a policy package aimed at restoring practically noninflationary conditions. In my appraisal the unavailability at present of this time-honored device will make the elimination of inflation more difficult, but it should not make the task unattainable. As for the longer-term future, I suggest keeping an open mind on the possible role of gold in the currency system of a group of countries. The argument behind my views on gold is developed in greater detail in the last chapter of Part One of the present volume.

Why Thought Should Be Given to a Fall-back Position

In various earlier writings I expressed the conviction that in the United States a consistent anti-inflationary policy that acquires sufficient credibility for conditioning price expectations and thus for modifying cost trends has a very good chance of success. A consistent disinflationary policy of this sort, when combined with incentive-strengthening adjustments of our tax structure, would still have a very good chance of restoring practical price stability at normal resource utilization levels within a period of roughly four years. Or, somewhat more loosely expressed, a policy of gradualism in this sense would still have a very good prospect of achieving its desired results after an adjustment period of a duration similar to that of a typical business cycle. In order not to lose credibility such a policy would have to reduce the annual increase of the money GNP to the neighborhood of 5 percent within approximately the time described above. In the recent past we have had oscillations of the inflation rate, during which the rate temporarily declined to the neighborhood of 5 percent before shooting up again into the two-digit range, but such oscillations merely add to the uncertainties of the economic environment. A credible policy of gradualism would have to eliminate inflation within a very limited period, and its progress must be perceptible.

The significance of what in earlier writings I suggested calling the credibility effect of a consistent policy is borne out by experience, and so is the validity of the proposition that sporadic demand-policy restraint, which is expected soon to be reversed even at high inflation rates, has very little cost-moderating effect. The conviction that we need a policy of consistent gradualism, carried out with perceptible speed, underlies also much of Phillip Cagan's analysis in the following chapter; and I share this conviction. Yet after the antecedents through which we have lived, there is inevitably enough uncertainty about the authorities' ability to acquire the credibility needed for a successful gradualist program to justify a professional interest in methods available if gradualism should fail, that is, if we should have to turn to sudden disinflation in one step to get rid of the disorder and the inefficiencies created by our inflationary process.

As for the February and March 1981 proposals of the Reagan administration,[1] it is uncertain as yet whether the implied scenario will qualify by the standards of gradualism with sufficient speed. On the one hand, the scenario describes a distinctly inflationary 9.6 percent rate of increase of the money GNP even as of four years from now; yet, on the other hand, it describes a course for monetary policy that is more compatible with reducing the nominal GNP expansion rate by that time to the neighborhood of the practically

---

[1] These are described in *A Program for Economic Recovery* (February 18, 1981) and in *Fiscal Year 1982 Budget Revisions* (March 10, 1981).

4

noninflationary level of about 5 percent than with keeping it close to 10 percent.[2] Gradualism would have a much better prospect for success if the nominal expansion rate were in fact reduced to the level suggested by the monetary-policy proposals included in the scenario. Such a policy would have a much better prospect of squeezing out the inflation component of nominal demand than would the course predicted for the money GNP, and thereby a better prospect of making the cyclical recovery of the early 1980s more durable. To the pronouncements of the Federal Reserve in this regard I will return.

The interplay of political forces along the gradualist route is unpredictable, and there continues to be reason to consider the possibility that the workings of the political process may not produce any period of, say, four to five years during which the authorities could be credibly consistent in completing such a program and that at some stage the process might nevertheless produce a very brief span in which disinflation could be brought about abruptly. In the introductory remarks to the 1980 volume of this series, I commented on the need to develop an alternative to gradualism, and I am here returning to this theme. I will limit myself to what I regard as the essentials; details could result only from the effort of a group of experts.

One reason why the implications of a fall-back position involving a deliberate strategy of abrupt disinflation might acquire practical significance is that forecasts of the relationship between the policy variables, on the one hand, and demand creation, on the other, are particularly subject to error when the policy regime changes. This is true, for example, during a period of transition from an inflationary to a noninflationary regime, when market expectations are not yet conditioned to the latter. During that phase the question which way the policy makers are "playing safe" acquires substantial importance. They may, of course, prove lucky in which case this dilemma would turn out to be of no decisive significance. But the fact remains that playing safe in the direction of the *avoidance* of abruptness implies the risk of not achieving the desired disinflation along the gradualist route and of losing the credibility required for making the cost trends gradually adjust to a noninflationary course. At the same time, playing safe in the other direction—in that of anti-inflationary restraint— implies the risk of an *unintended* adoption of the technique of abruptness. Unintentionally adopting a disinflationary policy in one big step would have the disadvantage not only of leaving the markets in uncertainty about the next policy moves, but also of precluding the

[2] This course of monetary policy is described in the first of the two documents referred to in the preceding footnote.

use of shock-reducing measures that could greatly improve the results obtainable by sudden and full disinflation. If the strategy of abrupt full disinflation is to be adopted, it should be done deliberately.

The pronouncements of the Federal Reserve leave much room for playing safe one way or the other. According to these pronouncements a one-half of 1 percent reduction of the targets for the increase of specific money aggregates is planned year after year. But because the width of the target ranges is 2.5 to 3 percent (depending on the aggregate) *and* because adjustments will be made for the increase in the demand for money in the narrower sense resulting from the spread of interest payments on checkable bank deposits, the question which way the authorities will be leaning remains wide open.

It will, I think, become clear from the reasoning I will develop that gradualism with perceptible speed would have the significant merit of avoiding the complications that would be necessary to face if policy makers attempted to move in one big step to creating merely the demand needed for a normal activity level with a practically horizontal price trend. The strategy of the one big step would have, however, the advantage of enabling the authorities to play safe in the direction of removing inflation and of coupling the approach with shock-reducing adjustments.

In the present stage of our inflationary process a strong case could be made for applying shock reducers in the event of sudden disinflation in one step because there exists a large volume of long-run payment commitments that have been accepted in the expectation of continued significant inflation. The reason why expectations of continued inflation at a significant rate pose a major problem is that these expectations are surrounded by quite a bit of uncertainty, and they do not remain stable. If firm expectations of some specific inflation rate did remain stable, it would be possible to gear the economy to an "inflationary equilibrium," with the welfare loss essentially limited to the equivalent of a tax on holding bank notes and coins. Yet it is impossible to achieve this result because once the public has adapted to some prevailing inflation rate, that rate ceases to provide a stimulus, and the same short-run considerations oriented to a Phillips-curve trade-off that have led to the accommodation of inflation in the first place then require accommodating a steepening of the inflationary process. This tendency toward steepening will soon get out of hand, however, unless its accommodation is occasionally interrupted, and thus an environment of substantial uncertainty and inefficiency is created.

The promise to stabilize an appreciable inflation rate, or merely to moderate it slightly and slowly, lacks the needed credibility for good reasons. Authorities now reluctant to face the anti-inflationary adjustment difficulties cannot induce the public to act on the assumption that they will lose this reluctance—and face the even greater difficulties of adopting anti-inflationary policies—at any higher inflation rate to be observed in future rounds. The vagueness of inflation expectations in an environment in which the process tends to steepen with occasional interruptions of the willingness to accommodate it, and thus with quite a bit of zig-zagging, is the reason why the restoration of our economic efficiency requires getting rid of inflation. Yet it is nevertheless true that as long as the process is at a stage such as that of the present American inflation, there is such a thing as a "typically" expected inflation rate, or of a narrow range of such rates, for the coming few years. At present a yearly rate in the neighborhood of 10 percent may be viewed as representing typical expectations, even if considerable uncertainty accompanies that expectation. In any event, 10 percent is the rate I will use for illustration at the present writing.

Payment obligations implying continued inflation at some such rate would, of course, prove very damaging to the parties committed to these payments if demand creation were suddenly reduced to the rate at which a normal level of activity could be maintained only with the price level held practically constant. These large damages would spread to other parts of the population. The sellers of goods would have a choice among two reactions and various combinations of these two reactions. They could keep their prices unchanged despite the cost increases, or they could charge rising prices in line with their rising costs, but in this case at very sharply reduced activity levels. In fact, they would balance these two methods of reacting to a sudden large demand insufficiency in relation to the output they had planned at the costs they have incurred, and the results would be very harmful. This is the reason why an abrupt restoration of nominal (current-dollar) demand to the level corresponding to noninflationary demand management would establish a strong case for shock reducers.

These remarks relate to the damage which sudden full disinflation would inflict on parties that have entered into long-run payment commitments. The damage already done to those *creditors* who made long-term loans some time ago at low nominal rates of interest belongs in a different category. These creditors suffer damage not as a result of any shift to anti-inflationary policy but, on the contrary, as a result of the inflation that has taken place since the time when they made the loans. In cases where stabilization came after a phase of runaway inflation, giving such creditors at least a small compensation for the practically complete loss of the real value of their assets was usually considered a requirement of fairness, but whenever such compensations were given they were small. In the neighborhood of the present American inflation rate this is not a problem I would suggest placing on the policy agenda. In the circumstances now prevailing in the United States, what matters for our analysis is the need to face the problems which, in the event of sudden full disinflation, would arise as a result of longer-run payment obligations that would become burdensome enough to cause serious dislocations because they were accepted in the expectation of continuing significant inflation. I will briefly describe here one of the possible lines of approach to the problem of shock reducers, not meaning to imply that other lines of approach lack merit. The problem itself deserves the attention of many economists, though so far it has received little attention.

In the preceding pages the reasoning has implied inflation rates such as those now prevailing in the United States, and in the next section I will continue to keep these conditions in mind. Later in my analysis I will, however, suggest that a more general appraisal of the outlook under sudden disinflation requires distinguishing *three stages* into which the inflationary process may have moved at the time of the policy shift—two stages in addition to our present one. This is a crude distinction which I believe to be fruitful in a first approximation. An analysis of finer details would require going beyond this threefold distinction.

The Problem of Shock Reducers in Ranges of Inflation Such as Ours

At these stages of inflation, making all long-term debts callable by the borrower—making them all similar in this regard to mortgages that can be repaid without significant penalties and similar also to many bonds that are callable by contract—would go a long way toward eliminating the harm that abrupt disinflation would do to debtors whose high nominal interest-rate commitments would otherwise change into equally high real-rate commitments. Bankruptcies of such debtors would, of course, hurt their creditors as well. Whether legislation establishing generalized callability should in such circumstances contain exceptions for debts involving interest-rate obligations that are automatically adjustable to changing market rates of interest is not a question I will consider in this discussion. This is a gray area. A gray area exists also as a result of contracts involving future deliveries and payments. Gray areas can never be covered with perfect consistency, and I will not try my hand at describing available compromises. Generalized callability should, however, in any event be limited to the phase of development in which abrupt disinflation is carried out. It would have to be subject to a deadline.

From debt obligations I now turn to wage agreements, which pose a more involved problem. The two problems overlap in one essential respect, in that under a policy of sudden full disinflation it would be desirable to ensure renegotiation of wage contracts, and this is analogous to the callability of debt obligations. What is not analogous is that if a debt is repaid by a borrower when market rates have become lower, he can turn to other creditors in a large market, while employers would often have to renegotiate their contracts with the same workers' representatives. It might turn out that the latter do not have the needed incentives to renegotiate contracts unless legislation were passed that prescribed the adjusted terms consistent with the new policy regime *in cases in which the parties fail to agree on the adjustments.* Such legislation, if needed, should in any event avoid introducing the rigidities of mandatory control schemes and/or the difficulties of administering tax-subsidy schemes, which none of the so-called incomes-policy proposals succeed in avoiding. Let us now first consider the contract adjustments suitable to the requirements of sudden full disinflation and then take a look at the legislative aspects that the problem may have in the absence of renegotiation.

In the event of abrupt disinflation at the present stage of our inflationary process, or at similar stages, it would be desirable to provide a strong incentive for renegotiating individual wage contracts now in force in such a way that after the reduction of the presently presumed inflation rate—its reduction, one would hope, from the presently presumed level of, say, 10 percent to a near-zero level— the contract should yield the same *real* increase which it is presently presumed to yield. This would involve for each contract *specifying the presently presumed real-wage change as a change in money-wage rates and adding a full cost-of-living adjustment (COLA) based on as short an indexation lag as is technically feasible.* The length of the lag between the increase in the price level and the wage payments for which a COLA compensates is normally the same as the length of the subsequent period during which the so-computed COLA is paid to the worker. The quarterly proportion (or the proportion computed for an even shorter period) of, say, a 10 percent annual inflation rate initially prevailing is small enough to justify the belief that in an environment of significantly tightened demand-management policy, the sellers of goods would typically *absorb*, rather than pass through, all or most of the carry-over of the initial inflation on

9

their current wage costs. At present the quarterly (or shorter period) installment of our yearly inflation rate would be somewhere in the range between 2 and 3 percent. *Under a policy playing safe on tightness,* absorption of much of such a cost increase by the employers over an equally short period is the likely outcome, and from there on deceleration would be rapid. Hence, no further carry-over effects would develop that would perpetuate the inflation.

As was said above, however, it should not be taken for granted that a sufficiently strong incentive for renegotiation along these lines could be created without legislation providing that in the absence of renegotiation the change is made compulsory. A strong incentive *might* exist in any event because in most cases the workers would receive a guarantee of at least somewhat rising real wage rates for the duration of the contracts in question—a guarantee they now do not have—and the employers would be spared the unintended very steep increase of real wage costs, with which they would be faced if sudden full disinflation were in prospect. Although the incentive to renegotiate might be strong in any event, the possibility cannot be excluded that putting into effect the new policy regime would require having legislated adjustments "in the background" for cases in which renegotiation would not take place.

It would be desirable—in my appraisal even essential—to limit any such legislation to the contracts in effect at the time the sudden full disinflating move is undertaken, that is, *not to force or even to encourage further indexation once the disinflation has been successfully carried out.* The indexation of payment obligations is helpful only when inflation is being reduced or eliminated; thereafter it can have very undesirable consequences in the event of otherwise temporary upward deviations from price-level stability, since it tends to magnify such upward deviations. There does exist the unwelcome possibility that spontaneous indexation would survive on a major scale after the phase in which indexation would be prescribed by legislation in the absence of renegotiation. But this is an unlikely spontaneous development, since in periods of reasonable price-level stability indexation was not a widely adopted practice.

Legislation of the sort here described would inevitably involve two elements of arbitrariness, yet these elements could presumably be reduced to minor size or at least to a size that may be considered tolerable. One inevitable element of arbitrariness would enter here because, in the absence of renegotiation, a general assumption would have to be incorporated into the legislatively prescribed change as to what inflation rate is implied by the contracting parties at the time of the legislation. This assumption would determine the interpretation of the "presently" presumed content of a contract in terms of real wages. To illustrate, recent major collective bargaining agreements[3] not including a COLA provision stipulate on the average a 10.4 percent annual increase of wage rates over the duration of the contract. On the somewhat arbitrary but reasonable assumption that a 10 percent annual inflation rate is at present implied by the contracting parties, an individual contract that happens to have the properties of the average contract would be changed in such a way as to involve, in the absence of renegotiation, a 0.4 percent average yearly increase plus full compensation for inflation with a short lag from the observed price increase to the wage payment.

Where the contract does include a COLA provision—recently obtained by 61 percent of the workers under major collective bargaining agreements—a second element of arbitrariness would be inevitable in the absence of renegotiation. This relates to the proportion of the price increase for which the COLA provides compensation. Yet in all cases in which the agreement in question is not entirely new—that is, already has a history even if this may as yet be short—the experience of the recent past with the contract could presumably be projected to obtain an estimate of the proportion of price increase for which the contract compensates the workers. To illustrate again with recent average results, the COLA provisions have provided compensation for 58 percent of the CPI increases; and in recent contracts, in addition to the COLA itself, workers obtained a 5.0 percent annual increase over the duration of their contracts (typically three-year contracts). On the assumption of 10 percent inflation, the workers in question would receive a 1.0 percent annual real increase.[4] Yet at zero inflation these workers would obtain a 5.0 percent average yearly real-wage increase, and such a real increase is clearly not intended by the contracting parties. In the absence of renegotiation a contract with these properties would therefore be changed legislatively to stipulate a 1.0 percent average annual increase, plus full compensation for inflation, with the shortest technically feasible lag from an observed price increase to the payment that includes an allowance for it.

The allowance for inflation, which the adjustments here discussed include, would inevitably involve lags and thus would inevitably involve some amount of carry-over of the *initially* observed

---

[3] These are the contracts signed in 1980.

[4] Given that 58 percent of 10 percent is 5.8 percent, these workers would receive a nominal increase of 1.05 times 1.058. The resulting 11.1 percent would have to be deflated by the assumed 10 percent inflation to obtain the increase in the real wage rate. This yields 1.0 percent.

price increases on subsequent cost. This inevitability makes it crucial for the approach here outlined to face a carry-over problem moving from past price increases to subsequent cost increases, with emphasis on the need to keep the lags very short. With a full yearly lag, even a 10 percent initial annual inflation rate would be too high to justify the assumption that, under a tight policy, the cost increase, extending in that case over a subsequent full year, would be absorbed by the sellers, rather than largely passed through at the expense of the sales volume. There is obviously a large difference between absorbing, under a tight policy, a 2 to 3 percent increase in wage costs for a quarter and absorbing a 10 percent increase for a year; or, alternatively expressed, there is a big difference between the degree of policy tightness that will accomplish these two results. To the extent that the cost-raising effect of the initially prevailing inflation is not soon absorbed by the sellers, the initial inflation will become built into a sequence of periods.

The reason why the lag problem plays such an essential role in this analysis is that strictly simultaneous price increases are largely determined by the indexed transactions themselves—hence, are not "given" at the time the payments are made—and to index on the basis of estimated (rather than observed) price increases of a period is a procedure that violates an essential requirement of the shock-softening method here under consideration. Legislation that, in the absence of renegotiation, would simply change a contract stipulating a 10.4 percent wage increase into one stipulating a 0.4 percent price increase and would stipulate no compensation for any future price increase, could not claim to have safeguarded the intended real content of the original contract. To adopt this procedure with the explanation that the authorities merely *estimate* the future price increase at zero would be arbitrary and unconvincing. Hence, any COLA in the sense proper within the domestic currency system inevitably involves lags.

The Changing Properties of the Problem When the Inflation Rate Is Zig-zagging in Higher Ranges

It is essential to realize that at appreciably higher inflation rates than those we now have in the United States, the line of approach here described would cease to achieve its objective. This is the reason why indexation is not the general cure-all that the foregoing presentation might appear to make it, but, on the contrary, can prove to be a very treacherous device.

The reasoning developed in the preceding pages cannot be repeated for the significantly higher inflation rates prevailing in several countries abroad, because at those higher rates, demand policies playing safe in the direction of tightness would not provide sufficient inducement to the sellers of goods for absorbing the quarterly (or even a somewhat shorter period) proportion of the initial annual inflation rate. Assuming that a substantial volume of long-run commitments is adjusted in such a way as to include a "real" component (for zero inflation) *plus* an inflation allowance with a short indexation lag, the effect of past inflation on current costs will, in much higher ranges of inflation, express itself not as a merely temporary carry-over effect on costs—one that becomes absorbed rather promptly—but as a *continuing* carry-over effect of past on subsequent inflation. In such circumstances indexation, even with very short lags, becomes a device perpetuating the inflationary process itself: a one-step reduction of demand-creation to the rate compatible with noninflationary normal activity levels does then not lead promptly to the desired disinflation of prices at approximately normal activity levels, but leads during a period of appreciable duration to significantly subnormal activity combined with continued price increases.

Where this higher range of inflation rates starts is not a question I could even try to answer in a general way. I do suggest that annual rates in the neighborhood of 10 percent, or even somewhat higher rates, are not likely to be subject to this difficulty, because the quarterly (or somewhat shorter-period) installment of these annual rates is small enough to avoid this impasse. A tight policy can in all probability suppress the cost-raising effect of, say, a quarterly 2 to 3 percent initial price increase, in which case the carry-over effect would not survive a brief span. The 100 percent or higher annual inflation rates that Israel, Turkey, and Argentina seem to have at the present writing do, on the other hand, clearly give rise to an inflation-perpetuation difficulty, because indexation lags cannot be made short enough to have the sellers of goods absorb the resulting cost increases instead of passing them through for a reduced sales volume.

Given the high probability that at these much higher inflation rates the indexation of contracts involving future payments will lead to a sustained carry-over of past inflation, indexation is likely to create an environment in which short-run oriented policy makers are tempted to generate the usual inflationary stimulus by steepening the inflation rate in order to "beat" the cost carry-over. If this is not to result in runaway inflation, the steepening must occasionally be interrupted and turned into temporary deceleration. The result is the same kind of zig-zagging of *upward tending but not continuously rising inflation rates* that we have come to know from our own experience, with the same kind of uncertainty developing in the markets. The difference is that in such circumstances the inflation rates around which this zig-zagging takes place are much higher.

There does exist a device by which the difficulties arising from indexation in these higher regions of inflation could in some cases be circumvented, and sudden disinflation could be carried out from these inflation levels without major and lasting shocks. But this is a device about which not much optimism can be expressed in the ranges with which we are concerned in the present section, in contrast to the ranges to be considered in the next section. The device consists of tying payment obligations to the *simultaneous* free-market exchange rate of a *foreign* currency such as is managed in an essentially non-inflationary way.

In the present American circumstances this device is obviously not available, and even in the higher inflation ranges we are considering in the present section, the applicability of the device is reduced by at least two circumstances. One of these is that, unless private contracts stipulate such spontaneous tying of payment obligations to a foreign currency, it is not easy to envisage a sovereign government enforcing terms that essentially raise a foreign currency to the official standard of value. The other circumstance reducing the applicability of this solution is that the movements of no foreign currency rate can be expected to serve as near-perfect proxies for domestic price-level movements. In the short run the relationship between currency rates and the domestic price level—essentially the purchasing power parity relationship—is apt to be very imperfect. This proxy relation would improve if valuation in a foreign currency were imposed on all parties entering into longer-run commitments, but it would still remain far from perfect.

Hence, the conditions existing in high-inflation economies with indexed long-term contracts, and with the inflation rate zig-zagging in high regions, may be particularly difficult to improve by sudden full disinflation supplemented by shock-reducing adjustments of contracts. In actual fact, in these regions of inflation rates, indexation within the domestic currency system itself is quite common, but it does not play into the hands of policy makers attempting to stabilize the price level. In these circumstances indexation does make the inflationary process somewhat less damaging than it would be if no part of the allowance for the ongoing rate of inflation were institutionalized. But this is a mixed blessing because a harmful process is thereby made politically somewhat more acceptable by a method that institutionalizes merely part of the allowance for an unstable inflation rate which it tends to *perpetuate*. In view of the indexation lags the proportion of the ongoing inflation for which indexation institutionalizes an allowance depends on the degree of stability or instability of the rate. The same tends to be true if the arbitrary device of indexing on the basis of an officially announced *expected* inflation rate is adopted.

"Runaway" Inflation

The conditions considered in the preceding pages change basically if the process moves into even higher regions in which inflation is steepening almost without interruption. These are the regions of what is usually described as runaway inflation or hyperinflation. In these circumstances indexation within the domestic currency system institutionalizes merely a negligible allowance for the ongoing inflation. That device comes to be generally recognized as being essentially worthless. In this kind of environment barter is spreading for "spot" transactions, and longer-term private commitments usually tend to become tied *spontaneously* (without any government intervention) to the simultaneous exchange rate of a foreign currency. The fact that movements of exchange rates may prove to be imperfect proxies for domestic price movements ceases to weigh heavily in comparison with the disorder caused by hyperinflation. Furthermore, in the most important cases of twentieth-century hyperinflation the relevant foreign currency was the dollar, and the dollar had in those cases an institutionally fixed equivalent in gold. When currency stabilization took place in the countries that had suffered hyperinflation, the value of their currency came to be fixed in dollars or in gold (which meant the same).

When inflation reaches the "runaway" stage, the economies experiencing it are severely hurt by the inefficiencies that the monetary disorder causes. The damages include the reduction to the neighborhood of zero of the real value of the assets of creditors who at an earlier stage had made loans at nominal interest rates amounting to a negligible proportion of the subsequent inflation. As was said above, however, these damages belong among those inflicted by the inflationary process itself, and they do not represent costs of the adjustment taking place when the price level is finally stabilized.

A demand policy determined to restore price stability after a period of hyperinflation is no longer faced to any major extent with long-run commitments carrying over the past price increases on subsequent costs and on subsequent prices. But the reason here differs essentially from that explaining why in an inflation range such as ours the carry-over difficulty caused by cost-of-living allowances with short lags could be reduced to minor significance by a tight demand policy. In the regions of runaway inflation the reason is that here the public almost wholly avoids entering into longer-run payment commitments in domestic currency, and the tying of longer-range payment commitments to foreign exchange rates, which takes place spontaneously, *can* be made lagless and hence need involve no carry-over effect. As for interest rates, debt obligations tied to the currency rate of another country are issued at the interest rates appropriate to loans denominated in the foreign currency in question, not the very high nominal rates at which loans denominated in the domestic currency would be made available.

The problems relevant to our present environment are those that were discussed in the first and second sections. The problems discussed in the third and fourth sections relate to higher ranges of inflation, but I believe that an understanding of the nature of the inflation problem at large requires at least a brief analysis of how the characteristics of various difficulties change as we move from one region to the next.

There exists also a substantial difference between the main reasons that have induced authorities to generate the high inflation rates described in the present section and the reasons that have led to lower-range inflations such as are plaguing us now. The intermediate ranges may typically be intermediate with respect to these reasons as well. Inflation in ranges such as ours has been generated mainly with the motivation to achieve high employment and output in the immediate future, disregarding the painful aftermath of such policies. The "hidden tax" (or its equivalent) resulting from the government's ability to acquire resources by borrowing directly or indirectly from the central bank, rather than through explicit taxation, has merely played a subsidiary role in most of these cases, and the same is true of the government's "inflation dividend," which it obtains through the inflationary bracket creep and through inflationary distortions of corporate taxation. Runaway inflations, unlike the lower-range inflations, have so far mostly developed after lost wars when the tax-collection system has very nearly collapsed and when governments were motivated *mainly* by the need to resort to the "hidden taxation" resulting from their ability to acquire resources by borrowing from the central bank.

Observations on the Role of Gold

In most cases of successful stabilization after major inflationary interludes, the "return to gold" played an essential role in establishing the credibility of the policy shift. As I explain in the last chapter of Part One of the present volume, I feel convinced that in a future now

16

foreseeable enough to be relevant to policy planning, restoration of a gold-based currency system as part of a noninflationary policy package will not be an option available to any group of nations. At the same time I feel convinced that this makes a return to noninflationary policies more difficult, though, in spite of the greater difficulty, it is imperative to accomplish this objective if the efficiency of Western market economies is to be regained. The more distant future of gold in the monetary system poses questions on which I suggest keeping an open mind, because the answers to these depend on factors that are at present unpredictable.

The proposition that tying currencies to a single commodity is irrational is not in itself convincing because whatever irrationality may be involved in such an arrangement needs to be compared with the irrationalities of the political processes under systems of "fiat money" (inconvertible paper currency). The basic question is whether, in the circumstances which we are considering, gold can be made to serve as a reasonably adequate proxy for goods in general, that is, whether the trend of the real price (relative price) of gold would remain close to horizontal and reasonably predictable. In circumstances in which this *is* the case, but only in those circumstances, the gold standard has the advantage that the prescription to use a stockpile of the authorities for keeping constant the price of the proxy (as which gold serves in this case) is much simpler and more straightforward than is the prescription to keep the general price level stable with inconvertible paper money. There is clearly a difference between bending or even essentially disregarding the content of such general prescriptions and defaulting on the obligation to enable the public to acquire gold at a given price.

In the last chapter in Part One, I will suggest an explanation of the reasons why, in a preceding historical era, systems falling in the gold-standard category could serve adequately as elements of a reasonably noninflationary policy package. Even that era included severely disturbed subperiods, but, insofar as the occurrence of these subperiods had to do with the gold standard itself, it is possible to make a fairly convincing argument in retrospect about the inadequate management of that system during those spans. It is possible also to identify the main reasons why under the present conditions no variety of the gold standard could perform the useful function which that system did perform in a past era and which it could have performed even better if specific mistakes had been avoided. It would be idle to speculate about whether these obstacles are or are not here to stay in the long run, and it seems unreasonable to me to resume the Treasury's gold sales amid these uncertainties.

Conclusions

1. The unavailability *in the now foreseeable future* of the time-honored method of coupling the restoration of price-level stability with a return to gold makes the task we are facing more difficult. The present unavailability of this method has resulted not from mere "prejudice" against gold, which also exists and is unhelpful, but from a change in the basic supply-demand relations in the gold market. The present task is to achieve a close approximation to price-level stability in spite of the greater difficulty caused by the unavailability, at least for the time being, of a method that played a major role in many past currency stabilizations after inflationary interludes. The task needs to be achieved by combining demand restraint with incentive-strengthening measures. Achieving this task is a vitally important requirement of putting an end to the uncertainties and the inefficiencies that have developed in the American economy.

2. Priority deserves to be given to achieving the objective by credible gradualism with perceptible speed. As concerns demand restraint, however, it may possibly turn out that the authorities are incapable of the tightrope walk required for erring *neither* in the direction of undue slowness, thereby losing credibility, *nor* in the direction of unintended abruptness of disinflation. This is a possibility for which we should be prepared. In that case *intentional* full disinflation in one big step would be far preferable to allowing the present inflationary disorder to continue. The latter strategy directs attention to desirable shock-softening measures for reducing the maladjustments which an abrupt procedure could otherwise create.

3. The main reason why the possible need for full and sudden disinflation directs attention to shock-softening measures is that the nominal (current-dollar) content of long-run payment obligations would turn out to be far out of line with their intended content in terms of real costs. It would then be clearly desirable to establish a much better approximation to the intended "real" content of contracts. This raises the question of adjusting in these circumstances the nominal content of contractual obligations by methods such as those outlined in the preceding pages, though alternative methods no doubt also deserve exploration. But the problem to which I am returning in this final paragraph would acquire timeliness only if what I have described as gradualism with perceptible speed should fail. For the time being, giving that method a fair chance—a better chance than it has been given so far—deserves to be regarded as the first item on the agenda.

Two Pitfalls in the Conduct of Anti-inflationary Monetary Policy

Phillip Cagan

Summary

A policy of gradually reducing inflation by monetary restraint is strongly supported by the new administration and is being pursued by the Federal Reserve. Yet many people remain skeptical that it can and will be carried through. A substantial reduction in inflation is thought to take more time than a presidential term, and in the meantime various supply shocks may arise to add to inflationary pressures. The skepticism reflects the repeated failures of monetary restraint over the past decade and a half to arrest inflation, which in each case ended with a further escalation of inflation. The present low credibility of monetary policy hardens the expectations of inflation, which increases the difficulty of reducing it and reinforces the skepticism.

A reduction of inflation through persistent monetary restraint is not viewed as impossible, however, and the chances of success can be improved by avoiding past mistakes. A repeated mistake was to allow cyclical expansions to overheat the economy and reignite inflationary pressures. Monetary policy relaxed restraint when it was still needed. The reasons for this can be traced to misinterpretations of cyclical fluctuations in the inflation rate and in interest rates, the two pitfalls discussed in this essay.

The first pitfall is the misinterpretation of declines in the inflation rate during business recessions. Most of these declines occur in market-sensitive prices that recover rapidly when business revives and are a misleading indicator of progress in curbing inflation. Lasting reductions in inflation require that the upward trend in wages and other insensitive prices be restrained, and this takes longer than the span of a business recession. A lasting reduction is indicated by a rate lower than the rate in the corresponding stage of the previous business cycle. Another indication is a reduction in the rate of increase in unit costs of production of finished goods—often considered the "underlying" rate of inflation.

The second pitfall is the misinterpretation of interest-rate movements. Interest rates have long served as a guide to the conduct of monetary policy. Although their role was downgraded in the new operating procedure announced in October 1979, they are not likely to be disregarded completely. Interest rates are considered useful to the Federal Reserve in achieving its monetary targets and in alleviating disturbances in financial markets. But, in an inflationary environment, movements in interest rates are extremely difficult to interpret.

It used to be taken for granted that short-run changes in monetary growth affected interest rates inversely, in reflection of a tightening or an easing of financial markets. In the past few years, however, financial markets have been interpreted as reflecting a relationship in which changes in monetary growth affect interest rates positively through changes in expectations of inflation. This is attributed to the so-called Fisher effect of inflation, whereby interest rates rise to compensate for the expected decline in purchasing power of fixed-dollar loans. This effect was once thought to occur over the very long run, but lately it is given as the explanation for short-run movements. The sharp swings in interest rates during 1980, for example, are attributed to changes in inflationary expectations.

An examination of past episodes of financial stringency suggests that inflationary expectations cannot be the explanation for the sharp increases in short-term rates that occurred at such times. Expectations of a coming rise in the inflation rate could lead to speculation in bonds, raising their yields, but could not affect demands and supplies for short-term credit so quickly. Hence such expectations would increase the differential of bond yields over short-term interest rates. Yet stringencies are characterized by a narrowing of this differential, indicative of a temporary tightening of credit.

In the late 1960s rising interest rates resulting from inflation were incorrectly attributed to monetary tightness. Now the opposite mistake is made of attributing every movement in interest rates to inflationary expectations. Expectations nevertheless appear to have played a greater role in 1979–1980 than formerly and may continue to do so. The usefulness of interest rates as indicators of financial developments is severely reduced by inflation, therefore, because it is difficult to determine the extent to which an increase reflects either monetary tightness or inflationary expectations—and such a distinction is crucial to the use of interest rates as a guide for policy.

Because of the long lag between a reduction in monetary growth and its effect on the inflation rate, a monetary policy of reducing inflation gradually is particularly vulnerable to mistakes of implementation. In addition, the inflationary environment itself creates a greater potential for error in the control of monetary growth and in the prediction of monetary effects on the economy. These difficulties make a gradualist policy less credible, which itself increases the difficulty of success. Credibility in a gradualist policy will be restored as developments indicate that progress is being made and that the pitfalls and other difficulties are being overcome.

Introduction

For many years after World War II the phenomenon first identified as creeping inflation, then later as persistent and recently as escalating inflation, brought forth endless discussions of its cause and cure. It was questioned whether excessive growth in the money supply was the major cause and whether monetary restraint was a cure. Price and wage controls, guidelines, and "jawboning" were proposed and tested. Economists researched all these questions and more. Few of the issues were ever completely settled, but monetary restraint is now generally recognized as essential to any cure, and less is heard of other causes and cures. The discussion has shifted to the implementation of monetary restraint, in the light of repeated failures to carry it through. In the place of causes and cures the outpourings on inflation now address the obstacles to ending it. These are varied and are sometimes viewed as being sociological or philosophical, though all are often lumped together as different manifestations of a basic lack of political consensus to incur the expected costs of ending inflation. Political consensus is certainly important, but whether it is lacking is itself a subject of controversy.

There are, however, other less controversial obstacles that can be avoided or that may with difficulty be overcome, if we can learn from past mistakes. Two obstacles in particular, which have been major pitfalls in the past conduct of policy, are singled out in this essay. These are the misinterpretations first of cyclical fluctuations in the inflation rate, which have led to overstimulations of business recoveries and the escalation of inflation, and second of movements in interest rates in an inflationary environment, which have made them a less reliable guide to the conduct of monetary policy.

The nature and past history of these two pitfalls are discussed in the two main sections of this essay. A final section puts these two pitfalls in the context of the tribulations encountered by monetary

21

policy in the attempts to reduce inflation over the past decade, particularly the self-reinforcing effects of low credibility.

Cyclical versus Sustainable Declines in Inflation

The most widely discussed obstacle to ending inflation is the expected large costs of protracted economic slack and unemployment. The present inflation, which began in the mid-1960s and has lasted for a decade and a half despite four major attempts to stop it,[1] has become highly resistant to mild and brief periods of monetary restraint. The experience in this country and abroad confirms that such persistent inflation can be eradicated only by an equally persistent policy of monetary restraint that is maintained through all stages of the business cycle. Past attempts to reduce the present U.S. inflation each began by precipitating a business contraction, but stimulative policies were then introduced to alleviate the resulting unemployment and allowed the ensuing business expansion to become excessive. The result was another resurgence of inflationary pressures that made the inflation more entrenched than before.

Cyclical Behavior of the Inflation Rate. In these past failures to end inflation, policy makers made mistakes in timing because they misinterpreted cyclical declines in the inflation rate. The economic slack of a business contraction has different effects on the various subgroups of prices. Fluctuations in basic commodity prices and other market-sensitive prices correspond to concurrent changes in business conditions and account for most of the cyclical fluctuation in the overall inflation rate. Many prices and most wages, on the other hand, show little immediate effect of business recessions. Thus the decline in the inflation rate during business recessions mainly reflects temporary weakness in the sensitive prices and is subsequently reversed as the economy recovers. Well before the economy reaches full employment these prices are rising again and soon match or exceed their rates of increase in the previous cycle, which largely eliminates the recession decline in the overall inflation rate.

The inflation rate is sustainably reduced by a recession if the rate is lower during the ensuing business expansion than it was at comparable stages of the previous cycle. This requires that slack markets during reduced levels of business activity affect the prices and

[1] These attempts were the major periods of monetary restraint in 1966, 1969, 1973-1974, and 1980. The monetary restraint of early 1981 can be viewed as the beginning of a fifth attempt.

costs in the economy that determine what is called the underlying rate of inflation. These are most wages and prices of services and manufactured goods, which tend to follow an expected long-run equilibrium path and respond slowly to deviations of demand from the expected path, though most changes in unit costs, even if unanticipated, will be passed through to prices fairly rapidly. Since all prices are subject to industry-specific influences, no one group of them provides a reliable measure of the underlying rate of inflation, which is to be viewed as a theoretical concept best represented by an index of the trend in unit costs of production of finished products.[2] The underlying rate of inflation changes slowly in response to demand pressures and accounts for the difficulty of reducing the overall rate.

The response of different prices to business cycles is illustrated by figure 1. It shows the price behavior of the three components of producer goods—crude materials, intermediate materials, and finished products—before and after business cycle peaks since the early 1950s (seven including the minirecession of 1966–1967). The price index for each component is based on unity for the peak month of the business cycle for ease of reference. Crude materials prices are the most volatile and respond sharply to shifts in demand and supply over the business cycle. These materials are largely traded on commodity exchanges or sold in highly competitive markets. For this reason they respond sharply to downward pressures in the first part of a business contraction and often start declining even some months before it starts. In the inflationary environment after the mid-1960s they followed a steep upward trend but still displayed cyclical fluctuations around the trend.

The price indexes for intermediate materials and finished products show little of the volatility of the crude materials index and far less responsiveness to cycles, though they have tended to decline moderately or rise less rapidly in business contractions. This tendency is weaker but still evident in the 1970s. In the 1973–1975 business contraction their cyclical response is strong but delayed, with little deceleration before October 1974 when industrial production plummeted and with little acceleration in the recovery phase until 1977 (not shown in the figure). Although disparate developments in intermediate materials and finished products caused their price movements to diverge in the cycles before the mid-1960s, their upward trends in the subsequent cycles became more pronounced and less divergent as the general inflation dominated industry-specific developments.

---

[2] See John L. Scadding, "Estimating the Underlying Inflation Rate," Federal Reserve Bank of San Francisco *Economic Review* (spring 1979), pp. 7-18.

FIGURE 1

Components of the Producer Price Index
before and after Business Cycle Peaks, 1953–1979
(peak = 1.00)

— Finished Products   – – Intermediate Materials   ······ Crude Materials

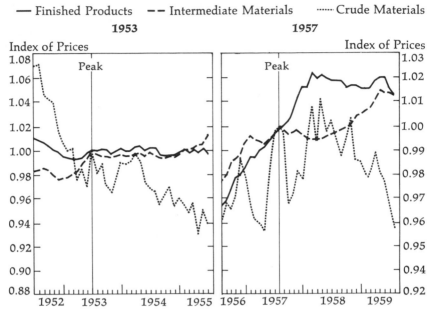

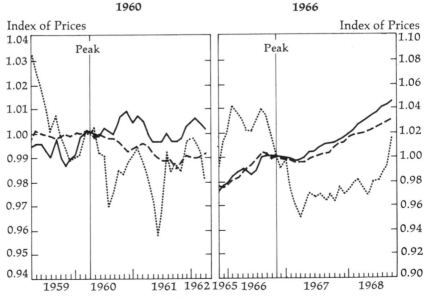

24

FIGURE 1 (continued)

1969

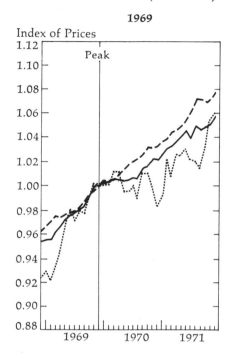

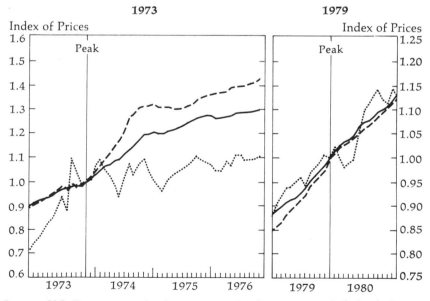

SOURCE: U.S. Department of Labor, Bureau of Labor Statistics, *Wholesale Prices and Price Indexes.*

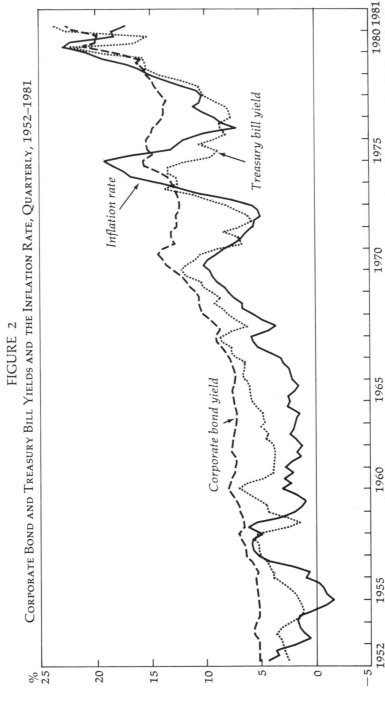

FIGURE 2

CORPORATE BOND AND TREASURY BILL YIELDS AND THE INFLATION RATE, QUARTERLY, 1952–1981

NOTE: Market yields are for Moody's Aa corporate bonds and three-month Treasury bills; the inflation rate is the logarithmic difference at an annual rate in the consumer price index for urban households between the current quarter and the average of the preceding four quarters.

SOURCE: *Federal Reserve Bulletin* and Bureau of Labor Statistics, *Monthly Labor Review.*

26

The consequences of the behavior of these price groups for one measure of the aggregate price level can be seen for the consumer price index (CPI) in figure 2, which covers finished consumer goods and services. The prices of services are generally the least responsive to business cycles. The rate of change of this index conforms to business cycles, though often with a lag because it takes time for fluctuations in more responsive materials prices to work through the price system to final products. After the mid-1960s, however, the cyclical declines in its rate of change did not last long and disappeared in the ensuing business recoveries. The later period lacked a sustained downward pressure on inflation, such as occurred from 1957 to 1960 to usher in the half decade of price stability from 1960 to 1965. Rather, overstimulation of the economy thereafter brought a chronic inflation, which has risen to new highs in each successive business expansion.

The Expected Rate of Inflation. Economic theory provides a simplified but adequate representation of the rate of inflation in terms of two variables, first the amount of excess capacity in the economy and second the *expected* rate of inflation in the near future (which is not likely to deviate much from the concurrent underlying rate of inflation). Excess capacity represents the upward or downward pressures on prices generated when current production exceeds or falls short of normal capacity output. Market-sensitive prices respond quickly to these pressures and account, as noted, for most of the cyclical fluctuation in the inflation rate. Other prices, being much less responsive to the current amount of excess capacity, tend to follow the expected long-run equilibrium path of prices in each industry as indicated by near-term projections of wages and other input costs per unit. Most wages and prices of services and manufactured goods are strongly influenced by these projections when contracts are negotiated between unions and employers or between raw material suppliers and users and when sellers set prices to remain competitive for the period ahead.[3] Fluctuations in demand are absorbed by inventories of storable goods or by the waiting time for services and custom-made products; this helps to avoid the disarray of uncoordinated short-run price changes among the firms in an industry, apart from discounts in times of distress.

[3] For an elaboration of the differences in behavior between market-sensitive and sluggish prices as an explanation of the persistence of inflation, see Arthur M. Okun, "Inflation: Its Mechanics and Welfare Costs," *Brookings Papers on Economic Activity*, no. 2 (1975), pp. 351-90, and Phillip Cagan, "The Reduction of Inflation by Slack Demand," in *Contemporary Economic Problems 1978*, William Fellner, ed. (Washington, D.C.: American Enterprise Institute, 1978), pp. 13-45.

27

The expected long-run equilibrium path of prices aggregated for all industries is represented in economic theory by the second term, the *expected* rate of inflation. It is not known precisely how expectations are determined, since they are not directly observable, but the expected rate presumably adjusts gradually to the actual rate of increase in costs and nominal demand per unit of output and therefore to the actual rate of inflation. The expected rate in turn helps to determine the actual rate in combination with but independent of the amount of excess capacity. The extended view taken in forming expectations explains the persistence of inflation in the face of sharp but temporary increases in excess capacity.

The Reduction of Inflation. A policy of reducing inflation must therefore bring down the expected rate. While cyclical fluctuations in excess capacity produce corresponding cycles in the actual rate of inflation, no lasting reductions in the inflation rate are achieved by symmetrical fluctuations around an unchanged expected rate. An anti-inflationary policy makes progress through sustained downward pressures on the actual rate of inflation via excess capacity. If the actual rate averages less than the expected rate over an extended period of time, the expected rate adjusts downward, which further reduces the actual inflation rate for the same level of excess capacity. The present high rates of inflation are the result of such a process that operated in the upward direction, though with more fluctuation than seems desirable in reversing it.

The cyclical behavior of the inflation rate makes policy vulnerable to the mistake of relaxing anti-inflationary measures prematurely. The mistake was prominent in the very first effort in 1966 to end the present inflation shortly after it began. A short period of monetary restraint was imposed that precipitated a business downturn and brought down the inflation rate with surprising speed—probably because it followed a half decade of relative price stability. This was interpreted as a successful reduction of inflation, allowing policy to stimulate a strong recovery of activity in 1967 supposedly without danger of reviving inflationary pressures. But the stimulus quickly reignited those pressures and the inflation soon reemerged with greater intensity. Policy makers appeared to mistake a temporary dip in the inflation rate for a sustainable reduction.

The same mistake was made following the second attempt to end the inflation in 1969. Monetary restraint again precipitated a business downturn, whereupon policy again shifted to stimulate a business recovery, even though this time no reduction in the inflation rate had yet become evident in the available data. Impatient with the lack of evidence of declining inflation despite weak business conditions, the administration imposed price and wage controls in August 1971. The controls were unfortunately a source of confusion because, by distorting the evidence on price changes, they fostered the misleading impression that the underlying inflation had come down further than in fact was true. Policy makers were lulled into becoming much too stimulative in 1972. This built up an inflationary potential that would have surfaced sooner than it did had it not been temporarily suppressed under the lid of controls. The stimulus also brought the economy to near full employment inopportunely, just as world prices were beginning to surge in grains and metals (and a year later in petroleum).[4] The controls were largely removed in January 1973 when world and domestic markets still seemed calm, but inflationary pressures soon exploded to send prices soaring. Although the imported part of this resurgence of domestic inflation was beyond the control of U.S. policy in 1973 and 1974, the overall resurgence and the contribution of world price increases would have been less if monetary expansion had not prepared the ground by overstimulating the economy during 1972.

Although the inflation rate fell appreciably during and for some months after the 1973–1975 recession, it began rising briskly again in 1977 and climbed back to a double-digit rate by 1979. Although the escalation of inflation in these years of expanding business activity was to be expected, a defeatist attitude took hold that, since the inflation rate comes back quickly when business recovers, little headway can be made against it by restraining economic activity. The administration appeared disheartened and resigned to the high inflation as being beyond its ability to control by traditional methods.

Such a defeatist attitude appears to misinterpret and overreact to the cyclical behavior of the inflation rate. Since declines in the inflation rate in business recessions are reversed when business recovers, this cycle gives the impression that whatever inroads a recession makes against inflation are quickly lost. But, just as temporary declines during recessions are not progress, their disappearance is not failure. Although a recession is often the first effect of imposing restraint, recessions are not crucial. Sustainable progress is made by keeping business expansions under control, thus avoiding the resurgence of inflation that is typical of their later stages.

[4] For further discussion of that episode, see Phillip Cagan, "Monetary Problems and Policy Choices in Reducing Inflation and Unemployment," in *Contemporary Economic Problems 1976*, William Fellner, ed. (Washington, D.C.: American Enterprise Institute, 1976), pp. 17-53, and "Imported Inflation 1973-74 and the Accommodation Issue," *Journal of Money, Credit, and Banking*, vol. 12 (February 1980), pp. 1-16.

The change in operating procedure by the Federal Reserve in October 1979 represented a new effort to prevent excessive monetary growth, as had occurred in 1977–1978. The change was an indication of an enhanced recognition that inflation, if not contained by a more activist policy, would become progressively worse. Given past failures, however, an extra margin of slack in the economy seems necessary to allow for the risk of unexpected inflationary forces. Such a firm policy is admittedly made difficult by the inherent cyclical fluctuations in economic activity and by political pressures to continue stimulating the economy so long as unemployment exists. The main problem, however, is that it takes so long to make sustainable progress. Estimates of the time needed to eliminate most of the present rate of inflation by a moderate policy range from a half to almost a full decade,[5] which requires a policy of perseverance that the political system in this country and most others has been unable to maintain. The time requirement to end inflation is a formidable obstacle that has discouraged policy makers and weakened their resolve.

Credibility and Expectations. The credibility of a policy to end inflation plays a role in the outcome. Credibility influences both of the terms in the theoretical equation of inflation described above—the response of prices to excess capacity and the expectations of inflation. A belief in relative price stability was once strong under the full-fledged gold standard. Under our present monetary system that has no standard and after the failures of anti-inflationary policy, credibility has declined. This increases the difficulty of ending inflation, because the expected rate of inflation adjusts more slowly to periods of restraint when the public believes that they will be reversed later by periods of strong demand.

No one knows how to improve credibility, though obviously some initial success in reducing inflation is crucial. If policy makers avoided past mistakes of overstimulus and convinced the public of their determination to persist in restraint, no doubt expectations would be more supportive, and the process of ending inflation would then proceed more rapidly and with less cost in terms of lower output and unemployment. While policy would have to work against adverse expectations in the beginning, as it began to show progress it could

[5] See George L. Perry, "Slowing the Wage-Price Spiral: The Macroeconomic View," *Brookings Papers on Economic Activity*, no. 2 (1978), pp. 259-91; Arthur M. Okun, "Efficient Disinflationary Policies," *American Economic Review*, vol. 68, no. 2 (May 1978), pp. 348-52; and Robert J. Gordon, "Why Stopping Inflation May Be Costly: Evidence from Fourteen Historical Episodes," National Bureau of Economic Research conference on inflation, Washington, D.C., February 27, 1981.

benefit from their increasing support. This means that estimates of the time and cost to end inflation based on past experience are too pessimistic. Yet how far credibility would in fact improve and support policy is unclear. The recent evidence of foreign countries suggests that restraint may still have to be firm and prolonged to be effective.[6]

Whether and how to gain credibility by pursuing a policy of firm and persistent restraint that at the same time is not too costly in terms of excess capacity and unemployment is a central and largely unsettled issue. What seems clear from the experience of 1980, discussed further below, is the negative finding that a volatile policy undermines credibility. Although the formula for positive results remains elusive, it is likely to help if the public understands that cyclical fluctuations in the inflation rate can be misleading and that progress toward ending inflation is made by keeping the average rate over the business cycle below the underlying rate, and if the public sees that policy makers also understand this and are acting accordingly.

Interest Rates as Guides and Constraints

The behavior of interest rates is a second potential pitfall for monetary policy. Under present inflationary conditions, when a sure-footed policy of reducing inflation is needed, the conduct of policy is disrupted and confused by large and unpredictable fluctuations in interest rates. These fluctuations are a product of the inflationary environment and will continue until inflation is substantially reduced. Although the use of interest rates as a tool of monetary policy has been downgraded, interest rates continue to guide and constrain the operation of monetary policy.

The Policy Role of Interest Rates. The conduct of monetary policy has long reflected a basic dependence on interest rates. They give the first sign of market responses to monetary operations, well before the repercussions spread through the economy to aggregate expenditures. The increasing specialization of financial instruments, combined with greater interdependence of financial markets, has further refined the use of interest rates as indicators for policy. The market in interbank borrowing of reserves on deposit at Federal Reserve Banks—

---

[6] Charles Pigott, "Wringing Out Inflation: Japan's Experience," *Federal Reserve Bank of San Francisco Economic Review* (summer 1980), pp. 24-42; Robert Solomon, "The Jury Is Still Out on Thatcher's Policies," *Journal of Commerce* (December 22, 1980), p. 4; and Leland Yeager, *Experiences with Stopping Inflation* (Washington, D.C.: American Enterprise Institute, 1981).

federal funds—which developed during the 1960s has provided an up-to-the-minute gauge of the tightness or ease of bank reserves. The interest rate on federal funds gradually became the object of Federal Reserve control to influence the entire spectrum of interest rates. Control over interest rates has been the means of counteracting undesired effects on aggregate expenditures of shifts in credit demands and supplies throughout the economy.

Growing dissatisfaction during the second half of the 1970s with the technique of conducting monetary policy by controlling interest rates led to a change in operating procedure in October 1979. Previously the Federal Reserve had kept the funds rate within a narrow band of a quarter to a half percentage point day to day and week to week, adjusting the band up or down a notch when developments called for a tighter or easier policy. The new procedure permits much wider fluctuations in the funds rate in the short run for the purpose of improving control over monetary growth, an objective that had previously been partially subordinated to interest-rate targets. The stronger commitment to a monetary growth target has not meant, however, that interest rates are to be ignored. A smooth functioning of financial markets is widely thought to benefit from a limitation of interest-rate fluctuations, which should be a policy goal to the extent it is consistent with long-run monetary targets. And interest rates are still thought to be useful as an indicator of the effects of policy actions on the banking system and financial markets and as a guide both to setting and to achieving the monetary targets.

The first year of the new operating procedure saw larger fluctuations than had been expected not only in interest rates, but in monetary growth rates as well. Some critics of Federal Reserve policy argue that it erred during 1980 by even attempting to restrain interest-rate movements within the widened bands and should abandon all such attempts in the future. While the extent to which concern with interest-rate fluctuations continues to influence monetary policy remains unclear, total abandonment of any such concern appears unlikely.

Yet a continued concern with interest rates, however necessary and however slight, poses difficulties in an inflationary economy. The cross currents of inflation make the interpretation of interest-rate movements treacherous and the guidance they used to provide for policy unreliable. It can no longer be taken for granted that changes in monetary growth always affect interest rates inversely in the short run, as was once the expected response, or positively, as is now a common view.

Monetary Effects on Interest Rates. That the short-run effect is inverse was long the standard view; the reasoning is as follows: When growth in the money supply is slowed by policy, for example, the supply becomes deficient relative to the growing demand for money balances that is determined by the ongoing growth in aggregate expenditures and income. As part of the reduction in monetary growth, the banking system curtails credit expansion and tightens lending practices; as a consequence of the reduction, the public seeks to meet the unsatisfied growth in its demand for money balances by selling financial assets. The resulting rise in interest rates moves the demand both for money balances and for credit into balance with the curtailed supply of each. A reduction in monetary growth will eventually contract aggregate expenditures, whereupon the rise in interest rates will disappear. An expansion of monetary growth works in the opposite direction.

Thus financial observers had long associated rising interest rates with slow growth in the money supply and falling rates with rapid growth, and monetary policy had long been guided and judged by its inverse effect on interest rates. The association is demonstrated most dramatically by extreme cases. In the banking panics of the pre-Federal Reserve era (and of the early 1930s), the loss of reserves through currency drains forced banks to contract loans and deposits, and interest rates rose sharply. The more recent financial "crunches" of 1966 and 1969 were produced by monetary restraint of the Federal Reserve, rather than by banking panics, but resulted in the same sharp rise in interest rates.

A positive effect of monetary growth on interest rates, opposite to the preceding standard response, is attributed to inflation, as follows: When prices are expected to rise, nominal interest rates tend to rise to compensate lenders for the expected depreciation in purchasing power over the term of loans. And borrowers are not disadvantaged. The theoretical explanation of this effect is based on the concept of a *real* rate of return on a fixed-dollar loan, which is equal to the nominal rate of interest *minus* the expected rate of change of prices of goods and services over the life of the loan. When inflationary expectations increase, the nominal rate of interest tends to rise to keep the real rate of interest at its equilibrium level. This effect of inflation on interest rates was first formulated by the Yale economist Irving Fisher around the turn of the century,[7] but it never received much attention in the United States until inflation escalated during the

[7] Irving Fisher, "Appreciation and Interest," *Publications of the American Economic Association*, vol. 11 (1896).

1970s. Previously the United States had experienced high inflation rates only in war periods and their aftermath, and the high wartime rates were not expected to last long. Although nominal interest rates appear to have declined during the long price deflation from the 1870s to the mid-1890s and to have risen during the ensuing uptrend of prices to 1920, these were mild movements except for World War I and its aftermath, and research has never clearly determined whether they confirmed the Fisher effect or not.[8]

Whatever the earlier situation, it was clear by the mid-1970s that the importance of rising rates of inflation in explaining the upward trend in interest rates since World War II could no longer be denied. Although part of this uptrend reflected a recovery from the low levels of the 1930s and 1940s, the continued rise eventually took interest rates well above historically normal levels. It was rightly claimed that "experience has finally caught up with Fisher's theory!"[9] Figure 2 shows that interest and inflation rates have generally been rising since World War II, with interest rates usually higher in most years to provide positive real rates of interest. In many of the years from 1973 to 1979 however, the inflation rate rose faster, producing a rare phenomenon of negative real rates of interest.

Financial Adjustments to Inflation. The adjustment of interest rates to inflation cannot be automatic, of course; it occurs when the price expectations of market participants affect the demands for and supplies of financial instruments. With a general expectation of higher inflation, either lenders or borrowers or both would shift their investment strategies. Until nominal interest rates rise far enough, lenders would withhold purchases of fixed-dollar securities to take advantage of alternative investments in real assets—commodities, property, equity—that provide a higher expected return in real terms after allowing for relative risks. Borrowers would step up demands for credit to take advantage of the discrepancy between the nominal cost of borrowing and the expected returns from financed investments in commodity stocks, working inventories, plant, and capital equipment. The result-

[8] Thomas J. Sargent, "Interest Rates and Prices in the Long Run," *Journal of Money, Credit, and Banking*, vol. 5, no. 1, pt. 2 (February 1973), pp. 385-449, and Irving Fisher, *The Theory of Interest* (New York: Macmillan, 1930), chap. 19. On the early controversy surrounding the Fisher effect and some evidence, see Phillip Cagan, *Determinants and Effects of Changes in the Stock of Money, 1875-1960* (New York: National Bureau of Economic Research, 1965), pp. 252-59 and appendix B.

[9] Milton Friedman and Anna J. Schwartz, "From Gibson to Fisher," *Explorations in Economic Research*, vol. 3, no. 1 (winter 1976), pp. 288-91; quotation from p. 289.

ing imbalance between the supply and demand for credit would raise nominal interest rates.[10]

The adjustment of interest rates to inflation is complicated by income taxes, which at today's high marginal rates are a major consideration for investors and borrowers. For lenders, interest payments at high nominal rates—even though mostly a compensation for inflation—are treated as income under the U.S. tax code, which means that lenders pay taxes on a part of their nominal investment income that in real terms is nothing more than a repayment of principal. It is not clear whether or to what extent the market adjusts interest rates to compensate lenders for the expected rate of inflation on an after-tax basis. No single adjustment will work for everyone, since individual lenders are distributed among different marginal tax brackets and financial institutions that are the major source of loanable funds pay relatively low tax rates. For borrowers, the burden of high nominal interest payments is mitigated by the deductibility of interest as a cost under the income tax for both individuals and corporations. For lenders, the net effect of taxes also depends on the alternatives available. If they invest in real assets, inflation-induced increases in dollar value are taxed as capital gains when the assets are sold; this tax rate, though lower than the rate on income, is not insignificant except on gains from the sale of owner-occupied houses.[11]

[10] An econometric model to explain bond yields finds that about two-thirds of increases in the inflation rate are put into bond yields, reflecting adjustments in both demands and supplies. See Benjamin M. Friedman, "Who Puts the Inflation Premium into Nominal Interest Rates?" *Journal of Finance*, vol. 33, no. 3 (June 1978), pp. 833-45.

Another study (Eugene F. Fama, "Short-Term Interest Rates as Predictors of Inflation," *American Economic Review*, vol. 65 [June 1975], pp. 269-82) reported that expected changes in the inflation rate are fully reflected by Treasury bill rates. This seems to suggest that anticipated effects of monetary growth on the inflation rate will produce corresponding movements in interest rates. While this does not rule out an *inverse* effect on rates of unanticipated changes in monetary growth, a recent study finds no indication of an inverse effect on bond yields (Frederic S. Mishkin, "Monetary Policy and Long-Term Interest Rates: An Efficient Markets Approach," *Journal of Monetary Economics*, vol. 7 [January 1981], pp. 29-55). Nevertheless, the inverse effect clearly appears in short-term rates and possibly also in bond yields at certain times. See Robert Shiller, "Can the Fed Control Real Interest Rates?" in *Rational Expectations and Economic Policy*, Stanley Fischer, ed. (Chicago: University of Chicago Press, 1980), pp. 117-56.

[11] One indication of a less than complete tax effect on the inflation premium is the change in the differential between corporate and municipal bond yields. The former yields are subject to federal income taxes and the latter are not. Moody's Aaa corporate yields averaged 4.49 percent in 1965 and 9.63 percent in 1979, while Standard & Poor's municipal yields averaged 3.27 percent and 6.39 percent, respectively. The marginal tax rate that would make the after-tax yield on corporates equal to that on municipals was 0.27 in 1965 and

Figure 2 shows that nominal interest rates more or less kept pace with the inflation rate in most years since World War II, though in many recent years interest rates slipped behind. Real rates of interest received by individuals *after taxes*, however, have declined substantially under inflation. Obviously financial adjustments to inflation have not been rapid or smooth, or yet entirely complete. Real rates of interest[12] have been negative for many years on passbook savings deposits subject to rate ceilings and often during the past decade on short-term credit market instruments. Negative rates attest to incomplete adjustments. Of course, no one can unfailingly predict the future, and expectations are subject to considerable error. But it seems unlikely that the negative rates can be attributed solely to lagging expectations of inflation, since it is difficult to believe that the majority of investors and borrowers continued year after year to expect inflation rates to be lower than the rates that actually prevailed.

The Fisher effect used to be considered of minor importance for monetary policy, because expectations of inflation before the mid-1960s were low and appeared to change slowly. At that time the generally accepted view concerning unexpected increases in the money supply was the standard one that they would lower interest rates and expand aggregate demand. But in recent years this view has been questioned and then reversed. An initial revision of the standard view began to occur in the early 1970s as unexpected increases in the reported money supply generated expectations of immediately rising interest rates. The expectation of rising rates was based on the presumption that, once an increase in money and its immediate effects had largely occurred, interest rates would move in the opposite direction as the Federal Reserve took steps to reverse the initial bulge in supply. This effect pertained only to week-to-week movements, however. In the past few years a further revision has occurred in the standard view to allow for the Fisher effect on interest rates. Although Fisher thought the effect would occur over an extended period as expectations adapted gradually to new developments, the new view

---

0.34 in 1979. A couple filing a federal joint tax return who were just below the 28 percent marginal bracket in 1965 would, if their income had increased by the amount of the rise in the consumer price index, be in the 43 percent bracket in 1979. If they were to be indifferent between these corporate and municipal bond yields in 1979, therefore, as they were in 1965, the 1979 differential between corporate and municipal bond yields had to be wider.

[12] The problems for an anti-inflationary policy posed by low or negative real rates of return are discussed in William Fellner, "Corporate Asset-Liability Decisions in View of the Low Market Valuation of Equity," in *Contemporary Economic Problems 1980*, William Fellner, ed. (Washington, D.C.: American Enterprise Institute, 1980) pp. 77-102.

is that unexpected monetary increases signal an easier monetary policy, which will expand aggregate demand and *raise* interest rates rapidly through immediate expectations of increased inflation to come. This view reverses the old adage that easy money will lower interest rates in the short run to claim that it will raise them because of the longer-run effect of increasing inflation, which telescopes future monetary effects on inflation into immediate financial adjustments. Thus the *Wall Street Journal* editorializes:

> One of our biggest problems in containing inflation is the wrong-headedness of the received wisdom about how interest rates are determined. . . . A reduction in money growth will constrict the supply of credit, but it will also lower inflationary expectations. If the markets are convinced the Fed is really serious about slowing money growth, the drop in the inflationary premium will swamp the impact on the real rate of interest, and nominal rates will fall.[13]

Inflationary Expectations and Yield Differentials. The new interpretation of interest-rate movements can be partially self-fulfilling, because it engenders the very expectations that will move interest rates in the postulated direction. But it involves some extreme assumptions about the speed with which expectations are revised and financial adjustments are made, which casts doubt on the accuracy of its interpretations of interest-rate movements.

Under what conditions would expectations produce a rapid positive effect of monetary growth on interest rates? An increase in monetary growth, or even an anticipated rather than actual increase, could generate expectations that inflation will be higher in future periods. Traders and forward-looking investors would expect the higher inflation when it came to force up interest rates, and expectations of the later decline in bond prices could therefore produce an immediate sell-off, thus raising bond yields.

Such speculation in bonds, however, should not carry over to short-term securities, say, those maturing in up to six months or even somewhat longer. Changes in monetary growth take much longer than that to affect the rate of inflation. While such expectations of monetary growth may affect prices in financial markets and commodity exchanges, expectations of *changes* in the inflation rate appear to have little effect on the anticipated trend of production costs, which changes slowly. Consequently, increases in monetary growth that raise expectations of future inflation do not affect the actual inflation

[13] January 7, 1981, p. 24.

rate until the monetary increases work through the economy to raise demand, and then not until the stronger demand affects prices. Based on the evidence, the lag in the effect of money on inflation is measured in years rather than months.[14]

Moreover, a rise in bond yields owing to expectations of higher inflation in future periods does not create an incentive to speculate on a rise in short-term rates. Although the higher bond yields are based on the expectation that future short-term rates will be higher, speculation on a rise in short rates is not profitable in the spot market, because the expected rise in short rates will occur, given the likely lags, after the outstanding short securities mature. Furthermore, sellers of bonds who were speculating on a later rise in yields would for the most part hold their funds in the interim in short-term liquid assets, thus temporarily driving short-term rates *down*. While some long-term borrowers discouraged from issuing bonds might then shift to short-term loans, their increase in demand for short-term funds would be more than matched by the shift on the supply side. It is therefore implausible to explain a collapse of bond prices as being primarily due to higher monetary growth and to expectations of *coming* higher inflation rates, unless the differential of bond yields over short-term rates were to rise commensurately. Yet at such times this differential, as is described below, tends to decline.

A flight from *both* bonds and short-term securities might be attempted, raising yields across all maturities, whenever, following upon a rise in the rate of inflation that is initially thought to be temporary, monetary growth also increases and creates expectations that the higher current inflation will continue for some time and per-haps even escalate. There might, for example, be a severe "supply shock" to the economy from an oil price increase to which monetary policy will be or is viewed as accommodating. Financial markets could conceivably adjust to such expectations without any major shift in the amount of credit demanded and supplied if all interest rates moved commensurately to a new equilibrium level that compensated for the rise in the expected rate of inflation. This would require, how-ever, an immediate and uniform shift in expectations by all market participants. Expectations often change quickly in the market, but hardly ever uniformly. Usually there is considerable diversity of

[14] Keith M. Carlson, "The Lag from Money to Prices," Federal Reserve Bank of St. Louis *Review*, vol. 62 (October 1980), pp. 3-10; Charles Pigott, "Expectations, Money, and the Forecasting of Inflation," Federal Reserve Bank of San Francisco *Economic Review* (spring 1980), pp. 30-49; and Peter I. Berman, *Inflation and the Money Supply in the United States, 1956-1977* (Lexington, Mass.: Lexington Books, 1978), chap. 3.

expectations, with convergence toward a single rate only when the actual rate has been fairly stable for some time.[15] It is more likely, therefore, that a sudden shock or development would produce a range of differing expectations, and therefore wide-ranging intentions to change the quantities demanded and supplied.

Since many of the intended changes in demands and supplies take time to accomplish and would occur gradually over a time period that exceeded the three- to six-month maturity of short-term securities, the adjustments in short-term interest rates would not be immediate but would also occur over an extended period. The outstanding supplies of investable funds and of securities are fairly fixed and quite large relative to new flows over a short period. An imbalance between offers to buy and to sell the existing stock of securities will not affect the quantities outstanding, of course, but will change their prices. For most suppliers of funds in credit markets, a decision to shift from financial assets to commodities or real property implies a radical restructuring of portfolios, which they would not undertake suddenly or attempt to complete rapidly. The only variable-priced assets that the major holders of fixed-dollar financial instruments would be able to shift into quickly, if large holdings were to be shifted, would be equities via the stock market. But the largest suppliers of funds are financial institutions which by and large do not purchase equities or real property, and the suppliers that do—primarily pension funds—are not known for attempting sudden large shifts in their investment policies. The partial shift of life insurance portfolios into equity participation loans has taken years and is unlikely to be quickly reversed or accelerated. Similarly, while demanders of funds who expect increased inflation might find it attractive to borrow more until interest rates rose commensurately, an increase in borrowed funds could not be profitably used for investment in inventories or capital without some advance planning. As the value of existing inventories rises because of inflation, more has to be borrowed in nominal amounts, to be sure, but not in real amounts. A change in

[15] The theory of "rational expectations" hypothesizes that all market participants base their expectations on the same general information. Even so, it does not follow that everyone will form the same expectations, because everyone possesses specific information not shared by everyone else and must form expectations of everyone else's expectations. As has been pointed out at least since Keynes, expectations that depend on others' expectations will not be uniform and, indeed, need not always even converge over time, though they usually will when markets are calm. For examples of the divergence of expectations, see Albert M. Wojnilower, "The Central Role of Credit Crunches in Recent Financial History," *Brookings Papers on Economic Activity*, no. 2 (1980), pp. 277-326.

inflationary expectations, therefore, is not likely to produce much immediate pressure on short-term interest rates. If demands and supplies are not much affected in six months, speculation in three- to six-month securities would also be limited.[16]

Speculative shifts from domestic to foreign securities would be limited by movements in foreign exchange rates. To the extent that exchange rates were fixed or constrained, substantial foreign capital outflows could raise domestic interest rates; but such outflows have not played a major role in recent U.S. financial stringencies.

In time, of course, expectations of increased inflation would tend to raise interest rates as investment and financing plans were altered. As these alterations were made, prices in equity and commodity markets would be bid up in real terms. The basis of Fisher's theory is that expectations of inflation, when formed, produce opposite movements in yields on fixed-dollar securities and variable-priced assets. To summarize the effect on the yield curve of fixed-dollar instruments, the timing of two adjustments is relevant. First, if an increase in monetary growth raises inflationary expectations, how soon is the higher inflation expected to occur? According to past evidence on this lag, it can take many quarters. Second, if the inflation rate has already increased and is expected to remain at the new level, how long will it take the demands for and supplies of funds to adjust? Short-term rates would not be affected until these adjustments began. While speculation might speed up the effect on bond yields, it would as noted tend initially to widen their differential over short-term rates. Notwithstanding the new view that both of these lags are essentially nonexistent, they are probably sizable and certainly not negligible. They will determine the main effects of monetary changes on interest rates whatever the transitory effects that may be introduced by market speculation.

---

[16] A revealing experiment of the short-run Fisher effect was provided by the three-month freeze on prices and wages imposed from mid-August to mid-November 1971. During these three months it was clear that the inflation rate would be practically zero, as it was, and goods and services were readily available at constant prices. (The reported three-month rate for the CPI of over 3 percent for the fourth quarter of 1971 in figure 2 is misleading, because the CPI involves some lag in the prices used in its construction.) Yet the rate on three-month Treasury bills, which was above 5 percent before the freeze and contained a substantial inflation premium, declined less than half a percentage point in the week after the imposition of the freeze—hence the real rate of interest temporarily rose sharply.

The implication is that the supply of funds available for short-term investment, and the demand for such funds, were unable to shift rapidly and on short notice. For other examples of the inelasticity of the short-term demand for credit, see Wojnilower, ibid.

The Evidence of Past Financial Stringencies. Historically most periods of financial stringency have displayed none of the Fisher effects of inflationary expectations. These periods were characterized by expanding economic activity and strong credit demands and by a tightening of the supply of credit usually because of declining monetary growth. Interest rates soared, short-term rates the most, producing the "humped" or inverted yield curve typical of stringencies. When the curve is inverted, intermediate rates of three months' to several years' maturity are above bond yields.[17] This was true in the banking panics of earlier periods, when the gold standard was in effect and the price level was relatively stable over the long run, and in the financial "crunches" of the late 1960s, when inflation was escalating. The inverted yield curves reflected a sudden curtailment of the supply of funds, which was viewed as being temporary, and indicated that short-term rates were expected to be lower in the future. The stringency ended when economic activity and the demand for credit contracted; in the ensuing business downturn monetary conditions became easy, and the yield curve reverted to its usual upward slope. The inverted yield curve of such stringencies reflected expectations opposite to those of a future increase in the inflation rate, because expectations of increasing inflation would produce a steeply rising yield curve indicative of coming increases in short-term interest rates.

Figure 3 plots a short-term interest rate and an average of bond rates, the rate of inflation, monetary growth, total funds raised in credit markets, and real money balances for the four periods of financial stringency since World War II. The first two in 1966 and 1969 provide casebook examples of the effects of a tightening of monetary policy. They occurred in the advanced stages of business expansions in which economic activity and interest rates had been rising for some time. To restrain growing inflationary pressures, monetary growth was contracted sharply, which gradually squeezed the supply of credit and raised interest rates far above their normal range. The credit squeeze did not subside for several months, until business activity and loan demand contracted and monetary policy eased. As figure 3 shows, total credit raised in financial markets declined relative to its upward trend in the months of peak interest

---

[17] In figures 2 and 3 the yields for corporate bonds fall relative to three-month Treasury bill rates during stringencies but never fall below them (except briefly in 1979-1980) because of differences in risk of default, while Treasury bond yields (not shown) did fall below bill rates at such times.

Apart from stringencies, the typical relation for securities alike in all respects but maturity is for yields to rise with maturity, because of the greater illiquidity of longer-term securities should they have to be sold before they mature.

FIGURE 3
Interest Rates, Inflation Rate, Monetary Growth, Real Money Balances, and Total Funds Raised in Credit Markets in Four Periods of Financial Stringency, 1965–1980

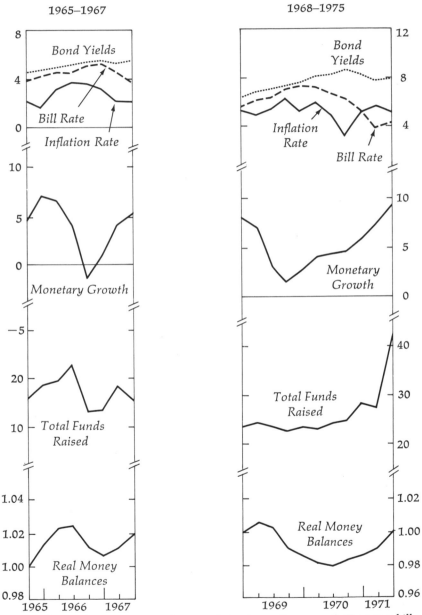

NOTE: Bill rate (percent per year) = market rate on three-month Treasury bills; bond yields (percent per year) = Aa corporate bond yields; inflation rate (percent

FIGURE 3 (continued)

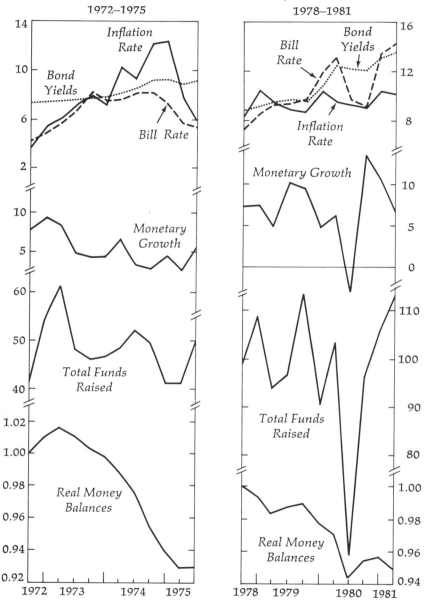

per year) = rate of change in quarterly averages of consumer price index; monetary growth (percent per year) = growth rate of M1–B; total funds raised (billions of dollars per quarter) = total funds raised by nonfinancial sector, flow of funds, seasonally adjusted; and real money balances (index, initial value = 1.00) = M1–B divided by the implicit price deflator (fixed weight) of gross national product.

SOURCE: *Federal Reserve Bulletin* and *Survey of Current Business.*

rates, indicating a tightened supply. It seems clear that both of these credit squeezes were primarily the result of monetary contraction; there was no other development to account for them.[18]

The delay of many months from the initial contraction in monetary growth to the peak in interest rates can be explained by the sequence of market responses to monetary restraint. A slowing of monetary growth relative to the ongoing rate of expansion of aggregate expenditures and credit demand leads to an increase in interest rates that induces the public to add to the supply of loanable funds through reductions in the demand for money balances. This reduction in demand does not change the nominal quantity of money outstanding, of course, but it makes the public willing to hold smaller money balances in relation to the expanding level of aggregate expenditures and transactions and the growing volume of financial assets. Thus the contraction in monetary growth is offset for a while by increases in monetary velocity, which require higher and higher interest rates. Gradually more and more borrowers are squeezed out of the market, finally precipitating a business downturn. The process is reflected in figure 3 by the declines in money balances in real terms while aggregate expenditures continued expanding until the cyclical peaks were reached.

The percentage decline in real money balances was extremely large in 1973–1974. Because of world price increases the inflation rate rose steeply while monetary growth was declining. This made the financial squeeze more severe than the decline in monetary growth would have produced by itself. The imported price increases reduced real money balances *below* the desired level, which was equivalent to reducing the supply of money. This differed from the usual case of domestic increases in the money supply coming first in the inflationary sequence to raise real money balances *above* the desired level until prices catch up.

For these first three episodes, figure 3 does show a rough correspondence between the rise and fall in interest rates and the inflation rate, but close inspection reveals discrepancies that argue against attributing the rise in interest rates primarily to changes in the expected rate of inflation. In 1966 interest rates reached a peak a quarter after the inflation rate began to decline appreciably. Conceivably this timing discrepancy could be consistent with the Fisher effect if expectations were slow to catch up with changes in the actual

[18] Flow of funds data for 1965-1967 and 1968-1970 indicate no major changes in household gross saving or expenditures on houses and consumer durables, as a percentage of disposable income. Net financial investment in the United States by the rest of the world was also fairly constant over these periods.

inflation rate. In the next two episodes, however, the discrepancy goes the other way and cannot be explained by a possible lag in expectations. Thus in 1969 the inflation rate did not fall appreciably below its 5–6 percent range (ignoring the large dip in the third quarter of 1970) until after the imposition of price controls in the third quarter of 1971, while bond yields had reached a peak earlier in the third quarter of 1970, and Treasury bill rates had peaked much earlier in the fourth quarter of 1969. In the 1973–1974 episode as well, bill rates rose during 1973 along with the inflation rate, but then held between 7½ and 8½ percent from the third quarter of 1973 to the third quarter of 1974, while the inflation rate escalated from 7½ to over 12 percent per year. Bond yields did rise during this period, but by far less than the inflation rate. Furthermore, short-term rates fell in the fourth quarter of 1974 when economic activity plummeted, yet bond yields and the inflation rate peaked a quarter later.

In all three of these episodes the differential between bond yields and short-term rates, which is indicative of expected future changes in inflation, fell as short rates were rising and rose as they were declining. (In figure 3 the vertical distance between the bond yields and bill rates narrows in the upswings and widens in the downswings.) The rise in the differential occurred only when short rates were pulled down by the contraction in business activity, at which point the inflation had reached its cyclical peak and was weakening. During these cyclical increases in the differential the corresponding expectations of inflation could not have been rising unless they were based on past rather than on the latest developments, which though not implausible means that they could not possibly explain the preceding sharp increases in both short rates and bond yields. These three episodes therefore do not have movements in the differential that conform to the implications of the Fisher effect.

Moreover, this effect requires a major attempt by investors to shift from financial instruments to real assets, primarily to common stocks and houses by households and to commodity inventories by businesses. The prices of these real assets did not generally exhibit a tendency to follow the movements in interest rates as such a major shift implies. Indeed, the prices of these assets were largely forced down as the soaring interest rates curtailed financing for their purchases.[19]

[19] Comparing the three months before and after the peak in bill rates in September 1966, January 1970, and August 1974, we find that common stock prices fell more or rose less before than after the peak in bill rates, indicating a financial tightness before, which then eased after. Precious metals prices also displayed this pattern, though indexes of spot commodity prices and of house prices were partial exceptions.

It is conceivable, in a period of high sensitivity to inflation, that a decline in monetary growth could squeeze credit supplies and raise short-term interest rates, and at the same time lower expectations of future inflation rates and, via the Fisher effect, reduce bond yields. This would narrow the differential between bond yields and short-term rates, as occurred in past stringencies. But, contrary to this hypothetical double effect of reduced monetary growth in past stringencies, bond yields did not fall but rose.

It is more plausible to interpret these episodes as conventional financial stringencies produced by tight monetary policies and, in 1973–1974, supplemented by the imported inflationary surge from grains, metals, and oil. In all three of these episodes monetary growth, real money balances, and total funds raised began declining before the sharp upward movements in interest rates began and were at or near their cyclical low points when interest rates peaked. These were not developments that would have caused or reflected expectations of higher inflation. The widening differential between bond yields and short interest rates during the business contractions can be attributed instead to expectations that the inflation rate and the short interest rates, though temporarily falling during the business contraction, would in the long run remain at the higher levels reached during the preceding business expansion. As figure 2 shows, bond yields have risen in rachet fashion, declining very little during business contractions and beginning each business expansion at the high levels reached in the preceding expansion. This rachet effect of inflation on bond yields was evident again in the first half of 1981, when bond yields remained at relatively high levels despite a decline in short-term rates.

The 1979–1981 Episode. The latest episode shown in figure 3 has strong similarities to the previous ones and some notable differences. The pattern of declining monetary growth, real money balances, and total funds raised was repeated in the fourth quarter of 1979 and first quarter of 1980 as interest rates rose sharply. But the usual lag between monetary contraction and rising interest rates was compressed, so that the quarterly movements in these variables shown here occurred simultaneously.

The peak in interest rates was sharper than usual even for such stringencies, and the subsequent contraction came sooner and pulled rates down faster. The stringency might have continued longer, however, if the credit controls imposed in March 1980 had not produced an unexpectedly strong curtailment of consumer installment debt and retail sales, which immediately took pressure off banks for loans (producing a drop in the money supply) and accounted for the steepness of the fall in interest rates. Indeed, the rapid return of interest rates to new highs in the fourth quarter of 1980, without a significant tightening of monetary policy, suggests that the decline in rates in the second and third quarters (due mainly to credit controls) was a temporary interruption of a move to higher rates that had started in late 1979.

The sharp runup in interest rates in February and March of 1980 was widely attributed in part to prospects of a larger federal deficit but mainly to heightened fears of a further escalation of inflation.[20] The inflation rate had indeed jumped up early in the first quarter of 1980, though most of this reflected the passing through of previous oil price increases and was temporary. A spurt in monetary growth in the first weeks of February also seemed to crystallize a widespread skepticism in financial markets of the Federal Reserve's control of monetary growth.

Fears of escalating inflation in early 1980 could have produced the speculative selloff of bonds and rise in their yields. If speculation also produced the even greater rise in short interest rates, there had to be a sharp expansion in the demand for loans to finance speculative purchases of real assets, since there was no indication of a sharp contraction in the supply of credit. There is some implication of strong loan demand in the skyrocketing prices of gold and silver and other commodities as a rampant inflationary psychology overtook these markets beginning late in 1979, and bank loans did expand strongly. Whether the increase in demands for short-term credit was mainly due to fear of escalating inflation or to a strong cyclical rise in business activity is unclear.

The rise in interest rates in the fourth quarter of 1980 was accompanied by a comparable escalation of inflation and also seems to present a case for the influence of inflationary expectations. But it seems unlikely that the rapid fall and subsequent rise in short-term interest rates during 1980 can be explained by a corresponding fluctuation in inflationary expectations and in the induced adjustments of credit market demands and supplies. It is more reasonable to interpret the failure of bond yields to fall very far in the second and third quarters as an indication that inflationary expectations remained on a high level throughout the year. When credit demands revived in the fourth quarter after the earlier credit controls were removed,

[20] "[The first weeks of 1980] had seen a very serious deterioration in public confidence in the government's ability and resolve to rein in inflation." Supplementary statement of Paul A. Volcker to the House Subcommittee on Domestic Monetary and Urban Affairs, November 19, 1980.

businesses shied away from the high long-term borrowing rates and shifted their demands to short-term credit, which pulled short rates up to and above the level of bond yields.

Uncertainties for Monetary Policy. The 1979–1981 episode therefore appears to reflect part stringency and part inflationary expectations in a combination that is difficult to interpret, particularly as it is unfolding. This poses additional new uncertainties for the use of interest rates in the conduct of monetary policy. It makes a considerable difference in interpreting and guiding policy whether interest rates are rising because monetary restraint is curtailing the growth of credit or because fears of higher inflation are stimulating the demand for credit and shifting the market supply. The uncertainty is compounded if, as in early 1980, the increase in the actual rate of inflation is due to earlier developments (the oil price hikes) that were tapering but set off fears of more to come.

Despite much current market opinion to the contrary, the positive Fisher effect of monetary growth and inflation on interest rates is a long-run phenomenon and not a dominant influence in cyclical fluctuations and financial stringencies. Nevertheless, it can still be a major source of confusion in judging whether nominal interest rates are viewed by borrowers and investors as high or low in real terms. And it can increasingly mislead the conduct of monetary policy, because interest-rate movements are now commonly interpreted as due to changes in expectations and many investors shift portfolios in anticipation of these effects. Such speculative expectations about the market's expectations are likely to be highly volatile and less tied to market fundamentals than are expectations of the underlying rate of inflation. Unfortunately for an anti-inflationary monetary policy, a little financial knowledge is a dangerous thing.

Conclusion: The Tribulations of Monetary Policy

The continuing struggle to end the inflation that began in the mid-1960s has been repeatedly set back by new obstacles that each time overwhelm the resolve summoned up to overcome the previous ones. In the late 1960s monetary restraint was widely criticized as being unduly disruptive of financial markets and the housing industry and as being ineffective in slowing a vigorous business expansion. The Federal Reserve nevertheless ignored the critics and imposed restraint twice. When this proved effective in contracting business activity, first inconclusively in 1966 and then conclusively in 1969, the achievement was thought to spell the end of the nascent inflation. But by 1969 inflation had developed strong roots, and it revealed an unexpected resistance to a slack economy. When policy recovered from the shock of failure and—after a useless experiment with price controls—was prepared to launch another attack, it had to deal in 1973–1974 and after with international supply shocks. The need to contain the price effects of supply shocks raised the cost of curbing inflation in terms of the amount of economic slack that had to be maintained.

When finally the resolve to conduct a firm anti-inflationary policy gained general acceptance in the late 1970s, policy makers found that their traditional tools had been weakened by the years of raging inflation. Financial markets had become volatile, with the consequence that interest rates were less easily controlled and, if controlled nonetheless, less certain in their effects on the economy. In addition, money substitutes were proliferating in large part because the effects of longstanding interest-rate ceilings and other regulations had become more severe under inflation. The substitutes increased the difficulty of conducting policy with prespecified monetary targets, making it less certain where such targets should be set or that they could be achieved. The dangerous erosion of monetary controls forced congressional passage in 1980 of long-blocked legislation to adapt regulations to the innovations in the financial system, but it remains to be seen whether the legislation has come too late and done too little, and whether the Federal Reserve will need further authority to regulate all money-like instruments that are important for controlling aggregate expenditures and the price level.[21]

Because of its past failures and these mounting obstacles, monetary policy faces a credibility crisis, in which the public is skeptical that monetary restraint can be effectively maintained long enough to curb inflation. Such skepticism hardens expectations that inflation will persist and perhaps escalate, which makes an anti-inflationary policy even more difficult. Greater difficulty validates the skepticism that in turn increases the difficulty, and so on in a descending spiral that has brought the credibility of anti-inflationary policy to its present low level. All this is enough to cause the staunchest inflation fighter to give up on monetary policy, except that the experience of the past decade leaves few to doubt that uncurbed inflation tends to escalate and that monetary policy "is the only game in town."[22]

[21] See the discussion of these innovations in Phillip Cagan, "Financial Developments and the Erosion of Monetary Controls," in *Contemporary Economic Problems 1979*, William Fellner, ed. (Washington, D.C.: American Enterprise Institute, 1979), pp. 117-51.

[22] "[Tight money is] the price we have to pay for the inflation this country finds itself in. It's the only game in town." Attributed to Donald T. Regan in an interview after he was designated to be secretary of the Treasury, *Newsweek*, December 22, 1980, p. 65.

Although there is no substitute for control over money in our economic system, monetary policy can be played in different ways. The lack of credibility of traditional policies has led to discussion of shock tactics. These would be decisive acts to end inflation and gain credibility in one fell swoop, either by a currency reform of the kind familiar from European history or by some other framework for drastically reducing monetary growth.[23] Despite the attraction of shock tactics to many former supporters of gradualism who are ready to give up on it, the United States is not yet ready, and perhaps never will be, for such strong medicine.

For the time being Federal Reserve policy remains committed to the gradual reduction of monetary growth. The implementation of this policy has failed for more than a decade and clearly could use improvement. A lack of persistence is the main deficiency. If this is overcome, the low credibility of traditional gradualist policies remains an obstacle but is not insurmountable. Of course, the credibility of a gradualist policy will not be greatly improved by preachings about the virtues of steadfastness to the policy makers, or about their suddenly acquired determination to a skeptical public. Apart from shock tactics, an improvement in credibility requires a couple of years of successful performance.

We can improve the technique of conducting policy straightaway, however, by learning from past mistakes. The misinterpretations discussed in this essay of movements in the inflation rate and in interest rates seem to underlie many of the past mistakes.

The inflation rate is subject to cyclical fluctuations that policy makers must distinguish from changes in the long-run underlying rate. Much of the decline in the overall rate during business contractions is not sustainable, and its reversal during the first stage of business recoveries is not a setback. Only reductions in the underlying rate are sustainable, and such reductions require that policy makers apply sufficient monetary restraint to hold the average rate of inflation for the business cycle as a whole below the concurrent underlying rate. The difference between them will gradually lower the expectations and cost trends that determine the underlying rate. But this takes time, and because of cyclical fluctuations it is easy along the

---

[23] "[T]here must be an abrupt change in the government policy for setting deficits now and in the future that is sufficiently binding as to be widely believed." Thomas J. Sargent, "The Ends of Four Big Inflations," National Bureau of Economic Research conference on inflation, Washington, D.C., October 10, 1980. See also William Fellner, "Introductory Remarks on Demand Disinflation: What If Gradualism Should Fail Despite Its Merits?" in *Contemporary Economic Problems 1980*, pp. 1-8.

way to misjudge whether gains are being made or lost. Consequently, the key to success of a gradualist policy is persistence and watchfulness to avoid an overstimulation of the economy that can reintroduce inflationary pressures and raise the underlying rate.

It is frequently claimed that such a gradual reduction of inflation by monetary restraint cannot succeed without controls over prices and wages or without a balanced federal budget. But these claims are based on misinterpretations of the historical evidence. The effect of monetary restraint in producing a lasting reduction in inflation cannot be reliably estimated from experience of the past decade and a half, when the effect does appear to have been small, because in that period the restraint was never applied for very long. If we look to earlier periods for evidence, such as the late 1950s, monetary restraint appears more effective. In any event, price and wage controls have never been more than marginally beneficial. Moreover, controls could undermine the credibility of an anti-inflationary policy if they were mistakenly given the credit for a reduction in inflation, because the public knows that controls cannot be imposed on the economy indefinitely. As for a balanced budget, it has never been a necessary condition for the imposition of monetary restraint. What is true is that monetary restraint combined with a federal budget deficit produces greater tightness in financial markets and squeezes a larger volume of private borrowing and investment out of the market. Such tightness is undesirable and is to be avoided as far as possible, but it should not be viewed as a deterrent to an effective anti-inflationary monetary policy.

The interpretation of interest rates is also more treacherous in an inflationary economy. The expected rate of inflation influences the long-run average level of interest rates and the differential between long and short rates but does not, contrary to current opinion, account for most short-run movements in interest rates. Nevertheless, these short-run movements are clearly more volatile and less predictable as a result of inflationary expectations. For this reason the use of interest rates as a tool of policy was downgraded by the change in operating procedure of the Federal Reserve in October 1979. Interest rates remain as a guide for policy, however, even though their increased volatility reduces their usefulness for this purpose as well. If policy makers will not or cannot ignore interest rates, they must interpret them with great care to avoid further policy mistakes.

In view of the obstacles to ending inflation and the damage to monetary controls that inflation itself has produced, it is no longer as obvious as it once seemed to be that an anti-inflationary monetary policy, even when firmly undertaken, will succeed. The Federal

Reserve nevertheless continues to affirm its commitment, with the support of a new administration, to subdue inflation. If policy can correct past mistakes and be persistent where it has previously wavered, it still appears capable of succeeding. That assumes, however, that new obstacles of which we are presently unaware will not arise. The need to end inflation before it creates new obstacles offers a strong incentive for getting on with the job.

The Chief Executive as Chief Economist

Herbert Stein

Summary

Presidents have been playing an increasingly active role in the management and exposition of economic policy, especially policy relating to inflation. Power and responsibility has moved to the president from the subordinate executive agencies, from the Congress, and possibly also from the Federal Reserve.

Presidents typically come into office little prepared for this function—less prepared than for the performance of their other functions. Such experience as they may have had with economic problems has usually not extended to macroeconomic problems but has been confined to the concerns of single states or to a few sectoral interests. Moreover, people who become presidents tend not to be the kind of people who have much interest in economics as a "scientific" subject, being more happy and more able at less abstract, more personal matters. The process of running for the presidency and of taking stands on economic issues does not serve to educate the candidate. It is more likely to enmesh him in commitments that have not been carefully thought out and that turn out to be embarrassing if he is elected.

A president will, therefore, be highly dependent on advice in the field of economics, more dependent than he is in the other major fields of his concern. How he organizes to get that advice is important.

In earlier times presidents seem to have relied on outside advice—advice from people outside the government in whose knowledge and judgment they had confidence. Some presidents have set up formal bodies of outsiders—such as labor leaders and businessmen— to advise them. And there are many self-designated study groups prepared to advise the president. The contribution of outside advisers has, however, been small. The outsiders usually do not learn enough about the current issues, or do not learn soon enough, to get into the decision-making flow in government. The outsiders can make a contribution insofar as they influence the general pattern of opinion in the country about the general and durable questions, and so affect the climate within which the president operates. But that always makes them irrelevant with respect to the decisions immediately before the president. Moreover, those close to the president often doubt the outsiders' loyalty to the president and therefore the trustworthiness of their advice.

The Reagan administration has established a body of economic advisers who could be called outside insiders. These people are not in the government but have been supporters of Ronald Reagan and, for the most part, have worked in previous Republican administrations. Whether this board will be valuable remains to be seen, but in the best of cases its influence is likely to be small relative to that of the people continuously on the scene.

New presidents always say that they intend to rely on the cabinet for advice. But experience with the cabinet or cabinet-size committees in several administrations shows that procedure not to be workable or durable. It involves too many people talking too much about subjects of which they know too little.

At the other extreme from the cabinet system of advice would be a one-to-one relation between the president and a chief economic adviser on whom he counts for information, discussion, and advice. This system has not existed in the case of economics as it has, for example, in the Kissinger-Nixon relation in foreign policy. The one-on-one system would be dangerous in the field of economics, where so much is in dispute and where it is essential that the president be aware of a range of views. Especially where the president is innocent of economics it can result in the adviser playing the role that should be played by the president.

The organization that seems always to emerge and that meets the needs of the situation is a small central committee of high-level economic officials who advise the president on what issues require his attention and on his options. The core of this committee is the secretary of the Treasury, the director of the Office of Management and Budget, and the chairman of the Council of Economic Advisers. In certain economic conditions other officials may be added more-or-less permanently to the group if their continuous participation is essential, as was the case when general economic policy was heavily affected by the price controls of the Nixon administration or by energy policy a little later. Other officials may be added on a case-by-case basis.

The effectiveness of this central committee will depend heavily on the way in which its members appreciate their relation to each other and to the president. The secretary of the Treasury is the senior economic official of the government and the natural chairman of the committee. He must not use his position to dominate the group or to exclude it from the decision-making process. The members of the group must be able to distinguish between the critical issues on which their differences need to be brought to the president's attention and those issues on which they should reach a consensus before approaching him. Each must be willing to work through the committee process and not to seek an end-run into the Oval Office. They must accept this process as part of their duty to the president and not try to manipulate him. This implies that they should be willing to give him a fair representation of all his eligible options, and not only the ones they prefer.

Since this committee process is very important, a major qualification for appointment to the positions that make up the committee, and especially for its chairman, presumably the secretary of the Treasury, is that they should be temperamentally suited for operating as members of such a consultative, advisory team.

The president will inevitably, and properly, be influenced in his economic decisions by considerations of political feasibility and attractiveness. The president's economic advisers cannot be expected to ignore such considerations. They should, however, try to make clear how much their judgments are based on economic factors and how much on political ones. The president will presumably look to others for advice on the political aspects of economic policy. He should seek political advisers who have a talent for giving political advice—a talent not necessarily demonstrated by long tenure in Washington or on the campaign trail. Also, an effort should be made to educate the political advisers on the main issues of economic policy before they give their advice to the president.

No relationship is of more potential value to the president in his conduct of economic policy than his relation with the Federal Reserve. There are abundant channels for the conduct of this relationship. On the whole, however, this relationship has been too distant, mistrustful, and even hostile. There should be much more recognition by both sides of their interdependence. The Federal Reserve needs the political support of the White House if it is not to be excessively vulnerable to public misunderstanding and congressional demagoguery. The administration needs the support of the Fed if it is to have a successful economic policy, and the administration cannot count on the Fed to provide a consistent policy, especially a consistently anti-inflationary policy, if the Fed cannot count on the political support of the administration. Developing a more candid and intimate relation between the president and the Federal Reserve is the most critical requirement for improving the process of economic policy making. The Federal Reserve and the administration should be able to agree on the objectives of macroeconomic policy for the next several years and on the way in which monetary policy would contribute to the achievement of these objectives. The agreement should also include recognition by the administration of the risks in the policy and of its obligation to stand by the Fed when it is attacked.

Forcing Presidents into Economics

Dissatisfaction with the performance of the economy, notably with the inflation, has increasingly focused attention on the performance of the president as the nation's chief economist. We are used to the idea that when there is a major national problem, and inflation surely is one, the federal government has a responsibility for solving it. Moreover, inflation is an especially "presidential" problem. Its consequences are so widespread, and the measures required to deal with it so comprehensive, that decisions cannot be delegated to cabinet secretaries, shared with Congress, or left to an independent agency, the Federal Reserve. Also, decision making about inflation and other macroeconomic problems is interwoven in a peculiar way with economics as a "science," if that is not too presumptuous a word. The usual qualities of a good president—foresight, persistence, judgment, persuasiveness, firmness, and so forth—are all important in dealing with inflation. Yet they are not sufficient. There must be an input from economics as a science. At the same time, the science is uncertain and divided. If the president cannot rely simply on intuition and native wit, neither can he look in the back of a textbook for reliable answers to his questions. He must use economics and not be used by it. Finally, since it is now generally recognized that the problem of inflation and its cure lie largely in the realm of public psychology, the president's unique role as communicator to the public has become a major aspect of anti-inflation policy.

All of these points are illustrated by the Reagan administration. Mr. Reagan has accepted, and asserted, responsibility for bringing down inflation. He has proposed a program whose success depends on the accuracy of forecasts of many economic magnitudes that most economists would regard as highly uncertain. He has chosen a rather eccentric school of economics and economists and has eschewed the opportunity of reducing his responsibility for error by staying close to the mainstream. In relations with Congress he has been unusually insistent that only the precise program he has proposed will solve the nation's economic problems. He has been unusually explicit in public advice and direction to the Federal Reserve. And he has vigorously played the role of public spokesman and salesman for the economic program.

Thus we see the president as the dominant decision maker in economic policy, as the judge of economics and economists, and as the major figure attempting to set the psychological tone of the economy. In those senses he is the nation's chief economist. But, of course, he is not an economist in the sense that 15,000 members of the American Economic Association are economists. That is, he is not a professional in this field. To be a professional economist is not a requirement for being a good president, although it is probably not a disqualification, either.

Few presidents have, when they enter office, even the level of understanding of economics one might find in an interested amateur or a fairly good third-year college student. Herbert Hoover was probably the most recent exception, the president in this century who was most abreast of the economics of his time. John Kennedy is said by his advisers to have been interested in economics and to have read some economics after his Harvard College days, but the evidence is weak and the authorities are suspect. Richard Nixon had a course in economics at Whittier College that he later described as having negligible intellectual content. Ronald Reagan is said to have read both Milton Friedman and Ludwig von Mises, but a reasonable guess is that it was the political and ideological writings of these authors rather than their scientific economics.

Even if future presidents have little book learning in economics, they have almost all been public officials and have had some experience in that capacity with economic problems and policies. A senator or congressman with twenty years of service will have acquired an amazing amount of knowledge of economic programs of government. Yet experience in Congress, or in a state governor's office, usually does not produce much knowledge of macroeconomics problems like inflation. Probably only two recent candidates had a useful background in this field. They were Richard Nixon and Hubert Humphrey, both of whom had been vice-presidents. Moreover, the value of this empirical background has been limited during a period increasingly dominated by a condition new to the United States, serious inflation, and less dominated by reverberations of the depression. In fact, one of the advantages of joining theory and history with personal observation is that it prepares one for the emergence of conditions outside one's personal experience. It must be confessed that economists trained in theory and history were not as quick as they should have been to adapt to the shifting state of the economy, but they were not the last to recognize the change.

People who run for the presidency usually have an idea of their general stance with respect to economic policy—a stance that may reflect their own convictions or their ideas of what the public likes to hear or, probably, a convenient marriage of the two. Thus, Kennedy thought of himself as a "liberal," Nixon regarded himself as a "modern conservative," and Reagan views himself as a "classical conservative." This kind of self-identification is not entirely meaningless. It does provide a president with some guidance in the choice of macroeconomic policies after he gets into office. Nevertheless, it still leaves a wide range of options open. Ronald Reagan's views of economic policy were probably more precisely defined than those of any other recent candidate who was not an incumbent. He wanted to free the private economy and revive the growth of total output and productivity, deemphasizing the reliance on public services and income redistribution as sources of the people's welfare and reversing the trends of the recent past. His various articulations of this theme before he became president, however, left open a great many possible strategies of macroeconomic policy. It was a tent big enough to cover supply-siders, monetarists, old-time-religionists, and probably many slightly chastened veterans of Kennedy's New Economics. It signified nothing about whether the candidate was for or against "the gold standard" or "balancing the budget," or, if it may be taken as Gospel that all politicians are "for" balancing the budget, when and under what conditions. It left open innumerable questions about the size of the budget and about monetary policy. The conspicuous exception, the point on which the Reagan philosophy had a concrete and specific embodiment, was a commitment to a 30 percent across-the-board tax cut to be put into place in three equal annual installments. Still, for those to whom that specific tax cut was not the totality of economic policy, that specific proposal raised many questions about the other measures that would have to be accommodated to it.

One might think that in an era when economic concerns such as inflation seem to dominate politics, a presidential campaign would provide the occasion and necessity for the candidate to formulate an economic policy, an exercise that would educate him and the public. But, of course, that is not the case. Candidates run on the economy, not on an economic policy. The candidates who are out of office run on the terrible state of the economy but do not get very specific about how they would make it better. The incumbent maintains that things are not so bad and were worse when he came in or are getting better.

Thus, the campaign is unlikely to be an educational experience for a future president. In fact, it is more likely to be a diseducational experience. For the purpose of getting votes, the candidate finds himself saying things that he comes to believe and that will interfere with sound policy if he does become president. With respect to inflation, specifically, he may be led into thinking that the problem is due to some obvious and peculiar deficiency of his predecessor that will be easily overcome by his own arrival in the Oval Office. This is, of course, a mistake that may for some time keep the new president from appreciating the gravity of his task.

Although the campaign will not be an educational experience for the president, at least not where economics is concerned, it may yet be a period of preparation for the job that lies ahead. It has become standard practice for a candidate who is not an incumbent to appoint a number of task forces of experts to work during the campaign preparing issue papers that will be available to the candidate and his top officials after the election if he should win it. The contribution of these papers to policy seems to have been small. They are generally not read by the new president or given much weight by his economic officials, if, indeed, they read them, either. On many matters the issue papers reflect much less information than will quickly become available to the new administration after it is in office or even during the transition, when it has access to the bureaucracy. If in the confusion of the transition they get into the hands of anyone in the new administration, it is likely to be either someone who already knows enough not to need the advice or someone who does not yet know enough to know that he needs it.

There is probably a more fundamental reason for the failure of these campaign-year issue papers to have more influence. The papers are the product of outsiders. During the campaign the candidate will have a group of economists traveling with him and advising him on the positions he should take in order to get elected. These are the insiders. They are the people who know what the candidate thinks and in whom he has confidence because they have demonstrated their usefulness and, above all, loyalty. The writers of issue papers are at some distance from these insiders. That is partly because the insiders are too busy and partly because some of the experts on the task forces do not want to become intimately involved in the political process.

Usually the task forces are established without any clear idea of how their product will get into the decision-making flow if the election is won. The task forces serve the purpose during the campaign of demonstrating that the candidate wants to draw upon the assistance of "thinkers" and that a certain number of "thinkers" are willing to help him. When the campaign is over, that purpose has been served. Then the issue paper commands no more attention from the people who are inside than would similar papers volunteered by, say, the American Enterprise Institute or the Brookings Institution or an editorial in the *New York Times* or *Wall Street Journal*. The issue paper does not command more attention because it is not regarded as coming from "us," from members of the team.

Conceivably the national committees of the political parties, especially the party that is out of office, could play a role in educating and preparing future candidates and presidents. They have not, however, been doing so. They have concentrated on the problem of getting elected and have ignored the problem of governing once elected. The party out of office commonly does establish a committee or council to think and write about issues. During the Carter administration the Republican National Committee established a large network of such committees, including one on economics with several subcommittees. Still, the work of these committees is not taken very seriously, because everyone knows that the program of the party will be the program of the next candidate, whoever he may be, and that he is unlikely to be much influenced by the work of the party and may be embarrassed by it. There may still be a role for the party committee to play if it will try to promote discussion of basic philosophies and policies rather than to formulate specific programs. This might at least alert the potential candidates to the options and uncertainties before they get themselves too much committed, and the potential candidates may be more receptive to such guidance if it comes from their own party than if it comes from some other source. To undertake such an effort would, of course, require the party to recognize that good policy will not automatically spring full-blown from the brow of the next president if only he is one of theirs. So far this condition does not exist.

We may take it for granted that a new president will arrive on the scene, on the day after the election, with little preparation in economics or in economic policy. (The day of transformation has, of course, become the day after the election, not the day after the inauguration, because that is when he stops running and starts governing.) The new president may have a fairly specific and comprehensive program—that is, a list of things he wants to do. Recollections of Roosevelt's Hundred Days have put a premium on "hitting the ground running." Still, having a program is not the same as having a policy. A policy is what tells you what to do when you cannot get your program, or when conditions change, or when the program does not work—all of which are things that are quite likely to happen. In that sense presidents do not come into office with an economic policy.

Of course, despite what may be suggested by higher criticism from the media and academia, a person does not become president without being intelligent and a quick learner. A president will certainly learn a good deal about economics and about economic policy on the job. How much and what he learns, however, will depend in part on how he organizes to do his work, which is the subject of this essay.

An example of the possibilities and problems of learning from experience is provided by a conversation I had with President Nixon in the spring of 1973. He was considering restoring a freeze on prices and wages such as that which he had imposed in August 1971. I said, quoting Heraclitus, that you cannot step into the same river twice. He replied that you could if it was frozen. My lesson from experience was that the success, economic and political, of the 1971 freeze depended on conditions that would not recur, partly because we had had that freeze. His lesson was that the 1971 freeze had been a great success. The decision went his way—a freeze was restored—and the outcome went my way—the new freeze was an instant flop. That experience tells something about advising, also.

The obvious consequence of a president's inevitable limitations in the field of economics is that he will delegate many decisions and depend heavily on advice. This is true in all fields, of course, but it is much more true with respect to economics than with respect to foreign policy, usually the other main area of presidential attention. There are several reasons why.

Presidents tend to be skillful in interpersonal relations and to enjoy them. Foreign policy seems to be an area in which much can be achieved by dealings with other individuals—"Brezhnev and I"—across the table. Economic policy deals with abstractions or statistics or masses. The president cannot confront the GNP eyeball to eyeball, or even "the consumer." Some presidents think they can deal with economic problems on a person-to-person basis, the opposite number usually being the president of the AFL-CIO, but that is a mistake and leads to disappointment.

Presidents like to associate themselves personally with dramatic events, for reasons of vanity as well as of politics. There is hardly anything in economic action that can compete with the televised picture of the president alighting from *Air Force One* on the Peking airfield. The only similarly dramatic event in the field of economics in the past forty-five years was President Nixon's announcement of the price-wage freeze and the closing of the gold window on August 15, 1971. Still, even on that occasion President Nixon doubted that the public would be interested in a speech about economics and was reluctant to speak on a Sunday evening for fear of annoying millions of citizens whose favorite TV program, "Bonanza," would have to be preempted. A later attempt to dramatize and to personalize economic policy, President Ford's Inflation Summit, was a great bore, and its accompanying WIN buttons became a subject of ridicule.

There are two other reasons why presidents have not wanted to become involved personally in economics. Economics has been the scene of more defeats than triumphs lately, and presidents do not like to be closely associated with failure if they can help it. There is comfort in having an inflation czar who can be removed or forgotten if things go wrong. Also, the gap between amateurism and expertise may be greater with respect to economics than with respect to foreign policy and most other fields with which a president has to deal, and therefore he may be more inclined to rely on economic "experts." Perhaps that is a parochial opinion of mine, but presidents seem to share it. Richard Nixon, for example, regarded economics as almost a "hard" science, unlike the other so-called social sciences.

President Reagan seems to be an exception to these generalizations in some respects. He has identified himself personally with his economic program to a greater extent than his predecessors have done and has taken the role of the chief spokesman and salesman for it to the Congress and to the public. He has made the economic program his "moral equivalent of war." Whether he is really an exception remains to be tested. As this is written the Reagan program is mainly promises. Whether he will retain close identification with it in 1982 if these promises are not being met will be the test. In any case, the Reagan administration is not an exception to the proposition that presidents rely heavily on advisers for guidance on economics.

Outsiders as Advisers

There are many ways in which presidents can organize to get the advice they require about economic issues, including which decisions are sufficiently important to receive presidential attention and which can be largely delegated to others. In the past, presidents may have obtained significant amounts of advice from outsiders—people outside the executive branch. One has the picture, perhaps apocryphal, of President Eisenhower consulting with friendly CEOs on the golf course or around the bridge table. If that ever did happen, it happens no longer. Perhaps it is more difficult to exchange ideas while jogging or riding horseback than while playing golf or bridge.

Later presidents have attempted more formal ways of getting outside advice. These are usually "commissions" of business, labor, and possibly "public" representatives (typically professors) with whom the president has met from time to time. Presidents Nixon and Ford occasionally met with small groups of private economists. Mr. Nixon once said that he wanted to run the whole gamut, from Friedman to Rinfret. Still, these exchanges were too infrequent, too brief, and too superficial to have much effect on decisions.

The president delegates the function of receiving advice from the outside to his insiders, which of course increases his dependence on them. On some occasions this outside advice can be extremely useful—I think particularly of the advice we received when we were planning Phase II of the price-wage control system in the fall of 1971. On the whole, however, this outside advice has not been very helpful. There are undoubtedly many reasons, but two seem especially interesting and important.

One reason has to do with the character of the advice. From the standpoint of the president and his team, the outsiders almost always engage in special pleading—that is, they attempt to advance some special interest, as distinguished from the national interest. That is even true of economists, whose personal reputations are often tied up with certain doctrines, which they therefore feel compelled to advance in all circumstances. Only a rare person fails to take advantage of an opportunity to promote his own interest if he has an occasion to advise the White House.

It may be naive to suggest that outside advisers represent special interests, in distinction to the national interest represented by the president. Perhaps it would be fairer to say that the outside advisers represent special interests that are different from the special interest that the president represents. Yet this formulation does not change the situation from the standpoint of the president and his people, which is that the outside opinion has to be discounted.

I do not know whether it was ever thus. I have the impression of an earlier time, in the first fifteen years after World War II, when some private citizens accepted a responsibility to give objective advice on national policy. That may be only a romantic recollection of my younger days, however, when I participated in an organized effort to provide such counsel.

63

The other reason for the limited usefulness of outside advice lies in the character of the decisions the government makes. Where lasting strategy—questions of principle—are concerned, outside advice can be timely and informed. Such decisions are made infrequently, they are usually changed slowly, and they rely on general attitudes and experience about the way the world is, not on inside information. Outside advice can influence such choices, but they are obviously not the bread and butter of government. Typically an issue arises, an ad hoc group is assembled to work on it, a body of information is hastily pulled together, the whole decision-making apparatus is seized with the question for a few weeks, a conclusion is reached, and then the process is repeated for the next issue. The wave rises, peaks, and subsides before the outside world can mobilize to offer opinions.

Outside Insiders

The Reagan administration has established an economic advisory unit that has some of the characteristics of an inside group and some of an outside group. That is the President's Economic Policy Advisory Board. The members—thirteen as of April 1981—are insiders in the sense that they are all Republicans and were all supporters of the Reagan candidacy. All but three of them held office in the Nixon or Ford administrations. Yet they are outsiders in that none of them holds office in the Reagan administration. Their inside quality may give them a credibility with the administration that a more diverse group might not have, although that is bought at the expense of limiting the range of views represented. Their outside quality may still expose the administration and the president himself to a variety and independence of advice that might not surface from inside sources alone.

No one knows how this will work, and although the conception seems excellent, the implementation could be delicate. Much will depend on the willingness of the economic officials of the administration to expose to outside criticism ideas on which they have not yet committed themselves and on which various ones of them may have taken different positions with the president. Effectiveness will also depend on the candor of the advisory board members in expressing disagreement with the president or with some of his officials. If the board is merely a council of elders called in to bless the president's decisions, it will not be very useful.

The basic problem here, as in other aspects of the advisory relationship, is that the president has little basis for judging the quality of economic advice. Even if he could tell who are the best economists, he could not be certain that they would be the best advisers. He therefore tends to give very great weight to loyalty as a test. Still, the value of the advice will depend on its independence. There is danger of confusing loyalty with dependence and independence with disloyalty. The outside advisory board, consisting of independent people, will succeed if it can exercise its independence without suggesting a lack of loyalty that will make opinions suspect.

One value of the board is that it will bring a body of experience that the new team will not have. That will be a transitory advantage, however, or it will seem so. The new group will acquire its own experience, which the board members will not have, and that may seem to make the older experience obsolete.

The Cabinet System

Despite these questions, the board of Outside Insiders may prove to be a highly valuable device. Nevertheless, we may expect the president to continue to rely primarily on insiders. If he follows precedent he will think, when first elected and confronting the problem, that he will rely on the cabinet for advice. Nothing seems more reasonable. The cabinet officer charged with a particular subject—the secretary of the Treasury, in the case of most economic questions—will explain the problem to the group of wise, objective, broad-gauged men and women gathered around the cabinet table; and out of their discussion the president will get what he needs for making a decision.

The trouble is that the cabinet is not like that. The cabinet usually consists of capable men and women, but being wise, objective, and broad-gauged is the lesser part of the qualities for which they have been chosen. They have been selected for knowledge of a particular subject, ability to manage a large enterprise, political influence, and fulfillment of the requirement that women, blacks, Hispanics, and so forth be represented in the top levels of the government. There is nothing wrong with these criteria, given the usual functions of a cabinet member, but these are not the people the president would most want to rely on for advice about fields not their own. Moreover, they tend to be ambitious and to see pleasing the president as one way to advance their aspirations. Some of them, through a lifetime spent on the stump, have become intolerably long-winded and are boring talkers in a small group. As a result, even a president who tries is likely to find soon that the cabinet is not a useful consultative body.

An effort to bring something like the cabinet into an advisory role on economic matters was made by President Nixon in 1969, when he set up the Cabinet Committee on Economic Policy (CCEP). This committee was not set up because anyone thought it would be the best way to make economic policy. It was created in part to comfort certain cabinet members who thought they were entitled to participate in the decision-making process.

The CCEP consisted of the president and vice-president, all the cabinet members whose main responsibility was economic, a representative of the State Department, the director of the Bureau of the Budget—later, the Office of Management and Budget (OMB)—the chairman of the Council of Economic Advisers (CEA), and the president's two counselors—twelve people in all. The two other members of the CEA participated regularly, as did some other people occasionally. The president carried through gamely, meeting with this crowd about once a month for a year. It served at least one purpose for him: It enabled him to watch in action some of his cabinet members whom he had not known before and to acquire some impression of their qualities. Still, it was not an efficient way to make decisions. Too many people spent too much time talking about subjects about which they knew too little. Moreover, the president was not going to share his thoughts with so many people who had no need to know them. At the end of 1969 the president turned the chairmanship of the group over to the vice-president. That was for all practical purposes the end of CCEP, because the cabinet members had no interest in attending meetings chaired by the vice-president.

Mr. Reagan's experiment with the use of the cabinet as a committee to discuss economic policy was even briefer. After about one month of his term he decided to use, instead of the cabinet, an economics group which, however, as initially established was almost as large as the cabinet. Nevertheless, it immediately appeared that this group was not the scene of the action either.

At the other extreme from using the cabinet as a source of advice on economic policy is the one-on-one system. The president meets regularly with one chosen adviser who serves as his source of information, ideas, and recommendations and with whom he discusses his thinking during the process of reaching a decision. This is the kind of relation that both Presidents Nixon and Ford apparently had with Henry Kissinger. No president has had quite that relation with anyone in the field of economics, although the relation between Richard Nixon and John Connally approached it for a time.

The one-on-one system can be dangerous. The president is likely to be, or at least to feel, quite inadequate in his understanding of economic questions, compared with his adviser. The result can be that the adviser becomes the policy maker, which is a mistake.

Even if the two parties are in the proper relation to each other, the two-handed decision-making process may be too unstable. That is, it may not take much of a change of mood or perception by the two people to produce a lurch of policy, which might have been avoided if a larger number of people, with different temperaments and viewpoints, had been consulted.

President Carter came into office with the idea that he was going to operate by what was called the "spokes-of-the-wheel" system. He would meet separately with each of his economic officials and advisers, obtain the views of each on the current economic policy issue, and make his own decision on the basis of what he had heard. This is a clearly unworkable process. It is wasteful of the president's time. More important, it deprives him of the advantage of seeing the interaction among his advisers. He does not get the assistance he should get from each of his experts in evaluating the arguments of the others.

The Central Committee

In recent years, although some administrators have made starts in other directions, the organization for giving advice on economic policy to the president has always boiled down to a small committee, of three to six people, which could be supplemented as necessary by others who had special knowledge or responsibility in a particular field. This committee set the economic agenda for the president and the executive office, made some decisions on its own, recommended decisions on other matters to the president, and on the most important matters, presented to him an analysis indicating the more eligible options and the arguments for and against them.

During the 1960s the central committee was called the Troika, consisting of the secretary of the Treasury, the director of the Bureau of the Budget, and the chairman of the Council of Economic Advisers. To some extent this composition of the group reflected the view that federal economic policy was fiscal policy. As Arthur Okun, chairman of the CEA in the later days of the Johnson administration, explained the rationale for the Troika: Treasury had the revenue, Budget had the expenditures, and CEA had the deficit. There were, however, strong reasons for these three to remain the core of the central committee even when presidential economics expanded far beyond fiscal policy. The secretary of the Treasury is the senior economic official of the government. The director of the OMB, with the assistance of an expert and mainly permanent staff, is the best-informed person in the administration on all the programs of government, by virtue of his agency's responsibility for monitoring the expenditures of all the agencies. Of all the economic officials in government, the chairman of the CEA is institutionally the most objective in the sense that he has no parochial departmental or agency interests. Of all the professional economists in government, the CEA chairman is the most presidential, and of all the presidential advisers he is the most professional.

As presidential economics expanded beyond fiscal policy, the Troika was also expanded, in two quite different ways. A new organization, the Quadriad, was established to join the chairman of the Federal Reserve with the Troika, in recognition of the importance of monetary policy. The Quadriad never achieved the intimate and operational character of the Troika. The relations of the president with the Federal Reserve have a special nature, which will be discussed below.

The other expansion of the Troika was the addition of other executive office people on a more or less equal basis with the original three, as the rise of particular problems dictated. In January 1971 a new White House agency, the Council on International Economic Policy (CIEP), was established in an effort to coordinate the often contradictory behavior of the State, Treasury, and Commerce departments and other agencies in matters of foreign economic policy. The director of CIEP then began regularly to attend meetings of the Troika. When price and wage controls were instituted in August 1971 and became a major expression of presidential economic policy, the director of the Cost of Living Council was added to the group. In 1973 when economic policy seemed dominated by energy policy, the official mainly responsible for energy was added.

This lineup has changed from time to time as economic conditions suggested a change of emphasis. Also, other agencies, such as Agriculture or Labor, might be added for the consideration of particular issues in which they had responsibility or competence. In general, as the situation has emerged, the Troika forms a continuous core. It retains exclusive jurisdiction with respect to budget policy and with respect to forecasting and analyzing the macroeconomic condition. There may be two or three other agencies that function as members of the central group on all other questions, and the identity of these agencies changes from time to time. Other agencies are brought into the circle on an ad hoc basis for the consideration of particular issues. The Ford and Carter administrations followed a similar pattern.

The secretary of the Treasury is the natural chairman of the central committee, since he is the senior official, and in ordinary circumstances the only "regular" cabinet member on the committee.

There was a period when another official, designated as assistant to the president, served as chairman. That is not likely to be a workable relation unless the designated person has quite unusual personal stature, relationship to the president, and skill in mobilizing a small group of near-equals. If he does not have these qualities, the secretary of the Treasury, at least, will not accept the committee as the normal channel through which his advice goes to the president. He will seek his own approach, known as the "end-run" in Washington, others will follow his example, and the committee system will break down. That can happen even if the Treasury secretary is the chairman; if he is not strong or respected by the others, they will try to function outside the system to the extent that the president permits.

A strong leader of the committee may operate either in an exclusive way or in an inclusive way. On the one hand, he may try to minimize the role of the other members and essentially use the committee as a facade for promoting his own ideas and influence. He will control the committee's agenda and be its most regular channel to the president. Thus, he can keep out of the committee's purview those subjects on which he wants the president to hear his views only, or first, and he can give the president his interpretation of the committee's advice.

Obviously, this exclusive approach forfeits the advantages of the committee system, however, and gets back to the difficulties of the one-on-one arrangement discussed above. The committee system works well only when the leader adopts an inclusive strategy, giving all members an opportunity to be heard in discussion of all major issues and to be represented in the advice that is communicated to the president.

In the Ford administration the executive committee of the Economic Policy Board, which was what I call here the "central committee," operated with divided, or shared, leadership. The secretary of the Treasury served as chairman and chief public spokesman. A presidential assistant provided the secretariat, managing the agenda, assuring that all relevant agencies had an opportunity to be heard, and supervising the drafting of position papers for the president. This arrangement seems to have worked well. Among other results, it keeps the secretary of the Treasury as the leader of the group but reduces the danger of his dominating it. The need for this arrangement, or its utility, was associated with rather special conditions in 1974. There was a secretary of the Treasury who had not been appointed by the new president and whose relation with the new president was uncertain—to the secretary, to the president, and to all the other people in the administration who need to know. At the same time there was a presidential assistant with long and close ties to the new president and with some background in the field of economics. The joint arrangement solved a number of problems. It is not, however, the ideal arrangement if there is a secretary who is close to the president and has his confidence and who is trusted by all the other participants to deal openly with them. In this case, as generally, the pattern of organization must be adapted to the persons on the stage.

The foregoing remarks have implications for the qualifications to be sought in a secretary of the Treasury. Secretaries of the Treasury are commonly chosen from the ranks of executives of large, successful financial or business firms. The qualities that attainment of such a position demonstrates are useful for the Treasury secretary. Still, it is not his only or even his principal function to run a large organization and exercise skill in dealing in the financial markets. At least as important is his role of leading but not dominating a group of diverse thinkers about economic policy, organizing and synthesizing but not settling issues, presenting issues fairly to the president, and representing his views persuasively to the Congress and the public. The qualities needed to perform this role may be found in Wall Street, but Wall Street success is not necessarily evidence of them.

The Options Paper

The key function of the central committee is to advise the president on what his critical decisions are, what the most eligible options are, and what the arguments for and against each of the options are. This advice can be presented in writing, orally, or in some combination, and the actual combination has depended on the preference of the president. President Nixon relied heavily on written presentations, reserving oral discussion for the most critical and difficult matters. President Ford preferred a larger element of face-to-face discussion with his advisers. Still, however much oral discussion there may be, a written basis seems essential. Writing down the options forces the committee members to concentrate on the main points and to specify the alternatives and arguments as precisely as they can. It also increases the opportunity for each member to see that his position is fairly stated. There is a danger that if the decision-making process relies too heavily on oral discussion, it may be too much influenced by persuasiveness and force of personality rather than by evidence and logic.

The options paper is the noblest work of the president's advisers—the most difficult and the most responsible. Its function is to help the president make a decision but not to make the decision for him. There are two dangers in writing an options paper. One is to tell too much, to include all information that is not demonstrably false or irrelevant and all options that might conceivably be chosen. That does not give the president the help he is entitled to have from his advisers. He is left floundering in a sea of facts and opinions that his advisers would have been more capable of dealing with than he is. It is the responsibility of the advisers to narrow the information and argument down to what is most probably true and relevant and the policy options that are most likely to be worth considering. Thus the preparation of an options paper requires the exercise of judgment about questions that cannot be conclusively answered by the facts. It is not only a prelude to decision making but also itself a decision-making process.

The other danger, which is more serious and more likely to occur, is that the options paper excessively limits the president's freedom of choice. One option can be described so much more attractively than the others that no reasonable person could fail to choose it. (The technique is suggested by Kissinger's Law of Options Papers, that the author should make his preferred policy "option B," because that is the one the president usually chooses.) This is likely to happen even if the authors of the paper do not consciously intend it. They will naturally attach more weight to the arguments for the option they prefer and present them more persuasively. One reason for relying on a committee rather than on a single person to advise the president is that differences among the members provide some protection against excessive restriction of the president's choices. More than that is required, however. The authors of the options paper must make a deliberate effort to give a fair presentation to the options worthy of consideration and not stack the deck in favor of their preferred option.

This points to some qualifications that a senior economic adviser should have. He should understand and share the president's general philosophy sufficiently that he does not exclude from consideration any options the president would want to consider if he knew about them. He should also be sufficiently loyal and responsible to the president, and sufficiently modest, not to try to force his own views upon the president by illegitimate means.

There is an anecdote that masters of ceremony who know little about economics love to use when introducing an economist as an after-dinner speaker: Harry Truman said that he wished he had a one-armed economic adviser, who would not say "on the one hand this and on the other hand that." But this longing for certainty reflects a mistaken conception of economics and economic advisers. On most of the issues that come to presidents, at least two possibilities should be considered, and often more. It is the responsibility of his economic advisers to inform the president of these possibilities.

Economics and Politics

Of course, the president's decision is not absolutely confined to the options presented in the options paper. If the president feels strongly enough he can certainly get his preferred option included in the paper and can even be sure that it is recommended by at least one of his advisers. If necessary he can broaden the circle of his advisers until he finds one who will recommend what he wants. Thus, it probably never happens that the president makes a decision that is not supported by some adviser.

Still, for the president to make a decision outside the range of options spontaneously suggested by his economic officials and to force his own preference into the range of eligible options is rare. There is a view, especially congenial to academic economists, that the president's economic advisers make suggestions to him that are sound economics and that the trouble begins when he departs from these suggestions for "political" reasons. This is a naive view of what happens. As I have already suggested, his advisers give the president a range of options from which to choose, which means that they are options that cannot be ruled out on economic grounds. The president must bring something other than economics into the decision-making process. He can exercise some judgment about the relative probability of the various possibilities and about the extent to which they conform to his vision of the way the world works or should work. He will probably also consider the political implications of the various options.

If the decision turns out to be wrong, it is unfair to attribute the error to the perversion of sound economics by politics or to attribute it only to that. The fault is usually with the economics in the first place. If the economics had been better, the erroneous policy would not have been included in the list of options from which the president chose. This is clearly illustrated by two seriously mistaken policy decisions that I had the opportunity to observe. One was the decision to impose price and wage controls in August 1971, and the other was the decision to push an expansionist fiscal policy at the beginning of 1972. Each of these decisions was politically useful to the president. Still, each of them was recommended by some of the president's economic officials, including economists, and was supported by a large number of economists outside the government. Probably neither of these decisions would have been taken if they did not have endorsement by some economists, especially by some the president regarded as part of his "team."

The presence of political considerations in presidential decisions about economics is certainly not surprising and is not necessarily to be decried. There are, however, three cautionary comments to be made about this.

1. The president should know when the advice that he gets is based on economic analysis and when it is based on political judgments. When President Truman's chairman of the Council of Economic Advisers, Leon Keyserling, told the president that a certain course of action should be taken because it was good politics, the president is said to have responded: "Don't try to teach your grandmother to suck eggs." It is probably unrealistic to expect that in their advice to the president, his economic officials will avoid considerations of political feasibility or political effectiveness. They live in an atmosphere where such considerations are always present. Still, they are not the people on whom the president would rely most for political advice, and they should try to make clear to him what they believe as professional economists and what they believe as political amateurs.

2. It should go without saying that when the president relies on political "experts" for advice about that aspect of economic decisions, he should seek the best qualified individuals he can find. The credentials of the people who can pass as political experts in the White House are quite uneven. Although some are people of experience and outstanding judgment, others have arrived at their position by serving as advance men in a victorious presidential campaign or by working as administrative assistants to defeated congressmen. The problem is not that there is too much politics in the decisions but that the politics is often too shallow. Also, the president's political advisers cannot well appraise the political implications of proposed economic policies if they do not understand their economic implications. This calls for a serious effort to explain these matters to the president's aides whom he is likely to call upon for political advice.

Efforts to bring the political advisers into the discussion of economic policy at an early stage are not likely to be successful. The economic officials will not want their recommendations to be influenced by the political judgment of this political adviser, whom they will certainly consider ignorant of economics, before those recommendations have gone to the president. They recognize that the president will make a political judgment and that he will be influenced by his political advisers, but they do not want the president's judgment to have been foreclosed by their prior agreement with a political adviser. At the same time the political adviser will not want his judgment merged with that of a group of economists before he has had a chance to present his views to the president. Responsible advising of the president will depend upon the effort of the economic advisers and the political advisers to understand the position of the others and to respect the differences in their functions.

3. Although the president must operate within the political constraints that exist and cannot adopt policies that the public will not tolerate, he can also to some extent change those constraints by using his unequaled opportunities to talk to the American people. The president is not confined to choosing the option that he considers most acceptable politically. He also has a responsibility to try to make the economically desirable policy politically acceptable. Presidents commonly take too defeatist a view of the possibility of moving public opinion and too readily accept the constraints imposed by the existing state of opinion. One reason is that they are too short-sighted and place more value on conforming to today's opinion than on trying to change tomorrow's. What is commonly called communication with the public is usually an effort not to change public opinion but to mobilize existing opinion in support of the president's program.

Speeches as Policy

One of the main instruments by which the president can try to influence public opinion or economic policy is his speeches. The importance of speeches and speechwriters in the formation and implementation of economic policy is usually underestimated. A speech is not only a way of influencing public opinion so as to make policy acceptable. It can also be itself a policy action in the sense that it can directly influence confidence and expectations and so influence economic behavior in the private sector. Moreover, the preparation of a speech can precipitate precise decisions on policy issues on which there would otherwise have been vagueness and differences of interpretation within the administration, and after the speech is delivered it serves as a guide throughout the government to the president's thinking.

Some presidents may make a large and specific contribution to their own speeches. This is unusual, however. A president will not get good speeches unless he wants them and recognizes one when he sees it, and he will usually rely heavily on a speechwriter. The success of the president's economic policy will depend greatly on the qualities and position of this person. He not only should be a good writer but also should have a good relation with the president, so that the president will communicate his wishes freely to him and be receptive to the writer's ideas. He should be able to work closely with the economic officials, be able and willing to receive instruction about economics from them, and have sufficient status to negotiate points of disagreement among the persons who participate in deciding on the form and content of a major presidential speech.

Relations with the Federal Reserve

No relationship is of more potential value to the president in his conduct of economic policy than his relation with the Federal Reserve and especially with its chairman. In principle this relation can run in both directions. That is, advice and influence can flow from the chairman of the Fed to the president and from the president to the chairman.

The advice that flows from the chairman to the president can be extremely helpful for several reasons. It will often be true that the chairman has much more experience with national economic policy than the president or any of his inside advisers. The chairman will have the services of a larger economic research staff than the Treasury, the OMB, and the CEA together contain. Through his contact with the twelve Federal Reserve Banks he will be informed about what is going on in the regions of the country, and through his contacts with foreign central banks he will be informed about economic conditions in the rest of the world. Also, the chairman has a degree of independence of the president, even if he has been appointed by the president then in office, which may make him more likely than other advisers to tell the president the bad news or to question the policies the president has adopted or is considering.

The flow in the other direction, the opportunity to influence monetary policy, can be even more valuable to the president. Nothing that happens in Washington is likely to be more critical for the achievement of the president's economic goals than the conduct of monetary policy. It is important that the president's goals and the Federal Reserve's policies should be in harmony with each other. The Federal Reserve's policy for monetary expansion should contribute to achieving the president's goals for the expansion of the economy. That does not necessarily mean that the Fed's policies should be attuned to the president's goals, but it does mean that there should be mutual adaptation. That is to be sought in the relation between the two parties.

Fairly elaborate procedures have grown up for the exercise of this relationship. The chairman of the Federal Reserve meets weekly with the secretary of the Treasury. The three members of the Council of Economic Advisers meet every two weeks with the seven members of the Board of Governors of the Federal Reserve. The Quadriad, consisting of the chairman of the Fed, the secretary of the Treasury, the director of OMB, and the chairman of the CEA, meets with the president on no fixed schedule but on the average eight or nine times a year. Other involvements have developed from time to time. When the administration's economic policy became focused on the Cost of Living Council during the Nixon price-wage control period, for example, the chairman of the Fed met with the council, although he did not become a member of it.

These procedures seem adequate to their purpose. Still, the relationship between the president and the chairman has not developed to its full potential value, the degree of the shortcoming varying with the personalities of the parties. On the side of the advice from the chairman about the administration's economic policy, the main problem seems to be one of trust. The same independence that makes the chairman's advice peculiarly valuable means that he is not a member of the president's team. His objectives will not be thought to be identical with the president's, and that will be correct. Moreover, the president's inside advisers may feel threatened if the chairman gains too much influence, and they may resent public statements by the chairman that are not supportive of the administration's policy. For these reasons there may be a tendency not to take the chairman's advice on the administration's economic policy at face value. These are not, however, very serious difficulties and can be largely overcome by persons who appreciate the importance of doing so.

The difficulties on the other side, the obstacles to achieving any specific and operational agreement between the administration and the Fed on monetary policy, or even to having any constructive discussion of monetary policy, seem more serious (although I must acknowledge that this view may be biased by my having been on the administration side of this relation rather than on the Federal Reserve side). The problems here are organizational and intellectual rather than mainly personal. Discussion with the chairman of the Fed is inhibited by the fact that he cannot speak for the board as a whole. Discussion with the board is inhibited by the unwillingness of the members to reveal to outsiders the differences among them. The Federal Reserve's tradition of secrecy is also an obstacle to discussion. An even more important difficulty is the Federal Reserve's posture, only now changing a little, that all decisions are open for review at least as often as every four weeks, when the Open Market Committee (the board's chief policy-making body) meets.

The main problem, however, is the usual interpretation of the Federal Reserve's independence. This has led to the extreme delicacy on the part of the administration in pushing any precise policy upon the Federal Reserve and extreme reluctance on the part of the Federal Reserve to enter into any specific discussion of monetary policy.

All of this is understandable, but its inadequacy is becoming clearer and clearer. The country urgently needs a moderate-term disinflationary economic policy in whose durability there can be confidence. President Reagan has promised such a policy. This policy will have to be a joint policy, agreed to by the administration and the Federal Reserve. If it is the president's policy alone, without commitment by the Federal Reserve, there will be real doubts that he can carry it out. If it is the Federal Reserve's policy alone, there will be real doubts that the agency will have the political strength to carry it out.

The Reagan administration, at least in its early months, seemed to have embarked on a new tack in the relations between the presidency and the Federal Reserve. Instead of the previous hesitancy about openly and admittedly giving advice or directions to the Federal Reserve, the new administration made strong public statements about what it thought the Federal Reserve should do, in highly specific terms, that not only were highly critical of the Federal Reserve's practice of the immediate past but also seemed at variance with the Fed's current conception of its proper policy. Specifically, the administration put much more emphasis on the stability of the rate of growth of the money supply in the short run than the Federal Reserve did. At the same time, the administration asserted its regard for the independence of the Fed and showed no wish to take over its responsibilities in a formal way.

It is doubtful that this confrontational approach will be more successful in getting the president and the country what they need than the previous more delicate approach was. There is a rationale for the independence of the Federal Reserve. That independence was given, or justified, by the need for the Fed to do politically unpopular things. Such need, in this time of dangerous inflation, is greater than ever. Ways to get around that need are conceivable—the gold standard or a constitutional amendment controlling the rate of growth of the money supply. But if these are solutions at all, they are not for the next few years. For now it is necessary to strengthen the resolve of the Federal Reserve to fight inflation, and that requires strengthening the ability of the Federal Reserve to resist the attacks that will be made upon it in the course of the fight against inflation.

The main reason for the failure of the Federal Reserve to restrain inflation is its fear of the popular dissatisfaction and congressional attacks that will ensue if the anti-inflationary process results, as is likely, in higher unemployment and higher interest rates for a time. Public criticism of the Fed by the administration weakens public regard for the independence of the agency—contributes to under-mining the idea that this institution should be treated with special respect—and increases the vulnerability of the Federal Reserve. The administration cannot expect to have a monopoly on criticism of the Fed. The danger that the Fed will be attacked when the less pleasant consequences of its disinflationary efforts appear, or that the Fed will be excessively timid for fear of such attacks, is increased if the administration has publicly discredited the monetary authority. That danger is especially great if the administration has given the public the impression that the disinflationary process need not involve any unpleasant side effects.

The Federal Reserve needs the political support of the White House just as the White House needs the economic leverage of the Federal Reserve if a national macroeconomic policy is to succeed. Developing a more candid and intimate relation between the president and the Federal Reserve is the most critical requirement for improving the process of economic policy making. Through such a relation the administration and the Federal Reserve should be able to agree on the objectives of macroeconomic policy for the next several years and on the way in which monetary policy would contribute to the achievement of these objectives. That need not include agreement on operating procedures or on day-to-day policy, although there is no reason why such matters should not be discussed between the parties. The agreement should also include a recognition by the administration of the risks in the policy and of its obligation to stand by the Fed if and when it is attacked. Such an agreement could do much to supply the confidence now lacking in the continuity and determination of anti-inflationary policy.

Inflation and Statistics—Again

Geoffrey H. Moore

Summary

Three of the more serious effects of inflation upon our statistical intelligence system are explored in this paper. The first concerns the method of allowing for changes in export and import prices in the calculation of real gross national product (GNP) and the GNP implicit price deflator. Because of the way this is handled in the Department of Commerce estimates, the faster rise in the prices of imports, especially oil, than in the prices of exports has converted a modest trade surplus in current dollars into a much larger surplus in 1972 dollars. As a result, the foreign trade sector of the accounts has been pushing up the growth of real GNP and holding down the implicit price deflator. An alternative method of deflating net exports of goods and services, which does not have this effect, is presented. Some striking differences in the recent history of real economic growth and inflation are revealed.

The second topic deals with the lag in the availability of inflation-adjusted estimates of retail sales, inventories, and certain other widely used monthly series. The delay has various consequences, including a lack of public awareness of what is happening to the real level of economic activity. An effort should be made, I believe, to release inflation-adjusted estimates simultaneously with figures in current dollars, so that the effect of inflation on the latter is readily discerned.

Finally, this paper suggests the need for an improved measure of the rate of inflation embodied in the consumer price index (CPI). The measure that is most commonly used, the percentage change from the preceding month, seasonally adjusted, is highly erratic in its movements. Other measures, such as those that cover a three-, six-, or twelve-month span, have various advantages and disadvantages with regard to their stability, timeliness, and ease of understanding. A new measure, which achieves considerable stability, is reasonably up-to-date, and is fairly simple, is proposed for consideration. The same measure can be applied to quarterly or weekly data and to rates of change in wages, money supply, etc.

A Perennial Problem

Statistical problems pertaining to the measurement of inflation and its consequences continue to plague us. Who would have forecast, in March 1980, that the 18 percent rate of inflation that the consumer price index was registering would hit zero briefly in July? How many are aware that the rising price of imported oil has reduced our most comprehensive measure of inflation? Why is it that, after fifteen years of experience with a worsening inflation problem, statistical agencies still release many of the numbers without, at the same time, allowing for the effect of changes in the value of the dollar? In view of these persistent problems, a sequel to my discussion of this subject in last year's volume may serve a useful purpose.

Inflation, the Trade Balance, and Real GNP

Inflation has been playing tricks with the trade balance. The trade balance—net exports of goods and services—is the only component of GNP that is larger in terms of 1972 dollars than in terms of current dollars.[1] In 1980, for example, the net export surplus was $23 billion in current dollars. One might suppose, since the dollar is not worth as much now as it was in 1972, that the surplus would be smaller than $23 billion when expressed in 1972 dollars. It was not. It was $52 billion in 1972 dollars. For the rest of GNP the relation is, of course, just the opposite. The 1980 figure for GNP excluding net exports was $2,602 billion in current dollars, but only $1,481 billion in 1972 dollars. The implicit price deflator for net exports last year was only 45 (1972 = 100), while the price deflator for the rest of GNP was 182. Many of us have thought we would never live to see a price index less than 100, but here it is.

One result of this anomaly is that net exports have been contributing a much larger percentage to real GNP (3½ percent in 1980)

---

[1] For brevity I shall use the terms "trade balance" and "net exports of goods and services" interchangeably. The merchandise trade balance is, of course, more limited in coverage, excluding the services component.

than to current dollar GNP (less than 1 percent). The net export figures have also been exerting a more potent influence than one might have expected on the rates of change in real GNP and its implicit price deflator.

From the fourth quarter of 1980 to the first quarter of 1981, for example, the implicit price deflator for total GNP rose at the annual rate of 10.0 percent. If one excludes net exports, however, and looks only at the rest of GNP, the implicit price deflator rose at the rate of 9.4 percent. That is, for the great bulk of GNP (99 percent of the total, in fact) the price level was rising somewhat more slowly than for the total. To put it differently, the 1 percent of GNP constituting net exports was causing the total deflator to rise more rapidly than it otherwise would have. The 1 percent tail wagged a big dog because *its* implicit price deflator rose very rapidly between the fourth quarter of 1980 and the first quarter of 1981. The reason for this rapid rise in the price deflator for net exports was that the prices of exports rose faster than the prices of imports. Hence the surprising consequence: the overall GNP price deflator, the most comprehensive measure of inflation that we have, was *pushed up* by the relatively slow rise in the prices we pay (for imports) as compared with the prices we receive (for exports).

Correspondingly, the movement of real GNP was also significantly affected by net exports. According to the official figures, real GNP rose at the annual rate of 8.4 percent in the first quarter of 1981. Excluding net exports, the rate was 7.1 percent. That is because real net exports, as officially measured, shot up at the annual rate of 53 percent. Thus, because net exports affect the statistics so markedly, one's appraisal of inflation and the performance of the real economy hinges to a large extent on how net exports are treated in the national accounts.

The official method of deflating the numbers, and a proposed alternative, are displayed in tables 1 and 2. In the official method, export values are deflated by prices of exports, and between 1979 and 1980 this deflator rose at the annual rate of 10 percent (table 1, line 2, last column). Imports are deflated by import prices, which rose at the annual rate of 18 percent (line 3, last column). Since 1972 import prices have gone up much faster than export prices, largely because of the enormous rise in the price of oil. Consequently, when the export and import values are expressed in 1972 dollars, import values are reduced much more than export values, creating a large export surplus in 1972 dollars. In the first quarter of 1981 (table 2), the export surplus in 1972 dollars was $54 billion at the annual rate, nearly half again as large as the $37 billion current dollar figure.

TABLE 1

ALTERNATIVE METHODS OF DEFLATING NET EXPORTS: EFFECT ON REAL GNP AND IMPLICIT PRICE DEFLATOR, 1979–1980

	Current Dollars (billions)				1972 Dollars (billions)				Implicit Price Deflator (1972=100)		
			Change, 1979–80				Change, 1979–80				Change 1979–80
	1979	1980	$	%	1979	1980	$	%	1979	1980	(%)
1. GNP, official	2,413.9	2,626.1	212.2	8.8	1,483.0	1,480.7	−2.3	−0.2	162.8	177.4	9.0
2. Exports	281.3	339.8	58.5	20.8	146.9	161.1	14.2	9.7	191.5	210.9	10.1
3. Imports	267.9	316.5	48.6	18.1	109.2	109.1	−0.1	−0.1	245.3	290.1	18.3
4. Net exports	13.4	23.3	9.9	73.9	37.7	52.0	14.3	37.9	35.5	44.8	26.2
5. GNP less net exports	2,400.5	2,602.8	202.3	8.4	1,445.3	1,428.7	−16.6	−1.1	166.1	182.2	9.7
6. Net exports, directly deflated[a]	13.4		9.9	73.9	8.1	12.8	4.7	58.0	166.1	182.2	9.7
7. GNP, including net exports directly deflated[b]	2,413.9	2,626.1	212.2	8.8	1,453.4	1,441.5	−11.9	−0.8	166.1	182.2	9.7
8. Terms of trade effect[c]					−29.6	−39.2	−9.6				

[a] Net exports (line 4) deflated by price deflator for GNP less net exports (line 5).

[b] Line 5 plus line 6.

[c] Line 6 minus line 4 (or line 7 minus line 1).

SOURCE: Center for International Business Cycle Research, Rutgers University, Newark, N.J.

TABLE 2

ALTERNATIVE METHODS OF DEFLATING NET EXPORTS: EFFECT ON REAL GNP
AND IMPLICIT PRICE DEFLATOR, FOURTH QUARTER, 1980–FIRST QUARTER, 1981

	Current Dollars (billions)			1972 Dollars (billions)			Implicit Price Deflator (1972=100)		
	Fourth quarter, 1980	First quarter, 1981	Percent change (annual rate)	Fourth quarter, 1980	First quarter, 1981	Percent change (annual rate)	Fourth quarter, 1980	First quarter, 1981	Percent change (annual rate)
1. GNP, official	2,730.6	2,853.8	19.3	1,485.6	1,516.0	8.4	183.8	188.2	10.0
2. Exports	346.1	376.8	40.5	157.4	166.8	26.1	219.9	225.9	11.4
3. Imports	322.7	339.8	22.9	108.9	112.9	15.5	296.3	301.0	6.5
4. Net exports	23.3	37.0	535.9	48.5	53.9	52.5	48.0	68.6	317.2
5. GNP less net exports	2,707.3	2,816.8	17.2	1,437.1	1,462.1	7.1	188.4	192.7	9.4
6. Net exports, directly deflated[a]	23.3	37.0	535.9	12.4	19.2	474.8	188.4	192.7	9.4
7. GNP, including net exports directly deflated[b]				1,449.5	1,481.3	9.1	188.4	192.7	9.4
8. Terms of trade effect[c]	2,730.6	2,853.8	19.3	−36.1	−34.7				

[a] Net exports (line 4) deflated by price deflator for GNP less net exports (line 5).
[b] Line 5 plus line 6.
[c] Line 6 minus line 4 (or line 7 minus line 1).

SOURCE: Center for International Business Cycle Research, Rutgers University, Newark, N.J.

It is the difference in the deflators that causes net exports in 1972 dollars to be larger than in current dollars. If the import and export deflators were at about the same level, then the usual relationship would hold, with the 1972 dollar figures for net exports smaller than the current dollar figures. It is ironic that the oil price explosion should have an arithmetic effect on the official GNP numbers that is just the opposite of what the economic effect is usually presumed to be. The arithmetic effect of the higher import price deflator is to reduce the implicit deflator of net exports, reduce the overall GNP deflator, and increase real GNP. This is because imports have a negative impact on GNP. The more rapidly they rise in price, the less rapid the rise in the GNP deflator. The slower the rise in import volume, the more rapid the rise in real GNP.

This result is a consequence of the method chosen to deflate net exports. It is true that, to measure the physical growth in exports, deflation by an export price index is appropriate. Similarly, to measure the physical growth in imports, deflation by an import price index is appropriate. But it does not follow that the difference between these two deflated numbers is the appropriate measure of the real value of the trade balance. If the trade balance in current dollars is negative, it is difficult to think of any real counterpart that would make it positive. Yet this can happen unless the balance is deflated directly, and until the latest (December 1980) revision of the GNP accounts, it was happening regularly (because the previous estimates of exports were much smaller than the revised ones). Quite apart from this, however, the separate deflation of imports and exports can and does produce movements in the trade balance that are very different from what they would be if the balance were deflated directly. Since the balance itself can be considered to be a component of GNP (it is net foreign investment), it is not unreasonable to deflate it directly, thus treating this component in the same manner as the other components, such as domestic investment or consumption expenditures.

A method for doing this that has been advocated for many years by Solomon Fabricant and other students of this subject is to deflate the trade balance (net exports) by a general price index and incorporate the resulting real balance in real GNP.[2] A general price

[2] See Solomon Fabricant, "Capital Consumption and Net Capital Formation," in Conference on Research in Income and Wealth, A Critique of the United States Income and Product Accounts, Studies in Income and Wealth, vol. 22 (New York: National Bureau of Economic Research, 1958), p. 447. Fabricant discussed this method in an unpublished memorandum, prepared for the National Bureau's Capital Requirements Study, June 1951, "Deflation of Foreign

index that seems suitable for this purpose is the price deflator derived from total GNP exclusive of net exports. This is a measure of general purchasing power—it covers virtually the whole of GNP—and its use for this purpose leaves the deflator of total GNP unaffected by the trade balance itself. That is, since the deflator used for net exports is the same as for the rest of GNP, the overall deflator is the same also. The calculation for net exports and GNP is shown in tables 1 and 2, and the effect on net exports in recent years is shown in figure 1. The level and trend of the real balance derived by this method (bottom line) is very different from that shown by the official method (middle line) and corresponds more closely to the current dollar measure (top line).

Lately, the use of this method makes a remarkable difference in the level and growth of real GNP, and an equally remarkable difference in the inflation rate. During 1979 and early 1980 the growth in real GNP is reduced to zero, whereas the official figures rose gradually until the peak level of real GNP was reached in the first quarter of 1980 (see figure 2). That is to say, the impact of the recession on real GNP developed sooner and more plainly in the modified figures than in the official numbers. In both the official and the modified figures the recession low was reached in the second quarter of 1980, and both show a substantial recovery since then, though it is more marked in the modified figures.

As for inflation, the alternative calculation shows that considerably higher rates were reached during 1979 and that there was a much sharper decline during the recession itself (see figure 3). Between the first and third quarters of 1980 the inflation rate dropped from 11½ percent to 6½ percent according to the modified measure, whereas the official measure remained around the 9½ percent level. In general, excluding the influence of net exports on the measure of inflation shows it to conform more closely to business cycle downswings as well as upswings.

What all this means is that the way the real trade balance is measured can substantially alter the behavior of the nation's most comprehensive measure of real economic activity and of inflation. This finding will not come as a surprise to students of national income accounting. They have argued about it for years and not only in this country, since in many countries foreign trade is a more important factor than in the United States. But the method of

---

Investment." Simon Kuznets used the measure in the final report of the study, *Capital in the American Economy* (Princeton, N.J.: Princeton University Press, 1961); see p. 492 for annual data, 1919-1955.

FIGURE 1
Net Exports in Current and in Constant Dollars, 1968–1981
(billions of dollars)

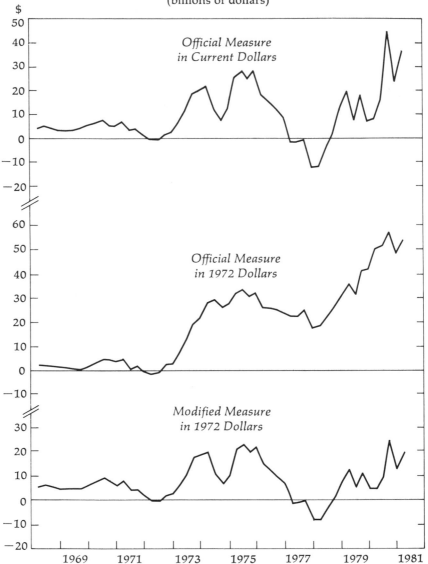

NOTE: In the official measure exports are deflated by export prices and imports by import prices. In the modified measure net exports are deflated by the GNP implicit price deflator excluding net exports.

SOURCE: Center for International Business Cycle Research, Rutgers University, Newark, N.J., based upon revised GNP data released in January 1981.

FIGURE 2
REAL GNP WITH ALTERNATIVE MEASURES
OF NET EXPORTS, 1978–1981
(billions of 1972 dollars)

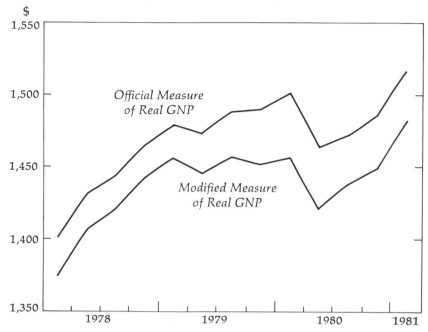

NOTE: In the official measure exports are deflated by export prices and imports by import prices. In the modified measure net exports are deflated by the GNP implicit price deflator excluding net exports.
SOURCE: Center for International Business Cycle Research, Rutgers University, Newark, N.J.

deflating the trade balance has recently become more important, partly because rates of inflation are higher and partly because trade balances are now greatly affected by imports or exports of oil.

In the United Kingdom, for example, the Central Statistical Office has since 1975 regularly published a measure, called "real national disposable income," which is distinguished from their real gross domestic product (GDP) chiefly by the fact that the trade balance is deflated by a single price index (the price of imports) whereas in real GDP, exports are deflated by export prices and imports by import prices (as in the United States).[3] At the time this

[3] J. Hibbert, "Measuring Changes in the Nation's Real Income," *Economic Trends*, no. 255 (London: Central Statistical Office, January 1975), pp. xxviii-xxxv.

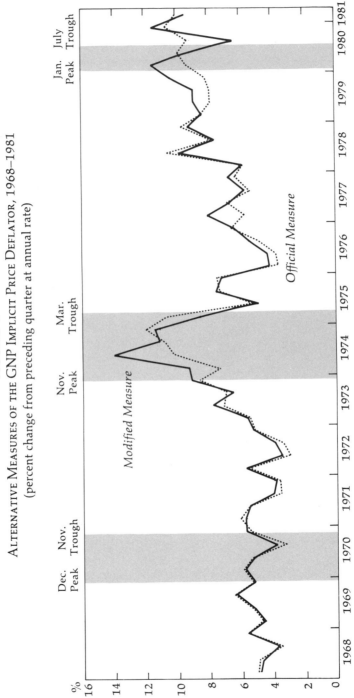

FIGURE 3

ALTERNATIVE MEASURES OF THE GNP IMPLICIT PRICE DEFLATOR, 1968–1981

(percent change from preceding quarter at annual rate)

NOTE: The modified measure excludes net exports. Shaded areas indicate business cycle contractions; the end of the most recent contraction is tentatively set at July 1980.

SOURCE: Center for International Business Cycle Research, Rutgers University, Newark, N.J.

88

measure was constructed in 1973–1974, the effect of directly deflating the trade balance was similar to what it has been in the United States: it reduced the measure of real output. Recently, however, the effect in Britain has been just the opposite, with the directly deflated measure exhibiting greater real growth and implying less inflation. This is because Britain is now exporting North Sea oil and getting the benefit of high oil prices, a benefit that is not reflected in the usual measure of real output (GDP).

Economists have usually discussed this issue in terms of whether a change in the terms of trade should or should not be considered to affect the nation's real output or income. If the same physical quantity of exports will no longer buy as large a physical quantity of imports, has the nation's real output been diminished? When exports are deflated by export prices and imports by import prices, a change in the terms of trade has no effect on the measure of output. When both are deflated by the same price index a change in the terms of trade is reflected in the measure of output. Probably the most widely accepted view is that a nation's real *income* is diminished when imports become more expensive relative to exports, but that its real *output* is not affected. That is why the British have two measures, one referred to as income, the other as output.

It can be argued, however, that a nation's output and income are conceptually the same. Virtually no one disputes this when both are measured in current prices. Indeed, from the outset of national accounting this position has been accepted and estimates based on measures of income and on measures of output (or expenditure) have been viewed simply as different ways of estimating the same total, the differences being referred to as a statistical discrepancy. Why then should real output be different from real income? Is a dollar's worth of output different from a dollar's worth of income when both are measured in relation to the general level of prices? Or is the general level of prices different when it is to be used to measure real output than when it is to be used to measure real income? In particular, which is the more relevant measure of the general price level, an index that goes up faster when the prices we pay for imported oil go up faster than the prices we get for exported wheat, or an index that goes up more slowly in that event?

I understand that by the time this paper appears in print the Department of Commerce may have enlightened us on these matters by producing a measure of real national product in which net exports of goods and services will be deflated directly by a price index, namely the price index for imports (as the British have already done).[4] The results, to judge from past experience, are not likely to differ much from those based on the method proposed here, where net exports are deflated by the price index for the rest of GNP. Whichever method persists, inflation will have stirred up an important issue.

Deflate Now, Revise Later

One of the merits of the national accounts statistics is that estimates expressed in constant prices are released at the same time as estimates in current dollars. Hence one can see what has happened to the physical volume of GNP and its components and at the same time observe the current dollar magnitudes and the implicit change in the price level. With many of our monthly statistics, on the other hand, deflated data are released only later. This is true, for example, of retail sales, of total manufacturing and trade sales, of inventories, and of new orders. One of the consequences is that the press gives almost exclusive attention to the current dollar figures, since these are up to date, despite the fact that the deflated numbers may give a very different impression of the trend of business (see figure 4).

Another consequence is that analysts make their own estimates of the deflated numbers, often on the basis of much less information than is available to the statistical agency. Of course, the agency does not have as much information on prices as it would like to have or will have at a later date, but this simply means that its preliminary estimates will have to be revised. The question is whether the preliminary estimates are sufficiently accurate to be useful. Judging from the efforts of analysts to provide their own preliminary estimates, the answer seems to be yes. When one is seeking evidence of recession or of recovery, under conditions of double-digit inflation, even rough estimates of the physical volume of sales, orders, and inventories are welcome. In appraising the effect of policies to fight inflation, promptly deflated statistics are a necessity. If the quarterly GNP figures can be deflated when they are first released, so can the monthly figures on which they are based.

Our statistical arsenal requires attention in another respect as well. Some figures are reported only in current dollars and are not published in deflated form at all. Examples are the monthly statistics on inventories by stage of processing, the stock of unfilled orders,

---

[4] I am indebted to Edward Denison of the Bureau of Economic Analysis for allowing me to examine his unpublished manuscript on this subject. See his "International Transactions in Measures of the Nation's Production," *Survey of Current Business*, May 1981, pp. 17-28.

FIGURE 4
Deflated and Undeflated Statistics
Prior to, during, and after the 1980 Recession
(billions of dollars)

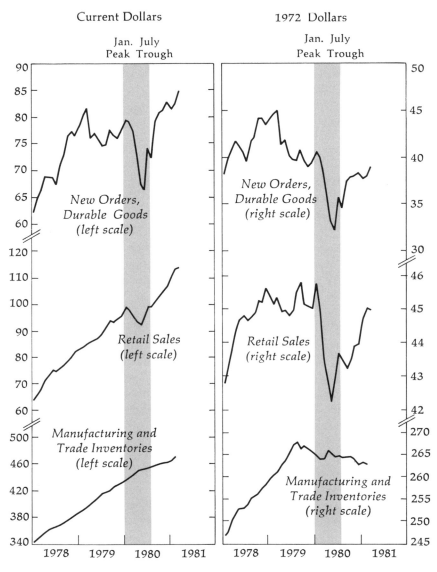

NOTE: The shaded area is the business cycle contraction beginning January 1980; the end of the contraction is tentatively set at July 1980.

SOURCE: Center for International Business Cycle Research, Rugers University, Newark, N.J.

and the volume of credit. Each of these can be linked, conceptually, with other statistics that are published in deflated form. Hence for analytical purposes they should be deflated also. The physical volume of materials inventories is needed to compare with output and to assess the extent of speculative buying in commodity markets. The physical stock of unfilled orders indicates how fully utilized capacity is and to what extent changes in inventories on order are offsetting or augmenting changes in inventories on hand. The flow of credit is related, of course, to both the physical volume of transactions and the price level. Adjusting the credit aggregates to allow for inflation distinguishes the physical component and facilitates comparison with other physical measures such as output and employment. How much credit is simply being used to pay higher prices?

What Is the Rate of Inflation?

Probably the most popular conception of the rate of inflation is a figure that is not even published by the statistical agency responsible for it. It is the seasonally adjusted month-to-month percentage change in the consumer price index, expressed at an annual rate. The Bureau of Labor Statistics (BLS) does publish the monthly percentage change, but does not express it at an annual rate. News writers and TV commentators usually prefer the annual rate, and convert the monthly rate to that basis. On the other hand, the BLS does publish several other rates in annualized form, over a three-month span, a six-month span, and a twelve-month span (that is, from the same month a year ago).

The BLS's reason for not annualizing the monthly rate was, and is, that monthly changes are highly erratic and, consequently, the assumption implicit in the annualizing procedure—namely, that the annual rate is what would be realized if the monthly rate persisted for twelve months—is very unlikely to hold true. Experience in 1980 vividly illustrated this point. In January, February, and March, the seasonally adjusted monthly rate was 1.4 percent. Annualized, this worked out to a rate of 18 percent. But these monthly rates did not persist and indeed dropped to zero by July. The zero rate was an extreme in the opposite direction and was widely recognized as such. Nevertheless, the monthly rates continue to receive much attention, and they continue to be highly unrepresentative of the persistent rate of inflation.

In the long run, I hope, statistical data disobey Gresham's Law. Good statistics do drive out bad. But the law has a certain power in the short run, and in the case of the rate of change in the CPI a single "bad" statistic has driven out a variety of "good" ones. It is easy to show that the three-month rate, or the six-month rate, or the twelve-month rate is less erratic than the one-month rate, and hence offers a better guide to what the underlying rate of inflation is. All these rates are published and available, but they rarely make headlines. Perhaps there are too many of them.

An alternative would be for the BLS to select and emphasize a single rate, which might become known as "the" rate of inflation. It would become known in the same way that "the" rate of unemployment is known. Naturally, other rates could be computed and used by analysts, but the public would be better informed than by a rate that swings from 18 percent to zero in the course of five months.

The candidate that I would propose for this honorable post is not now published by the BLS, nor is it widely used anywhere. But its newness may give it a novelty that existing rates do not have, and it has superior properties of stability. It is a rate determined by dividing the current month's CPI (seasonally adjusted) by the average CPI for the preceding twelve months. The span covered by such a rate is 6½ months—the twelve-month average precedes the current month by that length of time. Hence the annual rate of change is roughly twice the percentage change between the twelve-month average and the current month's index.

When, for example, the CPI in March 1981 was 265.5 (1967 = 100) on a seasonally adjusted basis, the average for the preceding twelve months (March 1980 through February 1981) was 251.5. The rate of inflation, therefore, was $[(265.5 \div 251.5)^{12/6.5}-1]\,100 = 10.5$ percent. What this method does is take the average of the preceding twelve months as a base, and compare the current month's index with it to see how much inflation has raised the current index. The twelve-month average is a more stable figure than any single month, such as the preceding month, which is the base for the month-to-month change. Last month's index may be affected by some special factor that raised or lowered the index in that month. The twelve-month average is much less subject to the influence of special factors. It is also not subject to revision because of changes in seasonal adjustment factors (which are revised every year), since over a twelve-month period the seasonal factors balance out.[5]

---

[5] It would be possible, and indeed preferable, to use original data rather than seasonally adjusted data to compute the moving twelve-month average, though ordinarily there will be little difference between the two averages. But the current month's index *must* be seasonally adjusted since the objective is to obtain a seasonally adjusted inflation rate.

FIGURE 5
RATES OF CHANGE IN THE CONSUMER PRICE INDEX, 1972–1981

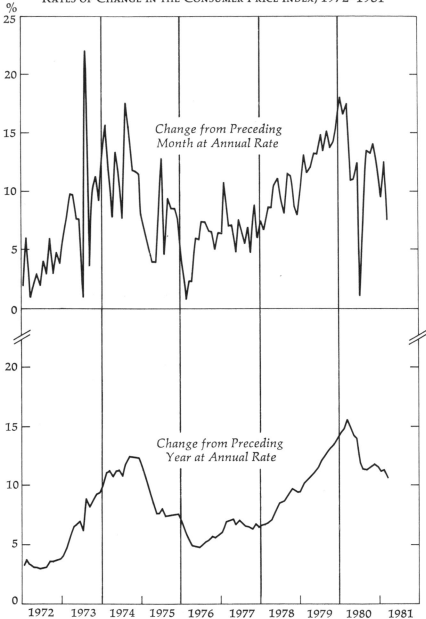

SOURCE: Based upon seasonally adjusted consumer price index for urban households, from the Bureau of Labor Statistics. Center for International Business
Cycle Research, Rutgers University, Newark, N.J.

How stable the new rate is can be seen in figure 5, which compares the month-to-month rate (annualized) with the proposed rate (also annualized). The wild fluctuations in the former are largely eliminated in the latter. The 18 percent rates in January, February, and March 1980 are reduced to about 15 percent, and the zero rate of July 1980 is raised to about 11 percent. Similarly, during the rise and fall of the inflation rate in 1972–1976, the new rate makes it much easier to see what was happening. In 1973, for instance, the monthly rate dropped as low as 1 percent (annualized, in July) and climbed as high as 24 percent (in August). In the same months, the new rate was 6 percent and 9 percent, respectively.

It is true that, if the month-to-month rate rose smoothly to a peak and then smoothly down again, the new rate would be likely to continue rising a month or two longer. That is, it would lag. Something like this happened in 1974, when the high in the monthly rate was reached in August (17 percent) while the high in the new rate was not reached until September (12 percent). A better example of the lag occurs at the next trough, in 1976, where the monthly rate hits its low (1 percent) in February while the new rate continued to drop until June (5 percent). But the fluctuations in the monthly rate make it very difficult, at any given time, to tell whether a true low has been reached or just a false bottom (as in 1973 or in 1975). The new rate is not perfect in this respect either, but it is surely better.

By computing and publishing a rate such as the one proposed (or one with equally good credentials) and eliminating all the other rates it publishes the Bureau of Labor Statistics would, in my view, be doing the public a service. It would tell the nation what the rate of inflation is, in terms of the most widely known price index, the CPI. With inflation recognized as the nation's number one economic problem, we need a number one inflation rate to tell us how we are getting on with it.

Gold and the Uneasy Case for Responsibly Managed Fiat Money

William Fellner

This is a slightly adjusted version of a paper contributed to the Festschrift in honor of Professor Herbert Giersch, director of the Institute fur Weltwirtschaft in Kiel. In the final section of the introductory remarks to Part One of the present volume, as well as in the summary preceding those remarks, I referred to the content of the study that follows here. In the present version of this paper I added a few critical comments on some modifications of the conception underlying the gold standard (see footnote 4 and the passage to which it is attached).

Introductory Remarks on a Controversial Theme

In a world in which short-run oriented policy makers persist in creating inflationary pressures at rates that cannot be predicted without large margins of error, floating describes the only acceptable exchange-rate arrangement. Lack of predictability is an essential property of such an inflationary setting, because even the limited, short-run stimulus derived from inflation would be unattainable if the inflation rate were correctly foreseen. Thus to maintain the stimulus, inflation must be accommodated for a while at an accelerating rate, but full accommodation must occasionally be interrupted to prevent the process from getting out of hand at a very early stage. The resulting environment is one of heightened uncertainty and of lowered efficiency.

To the requirements of such an undesirable environment, floating rates are much better suited than any other exchange-rate system. One of their several advantages is that they permit some countries to resist the inflationary policy pressures to a greater extent than that to which others are capable of resisting it. Furthermore, in such an inflationary world attempts properly to adjust "fixed" rates by occasional administrative decisions would miscarry. The attempt to avoid floating by that method would be apt to result in the rationing of currencies, and even in the occasional closing of exchange markets. This is because of the insufficient flexibility of administratively adjusted rates when excess demand develops.

Whereas in the present paper I take for granted the advantages of floating in an environment of this sort, I am not concerned here with the requirements of such an undesirable international setting. Instead, I am concerned with a specific problem relevant to the overdue effort to put an end to these difficulties by restoring noninflationary conditions. With that objective in mind, the paper argues for the validity of the following three propositions.

1. In a future near enough to serve as a basis for present policy planning, reestablishing the gold standard (to be defined for our purpose specifically later in this paper) can play no useful role in restoring a policy package that performed a significant function in an earlier era. This package included in the past, in addition to the gold standard, policies that can safely be called noninflationary compared with recent Western practices.

2. The unavailability at present of the gold standard as an element of such a package will make the return to an essentially noninflationary course quite a bit more difficult, though it is crucially important that we should make a determined effort to achieve the objective in spite of the greater difficulty.

3. The reasons why the techniques defining the gold standard cannot at present be used constructively by any group of countries are not necessarily "here to stay." I therefore consider it important to keep open the debate not only over the past performance of the gold standard but also over the possible future role of gold in the monetary system, and I feel opposed to the resumption of gold sales by our authorities.

I will refer to the foregoing three paragraphs as my three "numbered propositions."

Jointly these propositions are highly controversial. Those agreeing with the first proposition make up a large majority of my professional colleagues, but they are likely to disagree sharply with the third and in many cases even with the second proposition.[1] Those

---

[1] I believe that Robert Barro belongs among the exceptions, in that I would interpret one of his recent writings as expressing a spirit similar to that motivating my present paper. See his "U.S. Inflation and the Choice of Monetary Standard," Working Paper Series No. PPS 80-30, Graduate School of Management, University of Rochester. This working paper contains the text of a talk presented by the author on April 9, 1980. See also his "Money and the Price Level

agreeing with the second and the third propositions are likely to dis-agree with the first. I will argue for the joint validity of the three propositions.

Attributing significance to the second and the third propositions despite the validity of the first derives its justification from the sub-stantial element of truth involved in the assertion that fiat money has been misused in all history—has always led to the corruption of the currency. Further, it is no distortion of the truth to add that when conditions under inconvertible currencies deteriorated far enough, countries usually coupled a return to healthier monetary conditions with a return to the convertibility of paper money. The reason why the concept of convertibility into gold enters here in connection with the avoidance of monetary irresponsibility is that in modern economic history the essential method of debasing the currency has ceased to be the reduction of the metallic content of coins; instead, it has be-come the excessive creation of means of payment in the form of bank notes and particularly of bank deposits. These are created in terms of currency units for which under some systems it *is* and under others it *is not* possible to acquire an officially determined quantity of gold. If we had earlier phases of modern economic history in mind, we should presumably say "gold or silver," but for well over a century now this has amounted to gold.

The fact that, as an element of a package involving essentially noninflationary demand management, gold-convertibility did play an important role in the past and that at that time it added considerably to the credibility of such a policy package has to do primarily with the *simplicity and easy ascertainability of the behavioral rule pre-scribing constancy of the nominal price of gold.* That rule cannot be disregarded, or even bent more or less unnoticed, when short-run con-siderations would make it convenient to do so. Abandoning the rule is a major and "dramatic" political decision. This is an essential prop-erty of such a system. Yet it is equally important to remember that observing that rule is not a reasonable objective for its own sake. Whether it is a reasonable objective depends on whether its observ-ance serves other directly desirable objectives. This is the case in some circumstances but not in others, as will be argued in these pages.

---

under the Gold Standard," *Economic Journal*, vol. 89, no. 353 (March 1979), pp. 13-33.

A matter-of-fact recent analysis of the obstacles standing at present in the way of returning to gold, without (it seems to me) any attempt to judge the prospects for the more distant future, is found also in Edward M. Bernstein, "Back to the Gold Standard?" *Brookings Bulletin*, vol. 17, no. 2 (Fall 1980). For Bernstein's contribution to the debate, see also footnote 2.

As these introductory remarks may suggest to the reader, I propose to take an unemotional look at some of the main issues involved in a problem that has given rise to highly emotional controversies. Sometimes I have the feeling that the debate about gold has moved increasingly into a namecalling stage: "gold bugs" are facing "debauchers of currencies." From that stage the debate should progress into one of rational economic-theoretical analysis with reliance on the available data.[2]

I will end this section with a word about the concepts of rationality and irrationality. One may be inclined to the position that even if it were possible to return to the gold standard in the predictable future, or even if it should be possible to do so in some more distant future, such possibilities do not deserve detailed analysis, because tying monetary management to gold is an irrational arrangement in any event, even if such a system turns out to work satisfactorily most of the time. I have no quarrel with the "irrationality" thesis per se which is involved in that position, but I find it difficult not to be greatly impressed by the very large damage done to the economies of the industrialized world, and indirectly to other countries as well, by the "irrationality" of the monetary management that has *followed* the era of convertibility. In this newer era it has so far proved impossible to overcome the consequences of highly inflationary techniques focused on a short run that tends to become increasingly short, and that creates the need for uncomfortable adjustments which become increasingly uncomfortable as the political process postpones them further and further. This is the irrationality of the new era, and it has placed the Western economies in acute danger.

Yet, as concerns the options we are facing at present, I feel convinced of the validity of the first of my numbered propositions as well

[2] Aside from the sources listed under the table on p. 109, I made use largely of data found in W. J. Busschau, *Gold and International Liquidity* (Johannesburg: South African Institute of International Affairs, 1961); Peter A. Abken, "The Economics of Gold Price Movements," *Economic Review of the Federal Reserve Board of Richmond*, March-April 1980; W. C. Butterman, "Gold," in U.S. Department of the Interior, Bureau of Mines, *Minerals Yearbook 1978-79*; Hearings before the Senate Committee on Banking, Housing, and Urban Affairs on S. 2704, 96th Congress, 2d session, May 29-30, 1980, pp. 466 ff.; estimates used by Edward M. Bernstein in the *E M B Reports* and kindly put at my disposal; Phillip Cagan, *Determinants and Effects of Changes in the Stock of Money, 1875-1960* (New York: National Bureau of Economic Research, 1965, distributed by the Columbia University Press, New York and London); Joseph Kitchin, "Gold," *Encyclopedia of the Social Sciences* (1931; reprinted ed., New York: Macmillan, 1950), vol. VI, pp. 689-693; International Monetary Fund, *International Financial Statistics Yearbook 1979*. Abken and Bernstein as well as I have made substantial use *inter alia* of the estimates of Consolidated Gold Fields Ltd., London.

as that of the other two, and I believe I am able to provide here a somewhat detailed justification for all three.

Defining the Gold Standard for the Present Purpose

The gold standard is a somewhat ambiguous concept, the precise definition of which is often made dependent on the specific list of gold-related obligations which the monetary authorities accept under a system. I consider this an unnecessary difficulty. I will circumvent it by regarding a system adopted by a country (or by a group of countries) as a system belonging in the gold-standard category if the following condition is satisfied: the purchase and sale of gold at a fixed price by the monetary authority of any participating country keeps the price of gold continuously constant at that level not only in the transactions to which the authorities themselves are committed, but also in market transactions in general in which the public at large is free to participate.

Achieving this objective without interruption requires a stockpile ("reserve") of gold held by the monetary authorities not only for sales to and purchases from the monetary authorities of other countries, but also for sales to and purchases from private market participants. However, the institutionally prescribed or otherwise generally accepted rules of behavior must be such that very little room should be left for influencing the free-market price of gold by sustained reserve gains or losses of the authorities except for the influence exerted by gradual reserve accruals along the time paths of growing economies. As for the little room that can be left for *sustained* reserve movements beyond this, increases in reserves can be sterilized within limits over periods of considerable duration, and this can perform the function of diminishing the supply available to private holders. From this it follows that in some circumstances it is possible to engage in the inverse operation involving reserve losses over periods of considerable duration as a means of increasing the supply to the private sector. But continuing such operations in one direction indefinitely is even physically impossible, and, if the system is to function efficiently, reliance on them over periods of appreciable duration must be held within narrow limits. Such operations endanger the system particularly because the second of the two operations—reliance on major reserve losses for holding on to a price that would otherwise be changed by the market—removes the anti-inflationary discipline which the system is intended to create.

In other words, the general rule which the system enforces must be such that the gold-price support commitment, and the changes in reserves which the official support operations bring about, should induce the authorities to allow the overall demand for goods and services to rise and to fall along with the gold stock. The general rule requires making the official price acceptable to the market by an adjustment of the nominal demand for goods and services in such a way as to keep the real price (relative price) of gold corresponding to its official nominal price at the demand-supply equilibrating level in the market.

In the interpretation of the mechanism on which the proper functioning of such a system is based, the emphasis thus belongs on the influence of the overall demand for goods and services on whether a given nominal price of gold corresponds to the correct *real* price by market criteria. Reduction of the general price level will raise a real price of gold that was initially too low by the criteria of the market, and even if a general tightening of demand does not reduce the general price level, it reduces or eliminates any excess demand for gold at a real price that was initially too low (hence, will tend to make that real price reflect the changed market forces more nearly). For analogous reasons, general demand expansion will, by raising the price level, reduce the real price of gold corresponding to a given nominal price that was initially too high or will, even aside from this, diminish or eliminate the excess supply that develops at such a real price.

It is with the conditions faced by gold-standard countries in the aggregate (or globally) in mind that we stated the requirement that, given any official price of gold, central-bank policies must be such as to ensure that demand and supply in the gold market should tend to balance at the corresponding real price of gold. But the essential content of these propositions is not altered if the analysis is focused on the country-to-country aspect of the problem as this reflects itself in the balance of payments of individual countries.

The position of deficit countries can always be expressed by the statement that given the exchange rates, and given the international capital movements and the unilateral transfers, they have developed an excess demand for the goods of the surplus countries, that is, the latter have developed relative demand-insufficiency for the goods of the deficit countries (excess supply to these countries). This disequilibrium tends to lead to a change in exchange rates which, however, the gold standard suppresses. The method by which the exchange-rate movements are suppressed involves substituting gold for part of the other exports of the deficit countries since the demand-insufficiency of the surplus countries for the goods of the deficit countries cannot apply to gold as long as the monetary authorities of all countries concerned are willing to buy and sell gold in unlimited quantities at constant prices. Hence, while at the given exchange rates the deficit countries' goods *other than gold* are overpriced from the point of view of the surplus countries, the gold of the deficit countries does not exhibit the behavior of an overpriced commodity but shows the behavior of a commodity *in relation to which* the other goods of these countries are overpriced. At the official nominal price the real price of gold is too low in the deficit countries and too high in the surplus countries. If the system is to function properly, however, the resulting gold movements will lead to the adjustment of the demand for goods and services in general in such a way as to eliminate the deficit countries' excess demand for the goods (other than gold) of the surplus countries, and thus to eliminate the surplus countries' demand-insufficiency for the goods (other than gold) of the deficit countries. The overpricing and underpricing relative to gold will then also disappear. The real price of gold will be set right again by the criteria of the market and, given the nominal price of gold, its real price and the general price level are two sides of the same coin.

The gold-exchange standard, in contrast with what sometimes is considered the gold standard proper, is described by the practice of some participating countries to substitute for monetary gold reserves, in part at least, claims on the monetary authorities of other countries that are maintaining gold reserves for keeping the price of gold constant in terms of their own currency. Yet this raises no question of principle beyond that already pointed out, namely, whether there is a sufficient stockpile of gold behind the system as a whole to maintain the price of gold continuously fixed at the officially announced level, without permitting a discrepancy to develop between this price and the gold price tending to develop in the free market.[3]

As concerns the official dollar price and the private market price of gold, the Bretton Woods system kept the United States close to the

[3] This is not to say that in respects other than that stressed in the text the "gold-exchange" variety of gold-standard type systems is not worth distinguishing from other varieties. Even as concerns the ability of the authorities to hold the price of gold at a fixed level—that is, even in the context of the discussion in the paper—it is to be noted that all gold-saving devices have an effect on the proportion of the gold output available for satisfying the private demand. This is a point to which we shall return. Further, the adjustment mechanism under the gold-exchange variety of the system must satisfy specific conditions: whenever the manageability of the system requires a gradual increase in the gold-convertible reserves of participating countries, the countries whose money is held by others as a gold-convertible reserve must have a sum of current account transactions and of private capital exports or imports to which (jointly) a negative sign attaches. That is, they must have a balance of payments deficit in this sense. I am, of course, not opposed to distinguishing such special characteristics of the gold-exchange standard, but for the purpose of the analysis in this paper it is a variety of the gold standard.

requirements of the gold standard in the sense explained above, even if two qualifications will subsequently have to be added to this interpretation. In the entire post–World War II period up to the collapse of the Bretton Woods system in 1971, the official price of gold remained at $35 an ounce, and deviations of the free market price from this level did remain small in all years except 1968. Whereas the United States was obligated to buying and selling gold at this price only in its relations with foreign official agencies, and while the official agencies of the other countries were settling with each other mostly in dollars, the participating countries achieved near equality of the free market price with the official dollar price of gold by transactions in the world market whenever that was needed.

Yet if for this reason we interpret the United States as having been "essentially on gold" not only up to World War II but through the Bretton Woods era, two qualifications need to be added. One of these is that in the late part of that era quite a bit of pressure was placed on foreign dollar-holding agencies not to convert their dollar reserves into gold and thus not to speed the depletion of the American gold stock. This was an antecedent of the collapse of the system with a gold price that had been kept constant since 1934 and with a price level that had from that year more than doubled even by the early part of the 1960s. The other qualification is that from 1933 to the mid-1970s the ownership of unfabricated gold by American citizens was made illegal. Yet it is in the nature of such regulations that it is not very difficult to get around them even without violating the provisions of the law. Hence, by the criteria I am applying here, the United States was "essentially on gold" throughout the Bretton Woods gold-exchange standard era, with some qualifications of which the essential one relates to symptoms of an impending collapse at a time when gold was becoming increasingly undervalued relative to other goods and services. The undervaluation became particularly pronounced in the years following 1965 when the American inflation rate started steepening.

For most other countries the question arises with what frequency the fixed price of gold can be adjusted to a different level without the country being "off gold." In the United States the price of gold was adjusted only once in about nine decades beginning in 1879, and this happened in the 1930s. From 1879, when after the Civil War the country returned to gold, to March 1933, the official price was $20.67 an ounce; then, after about eleven months of inconvertibility of the dollar, the country was again on gold at $35 an ounce. I will deal with this by regarding the American system as one belonging in the gold standard category *up to 1933*, and then again as one belonging in that category *from 1934 on,* with a discontinuity developing at the time of the 1933–1934 revaluation. I favor the analogous terminological practice, postulating a discontinuity, also for countries that (unlike the United States in 1933–1934) moved from one specific gold parity to a different parity without an intervening period of inconvertibility; and I favor the same terminological practice also for countries that changed the official price of gold in terms of their currencies more frequently than the United States—changed it during as well as before the Bretton Woods era.

Leaving semantics aside, it needs to be stressed that adjustments of the official gold price express that "something has gone wrong" with the system. While adjustments on very rare occasions may simply suggest that no system can be expected to work perfectly, frequent adjustments by administrative decisions are a sign of malfunctioning.

The Real Price of Gold

I suggest that the usefulness of coupling a return to monetary stability with a return to gold depends on whether the *real price* (relative price) of gold would tend to remain reasonably stable in the market—at least in the sense of changing only very gradually in a more or less predictable fashion. In this case the general price level would tend to remain reasonably stable, or, at least, its slow and gradual movements would bring few surprises, so that the simple device of fixing the nominal price of gold would at the same time achieve what is usually meant by reasonable price stability. Alternatively expressed in terms of central-bank operations: With the *real* market price of gold tending to remain reasonably stable, or tending to show only a mild and roughly foreseeable trend, the degree of tightness or ease of monetary policy which is required for living up to a simple and well-defined obligation—that of keeping the nominal price of gold constant with reliance on a stockpile of "reserves"— *would be the same degree of monetary tightness or ease that would ensure reasonable general price stability.* Yet, with an underlying tendency of the real market price of gold to change at a significant rate, the gold standard would malfunction by becoming associated with significant changes in the price level, and these changes would be very likely to be sufficiently unpredictable to generate substantial uncertainty and inefficiency.

Occasionally suggested modifications of the general conception underlying the gold standard would aim at allowing one or the other modified system to function properly even if the trend in the real price of gold were not to prove mild. These systems would aim at achieving a stable general price level, regardless of the behavior of the real price of gold, by retaining in modified form the basic conception that the authorities need to default in some sense if they do not live up to the commitment to sell and to buy legally defined reserves at a stated price. For reasons commented upon briefly in a footnote, however, I consider these modified systems unpromising,[4] and I will limit myself in this paper to the gold standard conceived of as a system guaranteeing a fixed nominal gold price.

In the preceding pages it was explained that, by allowing the demand for goods and services to adjust to gold movements, the authorities of gold-standard countries are able to avoid discrepancies between the *real* price corresponding to the official gold price and the *real* price reflecting the market forces. Sustained discrepancies of this kind would make the official price untenable. At this point it needs to be added that the expansionary or contractionary moves required

[4] I will comment here merely on two such modifications. Irving Fisher suggested that whenever at the given nominal price of gold its real price changes—that is, whenever the general price level changes at the given nominal price of gold—the nominal price of gold should be adjusted in such a way that the new nominal price should correspond to the new real price at an unchanging general price level. As I see it, the difficulty into which such a system of frequent nominal gold-price changes would run is that trying to keep the general price level *strictly* constant all the time is not a feasible or even a desirable objective, and the system would therefore open the door for adjusting the nominal gold price frequently to make room for whatever changes in the general price level the authorities consider acceptable in view of their various political objectives (pretty much as with inconvertible paper). On Irving Fisher's views, see *Stabilizing the Dollar* (New York: Macmillan, 1925), pp. 96ff.

Various versions of another modification would substitute for the obligation of the authorities to supply gold at a given nominal price, and for their obligation to buy gold at that price, the obligation to deliver and to buy *at a fixed price* a comprehensive *bundle* of commodities the price behavior of which approximates the behavior of the general price level. One of several difficulties here is that neither the authorities nor the public would want actually to *store* such a comprehensive bundle (which concerning storability would be likely to be far inferior to the gold the public can acquire from the authorities under the gold standard), and that such systems would therefore be based on an idea the essential content of which is that the authorities need to pay to the public a *financial compensation* corresponding to a price difference if their demand policies tend to raise the market price of the bundle. The composition of the bundle would presumably have to be subject to rather frequent adjustments if, by inevitably vague criteria, its price behavior is to approximate the behavior of the general price level reasonably well. Also, governments accepting such an essentially financial obligation vis-à-vis the public would, of course, retain their power to tax the public. The system so described would be one of great complexity, and, quite aside from that, it would be very unlikely to create safeguards against loose demand management that would be comparable to those created by the gold standard whenever the real price of gold is subject to merely a mild trend.

for attaining these objectives are apt to become large, and the important requirement of a reasonably stable price level is apt to be violated in a major way, if the gold output shows little responsiveness to the demand for gold. It may be taken for granted that by market criteria the "correct" real market price of a *fixed supply* of gold would change significantly along the time path of growing economies and that predictions of the rate of change would be surrounded by substantial uncertainty. Hence, with the output irresponsive to demand and with the nominal price of gold held constant, large pressures would be generated on the price level in an environment of high risk.

This proposition places the emphasis on market forces, and on the supply as well as the demand which they generate, rather than on decisions of the monetary authorities to absorb more or less of the gold output and of the gold stock. One's inclination to place the emphasis in the analysis of trends on the public's preference functions rather than on the rate of change of monetary reserves along the time path of growing economies is supported by economic history. We shall soon see that in the United States the real price of gold had a moderate downward trend over a period of roughly ninety years, and that was a period during which the monetary authorities were absorbing a high proportion of the gold output—part of the time a rising proportion. More recently the real price of gold has been rising steeply, though the authorities have been decreasing their gold holdings. In the interpretation of these trends the emphasis belongs on private market behavior.

In a matter of such complexity, however, few generalizations hold without a qualifying comment. As for the emphasis on the demand-supply relations in the private sector, rather than on the demand originating in the monetary authorities, it must be taken into account that the reduction of the real market price of gold in the era of subtantially *rising* official holdings would have been smaller, or would have been turned into a rising real price, if various innovations in the management of gold-standard type systems as well as in the private financial markets had not gradually increased the amount of money compatible with any given official gold stock. The importance of these innovations must not be overlooked; but recognizing their importance does not contradict the statement that in the era of significantly rising official stocks the market forces generated a mild downward trend in the real price of gold and that in a subsequent period of declining official stocks the market forces generated a steeply rising real price. This directs attention primarily to the market forces, and to the large role that the private demand for gold

107

and the responsiveness of the output to the total demand have played in shaping these forces.

As concerns the general price trend, the record of our post–1879 gold-standard period up to 1965 was certainly far more satisfactory than our subsequent record has been. For the period 1879–1965 as a whole, during which there occurred one instance of gold revaluation, we obtain a 1.4 percent average yearly compound rate of increase in the consumer price index (CPI), as shown in the table below. This eighty-six-year period does, to be sure, include subperiods for which the behavior of the American price level cannot be properly described as expressing reasonable stability and for which the behavior of the real price of gold can also not be so described. But most of this instability of behavior during various subperiods can be explained by wars and events following wars. The inflation of World War I was followed by a downward moving price level with deflation becoming sharp and highly damaging during the Great Depression. Nevertheless, only partially did the cumulated deflation of the post–World War I subperiod offset the general price increases of the war years (that is, the earlier decrease of the real price of gold), and yet gold was not revalued until 1934. The inflation of World War II and that of the Korean war were never offset by any subsequent decreases of general price level—indeed, were followed by a renewed flare-up of the American inflation after 1965—and yet gold was not revalued during the quarter century following the war. Thereafter the system collapsed.

Furthermore, the difficulties caused by wars for American monetary management are given insufficient weight by any such account limiting itself to the United States. After World War I most major European countries took several years to return to gold, and they did so after going through a period of severe inflationary disorder. When stabilization did occur abroad, the gold parity of most currencies corresponded to a lower real price of gold than had been the case prior to the war, but lower to a different extent in different countries. In the 1930s many countries abroad went off gold again, and, with the greatly increasing likelihood of a new war soon, capital movements into the United States became very large.

I have not carried the table beyond 1965 because the span from that year to 1971 was the immediate antecedent of the collapse of Bretton Woods, with our average yearly rate of price increase already starting to accelerate noticeably and the real price of gold thus declining in those final years of the system at an average yearly rate of more than 4 percent. The collapse of Bretton Woods was followed by a brief period in which unsuccessful attempts were made to sta-

Gold Price Trends in the United States, 1879–1965

	Official Dollar Price of Gold per Troy Ounce	Average Yearly Rate of Increase of CPI (percent)	Average Yearly Rate of Change of Real Price of Gold (percent)
1879–1965[a]	Revalued in 1934 by 69.3 percent, from 20.67 to 35.00	1.4	−0.8
1879–1933	20.67	0.6	−0.6
1879–1929	20.67	1.2	−1.2
1879–1896[b]	20.67	−0.7	0.7
1896–1913[b]	20.67	1.0	−1.0
1913–1929	20.67	3.4 ⎱ jointly +1.3	−3.4 ⎱ jointly −1.3
1929–1933[b]	20.67	−7.0 ⎰	7.0 ⎰
1929–1965	Revalued in 1934 by 69.3 percent, from 20.67 to 35.00	1.7	−0.2
1934–1965	35.00	2.8	−2.8
1934–1951	35.00	3.9	−3.9
1951–1965[b]	35.00	1.4	−1.4

NOTE: Roughly the second half of the period 1934-1965 (the third period from the bottom of the table) falls in the Bretton Woods era in which the United States was committed to converting on demand into gold at the official price any dollar balances presented by the other central banks. The currencies of many other countries were devalued and some were revalued upward relative to the dollar during that period. While the central banks of the other countries were accumulating large dollar balances, several were converting part of their reserves into gold. From 1949 to 1965 the U.S. official gold stock declined from about 700 million to about 400 million ounces. In the remaining five years of the Bretton Woods era, when inflation started accelerating in the United States, there was a further rapid decline. The aggregate official gold stock in the system rose mildly up to 1965, and declined somewhat subsequently. Prior to 1971 the free-market price of gold differed significantly from the official price only in 1968 (though by the late part of 1970 there was again a nonnegligible 6 percent difference).

[a] For the entire period of 1879-1965 the cumulated decline in the real price of gold amounted to about 50 percent of its initial value.

[b] The four periods so marked are the only ones uninfluenced by major wars.

SOURCE: U.S. Department of Commerce, Bureau of the Census, *Historical Statistics of the United States* (1975). CPI data based on Series E135, pp. 210-211. Explanation of methods used for the computation of these and of wholesale price data to be referred to is found in *Historical Statistics*, pp. 183 ff. All yearly rates of change are continuously compounded.

bilize exchange rates at various administratively adjusted levels, and early in 1973 this period was followed by generalized managed floating.

The entire period, as broken down in the table, includes only four spans (designated in note b in the table) that are not affected by major wars. Two of these particular spans (1896–1913 and 1951–1965) show a decline of the real price of gold at a moderate yearly rate, while the other two (1879–1896 and 1929–1933) show a rise of the real price. The first of the latter two (1879–1896) shows a rise of the real price at a very moderate rate; the second of these two (the four-year span 1929–1933) brought a steep yearly rise of the real price. But this brief span, ending in 1933, coincides with the Great Depression, and the rise in the real price (reduction of the price level) during these four years of substantial hardship was insufficient to prevent gold's real-price trend from being negative for longer periods ending in 1933. For instance, the real price of gold was lower (the price level higher) in 1933 than either in 1879 or in 1913. After 1933 the price of gold was revalued upward belatedly by a substantial margin. Even with allowance for this revaluation we obtain a moderate yearly downward trend of gold's real price for the entire period covered in the table. But, as was suggested above, this real-price trend was greatly influenced by wartime inflations, followed in one case (after World War I) by partially offsetting deflation and thereafter by belated gold revaluation, and followed on the next occasion (after World War II) by a further increase of the price level. During the period 1951–1965, but not thereafter, this price increase remained mild.

The entire period covered by the table (close to ninety years) shows a 0.8 percent average yearly rate of decline of the real price of gold (see the first span listed). If, instead of using the CPI series referred to in the sources for the table, I had used wholesale price data based on Series E23 and E52 in *Historical Statistics* (p. 199 and p. 201), almost the same rate of decline of the real price of gold would have been obtained for the entire period 1879–1965. The average yearly rate of decline would have come out at 0.9 percent instead of the 0.8 percent yearly decline shown in the table.

The *cumulated* decline of the real price of gold over the long period covered in the table is, of course, large—about 50 percent. By the end of the Bretton Woods era (1971) the real price of gold had lost about 60 percent of its 1879 level, and this suggests one of the reasons for the insufficiency of the gold output to prevent a very steep price increase subsequently. But aside from interludes significantly affected by major wars, the long-run trend of the real price of gold was proceeding at a very moderate yearly rate.

There is no need to conclude that during the period covered by the table this record of the real price would have disappointed the expectations of the holders of gold. The record implies merely (1) that from the implicit rate of return which jewelry, art objects, and the like provided to the owners through their use value, a *deduction* needs to be made to reflect the gradual downtrend in the real price, and (2) that the price which hoarders of gold in the usual sense were paying for better protection of part of their assets from various risks in specific emergencies tended to include a real capital loss (as compared with full maintenance of their real wealth but, of course, not as compared with all available specific alternatives). This relates to the period ending in the late 1960s.

The record of the real price of gold becomes very different for the recent decade. From 1969, when the free-market price was still in the close neighborhood of $35 an ounce, to December 1980, the real price of gold rose *six to sevenfold* which corresponds to an average yearly rate of increase of 15 percent or more. The rise was exceedingly steep in several years of the 1970s, with occasional interruptions by phases of sharp but temporary decline. In December 1980 the real price of gold was 2.5 times as high as it had been at the end of 1978. In this brief interval of two years, the nominal price rose from about $220 per ounce to the $550 to $600 range (after having hit the $800 to $900 range in January 1980).

To put it differently, if at present the real price of gold were the same as it was in 1879, then its nominal price would be about $200 an ounce; if its present real price were the same as in 1929, then its nominal price would be not more than $100; and if its present real price were the same as in 1934, then its nominal price would be about $225. The nominal price would be in the neighborhood of $70 an ounce if from 1879 through 1980 the real price had declined at an average yearly rate of 1 percent which, according to the table, used to be more or less the rate characteristic of longer spans not affected by major wars.

For long intervals ending in 1980 we obtain in reality an *increase* in the real price at the average yearly rate of about 1 percent since 1879, about 3 percent since 1929, and 2 percent since 1934. The average yearly rise since 1879, or since the gold revaluation of 1934, corresponds to merely a mild upward trend in the long run, but the recent price increases have been sharp and the fluctuations of the price have been large. The belief that the recent sharp price increases and the fluctuations are explained almost entirely by inflationary psychology implies that it would be unreasonable to attribute a large part of these price increases and their effect on the long-run trend to changed market appraisals of basic demand-supply relations in the gold market. I will suggest that in view of what so far appears to be irresponsiveness of the gold output to a steeply rising real price, much of the emphasis does belong on changed appraisals of these basic demand-supply relations, which, even quite aside from inflationary psychology, are apt to produce instability of the real price of gold around a rising long-run trend. This change of appraisals is likely to have developed from the nature of the incentives to hold gold in the private sector of growing economies, on the one hand, and from the recent trend in the output of gold on the other.

Incentives to Hold Gold

I will distinguish two incentives motivating private owners to hold gold in one form or another, adding subsequently a comment on why a third incentive is not explicitly listed, and a further comment on the relation of the two listed incentives to each other. In this discussion gold money in circulation can by now be disregarded.

1. *Use-value incentive.* The first incentive is the attractiveness of the implicit rate of return developing to the owners through a flow of *use value* from highly durable objects containing gold. This is illustrated by jewelry and art objects.

2. *Asset-composition or "portfolio mix" incentive.* The second incentive is the attractiveness of including gold in the owner's portfolio of assets in view of a prospective change of the real value of gold or of gold-containing objects. This may provide a positive incentive over a considerable range of possible expected rates of real capital gain, often including even negative gains (losses). Even an asset with an expected moderate real capital loss may have a legitimate place in a portfolio if other assets expected to yield a positive real return carry a larger risk of major loss—a larger market risk *or* a larger political risk.[6] But other things equal, the second incentive will be more powerful the higher the expected rate of real capital gain is on gold.

Comment on why the motivation to hold industrial inventories is not added explicitly. Somewhere between 10 and 15 percent of the world's current gold output is conventionally classified as going to industry rather than as becoming incorporated into jewelry and art

---

[6] It must always be remembered that "expected" gain or loss in this sense means an expected value derived from a personal probability distribution which is known to involve also possible outcomes very different from the "expected" value, and this "variance" plays a different role for different assets. Depending on the preferences (the "utility function") of the owner, an asset with a somewhat negative expected rate and with small variance may have a legitimate place in a portfolio, particularly if the assets with a positive expected rate have a large variance.

objects or as being hoarded. Much of this industrial absorption requires no discussion beyond recognition that the gold held in response to the first and second incentives must, of course, be mined and processed, and that at the industrial level this obviously motivates enterprises to hold inventories as a corollary of behavior resulting from our first and second incentives. Even the gold acquired by industries such as that manufacturing dental products (rather than jewelry and art objects) falls in this category. Even that gold is ultimately incorporated into objects that yield the owner (patient) use value in the form of an implicit return from highly durable goods, and which the owner therefore holds in response to the first incentive. But if the matter is interpreted in this fashion, then the 10 to 15 percent of the world's gold output going to industries should be said to contain a component that does not fit a categorization limiting itself to the first and the second incentives. This component consists of the gold acquisition of industries incorporating gold into equipment used in the production of final goods containing no gold. The electronics industry illustrates this. The motivation leading to these particular gold purchases of industry is not simply a corollary of the first incentive, because here no implicit returns from gold-containing durable consumer goods are involved in the process: computers are not typically owned by consumers. But from the viewpoint of the analysis that follows in this paper the small proportion of the gold output and of the gold stock that does not "fit" in this sense has the same effect as do the gold holdings acquired in response to the two incentives listed in the preceding paragraphs. I will limit myself to those incentives.

Relation of the first to the second incentive. The first incentive is almost always either strengthened by the second incentive or is weakened by it (the latter if the second incentive is negative, suggesting disinvestment). In other words, the buyers of jewelry and of art objects containing gold are aware of the durability and marketability of these objects, which they do consider part of their "wealth." On the other hand, the second incentive may be effective without this having any bearing whatever on the first incentive. For instance, gold bars in a safe create no flow of use value for the owner. Yet, not all "hoards" are held exclusively in response to the second incentive, as is gold held in a safe. Old coins of various sorts are usually included in the estimates of hoarded gold, and these are not held exclusively in response to the second incentive. In part they are held in view of their aesthetic quality, and thus they yield also use value (implicit return to the owner) in a sense similar to that in which jewelry and art objects do.

Reasons for Stressing Output Limitations in the Analysis of the Process Generated by the Two Incentives

In the 1970s the average yearly gold production of the world—*declining gradually* from about 47 million to 40 million ounces including a crude allowance for the rising Russian component—seems to have been about 1.4 times as high as four decades earlier (in the 1930s). This corresponds to an annual rate of increase of only 0.8 percent over the four decades. Going back another forty years, we observe that the decennial output of the 1930s was 3.1 times as high as that of the 1890s, instead of the more recent increase of 1.4 times. This earlier increase corresponded to an average yearly rate of 2.8 percent, instead of the recent 0.8 percent.

Although we thus see that for the past four decades the world output has not risen at any substantial rate, the data to be surveyed indicate that the private gold holdings, now estimated at 1,650 million ounces, have been rising significantly. Of the 1,650 million ounces about 1,100 million ounces are estimated to be in jewelry, art objects, and industrial inventories and the remainder in "hoards." The privately owned gold stock could rise significantly in a period in which output rose little and, indeed, has recently declined, because, although in earlier times the monetary system of the world often absorbed more than one-half of the current gold output, the gold held by the monetary authorities has recently been declining. The monetary component of the stock has declined from about two-thirds of the world's total gold stock in 1959 to little more than 40 percent by the end of the 1970s, and since 1965 the monetary component has declined even absolutely.[5]

Over the past fifty years private gold holdings have risen at an average rate of 2.5 percent. The present yearly world output of 40 million ounces is barely sufficient for accommodating a continued 2.5 percent increase in the privately owned stock. The present Western output—that of the noncommunist countries—which amounts to about 30 million ounces, is sufficient for accommodating only a 1.8 percent yearly increase. Russian sales to the West, which along with sales of official agencies have been making up the difference

[5] The present total stock, including the component owned by the monetary authorities, is estimated at 2,800 ounces. From the 1930s on, the monetary gold stock is unequivocally the stock owned by the monetary authorities. Up to World War I monetary gold included a considerable proportion consisting of gold money in circulation, which became a small component after World War I and has played no role since the 1930s. The present privately owned stock is comparable to the nonmonetary part of the privately owned stock of the era prior to the 1930s.

between private accumulation and the recent Western output, have varied greatly from year to year. Given the rate of increase of the world population and, we hope, its standard of living, the growth rate of the private stock that the Western output or even the world output can accommodate is modest, particularly in an era in which substantial international uncertainties would presumably not disappear even if inflation were to be eliminated. But this leaves open the question to what extent the price at which the past accumulation took place has been raised by inflationary psychology and to what extent it has been raised by a reappraisal of future demand-supply relations in view of the irresponsiveness of output to demand.

If the price has been raised mainly by inflationary psychology—essentially by the expectation that the price of gold will keep up with inflation in an environment in which real returns on many other available assets tend to become negative—then the restoration of a henceforth noninflationary trend would lower the price of gold significantly. Even in that case, however, the growing demand for gold developing in growing economies would thereafter raise the real price of gold at hard-to-predict and probably variable rates *provided* the output remained irresponsive (or insufficiently responsive) to the growing demand. An output sufficient for a, say, 2 percent annual growth rate of the stock would have to rise at an annual rate of 2 percent to remain sufficient for that growth rate of the stock. Another way of expressing this is to say that if in such circumstances an attempt were made to return to the gold standard along with restoring a noninflationary general price trend, then feeling out the proper nominal price of gold would lead to setting the price at the outset much lower than any recent market price, but keeping the nominal price constant would from there on produce a downward tilted general price trend at hard-to-predict and probably variable rates.

In the next section it will be seen that even to the extent that the recent rise of the gold price has resulted from the reappraisal of normal demand-supply relations in the gold market in view of the irresponsiveness of output—that is, disregarding any additional role of inflationary psychology—the resulting price movement would in all probability still not be *monotonically* upward. The general outline of the price developments would in all probability be similar, and the essential conclusion would still be that after a phase of price fluctuations the relative fixity of the output in growing economies would dominate the trend. This would in any event be an upward trend in the real price of gold which under the gold standard would show in a downward trend of the price level.

115

Hence, if we take it for granted that transitional difficulties associated with initial price readjustments are inevitable, output limitations make up the core of the story. Quite aside from what could reasonably be called inflationary psychology, the basic facts suggest that the market participants have reason to anticipate the advent of a long-run upward trend in the real price of gold *provided* the prospect of significantly delayed major output-raising effects of the increased real price of gold is considered too uncertain to be weighted heavily. In this case they have reason to anticipate also that this trend will not reassert itself monotonically and, depending on their attitude to risk (variance about expected values), they will react to this differently.

It is possible to take the position that the consequences of tightness could be postponed over an extended period because at any gold price approximating those recently prevailing, and at any price that might initially seem "just right" by market criteria, the monetary authorities could afford to lose gold to private owners over an extended period, and thereby they could make up for any output deficiency. The authorities could indeed afford to do this, and if they wanted to depress the market price of gold they could obviously do so by selling part or all of the 1,100 million to 1,200 million ounces of gold they now possess. Thereby they could depress the market price significantly for a long time. But, as was already suggested, doing this outside the framework of the gold standard is very different from trying to operate a system belonging in the gold standard category by sustained losses of monetary gold reserves. Trying to rely on sustained reductions of the monetary gold stock for making the gold standard immune to the tightness developing from an inflexible gold output would be basically inconsistent with the proper functioning of any variety of that system. This is so not only because the functioning of the system would be based on a temporary makeshift, but also because, during the entire intervening period of gold-reserve losses, the extent to which the authorities engage in inflationary operations would depend on ad hoc political decisions, *as is the case with fiat money.*

As long as the system would be made to work by the makeshift of gold-reserve losses, the avoidance of inflation would have nothing to do with constraints imposed on the authorities by gold convertibility. The authorities could go on losing gold reserves during an intervening period so conceived by policies leading to a rise in the general price level, and by thus reducing the real price of gold, rather than by merely keeping the real price unchanged in the face of a demand that would be rising even at the unchanging real price. They could generate inflation without any dramatic and promptly observable departure from the behavioral rule making them responsible for the nominal price of gold. Reliance on the makeshift of gold-reserve losses over an extended period would destroy the discipline of the gold-standard mechanism up to the time when, following that period, the system would start relying on the responsiveness of the gold *output* to demand—or, in the absence of such responsiveness, would become faced with upward pressures on the real price of gold.

Barebones of the Process: Gold Stock Adjustment, Flow Effects, and Price Movements aside from Inflationary Psychology and from Gold Sales of the Authorities

Let us now briefly follow through the consequences of a newly developing expectation that the gold-output trend will be insufficient by a substantial margin to match the rising trend in the demand for gold at a real price that initially reflects the market forces. This problem will first be considered without regard to the question of inflationary psychology and to modes of behavior of monetary authorities—questions to which we shall return. The final section of the paper will stress the possibility of delayed output responsiveness such as could significantly influence the outlook for the role of gold.

With the output flow showing no or little flexibility, the price-raising effect of the rising demand for gold, as determined by population growth and by the rise in living standards, would become automatically supplemented by another price-raising effect which is apt to cause major upward and downward movements around a rising trend. This additional effect would be generated by gold purchases motivated by expected capital gains. In this context I refer back to the foregoing discussion of incentives for the private acquisition of gold. Once we assume that, given the supply of gold, the first incentive (use-value incentive) suggests a substantial change in the trend of the real price, the second incentive (portfolio-mix incentive) will reinforce the real-price effect (see p. 113). The price of gold would have to rise to the level at which the acquisition of the use value of objects containing gold becomes expensive enough to reduce purchases motivated by the first incentive to the extent needed for making room for purchases motivated by the strengthened second incentive (portfolio-mix incentive).

If the markets were heedless of the mechanics of the successive price developments so described, there would first take place a steep increase of the price to suppress a substantial amount of purchase motivated by the use-value incentive, and thus to enable the asset rearrangement toward gold to take place in response to the portfolio-mix incentive. After the completion of the stock adjustment the price would decline steeply to make room again for satisfying the use-value incentive; yet, subsequently, the price would rise as population growth and rising living standards raise the amount of gold demanded in response to the use-value incentive.[7] The more predictable the details of this time sequence become, however, the more the sequence will become modified by anticipatory market behavior, which, in the limiting case of full predictability, would lead to a monotonic rise of the real price from the outset. Market participants would obviously not shift to gold in view of a long-run rise of its real price if they knew that the future would bring a passing phase of a declining real price. With full predictability of the course of events, the monotonicity of the rise of the real price would result from slower portfolio rearrangement in the early phases and from subsequent substitution of a rising use-value-motivated demand for the portfolio-mix-motivated demand as the portfolio rearrangement is gradually completed.

Full predictability represents, of course, an unrealistic limiting case. On realistic assumptions concerning foresight, the initially described sequence of price movements—a very sharp *up and down* followed by a *gradual rise*—may be smoothed out to a considerable extent as compared with the account given above, but the instability will not be removed. And quite aside from the initial up and down, and from the extent to which it may become smoothed by foresight, it would be utopian to attribute to experts, or to markets in general, the ability to predict with much accuracy the rate of the subsequent gradual rise of the price—the rise resulting from an inflexible or insufficiently flexible gold output as against a gradually rising demand motivated by the use value of gold-containing objects and to some extent by the amount of hoarding that would take place even aside from inflationary psychology.

This alone suggests the emergence of an environment in which the present outlook is unpromising for associating a return to non-inflationary demand management with a return to a fixed nominal price for gold. The data here surveyed suggest that fixity of the nominal price of gold would run a serious risk of having as its corollary not a reasonable degree of price stability, but first major swings while the "present" appropriate price is felt out and *thereafter* general

---

[7] A small part of the portfolio-mix incentive would, however, continue to play a role after the completion of the stock adjustment, since somewhat more of the current *increase* of the asset holdings of each period will have a gold-price-raising effect.

price deflation at variable and unpredictable rates. It is inevitable that such general deflationary price trends should become associated with a fixed nominal price of gold whenever the real price of gold has a basic tendency to rise at rates that would be very difficult to predict for successive intervals.

So far we have paid no attention to several further complicating factors. The effect of inflationary psychology is clearly one of these, but, as will be argued in the next section, it is not the only complicating factor. In the final section it will be stressed that it would be a mistake to overlook an essential qualification to which the negative attitude concerning the future of gold is subject.

Additional Complicating Factors

While I do not believe that it is *logically* necessary to bring inflationary psychology into the picture to explain the recent instability in the gold market, it is safe to conclude that inflationary psychology has in fact played an additional role. Financial assets that in a non-inflationary world carry predictably positive (or at least nonnegative) real rates of interest, have in our recent environment often yielded negative real rates, and this must have tilted the desirable portfolio mix toward a number of physical assets including gold. This supplementary gold-price-raising factor, the weight of which cannot be appraised at present, must have accentuated not only the recent steep rise of the price of gold but also the instability of the price. Still, this factor is not at the root of the difficulties standing in the way of returning to any variety of the gold standard in circumstances such as the present. If the basic demand-supply forces in the gold market were compatible with a policy package aiming jointly for the restoration of general price stability and for that of the gold standard, then knowledge that such a policy package is about to be adopted would suppress the inflationary gold-price-raising and destabilizing factor, which in the present circumstances does play an additional role. As I see it, the real difficulty develops because the basic demand-supply forces are not shaping up the way they were in the era of the efficient functioning of the policy of fixed nominal gold price, at which time these forces were compatible with an acceptable approximation to long-run general price stability under the gold standard. The basic forces are apt to produce an upward tilted long-run trend of the real price of gold, but one that would not manifest itself in a monotonic rise of the real price, not even if changing inflationary expectations and possible major gold sales of the authorities could be disregarded.

119

Beyond this, there are further complicating factors in the present circumstances. One of these is the instability of the portfolio-mix preferences, including gold-holding preferences, of foreign owners of very large funds, some of whom are in a politically sensitive position and whose risk appraisals are apt to be highly variable. To the extent that these foreign owners are monetary authorities (in form or in essence), this further complicating factor can alternatively be expressed by saying that even adequate responsiveness of output to demand would not satisfy the requirements of the proper functioning of the gold standard as long as sudden large gold accumulations and sales by major gold-holding authorities are not excluded.

The other adverse factor not taken into account in the foregoing discussion is the additional demand for gold that would develop in the future if along the growth paths of economies the monetary authorities were gradually to acquire again part of the current gold output. Of this last-mentioned factor our discussion has not as yet taken account, since so far we have paid attention primarily to the possibility that the future era of gradually rising monetary gold stocks would be preceded by a period of gold-reserve losses on the part of initially "overstocked" authorities. That possibility introduces a different complicating factor discussed earlier in the paper, because during such an intervening period essentially the same kind of leeway would be created for inflationary policies as is created by inconvertible paper money; but what needs to be added here is that from some future point in time on, the monetary authorities of growing economies would have to absorb part of the gold output. Ultimately, the system would have to be kept going by significant responsiveness of the output to demand, that is, to the real price of gold.

Inconclusiveness of the Negative Argument for the Long Run and the Need to Keep the Debate Open

The reader might wonder why he was asked to go through a complex piece of reasoning with the purpose of doing justice to the case for a return to gold if the analysis ends with a negative note about the outlook for such a policy shift in any future for which it would now be possible to develop plans. The answer is that the unfavorable basic demand-supply conditions which were explained in my analysis and which were assumed to last into the predictable future *could* change, as supply conditions have on various occasions changed and have made a significantly enlarged quantity of gold available without much advance notice. Discoveries of new ore deposits, and major technological improvements enabling producers to win gold profitably from poorer quality ores, have after all played a very major role in modern monetary history, and these events have in large part been concentrated into periods during which the real price of gold had been rising in response to supply limitations. For the nine decades covered by our table the great discoveries of the late 1880s and of the 1890s illustrate this point. Even now about 70 percent of the Western output comes from South Africa, the gold mines of which were discovered in the final ten to fifteen years of the previous century, along with improved methods of obtaining gold from the ore there found. The South African discoveries of the late nineteenth century, and the subsequent Alaskan, Canadian, and other finds, came after a period of a significant tightening of the gold supply relative to the demand for gold as compared with the 1850s when the Californian and the Australian discoveries had temporarily put an end to the earlier tightness.

It is easy to find illustrations of positive output effects touched off by scarcities, even if with a lag. It is possible even to take a stronger position on those supply effects by stating that a large price-raising excess demand for gold has so far always led to technological improvements and new discoveries that brought the real price of gold down again. But the lags with which this has happened in different phases of history have been of very different duration. With any reasonable time horizon in mind it is therefore preferable to suggest here the existence of a major potential output-raising effect of gold scarcity rather than to predict such an effect on grounds of past experience.

The conclusions derived from the analysis presented in this paper were expressed in the three numbered propositions of my introductory remarks. To repeat briefly: at present the demand-supply conditions required for making gold a reasonably good "proxy" for goods in general, and thus for a successful return to gold-convertibility, are not satisfied; the possibility exists that for a group of countries these conditions will become satisfied in the future; the general argument against the gold standard that it is irrational to tie the currencies of a group of countries to gold (a single commodity) is inconclusive because the political process by which fiat money is managed also has major irrationalities which have proved highly damaging. These considerations make me feel opposed to the resumption of gold sales by the American authorities.

Part
Two

Productivity and Supply:
International Comparisons

International Comparisons
of Recent Productivity Trends

John W. Kendrick

Summary

This article presents new estimates of rates of change in real gross product, factor inputs, and productivity ratios for the business economies of the United States and eight other members of the Organization for Economic Cooperation and Development for the periods 1960–1973 and 1973–1979. In the earlier period, rates of growth of total factor productivity and of real product per labor hour were lower for the United States than for the other countries. Still, after 1973 the growth of real gross product and of the productivity ratios decelerated significantly in all nine countries, in some more so than here, so that the United States moved up to fifth place in terms of total factor productivity growth.

A Denison-type growth-accounting model is used to explain statistically the proximate determinants of the differences in rates of change of productivity among the nine countries and thus the causes for the slowdown in all of them. In five of the nine countries there was a decline in the rate of substitution between capital and labor (the reconciliation item between output per hour and total factor productivity), and in the others it remained virtually constant. The decline of real net capital formation in all the countries except Canada is ascribed to a less favorable investment climate due particularly to the oil shock and the associated acceleration of inflation. Investments in education per member of the labor force increased a bit faster after 1973 than before, however, in all countries except Japan. In about half the countries, changes in the age-sex mix of the work force, which affects average experience of workers, were slightly less favor-

NOTE: Cavan Capps assisted with the statistical work for this chapter.

125

able after 1973. In all countries, resource reallocations, particularly from agriculture, in which rates of remuneration are lower, were distinctly less favorable after 1973.

Reflecting slower growth, economies of scale contributed less to productivity advance after 1973 than before. Also, rates of utilization of capacity were lower in 1979 than in 1960 and 1973, with an adverse effect on productivity in the latter period. Increasing real unit costs as a result of environmental regulations also depressed productivity growth (as measured) after 1973.

The residual is interpreted to reflect chiefly cost-reducing technological progress, although the net effect of other, unmeasured forces would also be reflected. Rough estimates of the effects of cumulative research and development (R & D) outlays, and of declines in average age of fixed capital goods, narrow the residual further. For the eight countries other than the United States, however, the final residual is substantial in the 1960–1973 period, which is interpreted as reflecting to an important extent the international transfer of technology from the United States. Collateral data on U.S. direct investment abroad, patents granted, royalties, exports of technology-intensive goods, and the rate of diffusion of U.S. innovations abroad all confirm the importance of technology transfer from the United States.

The final residual declined in six countries after 1973, although the decline was modest in Japan, and there were small increases in West Germany, France, and Belgium. This suggests that most other countries did less technological catching up with the United States after 1973; by that time the productivity gaps between the United States and all the other countries had narrowed greatly, as compared with 1950.

Introduction

Concern over the productivity slowdown in the United States in the 1970s has been reinforced by the observation that productivity growth has been higher in other industrialized nations since around 1950. Yet there has been little analysis in recent years of the reasons for the differences in growth rates, nor is it widely recognized that rates of growth of real product and productivity have also declined in the other countries since 1973, in some of them even more so than here.

In this article, estimates of rates of change in real gross product, factor inputs, and productivity ratios for the business sectors of nine countries of the Organization for Economic Cooperation and Development (OECD) including the United States are presented for the periods 1960–1973 and 1973–1979. Using a Denison-type growth-accounting framework, I attempt to explain statistically the differences among countries in rates of change of output per unit of labor input and in total factor productivity for both periods and thus the sources of the productivity slowdown that all of them experienced after 1973. This discussion provides perspective on the meaning of the differentials before and after 1973 and helps in assessing the outlook for the 1980s.

The Estimates and the Record since 1960

The estimates and analysis are confined to the business sectors, since real product originating in the nonbusiness sectors is measured in terms of real factor costs without allowance for productivity change. Still, the business sectors account for the bulk of gross domestic product (GDP) in the OECD countries, and the rates of change of real gross product in the total domestic and business economies are quite close, except for Sweden and the United Kingdom after 1973, when the business sectors grew significantly less rapidly than the totals.

The estimates of real gross product, labor inputs, and real gross capital stocks are all from OECD sources.[1] The real product estimates are at 1975 prices, although relative price weights are from years as early as 1963 for some of the countries. Index numbers of labor hours and of real gross capital stocks (used to approximate the movements of the factor inputs) were weighted together by the factor shares of gross national income in 1970 (which averaged 0.65 and 0.35 for the nine countries).[2] Internal weights were not employed for either labor

---

[1] OECD, *Productivity Trends in the OECD Area*, CPE/WP2 (79), 1st rev. (Paris, April 1980), plus printouts of series not published in the OECD national accounts statistics. The real fixed capital estimates were available only in aggregate for each country. Real gross stocks are used, since it is believed that they provide a better measure of output-producing capacity than do the net stocks.

[2] The estimates subsume a Cobb-Douglas type of production function. It is one in which the exponents (elasticities of output with respect to inputs) sum to more than one, however, since we use economies of scale as an explanatory variable. It also implies that scale economies and shifts in the productivity scalar (due to technological progress and other factors discussed in the text) are neutral with respect to the other causal forces and factor shares of national income. The use of constant factor weights gives results very similar to those obtained with alternative weighting systems based on other forms of production functions. (See G. S. Maddala, "A Note on the Form of the Production Function and Productivity," in *Measurement and Interpretation of Productivity* [Washington, D.C.: National Academy of Sciences, 1979], pp. 309-17.) The gross capital weights for the various countries are as follows: United States, .371; Canada, .472; Japan, .334; France, .382; West Germany, .349; Italy, .316; Sweden, .383; United Kingdom, .348; Belgium, .356.

TABLE 1
REAL GROSS PRODUCT, FACTOR INPUTS, AND PRODUCTIVITIES IN THE
BUSINESS ECONOMIES OF NINE COUNTRIES, 1960–1973 AND 1973–1979
(average annual percentage rates of change)

Country	Real Gross Business Product	Factor Inputs			Factor Productivities		
		Total	Labor	Capital	Total	Labor	Capital
United States							
1960–73	4.4	2.5	1.3	4.5	1.9	3.1	−0.1
1973–79	2.9	2.3	1.8	3.1	0.6	1.1	−0.2
Canada							
1960–73	5.8	2.9	1.6	4.7	2.9	4.2	1.1
1973–79	3.2	3.3	2.2	4.8	−0.1	1.0	−1.6
Japan							
1960–73	10.8	4.2	0.9	10.9	6.6	9.9	0.1
1973–79	4.2	2.4	0.4	6.4	1.8	3.8	−2.2
United Kingdom							
1960–73	2.9	0.7	−0.9	3.6	2.2	3.8	−0.7
1973–79	0.5	0.2	−1.4	3.1	0.3	1.9	−2.6
France							
1960–73	5.8	1.9	−0.1	5.1	3.9	5.9	0.7
1973–79	3.2	1.1	−1.0	4.3	2.1	4.2	−1.1
West Germany							
1960–73	4.6	1.4	−1.2	6.1	3.2	5.8	−1.5
1973–79	2.2	0.1	−2.1	4.1	2.1	4.3	−1.9
Italy							
1960–73	5.6	−0.2	−2.2	4.3	5.8	7.8	1.3
1973–79	2.6	1.8	1.0	3.4	0.8	1.6	−0.8
Sweden							
1960–73	4.2	0.6	−1.6	4.1	3.6	5.8	0.1
1973–79	0.1	−0.2	−2.4	3.4	0.3	2.5	−3.3
Belgium							
1960–73	5.3	1.1	−0.8	4.4	4.2	6.1	0.9
1973–79	2.1	−0.5	−2.3	2.7	2.6	4.4	−0.6

SOURCE: Based on data of the Organization for Economic Cooperation and Development.

or capital, so that relative shifts of the factors among uses and industries with different rates of remuneration affect the productivity ratios rather than the factor input series. The real gross capital estimates were not adjusted for changes in rates of utilization of capacity, so that such changes also show up in the movements of the productivity ratios.

Table 1 shows the rates of change in real product, factor inputs, and productivity ratios for the two periods. The year 1973 was chosen as the boundary between the periods, since growth of both real product and productivity slowed markedly in all countries thereafter, although in the United States and Italy there was already some deceleration by the later 1960s (see figure 1). Factor input also increased less rapidly after 1973 in seven of the nine countries. Although this study is confined to nine OECD countries, it is of

TABLE 2

CHANGE IN REAL BUSINESS PRODUCT, TOTAL FACTOR INPUT, AND
PRODUCTIVITY IN NINE COUNTRIES, 1960–1973 AND 1973–1979
(average annual percentage rates, and percentages)

Country	1960–73 Rates of Change				1973–79 Rates of Change			
	Real product	Total factor input	Total factor prod.	Prod. as Percentage of Product	Real product	Total factor input	Total factor prod.	Prod. as Percentage of Product
Japan	10.8	4.7	6.1	56	4.2	2.4	1.8	43
France	5.8	1.9	3.9	68	3.2	1.1	2.1	31
Canada	5.8	3.1	2.7	47	3.2	3.3	−0.1	−3
Italy	5.6	0	5.6	100	2.6	1.8	0.8	31
Belgium	5.3	1.1	4.4	83	2.1	−0.5	2.6	124
West Germany	4.6	1.4	3.2	70	2.2	0.1	2.1	95
United States	4.4	2.5	1.9	43	2.9	2.3	0.6	21
Sweden	4.2	0.7	3.5	83	0.1	−0.2	0.3	a
United Kingdom	2.9	0.8	2.1	72	0.5	0.2	0.3	60
Average	5.5	1.8	3.7	67	2.3	1.15	1.2	50

NOTE: Prod. = productivity.
a Base is too small for percentage to be meaningful.
SOURCE: Author, based on OECD data.

130

FIGURE 1

CHANGE IN REAL GROSS PRODUCT, TOTAL AND PER LABOR HOUR,
DOMESTIC BUSINESS ECONOMIES OF NINE OECD COUNTRIES,
1960–1973 AND 1973–1979

(average annual percentage rates)

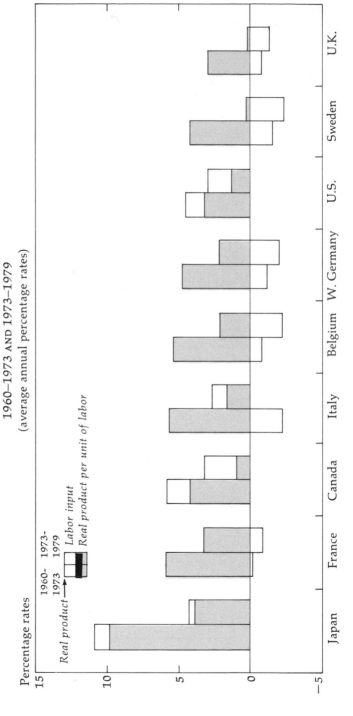

SOURCE: Table 1

interest that productivity and economic growth also slowed down in the 1970s in the U.S.S.R. and Eastern Europe, as documented in D. Gale Johnson's article in this volume.

There was considerable dispersion in rates of change of the several variables in both periods. This can be seen more clearly in table 2, in which the countries are listed in declining order of rates of growth of real business product in the first period. The growth rates range from 10.8 percent for Japan down to 2.9 percent for the United Kingdom, averaging 5.5 percent. The rankings with respect to changes in total factor productivity do not follow quite the same order. Japan is still first, with a 6.6 percent rate, but the United States is last at a 1.9 percent average annual rate of productivity growth. The average is 3.7 percent. Thus, changes in total factor productivity averaged two-thirds of the growth in real gross product between 1960 and 1973, the proportion ranging from 43 percent in the United States to 100 percent in Italy. There was a significant positive correlation between rates of change in real product and in productivity in the first period (see figure 2). There is also some degree of positive correlation between rates of change in real product and factor input, particularly capital input, since a higher rate of economic growth tends to be associated with a higher rate of capital formation.[3]

In the second period, 1973–1979, the average rates of growth of real gross product and of total factor productivity fell to 2.3 and 1.15 percent, respectively. Thus, productivity change accounted for half of economic growth, on average, and was slightly negative for one of the countries. The rankings of the countries changed somewhat with respect to both variables. Whereas Japan still showed the highest rate of economic growth, its productivity performance fell behind that of Belgium, West Germany, and France. Sweden fell to the bottom position on growth and Canada on productivity. The degree of correlation between rates of change in real product and in productivity was positive but low in the second period, as productivity growth fell less than proportionately to output growth in most of the European countries. Contrariwise, the correlation between rates of change in real product and in factor inputs was somewhat greater than in the first period.

The productivity slowdown is also clearly evident in the manu-

[3] The equations for the regressions between rates of change in total factor input (Y) and in real product (X) for the two periods are as follows: 1960-1973: $Y = 3.4391 + 1.1848X$; $\bar{R}^2 = .436$; t-statistics for a and $b = 3.339$ and 2.532. 1973-1979: $Y = 1.1731 + .8650X$; $\bar{R}^2 = .555$; t-statistics for a and $b = 2.325$ and 3.119.

FIGURE 2

RATES OF CHANGE IN OUTPUT PER UNIT OF LABOR VERSUS
RATES OF CHANGE IN REAL GROSS PRODUCT IN NINE COUNTRIES,
1960–1973

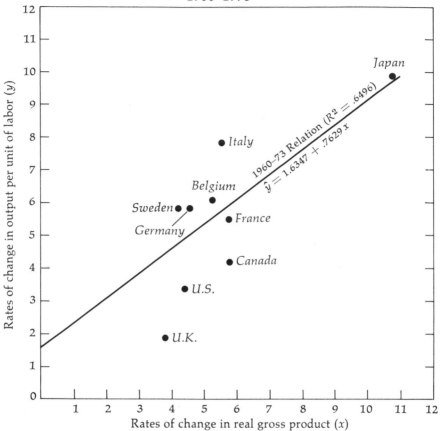

SOURCE: Table 7.

facturing sectors of the countries shown in table 3. The growth of
productivity in manufacturing was almost universally higher than in
the business sector as a whole, and the deceleration after 1973 was
less pronounced except for the United Kingdom.

Nevertheless, the deceleration of productivity growth was accompanied by an accelerated rate of increase in labor costs per unit
of output in all countries after 1973, as measured in national currencies. The acceleration was accentuated by higher rates of increase
in average hourly labor compensation in all countries except Japan,
Germany, and the Netherlands. In these three countries and in

132

TABLE 3

PRODUCTIVITY AND RELATED VARIABLES FOR MANUFACTURING IN
SELECTED OECD COUNTRIES, 1960–1973 AND 1973–1979
(average annual percentage rates of change)

Country	Output per Hour	Average Hourly Compensation	Unit Labor Costs National currency	U.S. dollars
United States				
1960–73	3.1	5.0	1.8	1.8
1973–79	1.4	9.4	7.9	7.9
Canada				
1960–73	4.6	6.2	1.5	1.3
1973–79	4.2	12.4	10.0	7.1
Japan				
1960–73	10.3	15.1	4.4	6.7
1973–79	6.9	12.8	5.5	9.4
Europe				
Belgium				
1960–73	7.0	10.9	3.7	5.8
1973–79	6.0	13.5	7.1	12.2
Denmark				
1960–73	7.0	11.5	4.3	5.4
1973–79	4.4	13.5	8.8	11.3
France				
1960–73	5.8	9.8	3.8	4.6
1973–79	4.8	15.8	10.5	11.3
West Germany				
1960–73	5.5	10.2	4.4	8.1
1973–79	5.3	10.0	4.5	11.1
Italy				
1960–73	7.2	13.6	5.9	6.5
1973–79	3.7	21.2	16.9	10.1
Netherlands				
1960–73	7.4	13.1	5.3	7.8
1973–79	5.3	11.5	5.8	11.7
United Kingdom				
1960–73	4.0	8.6	4.4	3.3
1973–79	0.5	19.2	18.6	15.7
Sweden				
1960–73	6.7	10.4	3.4	4.8
1973–79	2.4	15.0	12.2	12.5

SOURCE: U.S. Bureau of Labor Statistics.

Belgium, the increases in unit labor costs were less than in the United States after 1973, although from 1960 to 1973 the U.S. increase was the lowest except for that of Canada. In terms of U.S. dollars, however, which reflect changes in exchange rates and are the relevant measure for trade comparisons, the U.S. increase was still the lowest after 1973, again except for that of Canada.

The relative changes in manufacturing unit labor costs are roughly reflected in relative changes in industrial prices, as shown in table 4. The correlation is far from perfect, however, because of differential movements in unit nonlabor costs. The relationship is even looser for the broader price indexes also shown in the table, which reflect productivity and unit cost changes in the nonmanufacturing sectors as well as in manufacturing.

It is sometimes asserted that the lower productivity growth in the United States than in many other industrialized nations puts us at a competitive disadvantage in foreign trade. This is an ambiguous proposition in view of the other influences on relative price-level changes, however, and particularly so under a regime of floating exchange rates. Still, domestic industries whose relative productivity declines in relation to the same industries abroad would certainly become less competitive.

As a result of the more rapid growth of labor productivity in industrialized countries other than the United States since World War II, the productivity gaps have narrowed substantially. This is shown in terms of real GDP per employed person 1950–1979 in table 5. The smallest relative gains were made by the United Kingdom and Canada, the largest by Japan. Italy, France, and West Germany all more than doubled their productivity levels relative to the United States. The estimates were based on international price weights, which give somewhat different results from U.S. price weights or other weights of individual countries. Irrespective of the weighting system, however, there was a significant narrowing of the productivity gaps over the twenty-nine-year period.

Sources of Productivity Differences

The productivity estimates we have just reviewed lead to the questions: What accounts for differences in productivity levels among nations, and what factors explain the differences in rates of growth? In the section following this one we use a "growth-accounting" approach, based on that pioneered by Edward F. Denison, to try to explain statistically the differences in productivity growth rates among

TABLE 4

CHANGE IN UNIT LABOR COSTS, INDUSTRIAL PRICES, AND GENERAL PRICE INDEXES IN NINE OECD COUNTRIES, 1960–1973 AND 1973–1979

(average annual percentage rates)

Country	Unit Labor Costs, Mfg.	Industrial Prices[a]	Consumer Prices	GDP Implicit Price Deflator
United States				
1960–73	1.8	2.2	2.4	3.4
1973–79	7.9	11.1	8.3	7.7
Canada				
1960–73	1.5	2.7	3.3	3.6
1973–79	10.0	11.1	9.2	9.8
Japan				
1960–73	4.4	2.2	6.1	5.5
1973–79	5.5	7.2	10.0	7.4
United Kingdom				
1960–73	4.4	4.2	5.0	5.1
1973–79	18.6	17.1	15.6	14.6
France				
1960–73	3.8	3.8	4.6	4.4
1973–79	10.5	8.5	10.5	10.5
West Germany				
1960–73	4.4	2.1	3.3	4.2
1973–79	4.5	5.1	4.6	4.7
Italy				
1960–73	3.7	2.7	3.6	n.a.
1973–79	7.1	5.2	8.7	n.a.
Sweden				
1960–73	3.4	n.a.	4.7	n.a.
1973–79	12.2	11.5	9.8	n.a.
Belgium				
1960–73	3.7	2.7	3.6	4.1
1973–79	7.1	5.2	8.4	7.9

NOTES: Mfg. = manufacturing. n.a. = not available.

[a] Wholesale prices were substituted for industrial prices for Italy and Sweden.

SOURCES: Bureau of Labor Statistics, International Monetary Fund, and Organization for Economic Cooperation and Development.

TABLE 5

REAL GROSS DOMESTIC PRODUCT PER EMPLOYED PERSON, 1950–1979

Country	1950	1960	1973	1979
United States	100.0	100.0	100.0	100.0
Canada	85.0	90.4	94.2	92.1
Japan	15.6	24.1	55.2	68.4
United Kingdom	54.0	54.5	56.8	60.5
France	42.7	54.2	76.5	89.4
West Germany	37.5	56.6	74.2	88.7
Italy	25.7	35.3	54.7	60.6
Belgium	56.2	60.5	78.8	90.5

NOTE: Output based on international price weights; United States = 100.
SOURCE: Bureau of Labor Statistics, May 1981.

the nine nations after 1960. Unfortunately, Denison's initial study of international differences in growth rates ended with 1962 for all countries except Japan, for which estimates through 1967 were presented in a later work, and for the United States, for which his latest work presented estimates through 1976.[4] So our estimates in the next section represent an attempt to update Denison's estimates, with some modifications as explained subsequently.

First, it is useful to review Denison's estimates (somewhat rearranged) of the causes of the differences in levels of labor productivity in 1960, which was near the end of the period covered by *Why Growth Rates Differ* and is the first year of the periods for which we provide explanations for the differing growth rates. The categories used in explaining the level differences serve to introduce those used later in explaining growth differences. Although the estimates in table 6, based on Denison, refer to real national income per labor hour, whereas the Bureau of Labor Statistics (BLS) estimates shown in table 5 relate to real GDP per person employed, the two sets of estimates of the productivity gaps of the other economies in relation to the United States in 1960 (1970 for Japan) are remarkably close.

According to the Denison estimates, the shortfall for the several European economies other than Italy was about 45 percent in 1960

[4] See Edward F. Denison, *Why Growth Rates Differ* (1967); Denison and W. K. Chung, *How Japan's Economy Grew So Fast* (1976); and Denison, *Accounting for Slower Economic Growth: The United States in the 1970s* (1979), all published by The Brookings Institution (Washington, D.C.).

TABLE 6

Sources of Shortfall of Other OECD Countries in Comparison
with the United States, in National Income per Labor Hour
(percent)

	Canada	Japan	U.K.	France	W. Germany	Italy	Norway	Belgium
Total difference	21.1	49.1	44.1	45.1	44.9	64.9	44.4	42.2
Capital/labor ratio	0.7	9.6	10.4	10.0	11.5	14.3	5.7	7.5
Quality of labor	2.8	4.9	3.7	5.1	6.4	9.3	3.0	4.2
Education	4.4	2.6	3.0	4.0	4.1	8.5	2.9	4.1
Age-sex mix	−1.6	2.3	0.7	1.1	2.3	0.8	0.1	0.1
Misallocation of resources	0.9	9.3	−2.8	7.7	4.1	16.9	8.2	2.8
Volume	6.6	−0.8	3.3	3.1	3.0	3.1	4.4	4.1
Scale economies	5.2	3.5	4.6	4.8	4.7	4.5	6.2	5.9
Cycle effect	1.4	−4.3	−1.3	−1.7	−1.7	−1.4	−1.8	1.8
Technological gap, efficiency, and n.e.c.	10.1	26.1	29.5	19.2	19.9	21.3	23.1	23.5

Notes: n.e.c. = forces not elsewhere classified. The comparison is with U.S. national income per labor hour in 1960; the year 1960 was used for all countries except Japan, which is compared using 1970. Norway was substituted for Sweden, for which estimates were not available.
Source: Adapted from E. F. Denison and W. K. Chung, *How Japan's Economy Grew So Fast* (Washington, D.C.: Brookings Institution, 1976).

but for Italy was 65 percent; for Canada it was 21 percent, whereas for Japan it was 49 percent in 1970—and near 75 percent in 1960, according to BLS estimates.

Despite significant increases in the quantity of capital goods per unit of labor in the 1950s, both absolutely and relative to the United States, lower capital/labor ratios accounted for around ten percentage points of the shortfall in Japan, the United Kingdom, France, and West Germany, and somewhat more in Italy, but were a minor element in the Canada–United States differential. Differences in the quality of labor, primarily education per worker but also a less favorable age-sex mix except in Canada, accounted for an average of about five percentage points, ranging from three to nine points in Canada and Italy,

137

respectively. In none of the countries did labor quality advance as rapidly as in the United States in the 1950s.

Allocation of resources improved in all the countries relative to the United States in the 1950s, but misallocation was still a significant part of the differential in all except Canada and the United Kingdom, ranging from three percentage points in Belgium to seventeen points in Italy.

Smaller local and national markets and remaining barriers to international trade were still a significant element—averaging about five percentage points of the shortfalls in all countries. This was true despite major relative productivity gains stemming from economies of scale in all. Still, the shortfalls from volume factors were reduced somewhat in all countries except Canada as a result of stronger cyclical intensity of demand abroad in the year 1960.

The residual, interpreted to reflect primarily the gap in application of technological and managerial knowledge, was by far the largest part of the shortfall in real income per labor hour of all countries except Canada from that of the United States. It ranged from nineteen percentage points in France to twenty-nine points in the United Kingdom. In Canada it accounted for only ten percentage points, however. Surprisingly, the technological gap did not decline significantly in the European countries except for France and possibly Italy, during the 1950s. In the following analysis of sources of productivity gains, we shall see that it did become an important factor after 1960.

Sources of Productivity Growth

A comparison of the sources of growth in real product per labor hour among the eight business economies, as summarized in table 7, shows that the classification of sources is the same as in table 6, with two exceptions. A category for the effects of government regulations on productivity as measured, which grew in importance in the late 1960s and 1970s, has been added. The residual, interpreted to reflect mainly advances in cost-reducing technology, broadly defined, has been broken down into three parts: increases in productivity stemming directly from domestic R & D; changes in the rate of diffusion of innovations embodied in fixed capital goods; and a final residual interpreted for all countries other than the United States mainly as increases from international technology transfer, primarily from the United States. It should be noted that, in some instances, the estimating methodology differs from Denison's, and the estimates for the contributions of the various causal elements differ in quality.

Nevertheless, it is believed that the numbers indicate broadly what has been going on over the past two decades, and the exercise is useful as a framework for discussion of the important forces affecting productivity.

The model relates only to the *proximate* determinants of productivity change. Underlying these variables are the basic values and institutions of societies, changes that are generally gradual and difficult or impossible to measure or even to assess qualitatively (for example, changes in the "work ethic"). In any case, however, changes in underlying values and institutions would affect productivity through the proximate determinants, which will now be discussed by major groupings.

Capital/Labor Substitution. Holding other things equal, the growth of real capital per unit of labor input increases output per unit of labor. According to production function theory, the rate of growth of the capital/labor ratio weighted by the capital share of factor costs (which we call "capital/labor substitution") indicates its contribution to the growth of labor productivity. As shown in table 7, capital/labor substitution in the nine countries is also the reconciliation item between the growth rates of labor productivity and total factor productivity, which is the ratio of real product to a weighted average of labor and capital inputs.

In the period 1960–1973, capital/labor substitution accounted for an average of 34.5 percent of the increase of labor productivity in the nine countries (with an average deviation of 4.5 percentage points). A simple regression between rates of change in labor productivity and in the capital/labor ratio yields $\bar{R}^2$ with a value of .823; the equation indicates that a 1 percent increase in the ratio is associated with a 0.88 percent increase in real product per unit of labor input (see figure 3).

The reason why the regression approach indicates a much greater effect of changes in the capital/labor ratio on productivity change than is suggested by the growth-accounting approach is that the former variable is positively correlated with some other variables promoting productivity growth. In particular, outlays for research and development and the pace of technological progress are related to tangible capital formation. R & D help increase the marginal efficiency of new investments, and the economic climate that is favorable to capital formation in turn tends to promote R & D and innovation. Also, since new plants and equipment are the carriers of much technological progress, higher rates of replacement and expansion are generally associated with faster rates of advance in cost-reducing

139

TABLE 7

Souces of Growth in Productivity in the Business Economies of Selected OECD Countries, 1960–1973 and 1973–1979
(average annual percentage rates of change)

Productivity Measures and Growth Sources	U.S. 1	U.S. 2	Canada 1	Canada 2	Japan 1	Japan 2	U.K. 1	U.K. 2	France 1	France 2	W. Germany 1	W. Germany 2	Sweden 1	Sweden 2	Italy 1	Italy 2	Belgium 1	Belgium 2
Real gross product per labor hour	3.1	1.1	4.2	1.0	9.9	3.8	3.8	1.9	5.9	4.2	5.8	4.3	5.8	2.5	7.8	1.6	6.1	4.4
Capital/labor substitution	1.2	0.5	1.3	1.1	3.3	2.0	1.6	1.6	2.0	2.0	2.6	2.2	2.2	2.2	2.0	0.8	1.9	1.8
Total factor productivity	1.9	0.6	2.9	−0.1	6.6	1.8	2.2	0.3	3.8	2.1	3.2	2.1	3.6	0.3	5.8	0.8	4.2	2.6
Changes in labor quality: Education	0.4	0.7	0.5	0.6	0.6	0.4	0.6	0.9	0.4	0.7	0.1	0.1	0.3	0.4	0.8	0.9	0.4	0.5
Age-sex composition	−0.3	−0.2	−0.5	−0.3	0.2	−0.1	−0.1	−0.1	−0.2	−0.3	0.1	−0.1	−0.2	−0.2	0.1	−0.3	−0.2	−0.1
Reallocations of labor	0.2	−0.1	−0.2	−0.1	1.1	0	0.2	−0.1	0.4	0.1	0.3	0.1	0.5	−0.2	0.8	0.2	0.4	0.1

	1	2	1	2	1	2	1	2	1	2	1	2	1	2	1	2	1	2
Volume changes:																		
Economies of scale	0.4	0.3	0.6	0.3	1.1	0.4	0.3	0.1	0.6	0.3	0.5	0.2	0.4	0	0.6	0.3	0.5	0.2
Capacity utilization	0.1	−0.2	0.2	−0.5	0	−0.3	−0.1	−0.8	−0.1	−0.5	0	−0.1	−0.1	0	0	−0.2	0.1	−1.0
Government regulations	−0.1	−0.4	−0.1	−0.3	−0.2	−1.0	0	−0.2	−0.1	−0.3	0	−0.4	−0.1	−0.3	0.1	−0.2	−0.1	−0.3
Advances in knowledge and n.e.c.	1.2	0.5	2.0	0.2	3.9	2.1	1.3	0.5	2.8	2.1	2.4	2.1	2.8	0.6	3.4	0.1	3.1	3.1
Direct effects of R & D	0.5	0.1	0.4	0.2	0.5	0.3	0.2	0.1	0.4	0.2	0.6	0.4	0.2	0.2	0.3	0.1	0.3	0.2
Domestic technical diffusion	0.2	0	0	0	1.3	−0.1	0	0	0.7	0	0.1	−0.1	−0.1	−0.1	0.6	0	0.8	0.1
Final residual[a]	0.5	0.4	1.6	0	2.1	1.9	1.1	0.4	1.7	1.9	1.7	1.8	2.7	0.5	2.5	0	2.0	2.8

NOTE: n.e.c. = forces not elsewhere classified. Columns labeled 1 = 1960-1973. Columns labeled 2 = 1973-1979.

[a] Including international technology transfer.

SOURCE: Author.

FIGURE 3

RATES OF CHANGE IN OUTPUT PER UNIT OF LABOR VERSUS
RATES OF CHANGE IN CAPITAL PER UNIT OF LABOR IN NINE COUNTRIES,
1960–1973 AND 1973–1979

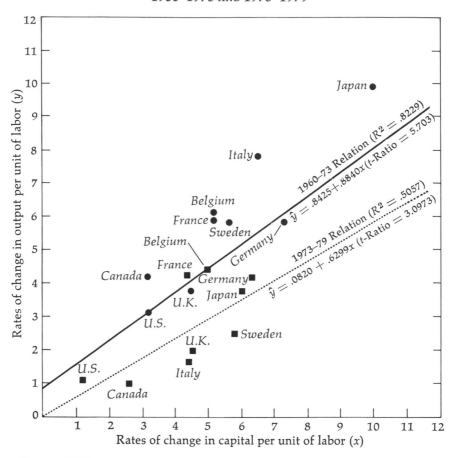

SOURCE: Table 7.

technology. It should be noted, however, that the stock estimates
were made using the perpetual inventory method, assuming constant
average lives for plant and equipment, which may introduce some
distortions.

Increases in capital/labor ratios and advancing technology may
also be associated with some of the other changes that promote productivity, discussed below: an upgrading of the skills and educational
levels of the labor force and shifts of resources toward industries
with above-average rates of factor remuneration. Also, periods of

strong capital formation and rapid technological advance generally provide greater opportunities for economies of scale and higher rates of utilization of capacity than prevail in less buoyant periods.

Even in more sophisticated multiple regression analyses, multicollinearity of the independent variables and specification problems make it necessary to interpret the coefficients with great caution. In my opinion, a growth-accounting approach, by which variables are weighted by their estimated marginal productivities, yields more reliable results.

In the second period, 1973–1979, capital/labor substitution accounted for a higher average proportion of the rates of change in labor productivity—about 72 percent—than in the first period, but with a higher average deviation of about eighteen points. This increase in relative importance reflected significant declines in the effects of productivity growth of most of the other causal forces. The correlation between rates of change in the capital/labor and output/labor ratios was not as high but still significant, with $\bar{R}^2$ with a value of .520. The line of relationship was lower and flatter, with a 1 percent increase in the capital/labor ratio associated with a 0.63 percent increase in labor productivity. Clearly, other forces were interfering more strongly with the productivity-enhancing constellation of forces associated with increases in real capital per unit of labor input than in the earlier period. Nevertheless, the effect was still somewhat greater than that calculated by the growth-accounting approach based on factor shares of gross income.

The rate of increase in real capital stocks declined between the two periods in all countries except Canada. Even in Canada the small acceleration in capital growth was less than the acceleration in growth of labor input, so that capital/labor substitution declined. In the United Kingdom and France the deceleration of capital growth equaled the slowing in growth of labor input. In the other five countries there was a decline in capital/labor substitution, which accounted for about one-fifth of the slowing in growth of labor productivity.

The differences in rates of capital growth, and in the derived capital/labor substitution measures, are associated with differences in the proportions of income and product devoted to saving and investment in the various countries. There is a significant positive correlation in both periods between rates of growth of real gross capital stocks and the percentages of GDP allocated to gross saving and investment, which in 1973 ranged from 19.5 percent in the United States to a high of 38.2 percent in Japan, as shown in table 8. Thus it is not surprising that there is a significant positive correlation

TABLE 8

Ratios of Saving and Investment, by Type,
to Gross Domestic Product, 1960–1979

Country	Saving Ratios			Total Saving-Invest-ment Ratio	Investment Ratios		
	Net saving	Capital con-sump-tion	Other[a]		Gross fixed invest-ment	Net change in stocks	Other[b]
United States							
1960	7.6	11.3	−0.1	18.8	17.6	0.8	0.4
1973	8.6	10.8	0.1	19.5	18.5	1.1	−0.1
1979	5.5	12.3	0.2	18.0	18.2	0.7	−0.8
Canada							
1960	6.7	11.2	0.4	19.3	21.9	1.1	−3.7
1973	12.8	10.7	0.3	23.8	22.4	1.3	0.1
1979	11.6	10.5	0.1	22.3	22.5	1.7	−1.8
Japan							
1960	25.2	10.3	−1.5	34.0	30.1	3.5	0.4
1973	24.5	13.7	0	38.2	36.6	1.7	−0.1
1979	16.9	13.0	2.6	32.5	30.2	0.6	1.7
United Kingdom							
1960	10.1	8.0	−0.4	17.7	16.5	2.2	−1.0
1973	8.8	9.6	1.0	19.4	19.7	2.0	−2.0
1979	7.8	11.7	−0.8	18.7	17.8	1.5	−0.5
France							
1960	14.6	9.9	−0.2	24.3	20.1	2.9	1.3
1973	16.5	9.6	−0.1	26.0	23.8	2.4	−0.2
1979	11.9	15.2	−0.1	23.0	21.3	1.6	0
West Germany							
1960	21.0	7.8	−0.2	28.6	24.3	2.9	1.3
1973	16.2	10.4	−0.1	26.6	24.5	0.8	1.3
1979	12.9	11.3	−0.2	24.0	22.7	2.1	−0.8
Italy							
1960	17.3	8.2	0	25.5	22.6	2.1	0.8
1973	14.0	8.4	0	22.4	20.8	3.3	−1.7
1979	13.4	9.7	0	23.3	18.7	3.0	1.6

TABLE 8 (continued)

| Country | Saving Ratios | | | Total Saving-Invest-ment Ratio | Investment Ratios | | |
	Net saving	Capital con-sump-tion	Other[a]		Gross fixed invest-ment	Net change in stocks	Other[b]
Sweden							
1960	14.0	10.2	−0.1	24.1	22.1	2.6	−0.6
1973	13.6	9.9	0.5	24.0	21.6	−0.6	2.2
1979	6.7	10.8	0	17.5	19.5	0.4	−2.5
Belgium							
1960	9.3	10.1	0.2	19.2	19.3	−0.1	−0.1
1973	15.4	9.2	−0.1	24.6	21.4	1.3	1.9
1979	9.5	9.0	−0.1	18.4	21.0	0.4	−3.0

[a] Net capital transfers plus statistical discrepancy.

[b] Net lending to the rest of the world, plus statistical discrepancy.

SOURCE: Organization for Economic Cooperation and Development.

between the saving ratios of various countries and rates of change in labor productivity, although the coefficients of correlation are somewhat lower than for the preferable regressions between changes in the capital/labor and output/labor ratios (see figure 4).

In all nine countries the saving ratios declined between 1973 and 1979, and averaged less than for the earlier period in all but Canada. This drop was obviously connected with the deceleration in the rate of growth in real capital stocks, although it is net saving and investment that is directly related to the growth of fixed capital. As shown in table 8, net saving ratios also declined in all countries. More relevant to the growth of real gross fixed capital, however, is saving and investment net of retirements. Fixed investment net of estimated retirements rose less or fell more than real gross fixed investment in all countries after 1973.

The crucial question in analyzing international differences in levels and changes in rates of growth of productivity is: What accounts for differences in saving ratios and capital growth and for the reductions in these variables that took place almost universally after 1973? I am not attempting a systematic analysis in this area but can offer some observations that seem pertinent. In the business sector, after-tax rates of return are important with regard to both inducements to invest and business saving, which helps finance pri-

145

FIGURE 4

RATES OF CHANGE OF OUTPUT PER UNIT OF LABOR VERSUS SAVINGS
AS A PERCENTAGE OF GROSS DOMESTIC PRODUCT IN NINE COUNTRIES,
1960–1973 AND 1973–1979

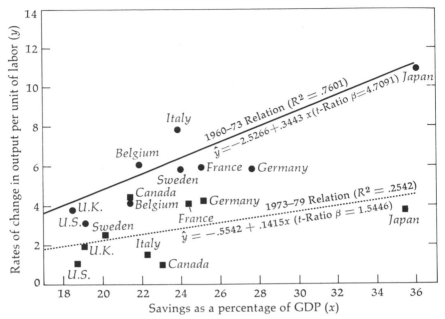

SOURCE: Tables 7 and 8.

vate investments. I would hypothesize that if estimates could be assembled on rates of return in the nine countries, they would be related to the differences in rates of growth of real capital stocks and the capital/labor ratios. A recent study, as yet unpublished,[5] of effective tax rates on capital for five of our nine countries, indicates that their rankings vary inversely with rates of productivity change. In 1970 the United States had the highest effective rate of about two-thirds, the United Kingdom was over 60 percent, France and Germany were a bit under one-half, and Japan was near one-third. Certainly, the net flow of investment funds from the United States to these other countries suggests that the after-tax returns were higher there.

Japan also had the lowest effective tax rate on labor income. A recent study by Price Waterhouse and Company shows that the

[5] George S. Tolley, William B. Shear, and Tim J. Bartik, "Effects of Taxation on National Growth Rates and Income Levels," typescript (prepared for U.S. Department of the Treasury, December 1980).

tax rates on personal income were much higher for the four countries that had lower personal saving rates and rates of productivity growth (United States, Canada, United Kingdom, and Sweden) than for the other countries.[6] In general, there is a mild negative correlation between the government share of gross income and product and saving-investment ratios.

With respect to the decline in saving ratios and real capital growth after 1973, the acceleration of price-level inflation, in which the increases in petroleum and other energy prices played a significant role, must bear part of the responsibility. As monetary policies sought to dampen accelerating inflation by holding price increases below increases in unit costs, profit margins were squeezed. After-tax rates of return were significantly lower in the United States, as indicated by readily available data, in the 1970s than in the 1960s, particularly after adjustment of depreciation allowances to replacement costs. The severe economic contraction of 1974–1975, which was aggravated by the oil shock, reduced the rate of net capital formation for the period 1973–1979 as a whole in all countries except Canada, which was the only net petroleum exporter.

More generally, the investment climate seems to have deteriorated in most of the advanced countries as uncertainties increased with accelerating inflation, surges in oil prices, incomes policies, recession, and increased regulations of business by governments. Friedman has hypothesized that high inflation rates reduce the efficiency of information transmission by relative changes in product and factor prices. Certainly, more resources are devoted to offsetting the unfavorable effects of inflation on various groups. Accelerating inflation has also tended to reduce personal saving rates, in part by reducing real interest rates, often to negative territory, and by reducing the nominal and/or real values of many types of financial assets.

After 1973 governmental deficits were higher, on average, in all of the countries than in the earlier period, reducing funds available for private investment. It is possible that the growth of productivity-enhancing public outlays increased, at least partially offsetting the deceleration of private investment, but I know of no evidence to that effect.

Changes in Energy Use per Factor Unit. In 1973–1974 the international price of oil increased almost fivefold, and by the end of 1979 it was about ten times the price that prevailed before the oil embargo

---

[6] Price Waterhouse and Company, "Tax Policy Incentives to Capital Formation," typescript (prepared for the N.Y. Stock Exchange, September 1980).

in later 1973. It is generally agreed that the oil shock and the sharp deceleration in the growth of production and consumption of energy associated with the sharp increases in the price of oil and of energy generally had negative direct and indirect effects on growth of real product and productivity. A major indirect effect in terms of the associated acceleration of inflation and the worsened investment climate was discussed in the previous section. In addition, sharply rising energy prices increased the costs of operating many types of capital goods in relation to wage rates, which contributed to the decline in substitution of capital for labor (as did various types of wage subsidies). Also, the huge increases in energy prices rendered some types of energy-intensive capital goods obsolete, a fact that helps account for the declining productivity of capital as measured—as does the increasing proportion of "nonproductive" capital goods required to meet regulatory standards. Finally, uncertainty as to future energy prices and availability was an additional inhibitory factor in long-range investment planning.

With regard to direct effects, table 9 shows the sharp deceleration in growth of energy consumption per unit of the factor inputs in each of the nine countries in our study. The rate of growth in energy consumption per unit of total factor input, which is most relevant to changes in total factor productivity, decelerated from an average of 4.1 percent a year in 1960–1973 to −1.2 percent in 1973–1979. If the average deceleration of 5.3 percentage points is weighted by the 5 percent average ratio of energy costs to GDP for the several countries for which data were assembled, the result suggests that it contributed a bit under 0.3 percentage point to the productivity slowdown. France and Sweden were close to the average; in Japan and Italy the greater deceleration contributed close to 0.5 percentage point; while in the others, including the United States, the deceleration contributed around 0.2 percentage point except for the United Kingdom, where the deceleration was smallest, contributing little more than 0.1 percentage point to the productivity slowdown.

These numbers were not included in the growth-accounting table for two main reasons. First, the energy consumption data relate to the total economy, whereas the factor input estimates are for the business sector. There is no assurance that the deceleration in energy consumption by business was the same as that for the nonbusiness sectors—households, private nonprofit institutions, and general government. Still, there can be little doubt that the deceleration in business consumption was sharp and significant. Second, it is possible that the increased conservation in energy use per unit of output, significant for all countries except Canada, did not have a propor-

TABLE 9

CHANGE IN ENERGY CONSUMPTION PER UNIT OF FACTOR INPUTS AND
OUTPUT FOR NINE OECD COUNTRIES, 1960–1973 AND 1973–1979
(average annual percentage rates)

Country	Total Energy Consumption	Energy Consumption per Unit of:			
		Labor	Capital	Total factor input	Real product
United States					
1960–73	4.2	2.9	−0.3	1.7	0.2
1973–79	0	−1.7	−3.0	−2.3	−2.9
Canada					
1960–73	5.8	5.9	0.7	3.9	0
1973–79	3.0	0.8	−1.8	−0.3	−0.2
Japan					
1960–73	11.1	10.2	0.2	6.9	0.3
1973–79	0.2	−0.2	−6.2	−2.2	−4.0
United Kingdom					
1960–73	1.6	1.6	−2.0	0.9	−1.3
1973–79	−1.4	0	−4.5	−1.6	−1.9
France					
1960–73	5.8	5.9	0.7	3.9	0
1973–79	−0.4	0.6	4.7	−1.5	−3.6
Belgium					
1960–73	4.4	5.2	0	3.3	−0.9
1973–79	−0.1	2.2	−2.8	−2.6	−2.2
West Germany					
1960–73	4.7	5.9	−1.4	3.3	0.1
1973–79	−0.2	1.9	−4.3	−0.3	−2.4
Italy					
1960–73	9.3	11.5	5.0	9.5	3.7
1973–79	0.3	−0.7	−3.1	−1.5	−2.3
Sweden					
1960–73	5.0	6.6	0.9	4.4	0.8
1973–79	−1.1	1.3	−4.5	−0.9	−1.2

SOURCE: United Nations for energy consumption; table 1 for real product and factor inputs.

tional effect on productivity. To the extent that energy conservation was not the result of reducing waste, or of the relative shift of demand and production to less energy-intensive goods and services, it represented cost-reducing technological progress, which we discuss as a separate factor in the next section.

The rough estimates presented above are of the same order of magnitude as those made by Denison for the United States and by Maddison for a number of OECD countries. They are considerably lower than estimates by Artus, Rasche and Tatom, and Hudson and Jorgenson, but they are somewhat higher than estimates for the United States prepared by G. L. Perry.[7] The impact is higher, of course, if indirect as well as direct effects are included, but we have chosen to discuss the indirect effects with reference to the other proximate growth determinants that were affected. Since we have not entered our estimates of the direct impact of the deceleration in growth of energy per factor unit in table 7, it is reflected in the residuals.

Changes in Labor Quality. Here we consider two different aspects of changing labor quality: the contribution by human investments, chiefly in education, that raise the marginal productivity of workers as reflected in relative compensation rates; and changes in the composition of the labor force and employment with respect to age-sex groups that have different average rates of compensation that reflect differentials in experience and other qualities (besides education) affecting marginal productivity.

All of the OECD countries in this study have increased educational outlays as percentages of GDP in both periods. What counts with respect to potential contributions to productivity growth, however, is the increase in average real educational capital per employed person or labor hour or, alternatively, the increase in real income and product due to the increase in the average education of the labor force as a higher proportion is employed at higher relative wage and salary rates.

The estimates of increased productivity resulting from higher educational attainment in 1960–1973 are those developed by Christensen, Cummings, and Jorgenson.[8] They appear to be generally con-

[7] See Angus Maddison, "Long-Run Dynamics of Productivity Growth," *Banca Nazionale del Lavoro Quarterly Review*, no. 128, March 1979. Maddison compares his own estimates with those of the other authors cited in the text (p. 36).

[8] Laurits Christensen, Dianne Cummings, and Dale Jorgenson, "Economic Growth, 1947-73: An International Comparison," in J. Kendrick and B. Vaccara, eds., *New Developments in Productivity Measurement and Analysis* (Chicago: University of Chicago Press, 1980), pp. 595-691.

sistent with those prepared by Edward Denison for the European countries in 1955–1962, for the United States in 1960–1973, and for Japan in 1960–1967, as well as with those prepared by Dorothy Walters for Canada.[9] The estimates for 1973–1979 are based on estimates by the OECD of average annual changes in average per capita educational attainment of the population aged twenty-five to sixty-four between 1970 and 1980 in relation to the changes between 1960 and 1970,[10] except for the United States, for which estimates are based on those of Denison.[11] It is noteworthy that except for Japan and Germany, education is estimated to have made a larger contribution to productivity in 1973–1979 than in the earlier period, despite the retardation in productivity growth generally. This phenomenon may reflect in part the very low effective tax rates on human investment because of the implicit writeoff of forgone earnings, as noted by Tolley.[12]

Theoretically, other increases in human capital resulting from investments in training, health, and safety also contribute to productivity advance. Still, we do not have separate estimates for these variables for countries other than the United States, so their effects are included in the residual. Our estimates for the United States indicate that the average annual effects are relatively small, since they averaged about 0.1 percentage point in both periods for training and somewhat less for health and safety.

Differences in age and sex are reflected in differential rates of labor compensation and value added per hour due to associated differences in average work experience and other characteristics affecting productivity. In the United States and Canada, increases in the proportions of youth and females (who also have less experience than their male counterparts) have tended to lower productivity growth in both periods. In the other countries except Japan there have been increasing female participation rates, but this has generally been partially offset by decreasing proportions of youth in the labor force in one or both periods.[13]

Reallocation of Labor. Changes in the composition of labor input among groupings with different levels of real product per unit of labor contribute to changes in aggregate productivity. In addition to the effects of changes reflecting educational attainment and age-sex

9 OECD, *Productivity Trends*, table 9.
10 OECD, *Productivity Trends*.
11 Denison, *Accounting for Slower Economic Growth*.
12 Tolley, Shear, and Bartik, "Effects of Taxation," p. 151.
13 OECD, *Productivity Trends*, tables 20 and 21.

composition, which we have reviewed, it is also desirable to measure shifts among occupational and industry groupings (holding other characteristics constant). Actually, the required occupational data are not available for most of the countries other than the United States, but to an important extent differences in occupational structure are reflected in industry differentials in income and product per worker or labor hour. Even the industry data are not available in great detail. Yet using estimates of real product per worker in seven to ten industrial groups for most of the countries, the OECD estimated the effect of relative shifts of employed persons for the two periods,[14] which we show in the table.

It will be noticed that the shift effect was positive in the 1960–1973 period in all countries and highest in Japan and Italy. The main contributor to this effect was the movement of labor out of agriculture into other sectors. In the second period the shift effect was reduced or eliminated because of slower declines in the agricultural share of employment in all countries. In some countries agriculture's share had reached a point—5 percent or less in the United States, United Kingdom, and Sweden—from which further reductions were relatively less significant, and the productivity differentials became smaller. In Japan, Italy, and France, on the other hand, 10 to 15 percent of employment remained in agriculture, where productivity levels were still two-thirds or less of those in other sectors. Shifts within the nonfarm sector had generally minor effect, although more might have been measured if industry data had been available in greater detail.

In principle, relative shifts of capital among industries with different rates of return could also have an effect on productivity. Industry capital data were not generally available, however, so this factor may affect the residual.

The reallocation of resources in response to changes in supply and demand conditions was enhanced both by high levels of demand relative to capacity through 1973 and by increased competition that made prices more sensitive to changing market forces. Aggregate demand is discussed below under volume factors. With regard to pricing, most of the countries, notably Japan and Germany, pursued procompetitive policies domestically. Particularly influential in promoting competition, however, was the increasing liberalization of foreign trade and investment. Internal trade barriers within the European Economic Community were gradually removed in the 1950s and early 1960s, and the several rounds of negotiations for the

[14] Ibid., table 9.

General Agreement on Tariffs and Trade reduced tariffs and other barriers more generally among the participating nations. The favorable impacts of these developments have been stressed by Angus Maddison, a keen student of comparative international growth trends. He points out that they promoted not only international specialization in production, with attendant reallocations of resources, but also technological advance and investment because of their favorable impact on growth expectations. The realization of strong growth, in turn, facilitated the transfer of resources out of agriculture and other industries in which rates of remuneration were low and labor supplies excessive.

Volume Changes. From Denison's rough estimate that the contributions of economies of scale are approximately one-tenth of growth rates,[15] it is clear that such economies contributed significantly less to productivity advance after 1973 than in the 1960–1973 period. The rates of growth of real product declined by somewhat less than half in the United States, Canada, and France. In the other countries the proportionate declines were greater. The drop in the contributions of scale economies amounted to 0.2 or 0.3 percentage point in all countries except two. In Japan a drop of 0.7 reflected the extremely high growth rate in the earlier period. In Sweden the decline of 0.4 was due to the virtual cessation of growth in real business product between 1973 and 1978.

Also contributing to the decline in productivity growth in all nine countries was the less than complete recovery by 1979 from the 1974–1975 economic contraction that affected all. A lower rate of utilization of capacity reduces the output/capital ratio proportionately and the output/labor ratio by about a quarter, which represents the average proportion of nonproduction, overhead-type workers who are generally not laid off in cyclical downturns. Given the relative weights of capital and labor, this decline means that total factor productivity is reduced by around one-half of the percentage drop in rates of utilization of capacity.

There was relatively little difference in rates of utilization in most of the countries in the years 1960 and 1973. In most of them, however, utilization rates were significantly lower in 1979 than in 1973, reflecting the slow recovery from the 1974–1975 economic contraction. The two exceptions were Italy, in which the unemployment rate was virtually unchanged, and Sweden, where the unemployment rate was lower in 1979 than in 1973, although public employment and work sharing increased.

[15] Denison, *Accounting for United States Economic Growth*, pp. 314-17.

Estimates of the ratio of actual to potential real GNP for the United States were available from the Council of Economic Advisers. For the other countries estimates were constructed based on unemployment rates.[16] Using a modified version of Okun's law, it was estimated that each percentage increase in the unemployment rate decreased productivity by 1.5 percent. The total effect between the boundary years was then reduced to an average annual rate.

Government Regulations. Changes in the legal and institutional framework for private enterprise, including the tax system, have been factors influencing some of the variables discussed above, particularly capital formation. Here we are concerned with the negative effects of governmental regulations in increasing business costs and inputs, without increasing real product as measured.

Although some environmental laws were on the books in the OECD countries prior to 1970 (see table 10), during the past decade the laws have been expanded, standards have proliferated, and enforcement has been strengthened. It is during this period that antipollution regulations have begun to have a significant effect on productivity growth by diverting both labor and capital from productive purposes. The same is true of certain other regulations, particularly in the health and safety area, effects of which are included in the estimates for the United States, although their impact is much less than that of environmental regulations.

As an increasing proportion of new investment has been required to meet standards, so has the proportion of real stocks of capital and the associated real capital costs and inputs for nonproductive purposes increased. Capital formation has been slowed because of the time required for approval of plant and equipment designs and because of land use regulations in new areas. Some new investment may have been discouraged because of risks and uncertainties due to possible changes in standards on short notice.

On the labor side there has been a diversion of managerial and engineering talent from production and innovation to complying with regulations. More labor has been required to operate the antipollution equipment. Reporting burdens and other administrative or legal costs of compliance have risen, often in inverse proportion to the size of firms. Although they are a minor factor in general inflation, rising regulatory costs have pushed up prices to some extent, although the impact has been uneven across industries, so that the composition of output has been somewhat affected.

[16] *Monthly Labor Review*, May 1979, table 2.

TABLE 10

DATES OF MAJOR ENVIRONMENTAL LAWS
PASSED IN SELECTED OECD COUNTRIES, 1956–1977

| Country | *Types of Laws* | | | | | |
	General	Water	Wastes	Air	Impact statement	Other
Canada		1970			1973	1975[a]
United States		1972	1965	1963	1969	1976[a]
		1977	1970	1970		
			1976	1977		
Japan	1967	1958	1970	1962		1973[a]
	1970	1970		1968		1974[b]
France	1976	1964	1975	1974	1976	1977[a]
West Germany		1957	1972	1974	1975	1976[d]
		1976				
Italy		1976		1966		
Norway		1970				1977[a]
Sweden	1969	1969	1975	1969	1969[c]	1964[d]
						1973[a]
United Kingdom	1974	1961	1972	1956		1975[b]
		1974				

NOTES: Some federal countries such as Australia and Austria have laws at the state level.

[a] Law on the general control of chemicals.

[b] Law on compensation.

[c] Essentially a specific administrative procedure.

[d] Law on nature conservancy.

SOURCE: Organization for Economic Cooperation and Development, *OECD Observer*, May 1979.

It has been estimated by Edward Denison that environmental and health/safety regulation reduced productivity growth in the United States by 0.1 before 1973 and by 0.3 after 1973. Estimates for the other OECD countries have been scaled to those for the United States using the relative proportions of GNP devoted to pollution control. OECD estimates indicate that Japan spent on regulatory compliance about four times the fraction of GNP spent

155

by the United States; Germany and Sweden spent about the same proportion; and the other countries somewhat less.[17]

If the beneficial effects of regulations could be accounted for in the GNP estimates, the negative effects on productivity would be less. In any case the trade-off between environmental improvement and lower productivity and production is a conscious one. Still, to the extent that costs have exceeded benefits and unnecessary requirements exist, productivity has been unduly depressed.

Residual: Advances in Technology and Other Sources. After we estimate the effects on output growth of the increases in inputs and the several sources of productivity growth discussed above, there is still a residual. Denison interprets the residual as reflecting primarily advances in technological knowledge as applied to the organization, instruments, and processes of production. The residual also reflects the net effect of other forces, which he judges to be minor, and of possible errors in the estimates.

In what follows we attempt to quantify the contributions to productivity growth of two of the chief factors affecting technology—domestic research and development outlays and the rate of diffusion of innovations as affected by changes in the average age of fixed capital goods. The final residual we interpret for all countries other than the United States as reflecting primarily the international transfer of technology. Still, for all countries, changes in labor and management efficiency and other forces not elsewhere classified may play a role, as discussed in the final subsection.

Before breaking down the residual it is instructive to look at its aggregate movement. Between 1960 and 1973, like total factor productivity, the residual was larger for all other countries than the 1.2-percentage-point figure for the United States, ranging from 1.3 for the United Kingdom to a high of 3.9 average annual percentage contribution in Japan. This suggests a significant narrowing of the technological gap with the United States that was indicated by the Denison estimates for 1960. The residual contributed 63 percent of the increase in total factor productivity in the United States; in the other countries it ranged from about 59 percent in Italy and Japan to around 75 percent in Germany, Belgium, and Sweden, averaging 67 percent.

The residual decelerated more in most other countries than it did in the United States, however, but not as much as total factor

---

[17] See OECD, *Economic Implications of Pollution Control: A General Assessment*, Studies in Resource Allocation, February 1974, p. 30; and *OECD Observer*, May 1979.

productivity in any of them. Although the average rate of growth of total factor productivity decelerated from 3.8 to 1.2 percent between the two periods, that of the residual slowed from 2.5 to 1.2 percent. This implies that the average contribution of all the other factors discussed earlier fell from 1.3 percentage points to zero. Thus, the residual, reflecting mainly technological progress, which accounted for 67 percent of total factor productivity growth in 1960–1973, accounted for all of it in 1973–1979. This underscores the extreme importance of the fundamental force of technological advance in economic progress in the 1980s, since the net effect of the other factors may well continue to be a lesser influence than it was before 1973.

We now attempt to measure and analyze the chief sources of technological advance, as well as the possible influence of residual factors.

Impact of domestic R & D. In the advanced countries a prime source of technological advance is organized research and development activity. Informal R & D—comprising the activity of lone-wolf inventors and innovative activities of workers and works-managers as a byproduct of production whereby many small improvements are made in the organization, instruments, and processes of production— are still significant but are subsidiary to the innovations developed by teams of laboratory scientists and engineers.

Using the argument that scientific and technological knowledge is international, Denison imputed the contribution made by this factor in the United States in the period 1950–1962, as measured by the residual, to the European countries he analyzed, since the United States led in technology in most fields. Nevertheless, even the adoption and adaptation of technology from abroad may often require domestic R & D in order to develop the necessary absorptive capacity. Also, at least part of the R & D of each country is devoted to technological areas and problems of special importance to each and may result in pioneering technological innovations. Accordingly, we depart from Denison's approach and base part of our estimates of advances in technological knowledge on the R & D outlays of each country, from which estimates of the domestically generated real stocks are derived.

Ratios of R & D expenditures to GDP are shown in table 11 for key years. The U.S. ratio, which had risen rapidly from about 1 percent in 1948 to 2.7 percent in 1960, peaked in 1964 at near 3.0 percent, then gradually declined to about 2.3 percent in 1977 and 1978 (and has remained there into 1980). The only country (besides

TABLE 11

RATIOS OF RESEARCH AND DEVELOPMENT TO GROSS DOMESTIC PRODUCT IN
NINE COUNTRIES, 1960–1979
(percent)

Year	U.S.	Canada	Japan	U.K.	France	W. Ger- many	Italy	Sweden	Belgium
1960	2.67	0.83	1.36	2.52	1.30	0.96	0.48	1.45	n.a.
1973	2.34	1.03	1.95	1.97	1.78	2.23	0.49	1.68	1.30
1979	2.32	0.92	1.94	1.83	1.74	2.39	0.86	1.80	1.48

NOTE: n.a. = not available.
SOURCE: National Science Foundation.

the U.S.S.R.) close to the U.S. ratio in 1960 was the United Kingdom, at 2.5 percent. Thereafter, the U.K. ratio declined slowly to about 2.0 percent in 1972 and 1.8 in 1979. The other countries all showed increases for a longer period than the United States. The ratio for West Germany rose from about 1.0 percent in 1960 to 2.4 percent in 1971 and has since remained between 2.2 and 2.4. The French ratio rose from 1.1 percent in 1959 to 2.1 percent in 1967, sagged to 1.8 percent in 1973, and has since stayed at about the same percentage. The Swedish ratio rose gradually from 1.5 percent in 1960 to 1.8 percent in 1979. The Italian ratio, which was the lowest for any of the countries studied, rose gradually from 0.48 in 1960 to 0.86 in 1979. Canada's ratio was near 0.8 in 1959 and 1960, reached a peak of 1.3 in 1967, and then settled back to around 1.0 percent in the 1973–1979 period. Finally, the Japanese ratio rose from 1.36 percent in 1960 to a high of 1.95 in 1973 and stayed close to that figure thereafter.

Thus the United States peaked earlier than the other countries except the United Kingdom and had a larger subsequent decline in the R & D ratio. Most of the decline came in the government-financed military and space area, however. When civilian R & D alone is compared, the United States has been behind Germany and Japan since the mid-1960s, was behind the United Kingdom until about 1970, and was only slightly ahead of France. There is, however, some spillover from military and space R & D into civilian technology that this writer believes to be substantial.

The rate of technological advance is not a direct function of real R & D outlays. Rather, it is related to the rate of advance in tech-

TABLE 12

REAL RESEARCH AND DEVELOPMENT STOCKS, 1960–1979

(index numbers and average annual percentage rates)

Year	U.S.	Canada	Japan	U.K.	France	W. Ger-many	Italy	Sweden	Belgium
				Index numbers (1960=100)					
1973	168.6	347.1	563.4	122.3	413.1	474.6	434.4	160.8	262.9
1979	181.8	451.0	1,090.5	129.9	560.1	802.8	659.2	227.7	405.9
				Average annual percentage rates of change					
1960–1973	4.1	10.1	14.3	1.6	11.5	12.7	12.0	3.7	7.7
1973–1979	1.3	4.5	11.6	1.0	5.2	9.2	7.2	6.0	7.1

SOURCE: Calculated from National Science Foundation estimates.

nological knowledge. The latter variable may be roughly estimated by cumulating real R & D outlays, after adjustment for lags between the outlays, completion of projects, and commercialization of resulting innovations, over the lifetimes of those innovations. This approach assumes that the R & D outputs in terms of technological knowledge are proportionate to the inputs, or real costs. Based on the methodology developed and applied to U.S. estimates,[18] real stock estimates were prepared for all the countries in terms of local currencies at constant prices, shown as index numbers in table 12.

The rates of increase in real R & D stocks slowed perceptibly in the second period in all countries except Sweden, reflecting the leveling or decline in R & D ratios. To the changes in the stocks during each period, an average rate of return was applied, and the resulting numbers were calculated as percentages of real GDP.[19] These are shown as percentage-point contributions to productivity growth in table 7.

In Sweden the contribution remained about the same in both periods, but it declined in all the other countries, particularly the

[18] In John W. Kendrick, *The Formation and Stocks of Total Capital* (New York: National Bureau of Economic Research, 1976), appendix B-3 on microfiche.
[19] Details of methodology discussed in John Kendrick, "Productivity Trends and the Recent Slowdown," in William Fellner, ed., *Contemporary Economic Problems 1979* (Washington, D.C.: American Enterprise Institute, 1979), pp. 60-64. A social rate of return of 50 percent on R & D investment was used to calculate its contribution.

TABLE 13

AVERAGE AGE OF REAL FIXED CAPITAL STOCKS IN THE
PRIVATE NONFARM ECONOMIES OF NINE COUNTRIES, 1960–1978

Year	U.S.	Japan	W. Germany	France	U.K.	Italy	Canada	Sweden	Belgium
1960	11.55	10.00	8.92	12.26	12.00	10.60	12.00	10.00	12.00
1973	9.73	4.87	8.39	9.26	12.48	7.81	12.20	10.71	6.26
1978	9.83	5.33	9.07	9.00	12.74	7.89	12.33	11.17	6.09

SOURCE: Organization for Economic Cooperation and Development.

United States, where the R & D ratio dropped sharply after 1964. If the percentage contributions seem low, it should be remembered that the innovations from R & D spur further, informal improvements, mentioned above. In addition, R & D raise the threshold beyond which technological transfer from abroad becomes more feasible. Indeed, the indirect effects of R & D may be greater than the direct, but these are captured by the final residual.

Diffusion of innovations. Innovations are diffused throughout an economy by various means: imitation, licensing, mobility of professional and skilled personnel, trade and professional literature and conferences, and promotional efforts of manufacturers of producers' goods, among others. If the rate of diffusion changes during a given period, this affects the rate of advance in technology and productivity.

To an important extent, cost-reducing innovations are embodied in new plants and equipment. There are measures of the stocks of many types of individual capital goods. At the aggregate level, estimates of the average age of real fixed-capital stocks provide a means of computing the rate of diffusion of embodied innovations. A decline in average age of one year may be assumed to contribute to productivity growth the equivalent of the average annual rate of increase in technological knowledge.

Estimates by the OECD of the average age of real fixed-capital stocks in the several economies are shown in table 13, from which the average annual changes for 1960–1973 and 1973–1978 were calculated. These were then multiplied by the average annual percentage contribution of advances in technological knowledge, as indicated by the residuals, or by the contribution of real R & D stock, if this was larger, as it was for several countries in the second period.

As shown in summary table 7, the contributions in the first period from more rapid diffusion due to declines in average age were appreciable for Japan, France, Belgium, and Italy and were modest for the United States and Germany. Slight increases in average age in Canada and the United Kingdom had no significant effect but in Sweden subtracted 0.1 from productivity growth. In the second period, reflecting lower rates of fixed-capital formation, average ages rose somewhat in all countries except France and Belgium, but the effect rounded up to −0.1 only in Japan, Germany, and Sweden.

Changes in the rate of diffusion due to factors other than changes in the average age of fixed capital would show up in the final residual, discussed next.

Technological transfer, changes in productive efficiency, and other residual factors. After quantifying the contributions of two of the forces behind technological progress, we are still left with substantial positive final residuals for all countries other than the United States for the period 1960–1973. In the subsequent period, the residuals are generally much smaller, with a small negative for Italy.

For the countries other than the United States we interpret the final residuals as reflecting largely reductions in the lag in application of worldwide technological knowledge, mainly from the United States. They may also be viewed as reflecting the narrowing of the technological gap between the other countries and the United States as a result of "catching up." It will be recalled that Denison's analysis indicated that more than half of the shortfall of labor productivity in most of the other countries relative to the United States in 1960 was due to lower levels of technology, organization, managerial skill, and other aspects of productive efficiency generally. His growth analysis for the period 1950–1962 suggested that "with the probable exception of France and possible exception of Italy the higher growth rates obtained by most European countries than by the United States were not due in any large measure to a catching up of technique to that of the United States." [20] Writing in 1967, Denison added:

> It is possible that the situation has changed materially since 1962. Descriptive evidence, and illustrative data such as those given . . . for the spread of self-service stores and supermarkets, suggests that only at the very end of the period were many changes becoming sufficiently general to importantly affect productivity in whole economies. The

[20] Denison, *Why Growth Rates Differ*, p. 285.

161

new generation of managers has only recently begun to attain positions of responsibility in a number of countries. A repetition of this study for the decade of the sixties might yield appreciably larger residuals.[21]

The final residuals obtained in this study for the period 1960–1973 definitely bear out Denison's prognostication of a significant catching up. They range from 1.1 percentage points for the United Kingdom to 2.6 points for Sweden. To the extent that the residuals truly reflect technology transfer and other sources of technological advance, the shortfalls from U.S. levels must have been substantially reduced by 1973. In fact, some observers have claimed that certain countries, even Japan, had virtually eliminated the gap by 1973,[22] although our evidence does not support so sweeping a conclusion. It must also be kept in mind that the residual reflects factors other than reductions in the technological lag, which will be discussed after some further observations and evidence on the latter factor.

There are at least nine major modes by which technology may be transferred internationally: [23]

- foreign direct investment and joint projects
- trade in goods and services, particularly producers' goods and consulting services
- licensing of patents and so forth
- performance of R & D abroad, either through subsidiaries or on a cooperative basis with foreign firms
- personnel exchanges
- publications
- international visits, conferences, and exhibitions
- teaching and training
- turnkey projects, international tender invitations, reverse engineering, and other.

After World War II the European Productivity Agency was established under the Marshall Plan; productivity centers were set up in the European countries and later in Japan and many other countries; foreign productivity teams visited the United States; and American experts worked abroad in an intensive effort to transfer American technology to aid in reconstruction and development.

[21] Ibid., p. 286.

[22] Christensen, Cummings, and Jorgenson, "Economic Growth, 1947–73."

[23] See Edwin Mansfield, "International Technology Transfer and Overseas Research and Development" in U.S. Senate, Subcommittee on International Finance, *Export Policy*, May 16, 1978.

TABLE 14

U.S. Direct Investment Abroad in Manufacturing, 1966–1978
(millions of dollars)

Area	1966	1973	1978[a]
All countries	20,740	44,370	74,207
Canada	6,697	11,755	17,625
Japan	366	1,399	2,317
Western Europe	8,906	20,777	36,426

[a] Preliminary.
SOURCE: National Science Foundation, *Science Indicators, 1980.*

American direct investment abroad increased rapidly, and know-how went with the investments, together with training of local personnel (see table 14). As a result in part of direct investments, U.S. exports of R & D–intensive goods rose even more rapidly (see table 15). Of these, the most important were machinery and equipment, often embodying the latest American technology. Also important was licensing of patents, frequently accompanied by technical services. As shown in table 16, U.S. receipts of royalties and fees rose dramatically, not only from foreign affiliates of U.S. firms, but also from unaffiliated foreign residents. The table shows, furthermore, that net

TABLE 15

U.S. Trade Balance with Respect to Research and Development Intensity, 1960–1978
(millions of dollars)

	1960	1973	1978
R & D intensive			
Export	7,597	29,088	63,908
Import	1,706	13,987	34,310
Balance	5,891	15,101	29,598
Not R & D intensive			
Export	4,962	15,643	30,627
Import	5,141	31,013	66,006
Balance	−179	−15,370	−35,379

NOTE: R & D = research and development.
SOURCE: National Science Foundation, *Science Indicators, 1980.*

TABLE 16

U.S. Receipts and Payments of Royalties and Fees, 1966–1978
(millions of dollars)

	1966	1973	1978[a]
With foreign affiliates of U.S. firms			
Total net receipts	1,163	2,309	4,364
Canada	246	394	698
Japan	43	153	401
Western Europe	496	827	1,854
Net payments	64	209	396
With unaffiliated foreign residents			
Total net receipts	353	712	1,065
Canada	30	32	61
Japan	70	273	343
Western Europe	186	297	465
Net payments	102	176	214

[a] Preliminary.
Source: National Science Foundation, *Science Indicators, 1980.*

payment by the United States, although much smaller than receipts, rose even more rapidly, attesting to the catching-up process. So do the patent statistics, which show a decline in the number issued to U.S. nationals and a relative increase in the number issued to foreign residents (see table 17).

It is also relevant that the proportion of foreign students in U.S. colleges and universities has been steadily increasing. At the doctoral level the proportion of degrees awarded to foreign students rose from 11.7 percent in 1959 to 16.1 percent in 1979, according to data in the National Science Foundation's *Science Indicators, 1980.* In science and engineering the proportion rose from 14.8 to 21.1 percent over the same period. One result has been an increase in international cooperative research and a relative increase of internationally coauthored articles.

Further evidence on the rate of international transfer of technology after World War II has been assembled by Edwin Mansfield.[24] He cites data showing that U.S. firms greatly accelerated the introduction of their new products abroad after 1950 or 1955 but that the

[24] Edwin Mansfield, "Technology and Productivity in the United States," in Martin Feldstein, ed. *The American Economy in Transition* (Chicago: University of Chicago Press, 1981), pp. 583-89.

TABLE 17

PATENTS GRANTED IN SELECTED COUNTRIES
BY NATIONALITY OF INVENTOR, 1966–1978
(thousands)

Country	1966	1973	1977	1978
United States				
To nationals	54.6	51.5	41.4	41.2
To foreigners	13.8	22.6	23.9	24.8
Japan	1.1	4.9	6.2	6.9
Canada	0.9	1.3	1.2	1.2
West Germany	4.0	5.6	5.5	5.8
United Kingdom	2.7	2.9	2.7	2.7
France	1.4	2.1	2.1	2.1
Foreign patents granted to U.S.	49.1	43.3	39.5	—
Japan				
To nationals	17.4	30.9	43.0	—
To foreigners	8.9	11.4	9.6	—
To U.S.	4.7	5.5	4.8	—
Canada				
To nationals	1.2	1.2	1.3	—
To foreigners	23.2	20.0	19.5	—
To U.S.	16.6	13.0	11.9	—
West Germany				
To nationals	13.1	11.2	10.8	—
To foreigners	9.5	12.7	10.9	—
To U.S.	3.7	4.9	3.5	—
United Kingdom				
To nationals	9.8[a]	9.4	7.7	—
To foreigners	28.9[a]	30.5	28.8	—
To U.S.	14.1	11.7	10.4	—

[a] 1969.

SOURCE: National Science Foundation, *Science Indicators, 1980.*

pace of acceleration slackened somewhat after 1965–1970 (see table 18). Foreign subsidiaries are used more frequently than was formerly the case. As of 1974, foreign subsidiaries (rather than exports, licensing, or joint ventures) were expected to be the principal channel of transfer in about 70 percent of cases reported.[25]

[25] Ibid., p. 583.

165

TABLE 18

PERCENTAGE OF NEW PRODUCTS INTRODUCED ABROAD
WITHIN ONE AND FIVE YEARS OF INTRODUCTION IN THE UNITED STATES,
1945–1975

Period	Number of New Products	Percentage Introduced Abroad	
		Within one year	Within five years
1945–50	161	5.6	22.0
1951–55	115	2.6	29.6
1956–60	134	10.4	36.6
1961–65	133	24.1	55.6
1966–70	115	37.4	60.1
1971–75	75	38.7	64.0

SOURCE: W. Davidson and R. Harrigan, "Key Decisions in International Marketing: Introducing New Products Abroad," *Columbia Journal of World Business,* winter 1977.

It is also significant that during the 1960s and early 1970s, the percentage of total company-financed R & D carried out overseas grew from 2 percent to about 10 percent. According to Mansfield, Teece, and Romero,[26] this R & D tended to be predominantly developmental, aimed at product and process modification to meet special design needs of overseas markets. This trend obviously helped accelerate the transfer of basic innovations.

The interpretation of our estimates that there was a significant degree of catching up in the 1960–1973 period seems well supported by the collateral data. What is perhaps surprising is Denison's conclusion that this was not a significant factor in the decade of the 1950s, except for France and possibly Italy. Still, it must be kept in mind that it took years after World War II for the reconstruction process, for rebuilding capital, expanding markets, expanding education and training programs, and increasing R & D outlays in order to enhance the absorptive and adaptive capacity of the other economies.

It is easy to ascribe the slower pace or apparent cessation of the catching-up process after 1973 to the fact that the prior dramatic narrowing of the technological gap made further gains more difficult. It must be remembered, however, that the residual reflects other forces that may have had a negative or less favorable impact after

[26] E. Mansfield, D. Teece, and A. Romero, "Overseas Research and Development by U.S.-Based Firms," *Economica,* May 1979.

1973. In Italy, which had a small residual, it is obvious that the net impact of the other forces was negative. Perhaps chief among these are changes in the ratio of actual to potential efficiency with a given technology, including the efficiency of management as well as of labor generally; changes in institutional forms and practices, including the degree of competition and of restrictionism; and the net effect of incompleteness and possible errors in the estimates of the specified determinants.

As to labor efficiency, in our more complete analysis of the slowdown in U.S. productivity growth, data were cited indicating that the ratio of hours actually worked to those paid for (used in the labor input estimates) declined at an average annual rate of 0.3 percent after 1966, helping to account for the smaller residual after 1973.[27] There is also a widespread impression that the work ethic may have weakened, reducing intensity of effort. Similar observations have been made with respect to Canada and Western Europe, although we do not have hard evidence on this rather elusive subject. Still, it is at least plausible that as the level of affluence rises beyond some point in a society, the intensity of drive and work effort may diminish somewhat. Also, with the increasing welfare orientation of most countries, the tendency is to maintain employment even when demand slackens. Social legislation in Sweden, Canada, and Italy, in particular, should be examined to see if it helps account for the small residuals after 1973.[28]

With respect to resource reallocations, the estimates of the effects of labor shifts were made only in terms of 10 or so sectors. Finer detail might produce somewhat different results, particularly with respect to the impact of the relative shift of employment into service industries. Also, we did not estimate the impact of reallocations of capital. Estimates by Jorgenson [29] for the 1960–1973 period indicate significant positive effects for some countries. Although estimates have not yet been made for the subsequent period except for the United States, it is possible that the effects were smaller.[30]

[27] See Kendrick, "Productivity Trends and the Recent Slowdown," p. 45.

[28] Maddison estimates that for France, Germany, and the United Kingdom between 1973 and 1978 "labor slack, other than unemployment, rose to 3 percent of the labor force on average." Angus Maddison, "Western Economic Performance in the 1970s: A Perspective and Assessment," *Banca nazionale del Lavoro Quarterly Review*, no. 134, September 1980, p. 281.

[29] Christensen, Cummings, and Jorgenson, "Economic Growth, 1947-73," table 11.13.

[30] See J. Randolph Norsworthy, Michael J. Harper and Kent Kunze, "The Slowdown in Productivity Growth: Analysis of Some Contributing Factors," in *Brookings Papers on Economic Activity*, no. 2 (Washington, D.C.: Brookings

Concluding Comments

Further improvements in data and estimates of outputs, inputs, productivity, and related variables are needed as a basis for further analysis. For example, only recently has OECD begun preparing estimates of capital stocks, which made possible the estimates of total factor productivity and capital/labor substitution that were important ingredients of the growth analysis presented here. When the capital estimates become available on an industry basis, estimates of total factor productivity by industry and the effects of 'interindustry capital shifts will become possible. The data on average and total hours worked need improvement in most countries. In addition, the price series for deflation of GDP should be strengthened and expanded.

Even with the present data base, more resources should be devoted to analyzing the underlying causes of changes in the proximate determinants used in growth accounting. In particular, we need to know more about the impacts of changes in energy supplies and prices, inflation rates, the structure and rates of taxation and public expenditures, and social and economic regulations.

Despite its limitations, however, the growth-accounting analyses of Denison and the present writer permit a number of broad conclusions. First, the quarter-century after World War II was a period of unusually rapid growth for the industrialized nations. The reconstruction and expansion of civilian productive capacity, associated with high rates of saving and investment in nonhuman and human capital, rising relative R & D outlays, reallocations of resources, expansion of domestic and international markets, and generally high rates of utilization of capacity all conduced to historically high rates of productivity advance. The U.S. productivity trend was somewhat higher than before,[31] but the acceleration in the other OECD countries reviewed here was considerably greater. Not only did most of the factors enumerated above operate more strongly abroad, but the rate of cost-reducing technological progress appears to have been considerably stronger than in the United States because of a significant degree of catching up with advanced levels of technology facilitated by rising R & D and the associated investments in fixed and human capital embodying the latest technology and know-how.

Institution, 1979). The authors find that translog aggregation of capital by type and sector in the U.S. business economy compared with direct aggregation has an effect of 0.82 in 1965-1973, as compared with 0.24 in 1973-1978.

[31] See Kendrick, "Productivity Trends and the Recent Slowdown," table 1.

Certainly the productivity and technological gaps between the other countries and the United States narrowed significantly in all of them, dramatically so in most.

It was probably inevitable that the period of unusually high productivity advance should come to an end. A slowing was already apparent in the United States after 1966 and even more so after 1973, as saving/investment rates declined, ratios of R & D to GDP declined, resource reallocations had less favorable effects, changes in the age-sex mix of the labor force were unfavorable, economic fluctuations became more pronounced, and expansion of government regulations diverted resources from "productive" uses. After 1973, our estimates show that the slowdown was universal. The same forces that affected the U.S. economy began to affect the other industrialized nations. The timing suggests that the oil shock and associated acceleration of inflation sharpened the negative effect of the proximate determinants of the productivity slowdown just enumerated, especially the decline in saving and investment rates associated with slower growth and a lower average rate of utilization of existing capacity.

All in all, the enumerated determinants accounted for about half of the deceleration in productivity advance in the other eight OECD countries 1973–1979, on average. It is our hypothesis that the other half was largely accounted for by a lower rate of technological transfer, mainly from the United States. The common-sense notion that the rate of catch-up would decline as the technological gap narrowed is supported by collateral data, such as the decline in patents granted to U.S. nationals after 1966 and the much slower growth of patents granted to foreign nationals after 1973. The situation varied considerably among countries, however. Our growth-accounting exercise indicates that the slowing of advances in knowledge, and particularly in the residual interpreted to reflect technology transfer, was much less pronounced in Japan, Germany, Belgium, and France than in Canada, the United Kingdom, Sweden, and Italy.

The findings of this study have obvious implications for growth projections. For example, it seems likely that the rates of total factor productivity advance in France, Germany, Belgium, and Japan, which averaged a healthy 2 percent a year for 1973–1979, will decline somewhat in the 1980s. Technology transfer was still a major element in that growth, but with productivity per worker in France and Germany about 90 percent and Japan over two-thirds of the U.S. level in 1979, catch-up will be less important in the decade ahead.

On the other hand, the slow rates of growth of total factor productivity in the other five countries, all below a 1 percent annual average, indicate major opportunities for improvement in the years ahead. My article in *Contemporary Economic Problems 1979* [32] suggested that the rate of productivity growth in the United States is likely to improve in the 1980s as some of the determinants, such as labor force composition and the growth of the capital/labor ratio, become more favorable. Generally, however, significant improvement will require the formulation of policies designed to promote saving and total investments, technological advance, resource mobility, and the other determinants of productivity growth. Continuing analyses of productivity developments in the United States and abroad are necessary to strengthen the knowledge base required for formulation of effective policies to promote growth.[33]

[32] Ibid., pp. 46-48.

[33] Around 100 policy options to promote productivity growth in the United States are presented in John W. Kendrick, "Policies to Promote Productivity Growth," in *Agenda for Business and Higher Education* (Washington, D.C.: American Council on Education, 1980). See also Kendrick, "Curriculum for Economics 1981: Productivity and Economic Growth," *AEI Economist*, November 1980.

Food and Agriculture of the Centrally Planned Economies: Implications for the World Food System

D. Gale Johnson

Summary

The Soviet Union, the seven "centrally planned economies" (CPEs) of Eastern Europe, and China substantially increased their roles in the international trade in grain and other agricultural products during the 1970s. At the beginning of the decade the Soviet Union was a small net exporter of grain, and the net grain imports of all of the centrally planned economies accounted for only 7 percent of the world's grain imports. By the end of the decade, however, these nine countries accounted for 30 percent of grain imports.

NOTE: For those readers who wish to add to their knowledge of the centrally planned economies generally and of agriculture in particular, the following publications may be of interest and value. Any person who has an interest in the economies discussed in this article owes a great debt to the Joint Economic Committee of the U.S. Congress for the impressive collections of articles that it creates every three years on the Soviet Union, Eastern Europe, and China. The most recent volumes are *Soviet Economy in a Time of Change*, 2 vols., October 10, 1979; *Chinese Economy Post-Mao*, 2 vols., November 9, 1978; and *East European Economies Post-Helsinki*, 1977.

For highly readable and authoritative discussions of a wide range of economic topics dealing with the Soviet Union and Eastern Europe, one should not miss two books by Alec Nove: *The Soviet Economic System* (London: Allen and Unwin, 1977) and *Political Economy and Soviet Socialism* (London: Allen and Unwin, 1979). Ronald A. Francisco, Betty A. Laird, and Roy D. Laird have edited two very good collections of articles concerning agriculture in the Soviet Union and Eastern Europe: *The Political Economy of Collectivized Agriculture: A Comparative Study of Communist and Non-Communist Systems* (New York: Pergamon Press, 1979) and *Agricultural Policies in the USSR and Eastern Europe* (Boulder: Westview Press, 1980).

Anthony M. Tang and Bruce Stone have collaborated to produce a most useful analysis, *Food Production in the People's Republic of China*, Research Report 15 (Washington, D.C.: International Food Policy Research Institute, 1980).

During the 1970s world grain trade increased by 95 million tons, or by about 90 percent. The centrally planned economies accounted for more than 55 percent of the increase in world grain imports.

Several factors have been responsible for the rapid growth of grain imports by the CPEs during the 1970s and did not operate with equal strength in the U.S.S.R., China, and Eastern Europe. The three most important factors have been the rapid growth of demand for meat and livestock products in the U.S.S.R. and Eastern Europe, the introduction of substantial food price subsidies, and the slow growth of agricultural production during the second half of the 1970s, especially in the U.S.S.R. In China the major source of increased demand for grain has been the growth of real and money incomes in both rural and urban areas as a result of policies adopted in 1977 and 1978.

The growth in the demand for livestock products in the U.S.S.R. and Eastern Europe was the result of a significant rate of growth of per capital incomes and relatively high income elasticities of demand.

The growth in demand for meat and other livestock products has been augmented by the food price subsidies. Starting in the 1960s and accelerating during the 1970s in the U.S.S.R. and five of the seven Eastern European countries, such subsidies resulted in low meat and milk prices; in some cases the subsidies equaled the actual retail price, and in numerous cases they amounted to half or more of the retail price.

The increase in per capita meat consumption in the Eastern European economies during the 1970s was remarkable, a gain of about one-fourth. To a degree, the feed required to produce the meat necessary to meet the growth in demand depended upon the increased importation of grain. This was especially true for Poland, which increased its annual level of grain imports from 2 million tons during 1966–1970 to 7 million tons during 1978–1980.

The Soviet Union, in contrast to the Eastern European CPEs, failed to achieve a significant growth in per capita meat production during the 1970s. In fact, in 1980 per capita meat production was the same as in 1974, which in turn was only 10 percent above the 1970 level. The expansion of meat and livestock production during the 1970s, and especially after 1975, was modest indeed, given the efforts made to increase such production. One means used to expand livestock production was the great expansion of grain imports, shifting from net grain exports of 4 million tons annually from 1969–1971 to net imports of more than 30 million tons in both 1979/80 and 1980/81. During the last half of the 1970s, grain fed to livestock increased by more than a fifth, although livestock output increased by only a third as much.

Grain imports by China increased significantly after 1975. The increase in grain imports was not due to poor grain crops in 1978 and 1979, which were years of very good crops; the 1980 crop was somewhat disappointing. Policy changes made in 1978 and 1979 provided for significant increases in prices paid to farms by the state, a reduction in the grain tax for poor farms, the introduction of food price subsidies that prevented an increase in the urban retail prices for the grains and vegetable oil, a significant increase in wages in the state sector, and a subsidy to urban workers to compensate them for the retail price increases permitted for farm products other than the grains and vegetable oil. All of these changes added to the demand for food and especially for grain. The rapid growth of grain imports resulted, in large part, from these policies, which both increased the demand for grain and held its price at a relatively low level in urban areas.

Continued rapid growth of grain imports by the CPEs could result in a substantial increase in the real prices of grain in international markets. It is not predicted that there will be rapid growth of grain imports by the CPEs during the 1980s. There is abundant evidence, however, that changing the food price and subsidy policies that have had a major role in increasing the grain imports will prove to be very difficult indeed.

Introduction

The "centrally planned economies" (CPEs) have 28 percent of the world's population and produce about a fifth of the world's gross national product.[1] In 1980/81 it is estimated that these economies consumed 39 percent of the world's grain and produced 35.5 percent.[2]

If these economies were self-sufficient in food, long their objective, the performance of their agricultures and the characteristics of their food policies would have little direct impact upon the rest of

[1] U.S. Central Intelligence Agency, National Foreign Assessment Center, *Handbook of Economic Statistics 1980*, ER 80-10452, 1980, p. 1. The "centrally planned economies" include the Union of Soviet Socialist Republics (U.S.S.R.) or the Soviet Union, the People's Republic of China, and seven Eastern European countries—Bulgaria, Czechoslovakia, German Democratic Republic, Hungary, Poland, Romania, and Yugoslavia. When the term "Eastern Europe" is used, it generally refers to the first six countries listed and thus excludes Yugoslavia.

[2] U.S. Department of Agriculture, Economics, Statistics, and Cooperatives Service, *World Agricultural Situation*, WAS-24, December 1980, p. 41. The Economics, Statistics, and Cooperatives Service will hereafter be designated ESCS.

the world. Until 1960 the CPEs were self-sufficient in grains or cereals and were net exporters of agricultural products. It now seems quite incongruous that two decades ago the Soviet Union was seen (and feared) as a major export competitor in the world grain and oil-seeds market and that the People's Republic of China was viewed as an important competitor in the international soybean market. During the 1970s the Soviet Union became the world's largest grain importer and China the third largest. Further, China has been a significant importer of oilseeds in some years, and recently China has even been a small net importer of soybeans. A striking indication of the changing agricultural fortunes of the CPEs is that during the 1970s they accounted for 55 percent of the increase in world grain imports and for 30 percent of world grain imports by the end of the 1970s, compared with 7 percent at the beginning of the decade.[3]

Why has this remarkable shift in the agricultural and food trading relationship occurred? This is the primary question that I wish to explore. I shall give emphasis to three factors: First, the income elasticities of demand for meat and other livestock products remain at levels near unity; second, during the 1960s in the Soviet Union and Eastern Europe and in the late 1970s in China there was a significant change in food price policies that encouraged the growth of demand for food; and third, the growth of agricultural production during the second half of the 1970s, especially in the Soviet Union, was significantly slower than for any similar period since the end of World War II.

First, the relatively high income elasticity of demand for meat and livestock products is important, since the Eastern European CPEs achieved significant growth in per capita incomes during the 1960s and 1970s, in both money and real terms. Consequently, in most of these economies the demand for meat has been growing at a rate significantly greater than could be met from local feed resources. The income elasticities of demand for meat in the European CPEs appear to be higher than in other countries with similar per capita incomes. There are probably several reasons for this, but one may well be the neglect of agriculture in the early years of collectivization. Livestock product, and thus meat supplies, were held to low levels. These economies may have been in a "catching-up process" in moving toward a level of meat consumption consistent with the demand patterns for their real income levels. In addition, the limited supplies of

---

[3] During the 1970s—from 1969-1971 to 1979-1980—world grain trade increased by approximately 90 million tons; net grain imports by the centrally planned economies increased by 50 million tons. See table 6 below.

174

quality consumer goods and limited amounts of poor quality and highly subsidized housing may have shifted demand toward meat and other livestock products.

During the 1960s the Soviet Union embarked upon a policy of increasing the prices paid to farms for meat and milk while at the same time leaving unchanged the prices charged at retail. In other words, a policy of subsidizing food consumption was instituted. As is so often the case in governmental programs, this policy was supposed to be temporary. The higher prices paid to farms were to generate sufficient expansion of production, through realizing efficiencies in production, that the prices paid to farms could soon be lowered to the prior level and could thus be consistent with the retail prices. As late as 1973 a Russian acquaintance said that the new policy was intended to be an emergency program; it was believed that the subsidies could be eliminated in a few years. History has refuted this expectation, and instead the amount of the subsidies has grown year by year and in 1981 will almost certainly exceed 30 billion rubles.[4]

Why were subsidies instituted? One reason seems to have been that Khrushchev did increase the retail prices of meat and milk significantly in 1962, and there was substantial resistance to the increase, with rumors of riots and other disturbances. In 1965 Brezhnev increased farm purchase prices but did so without increasing retail prices, and there have been no significant increases in official prices in the state stores since that time. The increase in prices received by farms after 1965 resulted both from increase in the base procurement prices and from introduction of bonus prices for deliveries in excess of procurement quotas. The premium for deliveries in excess of the required deliveries was 50 percent; this system was introduced for grains in 1965 and for livestock in 1970, with extensions to additional commodities in 1981.

In 1965 large zonal price differences were introduced as a means of maintaining production in high-cost regions and preventing high incomes in agricultural regions that would have been well endowed if prices for all farms had been increased to the level required to generate the desired level of output. Between 1965 and 1977 the average prices paid by the state, including the bonus prices for meat, increased by almost 60 percent without significant increases in the

[4] This is my estimate, based on a budget allocation of 25 billion rubles in 1977; the increase in such subsidies in 1979 by increased prices for milk, wool, potatoes, and vegetables estimated to cost 3.2 billion rubles; and further changes in farm prices in 1981 costing about 4 billion rubles. See U.S. Department of Agriculture, ESCS, *USSR Agricultural Situation: Review of 1978 and Outlook for 1979*, WAS-18 Supplement 1, April 1979, p. 25.

retail prices in the state stores. Between 1965 and 1979 milk procurement prices increased by even more, namely by 80 percent, with no increase in state-store prices.[5]

Similar subsidy policies were adopted in other Eastern European CPEs, especially in Poland and apparently in all of the countries except Yugoslavia. The consequences of the Polish government's attempts to reduce or eliminate the enormous and growing cost of food subsidies are well known as a result of riots and strikes that occurred subsequent to attempts to increase retail food prices in 1970, 1976, and 1980. In 1970 and in 1980 the disruptions that followed the food price increases were followed by major governmental shakeups. In February 1971 the new governmental officials rescinded the price increases announced in December 1970. Once again in 1976 the price increases were rescinded, and food subsidies continued to grow and may have reached 8 percent of national income by 1976.

The Polish experiences with efforts to increase food prices have influenced policies in other Eastern European CPEs. There is good reason to believe that an important reason why the Soviet Union has not increased meat and milk prices in more than a decade has been a fear that citizens might strongly protest. The Polish strikes in the summer of 1980 appear to have intensified the reluctance of other Eastern European governments to raise retail food prices. Since then Bulgaria, the German Democratic Republic (G.D.R.), and Romania have absorbed higher agricultural procurement prices in the state budget rather than passing the higher prices on to consumers. Romania may not have had significant food subsidies prior to 1981.

China had some food subsidies during the 1950s, increased them during the 1960s, and increased them again very substantially in 1978 and 1979. In 1979 procurement prices were increased significantly, and bonuses for deliveries in excess of established delivery quotas for each farm were also increased. Bonuses for excess deliveries are now 50 percent of the procurement price for grains and somewhat less for cotton.

The food price policies result in subsidizing food consumption in most of the CPEs. The price subsidies add to the relatively high income elasticities of demand, a second factor encouraging CPEs to become dependent on imports. Where there has been some significant degree of inflation, as there has been in most of the CPEs, the failure to adjust retail food prices to the level required by the prices paid to farms has meant that the real price of food has declined over the past decade or so. Consequently, one of the important reasons for

[5] Ibid., pp. 25 and 29.

more rapid growth of demand than of supply has been declining real prices for food products. The prices of meat products in state stores are especially out of line in the Soviet Union and some of the Eastern European economies. Subsidies have been paid for grain products and potatoes as well as for livestock products. In some instances, bread prices were set so low that bread was a cheaper livestock feed than grain.

The third factor has been the relatively slow growth of agricultural output in the Soviet Union and some Eastern European economies during the 1970s. For the U.S.S.R. agricultural output growth during the 1970s was less than half that of the 1960s. In Eastern Europe output growth declined significantly in the last half of the 1970s.[6]

For China a fourth factor has been important, namely a decision made in 1977 or 1978 to increase the real incomes of commune members by reducing required procurements as well as by increasing prices paid to farms. Since the rural population accounts for 80 percent of the total population, an increase in the real incomes of the rural population has a major impact upon the demand for food due to their high income elasticity of demand.

The CPEs do not have a monopoly on the use of food and agricultural subsidies. Many developing countries subsidize particular foods, whereas many industrial countries expend billions of dollars on direct subsidies to farms or to pay the cost of farm price-support programs.

Economic Performance of the CPEs

Some data on the overall performance of the economies may be of help in interpreting the analysis of factors associated with the sharp increase in reliance on grain imports required to meet demand in the CPEs. Table 1 gives data on the growth of real gross national product per capita for Organization for Economic Cooperation and Development (OECD) countries and the Communist countries for 1960–1965 to date. The data indicate that the general pattern of real growth in the CPEs for the past two decades compares favorably with the growth in OECD. There appears to have been a slowing down of growth after 1973 in most countries. It may be of interest to note that Poland, which seems to be in turmoil, has had a growth record that is equal

[6] Calculated from U.S. Department of Agriculture, ESCS, *Indices of Agricultural and Food Production for Europe and the USSR, Average 1960-65 and Annual through 1979,* Statistical Bulletin No. 635, p. 5.

177

TABLE 1
GROWTH RATES OF REAL GROSS NATIONAL PRODUCTS PER CAPITA,
1960–1979
(percent per annum)

Country	1960–1965	1965–1970	1970–1973	1973–1976	1976–1979	1960–1979
United States	3.2	1.9	3.8	0.2	3.2	2.5
Japan	8.9	10.9	7.2	1.1	4.7	7.2
Sweden	4.5	3.2	1.1	1.7	0.9	2.6
European Community	3.9	4.1	3.8	1.5	2.7	3.4
United Kingdom	2.6	1.9	4.1	0.4	1.7	2.2
West Germany	4.0	3.9	3.2	1.5	3.7	3.4
Eastern Europe	3.2	3.1	4.0	3.6	2.2	3.4
Bulgaria	5.5	4.1	3.5	4.5	1.2	4.0
Czechoslovakia	1.3	3.2	2.6	2.1	1.5	2.2
G.D.R.	3.1	3.2	3.5	4.1	2.8	3.2
Hungary	3.9	2.7	4.9	1.0	2.2	3.5
Poland	2.8	3.0	6.4	3.9	1.4	3.4
Romania	4.4	3.2	2.4	6.4	3.7	4.0
Yugoslavia	4.9	4.2	3.9	4.3	6.4	4.6
U.S.S.R.	3.6	4.2	3.4	2.5	1.7	3.2
China	3.3	4.2	5.5	1.6	7.2	4.2

SOURCE: Central Intelligence Agency, National Foreign Assessment Center, *Handbook of Economic Statistics 1980*, ER 80-10452, 1980, p. 29.

to the average of six Eastern European CPEs for the two decades. Climatic factors were responsible, at least in part, for the Chinese low growth rate for 1974–1976 and the high growth rate for 1977–1979. Some credit for the 1977–1979 growth rate may go to the general relaxation of regulations and increased incentives instituted after the fall of the Gang of Four in 1976.

Table 2 presents data on agricultural production since 1961–1965. These data bear out the statement made earlier that the rate of growth of agricultural output in the 1970s in the Soviet Union was significantly smaller than in the 1960s. In the Soviet Union the level of agricultural output during 1978–1980 was only 8 percent higher than in 1974–1976. Output growth during the 1960s was 3.9 percent, in the 1970s less than half of this. Agricultural output increased more in each of the Eastern European countries than in the Soviet Union, and for the group the performance compares favorably with any region in the world. Two countries performed very well—Hungary

178

TABLE 2

TOTAL AGRICULTURAL PRODUCTION, INDEXES AND GROWTH RATES OF
CENTRALLY PLANNED ECONOMIES, 1969–1980

Country	1969–71	1974–76	1978–80	Growth Rates 1969–71/ 1961–65	Growth Rates 1978–80/ 1969–71
Eastern Europe					
Bulgaria	126	138	—	3.4	—
Czechoslovakia	123	140	—	3.0	—
G.D.R.	112	133	—	1.6	—
Hungary	127	154	—	3.5	—
Poland	113	130	—	1.8	—
Romania	123	162	—	3.0	—
Yugoslavia	124	152	—	3.1	—
Total[a]	119	141	148	2.5	2.5
Soviet Union	131	143	154	3.9	1.8
China[b]	124	148	171	3.7	3.6

NOTE: 1961-1965 = 100. Dashes indicate data not available.

[a] For Eastern Europe and Yugoslavia.

[b] Base period for China is 1963-1965 to exclude low output at end of the Great Leap Forward years.

SOURCES: U.S. Department of Agriculture, Economics, Statistics, and Cooperatives Service, *Indices of Agricultural and Food Production for Europe and the U.S.S.R.*, Statistical Bulletin No. 635; *World Agricultural Situation*, WAS-24, December 1980; and A. M. Tang and C. J. Huang, "Changes in Input Relations in the Agriculture of the Chinese Mainland, 1952-1979" (Paper delivered at the Conference on Agricultural Development in China, Japan, and Korea, Taipei, Taiwan, December 17-20, 1980).

and Romania—whereas the other four Eastern European CPEs increased output at the respectable rate of 2 percent annually for the 1970s. The Chinese output index is subject to considerable uncertainty and should not be accepted as firm evidence of successful performance during the 1970s.

Table 3 gives an estimate of the hard-currency debt to the West of the Eastern European CPEs. In 1979 the debt was estimated to be $49 billion. Of this Poland owed approximately 40 percent. Table 4 presents some estimates of consumer prices for OECD countries and the Eastern European CPEs. As the table indicates, the centrally planned economies can have significant rates of inflation. Still, the indexes of consumer prices for the CPEs are presented more to indicate the potential for consumption substitution effects when the prices

TABLE 3

EASTERN EUROPE: NET HARD-CURRENCY DEBT TO WEST, 1971–1979
(U.S. billions of dollars)

Country	1971	1973	1975	1977	1979
Bulgaria	0.7	1.0	2.3	3.1	3.7
Czechoslovakia	0.2	0.3	0.8	2.1	3.1
G.D.R.	1.2	1.9	3.5	6.2	8.4
Hungary	0.8	1.1	2.2	4.5	7.3
Poland	0.8	2.2	7.4	13.5	20.0
Romania	1.2	1.5	2.4	3.4	6.7
Total	4.9	8.0	18.7	32.9	49.3

SOURCE: Central Intelligence Agency, *Handbook of Economic Statistics 1980*, p. 39.

of important foods have not been permitted to increase for a decade or more. The Soviet Union, as of 1978, had a gross debt to the West of about $10 billion. The Soviet Union has significant financial assets in the West, however, and its net debt may be about half the gross debt.

Exports and Imports of Agricultural Products. Although I have noted the dramatic increase in grain imports, the increasing deficit in grain trade of the CPEs is only the "tip of the iceberg." In times past the Soviet Union was a major net exporter of agricultural products. There has not been a single year since 1968 when the Soviet Union has had a net surplus in its agricultural trade (see table 5). The net deficit grew from a little more than $300 million in 1969 to almost $8 billion in 1978.

The Eastern European CPEs have had a deficit in the balance of their agricultural trade throughout the 1970s, but in contrast to the experience of the Soviet Union, the deficit for the region as a whole has increased very little during the 1970s. There are differences among the countries. Poland's deficit in agricultural trades increased from $283 million in 1971 to $1.3 billion in 1978. Hungary, on the other hand, has increased its export surplus in agricultural products from $188 million in 1971 to $650 million in 1979. Bulgaria and Romania have had small export surpluses in their agricultural trade. In spite of the very substantial growth of grain and cotton imports, China maintained a net positive balance in its agricultural trade throughout the 1970s.

TABLE 4

CONSUMER PRICE INDEXES, 1960–1979

Country	1960	1965	1970	1973	1974	1975	1976	1977	1978	1979
OECD										
United States	76	81	100	114	127	139	147	156	168	187
Canada	77	83	100	116	129	142	153	165	180	197
Japan	57	77	100	124	254	172	188	204	211	219
European Community										
Belgium	74	84	100	118	133	150	163	175	183	189
France	67	81	100	120	136	152	167	182	199	220
Italy	68	87	100	122	146	171	199	237	265	305
Netherlands	66	79	100	125	137	151	165	175	182	190
United Kingdom	67	80	100	127	148	184	215	249	270	306
West Germany	77	88	100	119	127	135	141	146	150	156
Communist countries										
U.S.S.R.[a]	88	96	100	106	108	109	111	113	115	118

(Table continues)

TABLE 4 (continued)

Country	1960	1965	1970	1973	1974	1975	1976	1977	1978	1979
Eastern Europe [b]										
Bulgaria [c]	73	86	100	109	114	116	120	126	132	135
Czechoslovakia	74	80	100	106	109	111	113	114	116	120
G.D.R.	87	92	100	100	103	103	104	108	109	110
Hungary	82	88	100	115	118	123	130	134	140	152
Poland	78	88	100	113	124	132	142	155	168	181
Other										
Yugoslavia	31	59	100	160	196	242	269	208	350	425

a Implicit price index obtained from a comparison of indexes of goods sold in the retail trade network in constant and in current prices. The current price index is based on the values of total retail and collective farm market sales in current prices regularly published in Soviet statistical abstracts. The index in constant prices is derived from the goods components of the CIA index of total consumption. A more complete explanation of the methodology and a discussion of the relative merits of an "official" or "alternative" price index are contained in "Soviet Economy in a New Perspective," U.S. Congress, Joint Economic Committee, October 14, 1976, p. 631.

b Calculated differently from that for the U.S.S.R.; the official index of personal consumption in current prices was deflated by a calculated index of personal consumption in constant prices. An explanation of the methodology used to calculate personal consumption is presented in T. P. Alton, "Index of Personal Consumption in Poland, 1937 and 1946-1967," Occasional Papers of the Research Project on National Income in East Central Europe (New York: L. W. International Financial Research, 1973).

c Price indexes are calculated from official figures for total consumption of the population, including estimates of health and education expenses.

SOURCE: Central Intelligence Agency, Handbook of Economic Statistics 1980, p. 43.

TABLE 5

NET BALANCE IN AGRICULTURAL TRADE FOR CENTRALLY PLANNED
ECONOMIES, 1969–1979
(U.S. millions of dollars)

Year	U.S.S.R.	China	Eastern Europe	G.D.R.	Hungary	Poland	Yugo-slavia
1969	−325	—	—	−505	195	−173	−9
1970	−1,046	380	—	−704	156	−149	−20
1971	−843	625	—	−665	188	−283	−142
1972	−2,048	645	—	−780	355	−115	−95
1973	−3,340	425	—	−873	556	−265	−275
1974	−6,786	240	−2,807	−1,314	442	−556	−735
1975	−7,415	1,500	−2,108	−1,308	588	−663	−287
1976	−7,257	1,720	−3,003	−1,634	515	−941	−301
1977	−6,403	625	−2,844	−1,611	593	−1,073	−545
1978	−7,910	1,655	−2,756	−1,596	652	−1,292	−444
1979	—	600	—	—	—	—	—

NOTE: A negative sign means net imports. Dashes indicate data not available.
SOURCES: United Nations, Food and Agriculture Organization, *Trade Yearbook*, various issues; U.S. Department of Agriculture, Economics, Statistics, and Cooperatives Service, *World Agricultural Situation*, WAS-21 Supplements 1, 3, and 6, 1974 to date.

Table 6 presents data on the grain trade for the CPEs for 1960 to date. To simplify the presentation, the figures are for net trade—imports are subtracted from exports to arrive at a net trade figure. Data are given for the Soviet Union, Eastern Europe, and China and for the CPEs as a whole. Data are not available for Cuba, North Korea, or Vietnam.

As noted in the introduction, net grain imports of the CPEs increased sharply during the 1960s and 1970s. In fact, much of the growth in grain imports occurred during the 1970s, with a large increase during the last two years of the decade. Given the small 1980 grain crop in the Soviet Union and the known import commitments made by the Chinese, the 1980/81 grain imports of the CPEs will be in excess of 60 million tons.

The data on grain trade for each of the Eastern European CPEs given in table 7 indicate that there are major differences among the countries. Hungary was a small net importer of grain during the late 1950s and early 1960s but has generally been a net exporter since 1966. Romania had a net export position from 1956 through 1970

183

TABLE 6

Net Grain Trade by Eastern Europe, the Soviet Union, and China,
1960–1981
(millions of metric tons)

Period or Year	Eastern Europe	Soviet Union	China	Centrally Planned Economies
1960/61–1962/63	−6.8	7.3	−4.1	−3.4
1969/70–1971/72	−7.5	4.0	−3.1	−6.6
1971/72	−9.2	−1.3	−2.5	−13.1
1972/73	−7.3	−21.0	−4.6	−32.9
1973/74	−4.9	−5.7	−5.7	−16.3
1974/75	−8.3	−0.5	−4.5	−13.3
1975/76	−8.0	−25.4	−1.3	−34.7
1976/77	−11.7	−7.3	−2.4	−21.4
1977/78	−9.8	−16.4	−8.7	−34.9
1978/79	−11.8	−13.2	−10.2	−35.2
1979/80	−13.3	−30.4	−9.8	−53.5
1980/81	−13.2	−33.6	−13.5	−60.3

NOTE: A minus sign indicates net grain imports; the year is from July to June.
SOURCE: Department of Agriculture, *World Agricultural Situation*, various issues.

but by the end of the 1970s seemed to have reached a rough balance between imports and exports. Bulgaria has a relatively minor role in grain trade, shifting from modest net exports to modest net imports from year to year. Yugoslavia has a somewhat erratic pattern of grain trade, with either small surpluses or deficits. Two countries, Czechoslovakia and the German Democratic Republic, were substantial net importers of grain over the entire period covered by the table. There appears to be no trend in the net import balance for Czechoslovakia, although there is an upward trend for the G.D.R. As will be noted later, these two countries have limited amounts of arable land for the size of their populations. Their grain yields are relatively high, have increased significantly over the past two decades, and are approaching those achieved in West Germany and France.

Poland is the source of a large part of the growth in net grain imports by the Eastern European CPEs; it has accounted for more than half of the grain imports during the 1970s. Poland is one of the two countries that have retained a large private agriculture sector consisting primarily of smallholders. The indexes of total agricultural

TABLE 7

Net Grain Trade of Eastern European Centrally Planned Economies, 1956–1980

(thousands of metric tons)

Country	1956–60	1961–65	1966–70	1971–75	1976	1977	1978	1979	1980
Bulgaria	−43	−255	210	93	15	266	−226	−532	−125
Czechoslovakia	−1,656	−1,889	−1,764	−1,488	−1,989	−1,173	−900	−870	−1,960
G.D.R.	−1,968	−1,908	−2,220	−2,834	−4,681	−2,443	−2,962	−2,482	−2,383
Hungary	−256	−533	23	601	1,440	721	446	719	250
Poland	−1,595	−2,663	−2,041	−3,140	−6,061	−5,732	−7,317	−6,783	−7,475
Romania	223	931	1,361	229	27	−100	729	−223	−359
Yugoslavia	−516	−904	21	−484	−395	−31	117	−1,202	−1,030
Eastern Europe	−5,811	−7,221	−4,410	−7,116	−11,659	−8,492	−10,163	−11,373	−13,082

NOTE: Data are for calendar years and thus differ from data in table 6, which are for July-June years. A minus sign indicates net grain imports. The data are annual averages.

SOURCE: Francis S. Urban, H. Christine Collins, James R. Horst, and Thomas A. Vankai, *The Feed-Livestock Economy of Eastern Europe: Prospects to 1980*, Foreign Agricultural Economics Report No. 90, U.S. Department of Agriculture, Economic Research Service, 1973, p. 101; Department of Agriculture, *World Agricultural Situation*, WAS-21 Supplement 3, 1980, pp. 28-29.

production given in table 2 show that Poland has had the smallest increase in total agricultural production from 1961–1965 to the present of any of the CPEs. Further, the increase in per capita food production of less than 15 percent since 1961–1965 has been much smaller in Poland than in any of the other countries; for all of Eastern Europe the increase in per capita food production has been about 35 percent.[7] Without the sharp increase in grain imports and other feed materials, the growth of food production would have been even smaller. In 1979/80 grain use in Poland for both food and feed was 26.3 million tons; of this, 7.6 million tons, or almost 30 percent, was imported.[8]

Some might argue that the relatively poor performance of Polish agriculture has been due to the persistence of the small private farms. I do not accept this view. I put primary emphasis upon the policies toward agriculture in general and toward the private sector in particular that have been followed by the Polish government. Yugoslavia, as indicated below in table 8, has only a slightly larger fraction of its land in the socialized sector than does Poland, yet growth of food production in Yugoslavia has been well above the average for Eastern Europe. What Polish experience does indicate, however, is that a productive agriculture depends upon much more than the form of land ownership or whether the agriculture is private or socialized.[9]

Some Characteristics of Agriculture in the CPEs. A limited number of facts about the agriculture of the CPEs may help in understanding the problems of agriculture and food in these economies as well as providing some basis for comparison among them. Table 8 gives

[7] Ibid., p. 8.

[8] U.S. Department of Agriculture, Foreign Agricultural Service, *Foreign Agriculture Circular: Grains*, FG-5-80, February 1980, p. 91.

[9] In an analysis for various factors that might explain the relatively poor performance of agriculture in the U.S.S.R., I concluded that the socialized organization was not the critical factor. The high percentage of national investment devoted to agriculture (more than a quarter during the 1970s), the high costs of farm products, and the instability of farm output were due much more to inappropriate farm price policies, to the use of quantitative plan indicators as criteria for distribution of bonuses for management, to the unwillingness of the Moscow planners to trust farm people to act in their own and national interest, to the continuing intervention of Moscow in the most minute details of farm operations, and to a very ineffective marketing and input sector with which agriculture must work. Almost none of these features of the setting within which agriculture must function is required by socialism; they result either from a particular ideology or from sheer ineffectiveness in the organization of resources that buys from and sells to the farms. See my paper "Agricultural Organization and Management in the Soviet Union: Change and Constancy," Paper No. 80:26 (Chicago: University of Chicago, Office of Agricultural Economics Research, 1980), revised.

TABLE 8

Agricultural, Population, and Labor Force Data and Gross National Product of Centrally Planned Economies, 1978

Country	Land (thousands of hectares)		Socialized Agriculture, Land (percent)	Population (millions)	Labor Force (millions)		GNP[a]	
	Agricultural	Arable			Total	Agriculture	Total (billions of dollars)	Per capita (dollars)
Eastern Europe								
Bulgaria	6,215	4,292	99	8.8	4.72	1.27	25	2,799
Czechoslovakia	6,952	5,246	94	15.1	7.57	1.12	71	4,673
G.D.R.	6,282	5,040	94	16.8	8.86	.86	81	4,834
Hungary	6,698	5,389	93	10.7	5.23	1.02	32	3,000
Poland	19,059	14,988	23	35.0	19.09	5.94	108	3,094
Romania	14,965	10,540	91	21.9	12.02	4.64	67	3,083
Yugoslavia	14,281	7,927	30	22.0	8.52	2.75	56	2,544
Total[b]	74,452	53,422	—	130.3	66.01	17.60	440	3,385
Soviet Union	605,706	232,306	100	261.2	131.8	32.80	1,046	4,004
China	343,500	129,500	—	997.2	(460.0)	(300.0)	324	323
CPE total	1,023,658	415,228	—	1,388.7	(657.8)	(341.4)	1,810	1,303

Note: CPEs = centrally planned economies. Dashes indicate data not available.

[a] In 1978 U.S. dollars.

[b] For Eastern Europe and Yugoslavia.

Sources: Department of Agriculture, *World Agricultural Situation*, WAS-21 Supplements 1, 3, and 6, 1980. Income data from U.S. Department of State, Bureau of Public Affairs, *The Planetary Product: Progress Despite "the Blues" 1977-78*, Special Report No. 58, 1979. Figures for the Chinese labor force are estimates by the author.

TABLE 9

Grain Production and Yields of Centrally Planned Economies, 1961–1980

Country	Annual Output (millions of tons)				Average Yield (centners per hectare)			
	1961–65	1966–70	1971–75	1976–80	1961–65	1966–70	1971–75	1976–80
Bulgaria	4.7	6.2	7.5	7.7	19.7	28.1	33.1	34.8
Czechoslovakia	5.5	7.0	9.4	10.2	22.2	27.0	35.0	37.9
G.D.R.	5.8	6.7	8.8	9.0	25.8	28.8	35.7	35.4
Hungary	6.7	8.2	11.5	12.4	21.0	26.5	35.0	42.1
Poland	15.0	16.8	21.2	19.7	17.2	19.9	25.1	25.1
Romania	10.9	12.7	14.0	18.9	16.1	19.5	24.1	29.8
Yugoslavia	10.3	12.9	14.5	15.5	19.3	25.2	29.9	34.9
Eastern Europe [a]	59.0	70.5	87.9	93.4	18.9	23.2	28.2	32.0
U.S.S.R.	130.3	167.6	181.5	204.9	10.2	13.7	14.7	16.0
China [b]	169.0	199.0	230.0	264.0	15.6	17.0	18.7	21.4
CPEs	358.3	437.1	499.4	562.3	13.4	16.2	18.0	20.0

Note: CPEs = centrally planned economies.

a Includes Yugoslavia.

b Chinese grain production data include paddy or rough rice and exclude tubers and legumes.

Sources: Urban, Collins, Horst, and Vankai, *The Feed-Livestock Economy of Eastern Europe*, pp. 79-82; *World Agricultural Situation*, WAS-21 Supplements 1, 3, and 6, 1980; and U.S. Department of Agriculture, Foreign Agricultural Service, *Foreign Agriculture Circular: Grains*, FG-11-81, March 12, 1981.

some general data about the nine economies—land, population, labor force, and GNP. Agriculture remains a significant employer of labor, utilizing approximately a third of the labor force in Poland, Yugoslavia, and Romania and almost a fifth in the Soviet Union. In China it is probable that 65 percent of the labor force is in agriculture. The G.D.R., at 10 percent, has the lowest percentage of its labor force in agriculture. Eastern Europe has 0.4 hectare (about one acre) of arable land per capita; the Soviet Union has 0.9 hectare. China has but 0.13 hectare of arable land per capita, though a significant part of the land can be cropped more than once each year and nearly two-fifths of the arable land is irrigated.

Per capita gross national products range from a low of $323 for China to a high of $4,834 for the G.D.R. The average for the Eastern European economies is $3,400, whereas the figure for the U.S.S.R. is $4,000.

Table 9 presents data on grain production and yields for five-year periods. Both production and yields increased significantly between the early 1960s and the late 1970s in each of the countries. The largest increase in yield was in Hungary, where yield doubled. Poland had the smallest increase, with 30 percent; Yugoslavia and the G.D.R. had increases of about 40 percent. Yield in the U.S.S.R. increased by 60 percent, approximately the average for Eastern Europe. For rough comparative purposes only, it may be noted that in the late 1970s the United States produced about one-half as much grain as the CPEs, and its yield was double that of the CPEs.

Table 10 shows the level of per capita meat consumption in the centrally planned economies. The highest levels in 1979 were in the G.D.R. and Czechoslovakia, with Poland and Hungary next. It is more than a little ironic that the Soviet Union is providing financial assistance to Poland to meet its trade deficit with the West. One of the alleged sources of the 1980 strikes and distrubances was the increase in the price of meat. There can be no doubt, however, that a significant part of the trade deficit is due to the purchase of grain for feed. As table 10 shows, the per capita meat consumption in Poland is significantly higher than in the Soviet Union. Soviet citizens would be somewhat more pleased with their food supply if per capita meat consumption were 72 kilograms per year, a level that will not be reached during the 1980s and perhaps not by the end of the century unless Soviet agriculture performs significantly better than it did during the 1970s.[10]

---

[10] Data on per capita consumption of meat and other foods since 1950 are given in U.S. Department of Agriculture, ESCS, *World Agricultural Situation*, WAS-21

TABLE 10

PER CAPITA CONSUMPTION OF MEAT IN CENTRALLY PLANNED ECONOMIES,
1965–1979 AND PROJECTED FOR 1980
(kilograms)

Country	1965	1971	1975	1979	Ratio 1979/1965	Projected 1980[a]
Bulgaria	40	44	58	62	1.55	58
Czechoslovakia	62	74	81	84	1.35	80
G.D.R.	59	68	78	87	1.47	78
Hungary	52	60	68	71	1.37	70
Poland	49	56	70	72	1.47	64
Romania	23[b]	29	46	52[c]	2.26	45
Yugoslavia	27	38	48	50	1.85	39
Eastern Europe[d]	43	54	—	67	1.56	60
U.S.S.R.[e]	41	50	57	56	1.37	—
China	—	—	—	10	—	—

NOTE: Dashes indicate data not available.

[a] As projected in the early 1970s in *The Feed-Livestock Economy of Eastern Europe: Prospects to 1980.*

[b] Average for 1956-1960.

[c] For 1977.

[d] Includes Yugoslavia.

[e] Includes slaughter fats; deductions for slaughter fat may not be uniform for other countries.

SOURCES: U.S. Department of Agriculture, Economic Research Service, *Agricultural Statistics of Eastern Europe and the Soviet Union, 1950-70*, ERS-Foreign 49, June 1973, pp. 100-106; *World Agricultural Situation*, WAS-21 Supplements 1, 3, and 6, 1980; and Urban, Collins, Horst, and Vankai, *The Feed-Livestock Economy of Eastern Europe*, pp. 28-29.

Estimates are available for the percentage of consumption expenditures devoted to food for four of the CPEs—Yugoslavia, Poland, Hungary, and the U.S.S.R. for 1977.[11] In Yugoslavia 40 percent of all expenditures was devoted to food and nonalcoholic beverages, in Poland the percentage was 31, and in Hungary, 30. In Poland the portion of expenditures on food, all beverages (including alcohol), and tobacco was 45 percent. For the Soviet Union, similarly, the figure

Supplement 1, April 1980, p. 43. My rather pessimistic estimate of the potential for expansion of meat production and consumption is based upon the slow growth of the past two decades and the very modest goals that have been set for the Eleventh Plan period, which ends in 1985.

[11] U.S. Department of Agriculture, ESCS, *World Agricultural Situation*, WAS-22, June 1980, p. 37.

was 47 percent; if tobacco and alcoholic beverages are excluded, the amount becomes 34 percent. In Hungary, food plus nonalcoholic beverages accounted for 30 percent of private consumption expenditures.

The percentage of total consumption expenditures for food in Poland is approximately the same as for two Western European countries with similar per capita incomes. In Greece, 35 percent of consumer expenditures was for food; in Italy, 31 percent. Yugoslavia and Ireland had similar per capita incomes—the Irish allocated only 27 percent of their consumption expenditures to food.[12] The percentage of consumption expenditures on food in the Soviet Union is clearly very high compared with the amounts for countries with similar per capita incomes. At most, given the per capita income of the Soviet Union, we would expect less than 30 percent of consumption expenditures for food and nonalcoholic beverages.

It is worth noting that the data on consumption expenditures exclude the large subsidies paid on food products in Poland and the Soviet Union and, to a lesser degree, in Hungary. Thus the real social costs of food are greater than indicated by expenditures on food as a percentage of consumer expenditures. Later we shall present data on the size of the subsidies, though it is not out of place to note that such subsidies amount to as much as a third to a half of consumer expenditures on food in the Soviet Union and Poland.

The amounts of food consumed in Eastern Europe and the U.S.S.R. are fully adequate to meet nutritional requirements,[13] nor is the consumption of animal products strikingly low, a fact shown by table 10. The Chinese, of course, have a much lower intake of animal protein than European countries. Still, it should be noted that a high intake of animal protein is not required for an adequate diet.

Horses and Tractors. Earlier I quite categorically stated that I did not agree that the continued existence of a large private sector in Polish agriculture, with its large number of small farms, was responsible for the recent rather poor performance of Polish agriculture. This poor performance was reflected in the low growth rate of output since 1961–1965 and the importation of 30 percent of grain used. Polish agricultural output grew at an annual rate of 1.6 percent from 1961–1965 to 1979, as compared with 3.0 percent for the six other Eastern European countries. Since Yugoslavia's rate of growth in

[12] Ibid.
[13] United Nations, Food and Agriculture Organization, *Production Yearbook, 1978*, vol. 32 (Rome: UN, 1979), pp. 247-51.

agriculture was 3.0 percent for the period, the source of the Polish problem had to be more than the country's reliance upon private agriculture for approximately three-fourths of its farm output.

Nevertheless, there may be some relationship between grain imports and the interaction between small private farms and Polish agricultural policy, broadly defined. Polish agriculture retains a large number of horses. In 1977 there remained 2 million horses in Poland, or 133 horses per 1,000 hectares of arable land. Hungary had but 26 horses per 1,000 hectares. Yugoslavia had 95 horses per 1,000 hectares.[14] The 2 million horses in Poland may have consumed about 1.6 million tons of grain.[15] This amount may be compared with the 7.6 million tons of grain imported in 1979/80. The nearly 800 thousand horses in Yugoslavia might consume about 450 thousand tons of grain. That Poland has a large number of horses is ironic because Poland has more tractors per thousand hectares of arable land than any of the other Eastern European countries except Yugoslavia and the Soviet Union.

There can be several explanations for the retention of such a large number of horses in Poland. One is that governmental policy has resulted in production of few tractors of the appropriate size for the small private farms. Instead, the government has tried to force most farms to obtain their tractor power from machine tractor stations. The other is that the farmers, at least many of them, simply do not accept the government and its agencies as reliable suppliers of power for their farms. In terms of fifteen horsepower units, the socialized sector of Polish agriculture has 55 percent of all tractors, even though it has but 25 percent of the arable land. The long-run objective of the Polish government is to achieve a socialized agriculture; this may well be the major impediment to efficient use of agricultural resources when the private sector still produces approximately three-fourths of total output.

A reasonably full explanation of the limited performance of Polish agriculture is not possible in a brief space, but some additional points may be worth noting. Poland's policy toward agriculture has vacillated. At times policy measures to improve the performance have been adopted, including increasing the amount of farm inputs, raising the level of investment, and increasing the prices paid to farmers. Yet at

[14] Ibid., pp. 199-200, 257-59, and 45-57.

[15] Francis S. Urban, H. Christine Collins, James R. Horst, and Thomas A. Vankai, *The Feed-Livestock Economy of Eastern Europe: Prospects to 1980*, Foreign Agricultural Economics Report No. 90, U.S. Department of Agriculture, Economic Research Service, 1973, p. 23. It is estimated that the feed requirements for a horse for a year under Polish conditions would be 0.79 metric tons of grain.

the same time that government officials reiterate their commitment to the maintenance of private agriculture, they also point to the socialization of agriculture as the ultimate policy goal. Farmers are thus skeptical of the credibility of official statements that private agriculture will be maintained indefinitely. One result of this skepticism is the effect upon private investment in agriculture.

Farmers have had other dissatisfactions. There is opposition to compulsory deliveries of farm products. Some inputs, such as coal, are made available to the private farms on terms that depend on meeting targets for selling output to the state. When an important input is controlled in this way, the authority of local officials over individuals is significantly enhanced.

The quality, quantities, and reliability of input supply to agriculture leave a great deal to be desired, and this is true of both the private and socialized agricultures. It has been stated, for example, that a quarter of the tractor fleet is idle at any one time for the lack of spare parts.

Causes of Growing Dependence

In the introduction I noted that three factors may explain the increasing dependence of the CPEs upon the rest of the world for grain and feed. These three factors were: first, the high income elasticities of demand for meat and other livestock products; second, food price policies that hold retail prices of food below cost; and third, a reduction in the rate of growth of agricultural output, especially in the Soviet Union, during the second half of the 1970s.

As indicated in tables 5, 6, and 7, the increasing dependence upon the rest of the world for food has not been uniform among the centrally planned economies. In fact, almost all of the increase in grain imports has been due to four countries—the Soviet Union, Poland, G.D.R., and China. These four countries account for all but 2 million tons of the increase in net grain imports between the early 1960s and the late 1970s.

Although four countries are responsible for most of the increase in net grain imports, the relative importance of the three factors differs significantly among them. In fact, the primary reason for the increased dependence of Eastern Europe upon grain imports has been the very rapid growth of meat consumption during the 1970s, whereas the Soviet Union achieved only a very modest increase in per capita meat consumption (none during the last half of the 1970s). The primary cause of increased grain imports by the Soviet Union has been slow growth of grain production and other feed supplies.

193

Eastern Europe. Table 10 depicts the very rapid growth of meat consumption in each of the Eastern European countries from 1965 through 1979. The increases in per capita meat consumption in Poland and the G.D.R. of 23 and 28 kilograms, respectively, were very large indeed. The increases were more than 47 percent for both countries. For all of the Eastern European countries per capita meat consumption increased by 24 kilograms, or 56 percent. This was a remarkable increase in consumption and was derived solely from the expansion of domestic meat production, since net exports of meat in 1978 (and for the last half of the 1970s) were slightly larger than during the mid-1960s.

It is true, of course, that some of the feed required to expand meat production at such a striking pace was imported, and the larger than anticipated growth in meat production and in the grain required to produce that meat has been a primary source of the increased imports of grain. In saying that the growth of meat consumption has been greater than anticipated, I rely upon the competent study undertaken by economists in the Economic Research Service of the U.S. Department of Agriculture (USDA)—*The Feed-Livestock Economy of Eastern Europe: Prospects to 1980.*[16] The study was published in late 1973 and made projections of per capita meat, milk, and egg consumption, livestock production, and feed requirements for 1975 and 1980. Projections were also made of uses of grain other than feed. The last column in table 10 gives the projected per capita meat consumption for 1980. Actual consumption of meat in 1979 exceeded the projected consumption for each of the seven Eastern European countries. The difference between the actual and the projected consumption for the Eastern European economies as a group was 7.2 kilograms, or 12 percent.

If estimates of feed requirements for livestock products in the USDA study are used to estimate the amount of grain required to produce the difference between actual and projected meat consumption, the amount would be approximately 4.7 million tons of grain. Milk output in 1979 was slightly less than the projected output, whereas egg output exceeded the projected level. The net effect of these two differences between actual and projected outputs was an additional grain use requirement of approximately 1 million tons. Thus livestock output in excess of projected 1980 levels required approximately 5.7 million tons of grain.

In the USDA study the 1980 projected level of grain imports was 3 million tons. Actual grain imports for 1980 were 13 million

[16] Ibid.

194

tons, or 10 million tons greater than projected. The projection for grain production for 1980 was 94.3 million tons. The average level of grain production for 1978 and 1979, the two years producing crops that supplied the feed for the 1979 production of meat and livestock products, was—surprisingly—94.2 million tons. Thus the increased grain imports were not due to a grain production shortfall. In the study, 1980 grain used as feed was projected to be 62 million tons. Actual use in 1979/80 was 72 million tons, or 10 million tons in excess of the projected level.

Consequently we can conclude that the substantial growth in imports of grain in Eastern Europe resulted largely from rapid growth of livestock output. The latter source was quite small, both absolutely and relatively. It would appear that the increased grain use per unit of livestock output amounted to but 4 million tons, or only a little more than 4 percent of actual grain use for feed.

The other important component of concentrated feed consists of oilseeds. The projections of both use and net imports were uncannily close to actual use in 1979. Thus differences in oilmeal availability did not affect the use of grain for livestock feed.

The projected levels of meat production and consumption for 1980 were reasonable. In the USDA study there appeared to be two offsetting errors that influenced meat consumption. One was an overestimate of growth of per capita real incomes; the other was an apparent underestimate of the income elasticities of demand. Since per capita incomes did increase, these two projection errors had offsetting effects. As is true of most such projections, it was assumed that the relative prices of livestock products would remain unchanged during the period. This was clearly not the case. In most, if not all, of the Eastern European CPEs the prices of meat and other livestock products were either unchanged during the 1970s or increased at a slower rate than the prices of other consumer goods.

I wish it were possible to show clearly how far prices of meat, milk, and eggs have been permitted to decline in real terms or relative to all other consumer prices. Much of the information required for such an exercise is not readily available. Still, it is possible to provide some insights. The data on consumer prices in table 4 indicate significant increases in consumer prices generally during the 1960s and 1970s. The indexes in the table are not the official price indexes but have been independently estimated. During the 1960s consumer prices in the G.D.R. increased by 15 percent; there was no increase between 1960 and 1970 in the prices of beef, pork, mutton, milk, or eggs or, for that matter, in bread or flour. In the 1970s there was a further increase in consumer prices of 10 percent, with no significant change in the retail prices of livestock products. Although consumer prices of food have been held approximately stable, prices paid to the farms were increased from the mid-1950s to the mid-1970s at an annual rate of more than 2 percent. As a result subsidies were required to cover the differences between the prices paid to farms plus transportation, processing, and marketing costs and the retail prices. One estimate indicated that in 1972 retail food prices in the G.D.R. were 23 percent lower than they would have been without government subsidy. By the end of the 1970s subsidies grew further both absolutely and relative to retail prices. The 1979 budget for the G.D.R. included 7.7 billion marks of subsidies for foodstuffs; during the same year the state's expenditure on all education amounted to 9.7 billion marks. At the end of the 1970s one-tenth of the national income was used to subsidize the same percentage as during the mid-1970s.[17]

Hungary has been one of the Eastern European countries that has been willing (and able) to increase food prices. In mid-1979, consumer prices of food were increased by 20 percent, including a 30 percent increase for meats and 50 percent for bread prices. Food prices had also been increased significantly in 1976, with meats increasing by a third. As a result of the mid-1979 consumer price increases, the price subsidy was reduced for a number of food products. One report indicates that the subsidy rate for pork fat declined from 38 to 11 percent; for cow's milk, from 57 to 38 percent; for sugar, from 24 to 13 percent; and one-kilogram loafs of white bread from 42 to 8 percent. The subsidy on pork meat increased, however, from 16 to 28 percent.[18]

Still, even with the price readjustments that occurred in 1979 and 1981, the Hungarian minister of finance in presenting the 1981 national budget in December 1980 noted that budget expenditures "in the form of consumer price subsidy will be 10 percent, that is, 7 thousand million forints more next year."[19] This statement indicates that consumer subsidies would cost 77 billion forints in 1981, or 16 percent of the entire budget. Not all of these subsidies are for food, though an OECD report indicates that in 1976 food subsidies

[17] Ibid., p. 19, and Ad Hoc Group on East/West Economic Relations in Agriculture, "Agricultural Production and Food Consumption in GDR," DAA/1731, Organization for Economic Co-operation and Development, Directorate for Food, Agriculture, and Fisheries, November 28, 1980, p. 32.

[18] United States Joint Publications Research Service, April 3, 1980, translation from Budapest *Figyelo* of February 20, 1980.

[19] *Nepszabadsac*, December 19, 1980.

alone amounted to 45 billion forints, or 10 percent of the budget.[20]

I have only limited information on food price subsidies in Bulgaria. Bulgaria increased food prices by large percentages in November 1979—prices for meat and eggs rose by 30 percent; for processed meat by 40 percent; milk, cheese, rice, and flour prices were increased by similar percentages. Butter prices doubled.[21] These increases were the first since 1956 for bread and the first since 1968 for meat, milk, and sugar. Since there had been increases in the prices paid to farms for cattle, hogs, and milk, subsidies were required during the 1970s prior to the sharp increase in consumer prices. Vankai in 1978 described the situation as follows: "Consumer prices of stable foods are fixed independently of producer prices and remain stable with the help of subsidies."[22]

At the beginning of 1981, purchase prices of many agricultural products were increased substantially in Bulgaria. Some examples are, in percent: wheat, 40; corn, 4; sugar beets, 15; cows' milk, 14.5; beef, 15; wool, 63; and poultry, 5.5. The cost of the increase in purchase prices will be paid from budget funds, costing approximately 3 percent of the planned budget for 1981.[23] Retail prices were not increased, however, and food subsidies were increased.

We know even less about the food subsidy in Romania than in Bulgaria. It is quite possible that there were no significant food subsidies prior to 1981. Retail price increases and shortages were reported to have resulted in labor unrest in 1980. Retail price increases that had been announced for 1981 were not put into effect. As a result, the cost of the increased farm procurement prices has

[20] Ad Hoc Group on East/West Economic Relations in Agriculture, "Agricultural Production and Food Consumption in Hungary," DAA/1712, Organization for Economic Co-operation and Development, Directorate for Food, Agriculture, and Fisheries, September 8, 1980, p. 14. The same report also notes: "The Hungarian government intends to diminish the subsidies for agricultural products gradually. As a first step, farms will increasingly be made, in 1981-90, to pay for the rapidly rising energy costs" (ibid., p. 48). Hungary's subsidy system is a complex one, involving a wide range of subsidies directly to agriculture, including investment subsidies, as well as subsidies for meeting the differences between prices paid to farms plus processing, transportation, and marketing costs and the retail prices.

[21] Department of Agriculture, ESCS, *World Agricultural Situation*, WAS-21 Supplement 3, 1980, p. 18.

[22] Thomas A. Vankai, *Progress and Outlook for East European Agriculture, 1976-80*, Foreign Agricultural Economics Report No. 153, U.S. Department of Agriculture, ESCS, 1978, p. 13. Vankai's next sentence was: "During 1971-75, real income increased 32 percent, causing difficulty in satisfying demands for goods and services."

[23] Foreign Broadcast Information Service, Bulgaria, December 23, 1980, translation from Sofia *Rabotnichesko Delo*, December 15, 1980.

been met from budget funds; it had been planned that the increased farm prices would be covered by higher retail prices.[24]

Czechoslovakia has had and continues to have a major program of food price subsidies. In addition to direct consumer price subsidies, subsidies are paid on agricultural inputs. For example, subsidies equal 13.5 percent of the wholesale prices of mixed feeds and 16 percent of the wholesale prices of chemical fertilizers. Milk and slaughter cattle subsidies were increased significantly in 1977 and again in 1979. For this group of products (presumably milk and beef only), subsidy expenditures increased by 16 percent, or 3.8 billion korunas, as a result of changes made in 1979. This indicates that the total subsidy had grown to over 27 billion korunas.[25] How much is a koruna worth? Its value is probably less than ten cents and more than six cents. Thus the cost of the subsidy might be about $2 billion. This is approximately $130 per capita, a not insignificant figure. Vankai reports that in 1977 the price subsidies for food accounted for "about one-fourth of the retail prices of meat, bread, and sugar."[26]

Yugoslavia has made little use of subsidies for agriculture and food. At times fertilizer has been subsidized, but such subsidies were supposed to have been removed in 1980. Price controls have been imposed on major agricultural products, but prices of farm products appear to have increased roughly in line with general price increases.[27]

The description of food price subsidies in Poland has been left to last. This was done in part because Poland has been the major cause of increased grain imports by the Eastern European CPEs. Further, we know rather more about the Polish subsidies than we do about those of other countries.

Poland increased food prices in 1970, but most of the increases were rescinded. Otherwise, retail prices of livestock products in the state stores in 1979 were little changed from the 1960 prices. Yet between 1960 and 1979 all consumer prices more than doubled. Since food prices in the state stores had changed little during the period, the official retail prices of livestock products relative to all goods and services declined significantly, perhaps by as much as 50 percent. Of course, the supplies of meat in the state stores did not meet demand

[24] In December 1980 it was announced that prices paid to the agricultural producer would be increased by 12 percent effective January 1, 1981 (*Economist*, February 28, 1981, pp. 46-47).

[25] Prague *Statni Statky*, vol. 12, 1979.

[26] Vankai, *Progress and Outlook*, p. 18.

[27] Ibid., p. 49.

at the official prices. Following the aborted attempt to increase meat and other food prices in 1976, the Polish government opened a significant number of "commercial shops," where meat and meat products of better than average quality were available at prices significantly higher than in the state stores. In 1979 approximately one-seventh of the market meat supplies were sold in the commercial stores at prices approximately double those in the state stores.[28]

In 1980 the direct consumer price subsidy for meat cost 67 billion zlotys. In 1979, however, it was estimated that total meat and poultry subsidies, including subsidies for livestock feed, amounted to 91.4 billion zlotys. In 1971 such subsidies totaled just 12.3 billion zlotys and were estimated to cost 100 billion in 1980. The cost of 91.4 billion zlotys equaled 11.2 percent of the wages fund.

The direct meat subsidies account for less than half of total food subsidies. In 1980 total food subsidies were 144 billion zlotys; additional subsidies to farmers for feed, fertilizer, and seeds equaled 28 billion zlotys. In the 1981 budget food subsidies were increased by 40 percent over the 1980 level, to 228 billion.[29]

In 1979 the government price subsidy (excluding subsidies paid to farmers) averaged 34.40 zlotys per kilogram; the average price of meat sold in the state stores was about 48 zlotys. Thus the subsidy amounted to more than 70 percent of the retail price or, put another way, the retail price was less than 60 percent of the cost of producing, processing, transporting, and selling the meat. If the subsidies paid directly to the farmers were included, the subsidy per kilogram of meat equaled the retail price of meat.[30]

Given that meat supplies were available, it is hardly surprising that per capita meat consumption in Poland increased by 40 percent during the 1970s. The prices of meat products have been held at exceedingly low levels. Using the tourist exchange rate for the zloty of thirty-one per dollar, which is at least double the black-market rate, the price of pork at retail in 1980 was $1.80 per kilogram, or

---

[28] *Polish News Bulletin*, translation from *Trybuna Ludu*, no. 126, May 28, 1980, p. 11.

[29] Ibid., pp. 10 and 11, and report by Radio Free Europe of the 1981 budget presentation by the Polish minister of finance on December 19, 1980, EE/6608/C/1 (B,W), December 23, 1980. If 91 billion zlotys in 1979 for meat and poultry subsidies equaled 11 percent of the wages fund, the total food subsidy bill estimated for 1981 of 228 billion zlotys must be at least 20 percent of the 1981 wages fund.

[30] Average retail price of meat estimated from data in *Polish News Bulletin*; subsidy indicated on p. 10. It was noted that between 1970 and mid-1980 procurement prices for livestock increased by 129 percent, whereas retail prices hardly increased at all.

about $0.80 per pound. The beef retail price in the state stores for the same year, was $0.97 per kilogram, or $0.44 per pound.[31]

In 1980 procurement prices for livestock products were increased, and it was assumed that retail prices would be increased to cover all or part of the increase. Taking all factors into account, however, the price subsidies for 1981 had to be increased significantly from the 1980 and earlier levels. The subsidies, in zlotys per kilogram, for 1981 are: pork, 53; beef, 48; butter, 101; sugar, 15.5; and flour, 7.3.[32]

One part of the summer 1980 agreement between the government and the labor groups was that the commercial stores would be closed or that the prices in these stores would be the same as those in the state stores. In a press conference held on December 5, 1980, it was stated that the retail trade would sell 1.1 million tons of meat at an average price of fifty-five zlotys per kilogram. A system of rationing was announced for the first of February but was later postponed until April, indicating that even at the higher prices imposed, the available supply would fall short of the demand. An average price of fifty-five zlotys per kilogram is a low price by comparison with prices in other countries. Using the tourist exchange rate, which certainly overvalues the zloty relative to the dollar, the meat price is $1.77 per kilogram ($0.81 per pound). Given this average price and the price subsidies indicated in the previous paragraph, in 1981 the meat price subsidies equal the retail price. In other words, the consumer is paying approximately half of the actual costs incurred in bringing the meat to the retail store.[33]

The Polish meat price subsidies have resulted in shortages in the stores and, finally, rationing. The substantial expansion in per capita meat consumption in the 1970s of twenty kilograms was based upon increased imports of feed. As one Polish writer put it:

> The balance sheet of the imports of grain, fodders and meat and of exports of livestock and meat is worsening from year to year. During 1970–79 the imports of grain and fodders

---

[31] Urban, *The Feed-Livestock Economy of Eastern Europe*, p. 21.

[32] Minister of finance, Radio Free Europe, December 23, 1980, p. 3.

[33] Radio Free Europe, December 18, 1980. It is reasonable to argue that the subsidy per kilogram of meat distributed through the retail network is greater than 55 zlotys per kilogram. The subsidy does not apply to meat produced and consumed by farm people; thus the amount of meat moving through the retail network is less than the total available supply. Assuming the 1981 subsidy cost will be 67 billion zlotys and the meat sold through the state stores will be 1.1 million tons, the price subsidy equals 61 zlotys per kilogram. Even more important than the difference in volume of meat produced, however, and that moving through the state stores is the effect of including the food subsidies. If these are added, the subsidy per kilogram is 100 zlotys, or perhaps $3.00.

increased three-fold in terms of volume and five-fold in terms of value. A steadily increasing part of meat consumption is based upon imported fodders. It has been calculated that last year about 1.1 million tons of meat (including fat), i.e., about 27 kg. of meat and 3.5 kg. of fat per capita, was produced from imported raw materials. To simplify the argument, it may be said that every one of us bought 27 kg. of meat abroad.[34]

Is there some important social purpose being served by these price subsidies? Two brief quotations indicate that at least some individuals have been unable to determine the existence of substantial benefits:

> Without risking to make an error, one may state that out of that 91.4 billion zl a lion's share were subsidies for the benefit of people in higher income brackets because the more affluent buy more meat. . . . The meat subsidies system and the extensive pumping of money into the meat market, creates a barrier to wage increases and necessitates the keeping of prices of products other than food at a relatively high level. Every wage increase, given the present price structure, increases the stresses on the market.

> I have already had occasion to tell the House the view that the problem of subsidies, despite their social motivation, arouses numerous controversies and reservations as regards their desirability as a form of social insurance. It is well known that they apply to all citizens, and thus the view that both those who earn more as well as those who earn less benefit from them, and perhaps those earning more benefit more, is correct. That is why we must not ignore the matter, but must search for methods which, while enabling us fully to guarantee incomes for lower and medium earners, will at the same time enable us to shape a more just distribution of goods among the nation.[35]

The meat and food price subsidies in Poland represent an additional confirmation of Director's Law that most actions of governments are for the benefit of the middle-class majority and at the expense of the poor and the rich. Farmers receive less direct benefit than urban workers with the same real incomes because much of

[34] *Polish News Bulletin*, translation from *Trybuna Ludu*, no. 126, May 28, 1980, p. 13.

[35] The first quotation is from *Trybuna Ludu*, ibid., pp. 11 and 12. The second quotation is from the finance minister's presentation of the 1981 budget in late December.

their consumption is derived from their own production. Further, low-income urban families derive less absolute benefit because they spend less on food than do higher-income consumers. Yet it is exceptionally difficult to abolish the subsidy system or to modify it to reduce its great cost significantly. The adverse economic effects are enormous, including major distortions in resource allocation and contributions to increased inequality in the distribution of income.

There are a number of ways in which the price subsidies distort resource use. Still, perhaps the most important is that the subsidies have resulted in excess imports of grain and other feeds, and the products derived from these materials are sold at prices that cover no more than half of the foreign exchange expenditures incurred. Thus a considerable part of the very large Polish foreign exchange debt can be attributed to holding the price of meat at too low a level. If meat and milk prices to consumers had covered the costs of producing these products over the past decade, grain and feed imports by Poland would have increased little, if at all, and the hard-currency debt could have been much smaller than it now is.

The summary of meat and food price subsidies reveals that more than 85 million of the 130 million population of Eastern Europe pay significantly less for meat, milk, eggs, and numerous other foods than the actual costs of bringing these products to and through the retail outlets. Only Romania and Yugoslavia have not engaged in major food subsidies—and the food subsidies can only be described as major, ranging from approximately a quarter to as much as half of the total retail value of food. For meat, a product with high income and price elasticities of demand, some of the subsidies have been equal to the retail prices of the subsidized products.

The growth of agricultural output in Eastern Europe has been at a satisfactory pace since 1960. Output growth was slowest in Poland, with no growth in production after 1973. It was quite unfortunate that the country with the slowest output growth was also the one with the largest subsidies for livestock products. In addition, it has been the rapid growth in consumption of livestock products that has resulted in the increase in grain imports of 10 million tons during the 1970s by the Eastern European economies.

I conclude that primary responsibility for the large grain imports and much of the foreign currency debt of Eastern European CPEs has been due to agricultural and food price policies. In Poland the difficulty is not only that food has been subsidized but that the continuing uncertainty about the future of private agriculture and the failure to provide adequate and appropriate inputs have extracted a high price in forgone opportunities.

Soviet Union. Of the approximately 50 million ton net increase in grain imports by the CPEs during the 1970s, the Soviet Union accounted for 35 million tons. Since this comparison is based on two years (1979 and 1980) when the Soviet Union had poor grain crops, a more appropriate comparison might be for a five-year period starting with 1976/77. If the most recent five years are used, the increase in net grain imports by the CPEs is reduced to 35 million tons. Still, the Soviet Union was responsible for 24 million tons of the increase, or 70 percent, the same percentage as above.

There can be little doubt that the demand for meat and other livestock products increased significantly during the 1970s. During the decade annual per capita growth in real GNP was approximately 3 percent. True, this figure was substantially below the 4 percent growth achieved during the 1960s, but even with the slower growth in real gross GNP, the per capita demand for meat increased by as much as 2 percent annually. Population growth of almost 1 percent per annum added to the demand, but demand growth is not the same as consumption growth.

A very important difference between the Soviet Union and the seven Eastern European economies is that the Soviet Union was not able to increase meat output, and thus meat consumption, significantly during the 1970s, whereas the seven countries increased their per capita consumption by about a fourth. Per capita meat consumption in 1980 in the Soviet Union was no more than fifty-five kilograms; this was the same as the 1974 figure and the lowest since that year. Per capita consumption in 1971 was fifty kilograms. Thus a decade of heavy investment in fertilizer and large imports of feeding materials achieved but a 10 percent increase in per capita consumption.

In passing, it may be noted that the Soviet per capita consumption refers to meat and fat, whereas the figures that have been presented for Eastern Europe exclude the slaughter fats. Thus, compared with per capita meat consumption in the Eastern European CPEs, the Soviet consumption figures are overestimated by at least 10 percent and perhaps by as much as 20 percent.[36]

The Soviet Union has a large and growing subsidy program for meat, milk, and certain other food products. As noted earlier, the total cost of the subsidy is probably now on the order of 30 billion

[36] If edible slaughter fat and offal are included in per capita consumption for Eastern Europe in 1979, the estimate was 89 kilograms. Although this estimate may not be strictly comparable with the Soviet one, it indicates a wide difference between what has been accomplished in the Soviet Union and in the Eastern European CPEs. Department of Agriculture, ESCS, *World Agricultural Situation*, WAS-21 Supplements 1 and 3.

rubles. The magnitude of these subsidies is indicated by the following quotation from a major Soviet journal: "In the USSR the state's outlay for the production, processing and sale of products were in the mid-seventies double the retail prices for beef, 1.4-fold higher for mutton, 1.3-fold higher for pork, 1.4-fold higher for butter and 1.3-fold higher for potatoes."[37] Since the prices of milk and potatoes were increased at the beginning of 1979 by 15 percent and 32 percent, respectively, with a simultaneous commitment not to increase the retail prices of these products, the total subsidy for food products was increased by 3.2 billion rubles annually. In 1981 there has been a further increase in farm prices and an increase in annual subsidies of 4 billion rubles.

As I noted earlier, a Russian acquaintance informed me that in the mid-1960s the meat and milk subsidies were thought to be temporary in nature. It is interesting to note that there remains, as of early 1980, a similar view that the current high subsidy rates can be gradually reduced and eventually eliminated. These sentences followed the quotation above:

> To a greater or lesser degree a similar picture is observed for all practical purposes in the other European CEMA countries as well. For instance, in 1975 subsidies in Poland covered 25 percent of the value of agricultural production. In order to raise the rate of profit of agricultural production, in 1978 the state allocated 60 percent more subsidies than in 1975. But in the future, as industrialization of agriculture is completed and as costs drop in the various branches of animal husbandry, this type of subsidy is to decrease or disappear altogether. This conclusion is specifically confirmed by development of industrial-type poultry raising in the CEMA countries, where production has been doing without subsidies for a long time now. Moreover, in a number of countries—the G.D.R. and Czechoslovakia, for example—purchase prices for eggs and broilers have dropped somewhat in recent years.

The assumption and hope that the cost trends for livestock generally will follow those exhibited by poultry during the past two or three decades have little foundation. The countries that contributed the management and technology required for the sharp reductions in the real cost of poultry products have not realized significant reductions in the real costs of producing pork and beef, nor does it seem

[37] Joint Publications Research Service 75754, May 22, 1980; translation of an article by M. Ye Bukh and L. V. Popova in *Izvestiya Akademii Nauk SSSR, Seriya Ekonomicheskaya* No. 1, 1980. Quotation from page 8 of JPRS.

likely that such will happen. It will not be easy to keep real costs from increasing for livestock products other than poultry and eggs. Consequently, there is no basis for officials' assumption in the Council of Mutual Economic Assistance (CEMA) countries that all they have to do is wait until declining supply prices for beef, pork, and milk make it possible to retain current retail prices without the use of price subsidies. The wait will be a very long one at best. Unless retail prices are increased, the cost of the subsidies will increase. In fact, one can say with a high degree of certainty that the only way the cost of subsidies can be held constant or reduced will be by increasing retail prices of subsidized products.

The poor output performance of Soviet livestock farms during the Tenth Plan is inexplicable, or at least it seems so to me. The Tenth Plan covered 1976–1980. Compared with the Ninth Plan, meat production and milk production increased just 6 percent. Egg production did increase by 22 percent, but overall livestock output increased no more than 7 to 8 percent. Although grain production did not increase as much as indicated by the Tenth Plan goals, it did increase by 13 percent over the average for the period of the Ninth Plan. With the very large increase in grain imports, it is reasonable to estimate that grain fed to livestock during the Tenth Plan rose 22 percent above the figure in the previous plan.[38] How can it be that there was such a small increase in livestock output? One possibility is that other sources of feed—hay, green feed, silage, straw, pasture—did not increase during the five years and may even have decreased in quantity and quality. Even if this were factually correct, however, one is left to inquire why there was no increase in the other types of feed.

Still, whatever the reasons for the poor performance of the livestock sector, there can be no denying that it was poor. The record of this sector, plus the meat and milk price policy, has induced the Soviet government to import large and growing quantities of grain. The 1980 grain crop brought no relief. That for 1979 was the smallest since 1974; that for 1980 was only a little larger and apparently of significantly lower quality because of wet weather during the harvest of much of the grain sown in the spring. In addition to the poor grain crop, the yield of potatoes (which is an important source of feed as well as food) was the smallest in nearly

[38] Department of Agriculture, ESCS, *World Agricultural Situation*, WAS-21 Supplement 1, p. 22, and Department of Agriculture, Foreign Agricultural Service, *Foreign Agriculture Circular: Grains*, FG-2-81, January 15, 1981, p. 4. For 1976/77 through 1980/81 the USDA estimates grain used for feed at an annual rate of 120 million tons; for 1971/72 through 1975/76, at 98 million tons.

three decades and more than a quarter below the 1979 crop. For the second year in a row there was a poor sunflower crop; the 1980 output was only 60 percent of the 1980 goal.[39] Sunflowers are a significant source of high-protein feed for livestock; a short crop results in a deterioration in the quality of livestock rations or requires significant increases in imports of oilmeals or oilseeds.

China. During the 1950s China imported no grain. As indicated in table 6, China became a net importer in the 1960s, with net imports ranging from a low of 3.1 million tons in 1969 to a high of 5.4 million tons in 1964. The early 1970s saw a slight downward trend in grain imports, with a low of 1.2 million tons of net imports in 1976. Since then net grain imports have increased rapidly, however, reaching 13.5 million tons in the 1980/81 marketing year.

The significant increase in grain imports in 1980/81 may have been due to a 1980 grain crop that was perhaps 12 million tons smaller than the record yield in 1979. Still, China has entered into a significant number of bilateral commitments with major grain exporters for periods that extend beyond 1980/81. The Foreign Agricultural Service of the U.S. Department of Agriculture has summarized the bilateral agreements and concludes: "Commitments under these agreements imply annual import requirements of 12.3 to 17.2 million tons, 1 to 6 million tons greater than the previous record."[40] The previous record level of grain imports had been gross imports of 11 million tons in 1978/79.

Why has China so substantially increased grain imports? Though there is some ambiguity about grain production data for China due to recent revisions in such data, the growth of grain production during the last decade has been at a reasonable rate and, in any case, is at least as high as the apparent long-term growth rate of approximately 2.5 percent annually. If one accepts the recently revised data for 1978–1980, the growth rate for grain production since 1969–1971 has been approximately 3 percent.[41] The apparent reason for increased grain imports must be found elsewhere than in a slowing of the rate of grain production growth in recent years.

[39] U.S.S.R., Council of Ministers, "Report on 1980 Plan Fulfillment," trans. in *Current Digest of the Soviet Press*, vol. 33, no. 4 (February 25, 1981), pp. 14-15.

[40] U.S. Department of Agriculture, Foreign Agricultural Service, *Foreign Agriculture Circular: Grains*, FG-5-81, January 28, 1981, pp. 5 and 8.

[41] The revisions for the year 1978 through 1980 may have added about 3 percent to grain output for the three years. Without the revisions, the annual growth rate would be approximately 2.8 percent.

It is my conclusion that the growth of grain imports has resulted primarily from policy changes and not from any reduction in the rate of growth of agricultural output in recent years compared with the rate since the mid-1950s. The policy changes that directly affected import demands were the following:

1. A significant increase in prices paid for agricultural products, estimated to cost 7.8 billion yuan, and some tax reductions that increased the incomes of communes. The effects of these and related changes, along with an increase in agricultural output, was to increase the per capita income from communes (including food received in kind) by almost 13 percent. The average price paid to farms in 1979 was 22 percent higher than in 1978.

2. Wages in state-run enterprises were increased significantly during 1979—by more than 9 percent.

3. The growth of grain procurements, largely used to supply the cities, appears to have slowed in 1979 and presumably in later years. In part this was due to the reduction of the agricultural tax, which was collected in grain and in 1979 was reduced by 2.4 million tons.

4. When farm purchase prices were increased in 1979, the consumer prices for grains and edible oils were not increased. While the prices of other food products were increased by about 30 percent, a five yuan per month subsidy was paid to most urban workers. Consequently the price of grain at retail fell significantly relative to other food products and worker incomes. The effect was to increase the desired consumption levels of grain.[42]

The effect of these and some other changes was a budget deficit in 1979 of about 10 billion yuan, or approximately 9 percent of domestic budget revenues. In the 1980 budget it was estimated that "a wide variety of price subsidies to offset price increases . . . will exceed 20 billion yuan in 1980."[43] Of this total, about 12 billion yuan was for consumer subsidies, mainly food products. Another 5 billion yuan was to cover the cost of the above-quota purchase prices for agricultural products; generally sales to the state in excess of required deliveries are paid at a price 50 percent in excess of the basic price. Finally, approximately 3 billion yuan was to be spent to provide preferential prices for agricultural inputs such as fertilizer and machinery. The subsidies listed above relate primarily to agri-

---

[42] Based on *Beijing Review*, no. 39 (September 29, 1980), pp. 11-18; Department of Agriculture, ESCS, *World Agricultural Situation*, WAS-21 Supplement 6, pp. 2-7, and *Agriculture Abroad*, October 1980, pp. 9-15 and 25-30.
[43] *Beijing Review*, no. 39, 1980, p. 16.

culture; the only specific exception appears to be coal. There are many other subsidies, for house rent and transport, which, it was said, would make the total subsidy figure much bigger. The actual outcome for 1980 with respect to these subsidies is not known as of the time of writing. In 1979 such subsidies turned out to be larger than anticipated.

In last year's article in this series, I devoted several paragraphs to a review of information generally disclosed by official sources concerning the recent food situation in China. To summarize briefly, per capita grain production had not increased between 1955 and 1977. Official reports indicated that peasants, except in better areas, had a hard life throughout the year. It was indicated that in a province not far from Shanghai, "there are many people in the villages who have not enough to eat or enough clothing to keep them warm." A high Chinese official reported in 1979 that 10 percent of the Chinese population did not have enough to eat.[44]

There is substantial evidence that famine has not been eliminated in China. During my visit to China in late 1980, reports of a famine in Anhwei Province in 1976 were verified by reliable informants. Information that I have received since writing last year's article, suggests, if anything, an even starker picture than was presented then. An article in the *People's Daily* on November 26, 1978, reported that living standards in northwest China, including Gansu Province, "are lower than those in pre-liberation days or the time of the war of resistance with Japan." Fox Butterfield, writing in the *New York Times*, reported that in 1976, communes in Gansu Province distributed only 354 pounds of grain per capita and that given the heavy reliance upon grains for calories (perhaps 80 to 90 percent), this was probably a hunger diet. The poorest production teams in the province were said to have earned about twenty dollars per year in 1976. Since 1976 grain distribution has increased to 500 pounds, a level providing for more than adequate calories and some excess for livestock feed.[45]

The *Economist* of April 4, 1981, carried the quite surprising story that the United Nations appealed for $700 million of disaster relief to assist China to provide food and other types of relief for

[44] See "The World Food Situation: Developments during the 1970s and Prospects for the 1980s," in William Fellner, ed., *Contemporary Economic Problems 1980* (Washington, D.C.: American Enterprise Institute, 1980), pp. 322-28. Note that in last year's article, Chinese grain production includes rice in milled form; in table 9 in this article rice is included as paddy or rough rice. The quoted statement appeared in *People's Daily*, January 20, 1979.

[45] *New York Times*, November 5, 1980.

20 million people. Hebei Province was said to have suffered the worst drought in twenty-six years and Hubei Province the worst flood in thirty-seven years. It was also reported that five other northern provinces had been adversely affected by drought. In Hubei Province the flood apparently destroyed as many as 200,000 homes. Although much of the relief was sought to help repair broken dikes and repair other flood damage, food relief was also requested. The *Economist* stated: "But [food] relief is being provided only in areas where more than 50 percent of the harvest was destroyed; this leaves some 100m[illion] other Chinese victims to fend for themselves." [46]

Given the food situation as it has been and is, it is not too surprising that the Chinese officials who succeeded Mao and the Gang of Four should make a serious effort to improve food supplies for a large fraction of the population. In addition, the unwillingness to pass on farm price increases for grains and edible oils as well as the introduction of the monthly subsidy to meet the costs of other food price increases indicates that governmental officials are seriously concerned about the support of populations in large urban centers.

Yet there is no doubt that urban incomes are much higher than rural incomes, almost certainly by a factor of more than two. The results of a recent survey of urban and rural incomes have been released. It shows an annual per capita income in urban areas of 392 yuan and 160 yuan for the rural population.[47] These data refer to income from all sources, including home consumption and private subsidiary production.

Urban and rural areas should not differ significantly in the purchasing power of a yuan. Urban workers pay very little for housing and transportation, and the subsidized retail prices of grains are no higher than the prices received by the farms and the prices that are probably used to value food products consumed in the farm households. Since commune members must pay most if not all of the costs of their housing, rural families may well spend more on housing than urban families.

Still, even if some adjustment to urban income is required to achieve purchasing power comparable to that of rural income, it remains true that urban real incomes are substantially higher than farm incomes. Thus the use of food price subsidies, available to all urban consumers but not to farm people, cannot be justified on the basis of the relatively low incomes of urban consumers. Urban consumers could have paid the full costs of the increases in farm prices and

[46] *Economist*, April 4, 1981, p. 17.
[47] Ibid., February 14, 1981, p. 69.

could still have had real incomes substantially higher than those of the farm people who produced the food. The same pattern of using food subsidies to benefit higher-income urban consumers prevails in almost all of the CPEs, however.

It should not be too surprising that the various measures adopted by the Chinese government in 1979 resulted in a significant growth in the demand for food. This is true in the urban areas, given the subsidized food prices, even with rationing of major food items, both because of some increase in ration allowances and because of a probable increase in the percentage of the ration allowance purchased with higher incomes, including the special subsidy as well as wage increases. Given the modest levels of food consumption for large numbers of farm people, higher farm incomes have certainly resulted in increased per capita consumption of all foods. It appears that the percentage of grain output procured by the state has declined in recent years, the response that one would expect if the steps to increase rural incomes were carried out. Most of the grain imports are consumed in the cities, presumably to minimize transport and distribution costs. It has been estimated that grain imports now provide for 40 percent of grain consumption in the cities.[48]

The significance of the food price policy of China for the rest of the world rests to a considerable degree upon the fact that China consumes about a fifth of the world's grain supply. Rather modest shortfalls in supply in China, if met by increased grain imports, can have a major impact upon world grain markets. Chinese net grain imports in 1980/81 were 13.5 million tons; this is only 4.5 percent of probable grain use during the year. If, because of low prices and money income growth, demand for grain should increase at a rate just 1 percent per annum faster than supply, Chinese grain imports would increase by approximately 3 million tons annually, or more than 30 million tons in a decade, to a level of more than 45 million tons. Even if the difference in annual demand and supply growth rates were as small as 0.5 percent, in a decade grain imports would be 30 million tons, or double the 1980/81 level of gross grain imports.[49]

The Chinese government is currently following food price, subsidy, and income policies that, it believes, are best suited to its

[48] Department of Agriculture, ESCS, *World Agricultural Situation*, WAS-21 Supplement 6, p. 10.

[49] Obviously if grain supply increases more rapidly than grain demand, even by as little as 0.5 percent annually, Chinese grain imports could decline to near zero in a decade. I am not in a position to predict whether it is more likely that demand will grow more rapidly than supply or vice versa. The example in the text is intended to indicate how large Chinese grain imports could become if their demand grew somewhat more rapidly than supply.

current situation. Yet these policies will most certainly result in a growing dependence of China upon grain imports. The consequences of such dependence will depend upon the Chinese capacity to provide the foreign exchange to purchase increasing quantities of grain and the availability of supplies at prices China is willing and able to pay. So far, or at least through 1979, China has had a small positive balance in its agricultural trade, even though it has run a deficit in its total trade since 1977.

Food and Agricultural Subsidies in the Market Economies. I do not want to leave the impression that food and agricultural subsidies are a monopoly of the centrally planned economies. There are some market economies with subsidies for particular commodities that are even higher than the subsidies in the CPEs. Japan, for example, pays its farmers prices for rice and wheat that are three to four times the prices charged to the first processor of these products. In recent years the agricultural subsidies of the European Community have equaled approximately an eighth of the value of its farm production. In 1978 farm production was valued at 96 billion units of account, and the farm fund spending was 11.5 billion units of account.[50] In addition the various member states of the community spent substantial amounts in agricultural subsidies.

The budget costs of farm price and income support programs in the United States have ranged from $3 billion to $5 billion in the later 1970s. In addition, food stamps, school lunch programs, and nutrition programs targeted for children and mothers have involved expenditures of $15 billion annually in recent years.

A number of developing countries subsidize the consumer prices of one or more food products. Egypt, for example, has priced wheat to the processors at about a third of the world market price in recent years. Ecuador, Brazil, Iran, Mexico, Peru, Korea, and Taiwan sell wheat to processors at prices significantly below either import prices or the prices paid to their own farmers.[51]

Still, the aggregate effects of the subsidy policies of the market economies upon the average level of world grain prices have been relatively small. Although some of the market economies have followed price policies that have encouraged a higher rate of food consumption than would have existed if internal prices had been at the world-market prices, other market economies have held internal

[50] *Economist*, November 1, 1980, pp. 51-54.
[51] U.S. Department of Agriculture, Foreign Agricultural Service, *Wheat and Corn Prices for Selected Countries*, FG-6-79, April 18, 1979, pp. 47-48. The price data are for 1977.

prices significantly above world-market prices. The very large subsidies in Japan for rice and wheat have not resulted in particularly low consumer prices, and by holding beef prices at levels well above import prices, Japan has discouraged the consumption of beef and has thus reduced use of grain as feed substantially below the amount that would be needed if Japanese consumers had access to beef at the same price as, say, consumers in the United States. The farm price policies of the European Community have also restricted the consumption of beef and pork and thus of grain as feed.

Concluding Comments

The experience of the centrally planned economies during the 1970s indicates how rapidly a country can shift from being self-sufficient in grain and food to a significant level of dependence upon grain imports. As has been shown, three factors were primarily responsible for the shifts that occurred—a relatively high income elasticity of demand for livestock products; a food price policy that resulted in lowering the price of food relative to other consumer products; and, in the case of the Soviet Union, very slow growth of agricultural output, including the products that are highly subsidized. In China the increase in money and real incomes since 1978 has contributed to a rapid growth in the demand for grain.

Four countries have been primarily responsible for almost all of the increased grain imports by the CPEs—Poland, the G.D.R., the Soviet Union, and China. In both Poland and G.D.R. meat production and consumption increased rapidly during the 1970s. Domestic feed production did not increase enough to support the growth of livestock production, however, and thus it was necessary to increase feed imports, including grains. In the Soviet Union the substantial increase in grain use as feed had seemingly little effect upon livestock production, and the large increase in grain imports was due, in part, to rather modest growth of grain production during the last half of the 1970s.

The increase in Chinese grain imports seems to have been associated with the institution of food price subsidies and the increase in the incomes of both rural and urban people. It appears that China has embarked upon an inflationary path, with significant implications for the desired consumption levels for grain and edible oils, products whose retail prices have been kept at low levels by the use of price subsidies.

The poor people of the world in countries outside the CPEs have some stake in the food and agricultural policies of the CPEs. If the current policies of the CPEs are continued without change for this decade, the growth of their grain imports could result in a significant increase in the real prices of grain in international markets. I do not predict that the policies will remain unchanged and that grain imports will continue to grow for another decade. Still, the available evidence indicates that it is very difficult to reduce food price subsidies significantly and thus stem the growth of grain and food imports.[52]

[52] There is another way in which the price policies of the CPEs have an effect upon the rest of the world. Since these economies attempt to stabilize their domestic prices by varying net trade, they impose the instability arising from variations in their production and demand upon the international markets. In addition, these countries absorb very little of any variations in supply and demand in the rest of the world. Thus the CPEs follow policies that contribute significantly to international price instability. Similar policies of domestic price stability are followed by the European Community and other Western European countries, however, as well as by a number of developing countries. Consequently the instability of international market prices is both substantial and increasing as an increasing percentage of international trade is undertaken to stabilize domestic prices. For further discussion of this topic, see my article "World Agriculture, Commodity Policy, and Price Variability," *American Journal of Agricultural Economics*, vol. 57, no. 5 (December 1975), pp. 823-28.

The Economic Malaise of the 1980s: A Positive Program for a Benevolent and Enlightened Dictator

Gottfried Haberler

Summary

The economic malaise that gripped the Western world in the 1970s, after the euphoria and optimism of the 1950s and 1960s, continued and deepened in 1980. All recent economic reports by national and international agencies are tinged with pessimism and gloom—seemingly intractable inflation and low productivity and GNP growth are the outlook. How would a benevolent and enlightened dictator deal with this problem?

The monetary authorities would be instructed to reduce monetary growth to the potential growth of real GNP. Although it is true that sufficiently tight money can bring down inflation irrespective of the size of the budget deficit, our dictator would realize that the combination of tight money–soft fiscal policy would drive up interest rates, crowd out private investment, and slow productivity growth, which in turn would make the fight against inflation more difficult. This is why most monetarists insist that anti-inflationary monetary policy must be supported by tight fiscal policy. Easy money–tight budget is the appropriate anti-inflationary policy.

The importance of fiscal policy, however, goes far beyond balancing the budget. The growing size of the budget, the mounting tax burden, and the inflation-distorted tax structure have become a formidable roadblock for economic growth. Tax reduction and tax reform—especially lowering of high marginal tax rates, which blunt the incentives to work, to save, and to invest—would be part of the

NOTE: An abbreviated version of this paper will appear in a Festschrift for Herbert Giersch, *Reflections on the Troubled World Economy: Essays in Honor of Professor Herbert Giersch* (London: Macmillan, forthcoming 1981).

program. But our dictator would realize that the beneficial effects of lower taxes would be slow in coming. Therefore, in order to avoid larger budget deficits, tax cuts must go hand in hand with expenditure cuts. This amounts to saying that our dictator would practice supply-side economics in the broad sense of the term, to wit, that he would take steps to stimulate output and employment. He would, however, reject supply-side economics in the narrow sense, now so popular, which claims that the beneficial effects of tax cuts on output and employment will materialize so fast that no reduction in tax revenues will result.

Growing rigidity of wages and prices has become a more serious obstacle to a successful anti-inflationary monetary policy than soft fiscal policy. Money wages are almost totally rigid downward, and real wages, too, have become rigid through formal or de facto indexation. Labor unions are not the only culprits. Numerous other pressure groups do for their constituents through political pressure what unions do for workers. Organized agriculture is the most important example. As a consequence, monetary restraint causes so much transitional or even long-lasting unemployment that it is almost impossible to bring it to a successful conclusion. In a truly competitive economy stagflation on the present scale would be impossible.

In this paper, the view of some monetarists that stagflation and persistent unemployment are possible even in a perfectly competitive economy is analyzed and found invalid, because of the failure to make the crucially important distinction between involuntary and voluntary unemployment.

Measures to make the economy more competitive are discussed. The most difficult problem will be curbing union power. Withdrawing special privileges will go a long way toward reducing wage pressure, but more drastic measures, such as abrogating inflationary wage contracts, should visibly be kept in reserve.

As far as nonlabor monopolies, oligopolies, and price rigidities are concerned, free international trade is the most potent and administratively easiest measure for restoring and maintaining competition. Deregulating industry and eliminating farm price supports and output restrictions would help to restore flexibility, to stimulate output, and to smooth the transition to a noninflationary growth path.

Two other reasons for chronic inflation and near-zero productivity growth that are often mentioned are the enormous rise of crude oil prices by OPEC and a dearth of entrepreneurial talents combined with a slowdown of technological progress. On closer analysis these explanations of intractable inflation are found invalid.

International complications are next considered. For the United States the proper policy is to concentrate on domestic stability and growth. If inflation is curbed, the dollar will strengthen all by itself, and the foreign exchange market can be left to manage itself. A unilateral return to a Bretton Woods–type regime of "fixed but adjustable" exchange rates, let alone the gold standard, is out of the question. Such a reform would require consensus among the leading industrial countries that does not exist.

Our dictator would cooperate with the International Monetary Fund to see that other countries keep their currencies freely convertible in the foreign exchange markets either at fixed rates (if they prefer to peg their currency to that of a major country) or at floating rates. The many countries that peg their currencies will have to keep their inflation rates approximately to the level prevailing in the country to whose currency they peg. The numerous highly inflationary countries, mostly in the third world, have no choice but to let their currencies float in one form or another.

The problems of the industrial countries other than the United States are more complicated. As an example, recent dramatic changes in Germany's international exchange position are discussed in some detail. After thirty years of almost uninterrupted current account surpluses, large current account deficits developed in the last three years, and the deutsche mark weakened in the foreign exchange market. This development, combined with rising unemployment and, by German standards, excessive inflation—about 5.5 percent currently— has been very unsettling. It has given rise to an interesting policy debate swirling around the orthodox reaction of the central bank, the Bundesbank. The policy of the bank has been criticized by the left and the right as being too restrictive.

In conclusion, it is pointed out that concern, in the present paper as well as in other contributions to this volume, with inflation as the most serious economic problem confronting the United States and other industrial countries is not meant to deny that the real economy, output and employment, are intrinsically more important than price stability. But we have learned that satisfactory, steady real growth and full employment cannot be achieved in an inflationary environment. There is a widespread view that the "North-South" confrontation is a more serious problem than inflation and slow productivity growth. This view, which has been dramatized by the Brandt commission report on international development issues, is briefly analyzed and rejected.

217

Introduction

In my contribution to the 1979 edition of *Contemporary Economic Problems*, I analyzed the economic malaise that in the 1970s had gripped the United States and other Western industrial countries after a long period of rapid growth, optimism, and euphoria in the 1950s and early 1960s. The malaise continued and became more intense in 1980. All recent reports on the state of the world economy and the prospects for the coming year from national and international agencies—the International Monetary Fund, the Organization for Economic Cooperation and Development, the European Community, the Bank for International Settlements, the Kiel Institute, and so forth—are tinged with pessimism and gloom, predicting more inflation, near-zero productivity growth, stagnating or declining GNP, and high unemployment.[1] The Reagan administration has been warned of the danger of an "economic Dunkirk," requiring the declaration of an economic emergency. Even some of those who, rightly in my opinion, reject the idea of declaring an economic emergency call the present outlook frightening.

In my 1979 article I traced the malaise to two related developments, first, a seemingly intractable chronic inflation in its modern vicious form of stagflation and, second, near-zero productivity growth and GNP stagnation. I argued that these twin afflictions are not due to a basic flaw of the free-market, free-enterprise capitalist system; on the contrary, they are the result of the fact that the Western industrial economies have moved too far away from the competitive ideal.

In the present article I discuss how a benevolent and enlightened dictator would deal with the problem. This approach permits me to concentrate on the economics of the problem and to bypass the admittedly important question of the political feasibility of such a program in a democracy.

A benevolent dictator is one who respects consumer sovereignty, who does not, as actual dictators usually do, impose on the people his own views of what is good for them. An enlightened dictator is one who realizes that to get the best results, to achieve rapid growth, full employment, and price stability, he has to rely on free, competitive markets—that is, real competition with private property of the means of production and respect for adequate profit margins. In other words, an enlightened dictator does not try to substitute

[1] A lame-duck economic report is an exception. An outgoing administration likes to depart on an at least moderately cheerful outlook, leaving the blame for future troubles and disappointments squarely on the shoulders of its successor. Of course, the incoming party has the opposite bias.

central planning for free markets and recognizes the theories of democratic, competitive socialism à la Oscar Lange and H. D. Dickinson [2] as what they are—unrealistic utopias.

How Much Power to the Dictator?

The power of the enlightened dictator must be circumscribed in a reasonable way. Simply to endow him with omniscience and omnipotence would beg too many questions and would stamp the approach as a utopian exercise.

It is not unreasonable, however, to assume that the dictator would be in full control of monetary and fiscal policies. That would make it possible for him to solve the credibility problem. It would exclude political interference by a recalcitrant parliament swayed by pressures from special interest groups. Thus, the public could be persuaded that the announced policies will be carried out consistently.

Monetary Restraint. The central bank would be instructed to reduce monetary growth to approximately the potential or normal rate of growth of real GNP.[3] That leaves open technical questions such as the choice of the monetary aggregates, the speed of the reduction of monetary growth, and occasional minor deviations from the norm. These decisions can be left to the monetary experts, who would be freed from political interference and the pressures of special interest groups.

The Need for Fiscal Restraint. The enlightened dictator would realize, however, that for optimum results monetary policy needs to be

[2] H. D. Dickinson, *The Economics of Socialism* (London: Oxford University Press, 1937), and Oscar Lange, "On the Economic Theory of Socialism," in B. E. Lippincott, ed., *On the Economic Theory of Socialism* (Minneapolis: University of Minnesota Press, 1938).

[3] A few words should perhaps be said about the meaning of "potential" GNP growth. This concept refers to long-run growth, abstracting from cyclical fluctuations. "Potential" growth should not be interpreted as growth under ideal conditions such as perfect competition, absence of institutional rigidities, and optimal government policies. Normal long-run growth would perhaps be a better description. On the difficulties of estimating potential output, see William Fellner, "Structural Problems behind Our Measured Unemployment Rates," *Contemporary Economic Problems 1978*, pp. 84–93. Successive reports of the Council of Economic Advisers, under both Democratic and Republican administrations, have estimated potential GNP growth to be between 3 and 4 percent per year. Whatever the defects of these estimates, monetary growth of 3 to 4 percent surely would not have been inflationary.

supported by fiscal policy. Inflation can be brought down by different monetary-fiscal policy mixes: tight money (high interest rates)—easy budget (large budget deficits), or easy money (low interest rates)—tight budget (low deficits or budget surpluses). Consider the first alternative. It is true that sufficiently tight money could do the job of bringing down inflation irrespective of the size of the budget deficit. Still, side effects on productivity and investment of tight money and an easy budget (large deficits) would be serious. This policy mix would drive up interest rates and would crowd out productive private investment, thus slowing down the growth of productivity and GNP.[4] This in turn would make the fight against inflation more difficult, for in a stagnating economy it is much harder than in a growing one to accommodate rising claims on the national product and to shift resources from obsolescent, declining industries to those showing new growth.

It follows that the other alternative, easy money—tight budget, is much to be preferred; large budget deficits must be scaled down. It could even be argued that in order to stimulate investment and productivity growth, the most effective policy would be to aim at a budget surplus, channeling the surplus funds through the capital market into productive private investments. This policy option,

---

[4] Two possible objections should be considered. First, the question may be asked whether the crowding out of private investment by large government deficits can be prevented by easy money; in other words, whether "easy money and easy budget" would be a viable option. The answer is that from a narrow static viewpoint the impact of a given government deficit on private investment can always be offset by sufficiently easy credit to private industry. But this policy is, in general, incompatible with a stable price level; in other words, it is possible only at the cost of rising inflation. I say "in general" to allow for the exception of a Keynesian situation of high unemployment. In that case public deficit spending need not crowd out private investment. This was the case in the 1930s, when Keynesian theory was born. In the 1980s, however, we do not live in a Keynesian world. True, we have over 7 percent unemployment, but there is general agreement that the "natural" (incompressible) unemployment rate is higher than it used to be, perhaps as high as 5 or 6 percent. And equally important, inflationary expectations have become very sensitive, so that an expansionary policy quickly translates into higher prices; in other words, the Phillips curve has become almost vertical, even in the short run.

The second objection is that the larger deficit caused by the tax cut need not drive up interest rates and crowd out private investment because the taxpayers will be induced to save all or almost all of the additional disposal income resulting from the tax cut. This is, however, unlikely to happen on a sufficient scale, especially since the tax reduction is intended by the policy makers to be permanent and is so regarded by the taxpayers. A temporary tax reduction would be much more likely to elicit substantial savings than a permanent one because taxpayers would not want to raise the level of consumption if they knew that the higher level of consumption could not be maintained.

however, has gone out of fashion.[5] Today a balanced budget is regarded as the maximum achievable.

The importance of a tight fiscal policy as a supplement to anti-inflationary monetary policy goes far beyond balancing the budget. The size of the budget and the tax structure are equally important for productivity growth and thus indirectly for the fight against inflation. Therefore our enlightened dictator would do his best to reduce government expenditures, expenditures on goods and services as well as transfer payments, in order to free resources for productive investment in the private sector and to lighten the tax burden. The magnitude of the tax burden and the tax structure have become a major impediment for the attainment of maximum growth. The tax structure has been greatly distorted by inflation. Inflation has pushed taxpayers into higher and higher tax brackets and has led to the taxation of inflationary phantom profits and of negative interests— thus discouraging saving and investment. A radical reform of the tax system to eliminate the existing distortions would be a high-priority task. Reducing the progressivity of the income tax, indexation of the income tax, and realistic depreciation allowances would go a long way to reforming the tax structure.

The beneficial effects of such reform measures on the flow of savings and investment, on productivity and GNP growth, would be substantial and thus could be expected eventually to result in an increase in tax revenues. Still, our enlightened dictator would realize that these beneficial effects are likely to emerge only slowly. He therefore would carefully watch the impact on the budget. In the short and medium run, tax revenues will decline, and the budget deficit will increase. Therefore, to avoid inflationary effects, tax reductions and tax reform should go hand in hand with expenditure cuts.

In other words, our dictator would practice supply-side economics in the broad sense of adopting measures, in the tax field and other

[5] This policy raises, moreover, several difficult problems of which only two can be briefly mentioned. First, the policy obviously requires that the surplus be achieved without reducing the flow of private savings and investment and without impairing essential productive public services. Second, the question may be asked whether in a free market economy the determination of the volume of savings and investment should not be left to market forces, that is to say, to the collective decisions of households and firms to save and invest. This raises the deeper question: Is a growth policy justifiable that goes beyond removing impediments to growth created by public policies and tries to raise the rate of growth to a higher level than that implied by the collective savings and investment decisions of the market participants? In other words, is a policy of compulsory saving defensible in a free enterprise, capitalist economy? I have tried to give an answer in my book *Economic Growth and Stability: An Analysis of Economic Change and Policies* (Los Angeles: Nash, 1974), pp. 26-29.

areas, that stimulate productivity growth and increase supply. In particular, he would remove existing obstacles to innovative investment, such as overregulation of industry and taxation of inflationary phantom profits and of negative interest rates. This approach does not imply acceptance—on the contrary, it means rejection—of supply-side economics in the narrow (extreme) sense that has become popular in recent years, namely, in the sense that reduction of tax rates will almost instantaneously induce a greater work effort and stimulate savings and investment to such an extent that tax revenues will not decline and the budget deficit will not increase.

Monetarists, who rightly stress the monetary nature of inflation and the primary responsibility of monetary policy for winding down inflation, usually add that it is imperative that tight money be supplemented by a tight fiscal policy. They concede that in order to avoid side effects of monetary restraint on output, employment, and investment, and to improve the growth performance of the economy, budget deficits must be scaled down, the size of the government reduced, and the tax structure reformed.

The Role of Wage and Price Rigidity. This qualification of pure monetarism has very important implications. It raises the question: Are there no factors other than a soft fiscal policy that also aggravate the side effects of an anti-inflationary tight money policy on output, employment, and productivity? The answer is: There are indeed such factors, and in a sense that will become clear presently, they are even more basic and important than the budgetary and fiscal-policy problem. Our enlightened dictator would understand that the fight against inflation would not be so difficult, in fact, that stagflation on the present scale would be impossible, if our economy had not moved so far away from the competitive ideal. He would realize that changing that trend, making the economy more competitive and flexible, is of great importance for curbing inflation and promoting growth.

Let us compare the solution of the problem of unemployment in an ideally, or even a moderately, competitive economy with the actual situation. If monetary-fiscal restraints initially cause unemployment, in a fully competitive economy money wages and labor cost would decline, so that the level of employment could be quickly restored. In a moderately competitive economy, money wages would at least stop rising and would gradually decline so that wage costs could decrease. Actually, money wages have become almost totally rigid downward, both in the aggregate and in particular industries. Striking examples are provided by the U.S. automobile and steel industries. These industries pay the highest union wages in the economy, although they are in deep trouble and suffer from high unemployment and slack. Wages in these industries are more than 50 percent higher than the average wage in manufacturing industries. This would be impossible in a competitive economy. Furthermore, real wages, too, have become increasingly rigid downward through formal and de facto indexation, and unions often push up real wages in the face of substantial unemployment. Labor unions are, of course, not the only culprits. Other pressure groups often force the government, through political action, to do for their members what unions do for workers. Organized agriculture is the most conspicuous and important example.

Monetarists in general have neglected, ignored, downplayed, or even denied the importance of this development for the fight against inflation. Still, there are exceptions. For example, the great monetarist Harry G. Johnson in one of his last papers wrote:

> Over the period since World War II governments have been assuming wider and wider responsibilities. In particular, their commitment to full employment has been carried to absurd lengths, well beyond the limits of feasibility. In some countries, there now appears to be a commitment not only for every man to be employed, but for him to be employed in the occupation of his choice, in the location of his choice and, it would sometimes seem, at the income of his choice.

In a footnote to the second sentence of this passage, Johnson added: "This has been a significant factor in the inflationary tendencies that have developed in a number of industrialized countries—especially in the United Kingdom."[6]

The older generation of Chicago economists, Frank H. Knight, Henry Simons, Jacob Viner, and others, unlike most modern monetarists did not ignore or minimize the great importance of the growing rigidity of wages and prices for the smooth working of the monetary system. Frank H. Knight wrote: "In a free market these differential changes [between prices of "consumption goods" and "capital goods" on the one hand and the prices of "productive services, especially wages," on the other hand] would be temporary, but even then might be serious, and with important markets [especially the labor market] as unfree as they actually are, the results take on

---

[6] Geoffrey Denton, Seamus O'Cleireacain, and Sally Ash, *Trade Effects of Public Subsidies to Private Enterprise* (London: Holmes and Meier, 1975), pp. xiii, xxxiii.

the proportion of a disaster." [7] Knight wrote with the *deflation* of the 1930s in mind, but what he says about wage and price rigidity applies equally to the case of disinflation, and the rigidification of wages and certain prices has made much progress since Knight wrote.

A good example of the neglect of the problem of institutional rigidities by most monetarists and rational expectations theorists is provided in an article by Karl Brunner, Alex Cuikerman, and Allan H. Meltzer.[8] The gist of the article can be given and evaluated without wading through the flood of mathematical formulas with which the argument is presented. According to the authors, "persistent unemployment" and stagflation "can occur in a neo-classical framework . . . in which all expectations are rational and all markets clear instantaneously." [9] In other words, perfect competition is compatible with persistent unemployment and stagflation.

For the problem at hand, the relevant part of the authors' theory is the supply function of labor. It goes like this: To determine the amount of labor that workers are willing to supply, they "compare the currently prevailing wage to the wage they currently perceive as permanent." If the prevailing wage is equal to the perceived permanent wage, there is full employment. Now suppose the economy is subjected to a "shock"—the authors usually speak of "a change in productivity." If productivity goes up, the actual real wage is raised "on impact." Still, the workers cannot know immediately whether the change is permanent or transient. Therefore, "the currently perceived permanent wage" will for some time be below the actually ruling wage. This will induce workers to supply more labor, which means "to work now and substitute future for current leisure," resulting in "negative unemployment." [10] In other words, there will be what is usually called "overfull employment."

If the shock is unfavorable, if productivity declines, the actual real wage will be reduced "on impact." Again, however, the workers cannot be sure what the permanent wage will be. Therefore, the actual wage will for some time be below the currently perceived permanent wage. This will induce "part of the labor force which looks for work [to] abstain from accepting current employment. This

---

[7] Frank H. Knight, "The Business Cycle, Interest and Money," in Frank H. Knight, *On the History and Methods of Economics* (Chicago: University of Chicago Press, 1956), p. 224. See also p. 211: "Wages are notoriously sticky, especially with respect to any downward change of the hourly wage rates."

[8] "Stagflation, Persistent Unemployment and the Permanence of Economic Shocks," *Journal of Monetary Economics*, vol. 6, no. 4 (October 1980), pp. 467-92.

[9] Ibid., pp. 483, 490.

[10] Ibid., p. 470.

group is counted as unemployed in the official statistics." [11] If "negative unemployment" means "substitution of future leisure for current leisure," then positive unemployment means substitution of current leisure for future leisure.

To describe unemployment as leisure is rather odd. At any rate, it is voluntary unemployment: If workers "substitute current leisure for future leisure" or vice versa, the leisure that they freely choose because they expect the future wage rate to be different from the current one represents *voluntary* unemployment and has nothing to do with real, *involuntary* unemployment.[12] But the authors do not mention the indispensable distinction between voluntary and involuntary unemployment.

The essential distinction between voluntary and involuntary unemployment has been made popular by Keynes's *The General Theory*. Keynes criticized the "classical school" for recognizing only voluntary unemployment. As far as his contemporary classical economists were concerned, Keynes's criticism was clearly unjustified. For example, A. C. Pigou makes the distinction between voluntary and involuntary unemployment,[13] although using different words. Still, Keynes's criticism was prophetically right as far as many modern monetarists are concerned.

That Brunner, Cuikerman, and Meltzer are a little uneasy about their definition of unemployment is suggested by the fact that al-

[11] Ibid.

[12] The authors seem to assume that there is a basic symmetry between negative and positive unemployment in the sense that deviations of actual employment from the full employment level, what they call the "zero unemployment" level, are of the same order of magnitude on both sides of full employment. This surely is unrealistic, although it is consistent with the authors' neglect of institutional rigidities. In the real world there is a strong asymmetry between deviations on the up side and the down side of full employment, due to the fact that wages (and to a lesser extent, prices) are rigid downward but more or less flexible upward. With labor unions and other pressure groups as strong as they are now, this asymmetry is pronounced. Still, it existed even in earlier periods when labor unions were weak. (See below.)

[13] See Pigou's excellent discussion of the problem in his monograph *The Theory of Unemployment* (London: Macmillan & Co., 1933), chapter 1, "Definition of Unemployment." Actually, Keynes's definition of involuntary unemployment is unnecessarily complicated. The entirely satisfactory common-sense definition is: A worker is involuntarily unemployed if he cannot find a job, although he is willing and able to work at the ruling wage for the type of work for which he is qualified. A man is voluntarily unemployed if he does not work because he finds the ruling wage too low and prefers leisure. For the actual application of these concepts, further specifications are required, and the borderline between voluntary and involuntary unemployment is not always clearly marked. On this point, see the careful analysis by Herbert Giersch, *Konjunktur- und Wachstumspolitik in der offenen Wirtschaft* (Wiesbaden: Dr. Th. Gabler-Verlag, 1977), pp. 254-57.

though they speak repeatedly of *persistent* unemployment, in a footnote they suddenly say: "Since the focus of the paper is on cyclical unemployment, we do not discuss types of unemployment that arise for other reasons." [14] It seems that despite the talk about *persistent* unemployment, the authors had all along the comparatively mild and short-lived postwar recessions in mind. It is true that in these recessions, due to generous unemployment benefits and welfare payments, the official unemployment figures contain a significant amount of spurious, that is, voluntary, unemployment. It is also well known that generous unemployment benefits have increased frictional unemployment (which occurs when workers who have lost their jobs take more time to look for suitable new jobs) and have reduced the hardship of unemployment. Still, it is surely an exaggeration to say, as the authors seem to imply, that all or the great bulk of registered unemployment is of the voluntary kind and that unemployment no longer involves any hardship.

In defense of the proposition that unemployment can occur even in the absence of strong unions, it can be argued (and has been argued, though not in the article under discussion) that unorganized workers often behave as if they were organized. Thus, in the depression in the nineteenth century, or in the 1930s, when unions were nonexistent or weak, workers resisted wage cuts. Declining demand for labor in a depression is a strong inducement for workers to organize themselves in order to strengthen their bargaining power. For this and other reasons, employers, on their part, are reluctant to push hard for wage cuts. The reason for the stickiness of wages even in the absence of powerful labor unions—why there is rarely "thoroughgoing competition" among workers—was thoroughly analyzed by A. C. Pigou in *The Theory of Unemployment*, a pre-Keynesian work, and repeated in the post-Keynesian *Lapses from Full Employment*. Pigou, of course, attributed much importance to the activities of labor unions and to government policies, especially generous unemployment benefits. In the preface to *Lapses* he says, "Professor Dennis Robertson has warned me that the form of the book may suggest that I am in favor of attacking the problem of [mass] unemployment by manipulating wages rather than by manipulating

---

[14] "Stagflation, Persistent Unemployment," footnote 12, p. 470. What the other types of unemployment are is not explained. Could it be that the other types of unemployment are nothing else but real, involuntary unemployment? In this connection it would be interesting to know whether the authors regard the mass unemployment of the depression of the 1930s as cyclical. Can that unemployment be described as a "substitution of present for future leisure?"

demand. I wish therefore to say clearly that this is not the case."[15]

In recent years the problem of wage rigidities, the seeming collusion of employers and workers, has been thoroughly examined by Arthur Okun. He speaks felicitously of the "invisible handshake" and the "implicit contract" between management and labor, both being fully aware that they have a valuable investment in their amicable relationship.[16]

In short, wages were not entirely flexible downward even before unions became as powerful as they are now. This is what Knight had in mind when he wrote that even when the economy was more free than at the time of his writing, monetary deflation was a serious matter.[17]

There surely is truth in all this, but the point must not be pushed too far; we must keep a sense of proportion. After all, in the great depression of the 1930s and the depression of the nineteenth century, money wages did decline sharply despite the workers' resistance. This situation has changed completely. Today's almost total downward rigidity of money wages, both in the aggregate and in particular industries, combined with real wage push, often in the face of heavy unemployment, would be inconceivable without the existence of strong unions, fostered and abetted by government policies.[18] The power and aggressiveness of other pressure groups, too, has increased sharply. This accounts for stagflation on the present scale. To ignore these institutional changes and rigidities is like playing Hamlet without the Prince of Denmark.

How to Make the Economy More Competitive. Since government policies are to a large extent responsible for the power of the various pressure groups to push up wages and prices, our enlightened dictator should be able to reduce the pressure on wages and prices considerably without taking such drastic steps as prohibiting collective, industrywide bargaining, outlawing indexation of wages, abrogating existing union wage contracts, and the like. Merely withdrawing privileges, protective measures, and subsidies that are now lavishly accorded to numerous pressure groups would go a long way to pro-

---

[15] A.C. Pigou, *Lapses from Full Employment* (London: Macmillan & Co., 1944), p. v.

[16] See especially Arthur Okun's posthumously published book *Prices and Quantities: A Macroeconomic Analysis* (Washington, D.C.: Brookings Institution, 1981).

[17] Knight, *On the History and Methods of Economics.*

[18] For statistical evidence of the changes that have taken place, see Jeffrey Sachs, *The Changing Cyclical Behavior of Wages and Prices, 1890-1976*, National Bureau of Economic Research, Working Paper 304 (Cambridge, Mass., 1978).

mote price stability and to reduce the transitional unemployment resulting from monetary-fiscal restraint, thus taking some of the burden of fighting inflation off the shoulders of the monetary authorities. But keeping visibly in reserve to be used if necessary some of the drastic measures, such as the possibility of abrogating or modifying inflationary wage contracts that run for several years, would have a restraining effect on wage contracts and thus would help to smooth the transition to a noninflationary growth path.

As far as industrial monopolies and oligopolies are concerned, freer trade is the most powerful and administratively the easiest method of restoring and strengthening competition. Given the enormous growth of world trade in manufactured goods during the postwar period and the fact that numerous new industrial centers have sprung up in developed and less developed countries, few significant monopolies or oligopolies could survive under free trade (outside the public utility area, where prices are controlled anyway). In addition to ensuring competition, freer trade would also increase GNP through more extended international division of labor. The increased flow of goods would have an anti-inflationary effect. Since high tariffs, import quotas, and other nontariff barriers to trade are still widespread, despite the liberalization of international trade that has taken place under the aegis of the General Agreement on Tariffs and Trade (GATT), there is here a rich field for our enlightened dictator to exploit in moving the economy closer to the competitive ideal. The concept of nontariff barriers should be interpreted broadly to include "voluntary" restrictions imposed on foreign exporters (often called "orderly market agreements," or OMAs) and subsidies to noncompetitive firms and industries, including subsidies in the form of taking over noncompetitive firms and operating them with great losses at the expense of the taxpayer.

Curbing the power of labor unions is the most difficult part of a policy of liberalization of the economy. Still, opening up the economy to foreign competition would go a long way to reducing the power of unions. Unions know, or find out quickly, that striking against world markets is risky. This is the reason why in small countries, where international trade is a large fraction of the economy, labor unions are usually much more moderate than in large countries.

Specific measures to reduce the power of unions to push up wages are abolition of the Davis-Bacon Act, which forces the government to buy exclusively from industries paying the highest union wages; elimination of minimum-wage laws; [19] prohibition of closed-

[19] Minimum wages are largely responsible for the shockingly high unemployment among teenagers, especially black ones, and other underprivileged un-

shop agreements; restriction of the right to picket; and withdrawal of unemployment benefits from striking workers. Deregulation of industries will obviously rank high on the list of urgent tasks. The regulatory explosion of the last ten years or so should be stopped and rolled back as far as possible.

Doing all these things would reduce monopolistic wage and price pressures, promote labor mobility, enlarge international division of labor, stimulate growth, and reduce government expenditures by eliminating the vast bureaucracies that are now needed to administer the existing restrictions, privileges, subsidies, and controls.

The question arises—is that all there is to it? Or are there other causes of inflation that have not been mentioned so far? Does our dictator not need additional power to deal with those factors?

The Oil Price Rise. What comes to mind first is the Organization of Petroleum Exporting Countries (OPEC) and the recent and prospective rises in the oil price. In the United States, and lately also in Germany, the second oil shock of 1979–1980 is frequently mentioned as the major, if not decisive, cause of inflation and stagnation.

That the rise in the oil price as such was not decisive is demonstrated by the fact that some countries that depend much more on imported oil than the United States—for example, Germany, Switzerland, and Japan—have managed to reduce the rate of inflation far below the American level despite the increase in the oil price. Furthermore, there are other energy-rich and oil-exporting countries that had even more inflation than the United States, for example, Canada and Venezuela.

According to OECD, "The quadrupling in 1973, and the more than doubling of the oil price between the end of 1978 and early 1980 represented a shock on the OECD economies equivalent to roughly 2 percent of GNP on each occasion." [20] After the first oil shock in 1973, the burden was lightened by inflation, because the dollar price of oil was kept stable for several years; this is not likely to happen after the second oil shock.[21]

---

skilled workers. The victims of this antisocial legislation are thus deprived of the on-the-job training that is essential for their future careers. See Masanori Hashimoto, *Minimum Wages and On-the-Job Training* (Washington, D.C.: American Enterprise Institute, 1981).

[20] OECD, *Economic Outlook*, July 1980, p. 114. For the United States it is less than 2 percent.

[21] I ignore another factor that postponed and potentially lightened the burden for some countries (for example, the United States), namely the fact that they received a large share of the petrodollars, in other words, that they could run a balance-of-payments deficit corresponding to the OPEC surplus.

A 2 percent reduction in real GNP is a shock, but it is not a crushing burden. In an ideal, fully competitive economy, if the monetary authorities keep the price level stable, prices of commodities other than oil and oil-related commodities would decline slightly, and there would be a once-for-all roughly 2 percent decline of money wages (or, more generally, money incomes). In a growing economy a short pause in the growth would take care of the problem. In a perfectly competitive economy, there would be no unemployment, or if we relax the assumption and assume some stickiness of wages, there would be some transitional unemployment.

Now suppose money wages are rigid downward, whereas real wages are not (the Keynesian assumption). In this case, to maintain full employment, a small once-for-all increase in the price level, a slight extra spurt of inflation, would be necessary to accomplish the unavoidable once-for-all reduction in real wages. At the other extreme, if *real* wages too are rigid downward through indexation, the only remedy, that is to say, the only way to maintain equilibrium in the balance of payments, would be unemployment and slack, which would reduce the demand for oil. In the real world the outcome will probably be somewhere in the middle, some unemployment, merely transitional it is to be hoped, and some inflation.

This analysis, rough and simple though it is, permits us to draw an important conclusion: If, and to the extent to which, our enlightened dictator is able to bring the economy close to the competitive ideal, he will also solve ipso facto the problem of the oil shock. No additional powers are needed.

Secular Stagnation? Another factor that is often mentioned as a cause of low productivity growth and indirectly of inflation is reminiscent of the theory of secular stagnation that flourished in the 1930s. Today, no one would argue, as the proponents of secular stagnation did, that we are suffering from oversaving, that is, an excess of saving over investment with deflationary consequences. Still, it is said, as in the 1930s, that investment has declined partly because of a lack of entrepreneurship, the absence of a technological breakthrough, or the slowing down of technological progress. Symptoms or aspects of this development are a declining trend in expenditures on research and development and an increasing share of lawyers and accountants among corporate executives, reflecting a decreasing share of businessmen.

The enlightened dictator would strongly doubt that there is a lack of entrepreneurial talents [22] and a decrease in the flow of usable

[22] A striking example of lively entrepreneurial activity is the economic rejuvena-

inventions, as distinguished from actual innovations.[23] But, he would recognize that innovative investments by Schumpeterian entrepreneurs have been seriously impeded and reduced by the growing web of government controls and regulations, the low level of profits due to chronic inflation and stifling taxation, and the growth of government expenditures. This is the reason for the decline of expenditures on research and development and the tendency of lawyers and accountants to replace businessmen as directors of corporations.[24] These same factors are responsible for stagflation and low productivity. Therefore, our dictator would redouble his efforts to reduce the size of the public sector, cut government expenditures, reform the tax structure, deregulate industry, and so forth and thus would make the economy more competitive and flexible.

The enlightened dictator would understand that the creative job of introducing innovations, of "revitalizing industry," as the modern phrase goes, is best done by private entrepreneurs, large and small. Our dictator would resist the temptation of trying to speed up growth by government interventions, government commissions, or bureaucrats trying to identify growth industries as candidates for special subsidies, tax rebates, and other privileges. Such attempts almost always lead to the creation of white elephants and waste of resources. The dictator would also understand that the widespread practice of propping up uncompetitive, obsolescent firms and industries by sub-

---

tion of New England. In the last two decades or so the economy of the region has undergone a basic transformation. It has emancipated itself from the traditional, obsolescent textile and shoe industries. Their place has been taken by high-technology industries—micro–ball bearings, computer hardware and the like. These industries are composed of numerous small and medium-sized firms. See John R. Meyer and Robert A. Leone, "The New England States and Their Economic Future: Some Implications of a Changing Industrial Environment," *Papers and Proceedings of the American Economic Association,* 68 (May 1978), pp. 110-15, and Lynn E. Browne and John S. Hekman, "New England's Economy in the 1980s," *New England Economic Review* (Federal Reserve Bank of Boston), January/February 1981.

[23] It will be recalled that since Schumpeter, economists distinguish between inventions, that is, discoveries of new or improved products or methods of production in the scientist's study or laboratories on the one hand, and the actual production of new products or use of new methods of production or marketing by innovating, risk-taking entrepreneurs on the other hand. (J. A. Schumpeter, *The Theory of Economic Development,* trans. Redvers Opie [Cambridge, Mass.: Harvard University Press, 1934]; first German edition, 1912).

[24] Since business management has to spend more and more time and effort to cope with the rising flood of government regulations and to find ways to reduce the tax burden, it is quite natural for lawyers and accountants to play an increasing role in corporate board rooms. These basically unproductive activities drain scarce human resources away from the creative and productive entrepreneurial activities.

sidies and import restrictions is the very opposite of a rational growth policy.

The proper method to stimulate saving, investment, and growth is to provide a favorable climate for saving and investment through cutting government expenditures, lowering taxes, curbing inflation, and dismantling controls and regulations.

Problems of an Open Economy

So far I have assumed essentially a closed economy. In an open economy with substantial foreign trade and capital flows across the border, there arise additional complications the importance of which varies from country to country, depending on the size and structure of the economy.

The Case of the United States. In a large country where the foreign trade sector is relatively small, the additional complications are minor. Thus, in the United States, if our enlightened dictator is successful in subduing inflation, there would be no reason to worry about the foreign exchange value of the dollar and the balance of payments. The dollar, as the world's foremost international reserve currency, weakened by the long period of high inflation, would be restored to its former strong role. A larger inflow of foreign official funds could be expected. The U.S. share in "petrodollars" from OPEC countries would increase. The United States may have to accept a larger current account deficit corresponding to the OPEC surplus, but that should be regarded as a blessing rather than a burden.

Of course, there could be changes in that picture. The OPEC countries may again turn out to be better spenders than was expected. That is to say, their surplus may shrink, and the flow of petrodollars may contract, and other countries may draw down their dollar reserves. Still, given the huge size of the U.S. capital market, such changes would hardly cause more than a ripple. No massive switches from the dollar to other currencies are likely, so long as reasonable price stability is maintained.

Our dictator would continue the present system of floating exchange rates. The United States could not, even if it wanted, unilaterally return to the Bretton Woods system of "stable but adjustable" exchange rates, let alone to fixed rates under the gold standard. This would constitute a major reform of the international monetary system. It would require agreement among the leading industrial countries and would take years to negotiate even if there existed a basic consensus that a move in that direction was desirable—a consensus that surely does not exist at the present time. If miraculously an international agreement on the restoration of a system of fixed exchange rates could be reached, the successful operation of such a regime would require continuous extremely close coordination of macroeconomic policies. Postwar experience has shown that in the present-day world this is impossible among sovereign states. The closely linked members of the European Community (EC) have not been able to reach the required degree of policy coordination. Nor has the problem been solved by the members of the European Monetary System (EMS), an even more tightly knit subgroup of the EC.[25]

Our enlightened dictator would conclude that the best strategy is to concentrate on domestic policy objectives—price stability, growth, employment—and leave the foreign exchange market to manage itself. He would cooperate with the International Monetary Fund, helping the Fund to discharge its statutory duty of "exercising firm surveillance over the exchange rate policies of members,"[26] to make sure that countries keep their currencies freely convertible in the foreign exchange market either at fixed rates (if they wish to peg their currencies to some major currency or to a basket of currencies) or at a floating rate and refrain from imposing exchange control and from "manipulating exchange rates . . . in order to prevent effective balance of payments adjustment or to gain an unfair competitive advantage over other members."[27]

The Case of Smaller Countries. I will now discuss very briefly some of the complications arising for some other countries or groups of countries from the openness of their economy.

There are, first, many, mostly medium-sized or small, countries that peg their currencies to the dollar or to some other major currency or basket of currencies. To stay out of balance-of-payments troubles, these countries have to keep their inflation rate approximately at the level prevailing in the country or countries to whose currency their own is pegged. I say "approximately" because comparative inflation rates, like purchasing-power parity, are but a very

[25] It has often been demonstrated that a system of "stable but adjustable" exchange rates à la Bretton Woods is in the long run unworkable because it opens the floodgate to destabilizing speculation. See, for example, Gottfried Haberler, "The International Monetary System after Jamaica and Manila," in *Contemporary Economic Problems 1977*, William Fellner, ed. (Washington, D.C.: American Enterprise Institute, 1977), pp. 244-45.

[26] *Articles of Agreement*, article IV, section 3.

[27] *Articles of Agreement*, article IV, section 1.

rough criterion of equilibrium. There is, furthermore, the large group of countries, mostly developing countries, with very high inflation rates, such as Argentina, Brazil, Israel, and Turkey. These countries have no choice but to let their currencies float in one form or other, including a crawling, trotting, or galloping peg. Much more complicated is the situation in Japan and the industrial countries in Europe. Especially interesting, in fact dramatic and puzzling, are recent developments in the Federal Republic of Germany. These changes merit special attention.

The German Case. For thirty years Germany enjoyed an almost uninterrupted series of current-account surpluses that enabled it to accumulate huge official reserves of gold and foreign exchange. In 1978 the surplus was about $8.7 billion; in 1979 a deficit of $5.5 billion emerged, which swelled to $16 billion in 1980. For 1981 again a large deficit of the same order of magnitude as in 1980 is expected.

The German mark had become one of the world's hardest currencies. This, too, has changed in the last year. The value of the mark in terms of the U.S. dollar rose (with some fluctuation) from 100 at the end of 1972 to 187 in January 1980. From the end of 1979 to February 1981, however, the mark depreciated by 23 percent vis-à-vis the dollar, 33 percent vis-à-vis the yen, and 24 percent vis-à-vis the British pound. Overall, the decline of the mark was, of course, much less. The effective exchange rate declined by about 5.07 percent and the real effective exchange rate by 5.35 percent.[28]

Since March 1979 Germany has been a member of the European Monetary System along with France, Italy, Belgium, the Netherlands, Denmark, and Ireland. In the EMS exchange rates are fixed in a narrow band of permissible fluctuations. It was expected that the mark would stay at the top of the band; actually it was for most of the time near the bottom of the band [29] and had to be supported by official interventions.

In fact, the large current-account deficit of about DM 28 billion in 1980 was financed largely by drawing on the central bank's—the Bundesbank's—international reserves. The Bank's reserve, consisting of gold and foreign exchange, dropped from DM 90 billion in January 1980 to DM 79 billion in January 1981; [30] and foreign liabili-

---

[28] See *World Financial Markets* (New York: Morgan Guaranty Trust Company of New York, 1981).

[29] This has changed recently. See below.

[30] At the end of 1978 it was DM 103 billion.

ties of the Bundesbank increased from DM 4.3 billion to DM 15 billion, resulting in a decrease of about DM 22 billion in what is called the net external reserve position.

These events have been very unsettling, especially because the external weakness has been combined with adverse internal developments. Unemployment went up from 3.8 percent in 1979 to 5.8 percent in January 1981, and the inflation rate as measured by the cost-of-living index rose from 2.7 percent in 1978 to 5.5 percent in December 1980.[31] Official statements by representatives of the Bundesbank and the government have become very gloomy, and the official pessimism has been greatly amplified in the news media, including serious newspapers. Economic policy seems to be faced with a double dilemma: the internal stagflation dilemma—inflation and unemployment going up simultaneously—and the divergent requirements of external and internal equilibrium. The weakness of the mark in the foreign exchange market is supposed to require monetary-fiscal restraint, whereas the recession calls for monetary-fiscal expansion.

Before discussing the policy options and policy reaction to this state of affairs, let me point out that the explanation of the sudden appearance of the large deficits is not at all easy. The large deficits are puzzling in view of the fact that although the German rate of inflation has gone up, as we have seen, it is still very low compared with that for most other industrial countries. It is less than half the U.S. rate, a third of the French, and so on. It is about the same as the rate of inflation in Japan.

Several reasons for the large German deficits have been given. One is that the German deficit simply represents Germany's share in the oil-importing countries' global deficit, the counterpart to OPEC's surplus. The idea is that the OPEC countries elected to invest a large part of their petrodollars in marks. But, if they had done that, their action would have strengthened the mark.[32] This explanation is, therefore, inconsistent with the weakness of the mark.

Other factors mentioned are a cyclical divergence between the major countries, delayed effects of the previous appreciation of the mark, and the large government budget deficit stemming from the fact that the German government, after some resistance, in the end gave in to the urgings of the United States and other countries to act

---

[31] The figures give the change from the year before. On a seasonably adjusted monthly basis the last figure is somewhat lower.

[32] It is true, however, that the German authorities borrowed substantial sums in Saudi Arabia to bolster the mark.

as a "locomotive" for the world economy by pumping up its own economy.[33]

As far as the weakness of the mark is concerned, the large external deficit and the loss of reserve are in themselves a depressing factor. The proximate cause of the decline of the mark that is always mentioned is the interest differential between Germany and the United States and other industrial countries. For some time nominal interest rates have indeed been much lower in Germany than in the United States, Britain, and other countries. This difference reflects the inflation differential, but in 1980 the difference in nominal interest rates exceeded the currently prevailing inflation differential.[34] Also significant are the expectations for the future. Thus, the strength of the dollar is partly due to the expectation that the new administration will bring down the rate of inflation.

Another factor, often mentioned, that accounts for the weakness of the mark not only vis-à-vis the dollar but also vis-à-vis the EMS currencies is the fact that the mark has become an important international reserve currency. As a consequence, it is said, the strength of the dollar affects the mark more than other currencies, because it triggers reserve switches from the mark into the dollar. Still another reason for the strength of the dollar and the weakness of the mark is said to be the threatening Russian intervention in Poland and the proximity of Germany to the Eastern cauldron. In other words, the United States is again becoming an attractive haven for cautious investors. The attractiveness of the dollar for apprehensive investors in Europe has been greatly increased by the sharp move to the left in French presidential and parliamentary elections in May and June 1981.

None of these various factors clearly stands out as dominant. In combination, however, they may well be capable of explaining the sudden development of large current-account deficits and the weakness of the mark, although it is hard or next to impossible to determine their comparative strength.

Fortunately, it is possible, without having disentangled the impact of the various causal factors involved, to describe and evaluate the principal policy options that have emerged from recent discussions of how to deal with the existing situation.

The reaction of the Bundesbank to the external deficit and the weakness of the mark has followed traditional central bank maxims.

[33] The decision to give in to the pressure to act as a locomotive was probably made easier by the realization that pumping up the economy was bound to help the government in the upcoming election.

[34] This situation changed in February 1981. See below.

Monetary policy was tightened, and the importance of fiscal restraint and of moderation in wage negotiations have been stressed again and again in statements by directors of the Bank and in the Bank's monthly reports. The target range for monetary growth, which was 5–8 percent of central bank money from the fourth quarter of 1979 to the fourth quarter of 1980, was reduced to 4–7 percent for the following four quarters, and monetary growth was kept near the lower end of the target range until very recently.

Since the drain on the reserves continued in 1981, and the current account showed a large deficit in January 1981, on February 20, 1981, the Bundesbank took a major step to tighten credit, an action described in the press as "pulling the emergency brake." The Bank suspended, "for the time being," the so-called lombard credit facility.[35] This facility permitted the commercial banks to borrow from the Bundesbank practically "without limit" (according to Pöhl) against suitable collateral at the "lombard rate," which was usually one to two percentage points above the discount rate. The fixed lombard-rate facility was replaced by "special lombard credits," which may be made available from time to time at "special lombard rates." These special credits are for very short periods only, subject to change at short notice, practically on a day-to-day basis. On February 25, 1981, such special lombard credits were made available, and the variable special lombard rate was set at 12 percent, up from the 9 percent of the previous fixed rate. On February 27, 1981, "the granting of these special lombard credits was discontinued."[36]

These steps were designed to bring about, and have in fact resulted in, sharply rising interest rates. Thus, the German *real* short-term interest rates rose sharply, and the foreign exchange markets reacted favorably. The mark appreciated sharply against the dollar and other currencies and climbed back to the top of the EMS band of permissible fluctuations.[37]

The Bank's restrictive policy has come under criticism from both the left and the right even before the latest tightening in February

[35] For the text of the decision and the explanation given by the president of the Bundesbank, Karl Otto Pöhl, see Deutsche Bundesbank, *Auszüge aus Presseartikeln*, no. 16, February 20, 1981.

[36] See Deutsche Bundesbank, *Auszüge aus Presseartikeln*, no. 17, February 26, 1981, and no. 18, February 28, 1981.

[37] The lurch to the left in France and the economic program of the socialist government have put heavy pressure on the French franc. Through the EMS the weakness of the franc has been transmitted to the mark and other member currencies. Thus, the mark reached a new low vis-à-vis the dollar in June (after this paper was written). High U.S. interest rates have provided European politicians with a convenient opportunity to divert attention from the basic European causes of their economic troubles.

1981. Attacks by left-wing members of the ruling Social Democratic party and by the trade unions were predictable, but criticism has come also from monetarist circles, that is, from the right, if I may say so.[38]

The critics believe that the Bundesbank has overreacted to the external deficit. The "extra-tight monetary policy," as Professor Gutowski puts it, has unnecessarily exacerbated the recession. The critics on the right agree with the Bundesbank that inflation must be brought down by monetary restraint, but they think that it should be done in a more gradual fashion. Thus, the dispute is fundamentally about shock treatment versus gradualism, or more precisely about the degree of gradualness. The disputants themselves have, as far as I can see, not stressed the to my mind very important issue of shock treatment versus gradualism.[39]

Concretely, the Kiel Institute recommends the adoption by the Bundesbank of a "potential-oriented" monetary policy; that is to say, the quantity of money should increase at the potential rate of growth of real GNP. Professor Gutowski concurs: The Bundesbank should restrict "the expansion of base money supply to the rate of growth of productive capacities plus an allowance for a still unavoidable—but over time decreasing—rate of inflation."[40]

How much more liberal the critics want the Bundesbank to be is not quite clear. Still, they seem to envisage a monetary growth at least at the upper limit of the Bundesbank's target band, 7 percent of central bank money, while the Bank appears to have aimed at the lower end of the band, 4 percent.[41]

[38] See especially Enno Langfeldt and Peter Trapp, "Fehlleitung der Geldpolitik durch Leistungsbilanzdefizit und D-Mark-Schwäche," in *Die Weltwirtschaft*, vol. 2 (Kiel, 1980). The same criticism of the Bundesbank's policy has been voiced by Armin Gutowski, "The 'Dilemma' of German Monetary Policy," *Wall Street Journal*, January 28, 1981.

[39] See William Fellner's introductory essay in this volume.

[40] The same recommendation, that the Bundesbank should reduce the pressure on the monetary brake and adopt a "potential-oriented policy," has been made by the Berlin Institute. (See "Zahlungsbilanzorientierte Geldpolitik verschärft Rezession," in Deutsches Institut für Wirtschaftsforschung, *Wochenbericht 7/81*, February 12, 1981.) The Berlin Institute has been described as the "most Keynesian of the leading German economic institutes" (the *Economist*). A better description would be "the most unconcerned about inflation." Thus the institute expresses pride in having recommended an international agreement to reduce interest rates simultaneously in the major countries (ibid., p. 82)—a recommendation that amounts to a call to give up the fight against inflation. The Bundesbank rejected this advice, but it found receptive ears among German politicians. Chancellor Helmut Schmidt called U.S. interest rates intolerably high and destructive of the world economy (*Washington Post*, February 26, 1981).

[41] The Kiel Institute prefers M1 to central bank money as an indicator and recommends a much narrower band than that of the Bundesbank.

The critics realize, of course, that the adoption of a less restrictive policy would initially mean more inflation; they hopefully speak of a slower decline in the rate of inflation rather than of an increase of the rate, assuming apparently that the inflationary tide is actually receding. Yet, they are confident that the rate of inflation would continue to go down and that the economy would gradually approach a sustainable near-zero-inflation growth path.

The critics are also fully aware that the weakness of the mark in the foreign exchange markets may continue longer or even be temporarily exacerbated if monetary restraint is relaxed; in other words, that the mark may have to be further depreciated and that it might be necessary to loosen the corset of the EMS or abandon it altogether. Still, they argue that the resulting rise in import prices (they should have added "export prices") need not result in significantly higher general inflation rates, let alone in a wage-price spiral, unless accommodated by an excessively expansionary monetary policy. Furthermore, they are confident that after a while the low German inflation rate and the depreciation of the mark vis-à-vis the dollar and the yen will reduce the current-account deficit, which in turn will strengthen the mark.

All this reasoning is very well argued, but it is based on a number of optimistic assumptions and presupposes a delicate calibration of the expansionary measures. The Berlin Institute, in fact, acknowledges that "the success of the recommended strategy cannot be guaranteed, although it is the economically best founded one."[42]

It is not surprising that the Bundesbank has not changed the restrictive stance of the policy. On the contrary, as was mentioned on February 20, it has tightened credit. The bank insists, however, that it has pursued all along a "production-potential oriented policy." The targets for monetary growth have been set in such a way as to bring about a rate of monetary growth approximately equal to the potential growth of GNP.[43] The president of the Bundesbank, Karl Otto Pöhl, replying to leftist critics of the Bank's restrictive policy, stated that the aim of the policy is to achieve price stability. The legal mandate of the Bundesbank, he said, is "stability of the value of money"; in other words, price stability, and not "Konjunktursteuerung," management of the business cycle. (This policy seems to rule out fine tuning.) He argued that in the longer run, price stability is best also for real growth and employment.[44]

[42] The Berlin Institute, *Wochenbericht 7/81*, p. 82.

[43] See the monthly report of the Bundesbank, March 1981, German edition, p. 7, which also gives reference to earlier statements of the same principle.

[44] See *Auszüge aus Presseartikeln*, no. 27, March 17, 1981, p. 1. Pöhl's remark

To demonstrate that it has been practicing a potential-oriented policy, the Bank pointed to the fact that in 1980 when the large external deficit drained reserves from the banking system, the loss of central bank money was "compensated or overcompensated by credits to the commercial banks." [45]

Early in 1981 the question arose, so the report goes on, whether the policy of offsetting the external drain of liquidity could be continued, in view of the fact that the current-account deficit seemed to widen and that the weakness of the mark on the foreign exchange markets became more pronounced. Thus, as mentioned above, on February 20 the Bank stepped hard on the credit brake, short-term interests rose sharply, and the mark rose in the foreign exchange markets. Although the report does not say it in so many words, this was clearly a deviation from the strict norm of a potential-oriented monetary policy. At this writing (April 1981) the precise impact on monetary growth is not yet clear.

The Bank justifies the change in policy by saying that there was great danger of a serious loss of confidence in the mark, especially among foreign holders of marks, both private and official. A further depreciation of the mark would have had adverse effects on price stability through the rise of import prices, especially of the oil price. This argument is not accepted by the monetarist for the reason mentioned above.

Be that as it may, there is another way to justify the hard step on the credit brake that I find more persuasive, namely, that it was necessary to persuade market participants at home and abroad, including the "social partners" (employers and labor unions), that the Bundesbank was determined to bring inflation down quickly. In other words, a mild shock treatment was necessary to make the anti-inflation policy credible.

The policy of the Bundesbank appears to find considerable support from economic experts. The German Council of Economic Experts in its annual report for 1980 seems to take the same position as the Bundesbank. [46] On February 25 a large group of leading economists issued a memorandum in which they asked for a "wage pause." They painted a rather gloomy picture of the present state of the German economy and urged that the social partners, employers

---

reminds us of a blunt statement attributed to one of his predecessors, Wilhelm Vocke, the first president of the new German central bank (1948-1957) after World War II: "Employment and unemployment are none of our business. The central bank's task is to protect the stability of the mark."

[45] See the monthly report of the Bundesbank, March 1981, German edition, p. 8.
[46] *Sachverständigenrat*, annual report 1979/80.

and labor unions, agree to postpone the ongoing negotiations for new wage contracts until the autumn of next year, leaving the existing contracts in force until new agreements could be reached.[47] The group argues that a wage pause would greatly strengthen the confidence in the future of the economy, bolster the mark, and so result after a while in a decline in interest rates. If this happens, "the Bundesbank should not resist the trend." This clearly supports the refusal of the Bundesbank to reverse its policy of restraint at this time.

What would be the reaction of our dictator? Which policy option would he prefer—that of the Bundesbank or that of the Bank's monetarist critics? Looking at the German scene from the outside, he would be impressed by the high level of the debate. He would be astonished, however, by the widespread pessimism and gloom. After all, compared with other countries, for example, the United States and the United Kingdom, the German economy seems to be in fairly good shape. The inflation rate is low by international standards, though too high by German standards. The same is true of the unemployment rate. The absence of index clauses in wage contracts and the nonexistence of wage contracts that provide large inflationary wage increases for the next several years should make it easier to regain stability. True, there is the large current-account deficit. Still, the monetarists are probably right that the deficit will decline or disappear if the inflation rate stays low. The large depreciation of the mark vis-à-vis the dollar and the yen, too, will have a favorable effect. Moreover, Gutowski is right when he says that under flexible exchange rates there should be no problem of financing the deficit by capital inflows rather than by depleting the Bank's reserves. If the "external value of the currency" declines "enough, people will believe that buying the mark will be profitable"—provided, I would add, that a credible anti-inflation policy is pursued.[48]

This, of course, is the crucial question. Fortunately, on this matter there is agreement in principle, as we have seen. Both the Bundesbank and its monetarist critics want to bring inflation down by monetary restraints. There is also agreement in principle that in the medium and long run the norm for noninflationary monetary

[47] See Deutsche Bundesbank, *Auszüge aus Presseartikeln*, no. 17, February 17, 1981, p. 5. It is interesting that among the signers of the manifesto are two professors from Kiel, Herbert Giersch and Gerhard Fels. It should be mentioned that unlike most American wage contracts, German contracts do not contain index clauses and do not run for longer than one year. In fact, index clauses in wage and other contracts are forbidden by the "currency law," except if specifically authorized by the Bundesbank.

[48] Gutowski, "The 'Dilemma' of German Monetary Policy."

policy should be a steady expansion of the money stock approximately in proportion to the potential rate of growth of real GNP. That leaves open such technical questions as the choice of the monetary aggregate (for example, central bank money versus M1) and the width of the target band. There is room for disagreement about those questions as well as about the magnitude of allowable temporary deviations from the norm. The main disagreement seems to be about the timing and speed of the disinflation. The monetarist critics think that the norm of noninflationary steady growth should be approached gradually. In Gutowski's formulation, initially the monetary growth target should be the growth of productive capacity plus an allowance for the still unavoidable inflation, but this allowance should gradually be reduced.

The Bundesbank evidently believes that the monetarist prescription is too finely spun and risky. To make the anti-inflation policy credible, to restore confidence in the stability of the mark, to douse inflationary expectations, an initial mild shock is necessary. A supporting motive for this approach is probably the wish to persuade the social partners, employers and unions, that the monetary authorities will not accommodate large wage increases, that rising unemployment will be the consequence of higher wages. This will, it is hoped, induce the social partners to reach moderate wage settlements in the impending wage contract negotiations. Indeed, according to the latest report, important wage settlements reached in the first quarter of 1981 provide for rather modest wage increases of about 5 percent.[49]

There is much to be said for the resolve of the Bundesbank to stop inflation quickly. Excessive gradualism has resulted in failure too often, each failure leaving behind a situation that requires sterner measures of restraint under less favorable circumstances. (See in this volume Phillip Cagan's chapter on the U.S. experience.) The case for a sharp step on the monetary brake, as against a more gradualist approach, is stronger in Germany than in the United States and other countries because the absence of inflationary wage contracts running for several years facilitates quick adjustment and thus reduces the cost of an abrupt stop.

Concluding Remarks

The emphasis in this chapter, as in other contributions to the present volume, has been on inflation. This is not to deny that the *real* economy—output, employment, income distribution, and so forth—

---

[49] *Economist*, London, May 18, 1981, p. 79.

is intrinsically more important than a stable price level. But, we have learned that the prospects for attainment of maximum growth, full employment, and price stability are inextricably interrelated. Whatever is true in the short run, in the long run inflation is incompatible with satisfactory growth. The longer inflation lasts, the less can be achieved even in the short run by sudden unexpected spurts of inflation. In technical terms, even in the short run the Phillips curve tends to become vertical. Moreover, as we have seen, largely the same type of policy is indicated for bringing down inflation and for promoting growth.

The statement that inflation and the associated low productivity growth is the major problem confronting the industrial countries will perhaps be questioned by the many people who have become greatly alarmed by what is now called the North-South dialogue or confrontation allegedly resulting from a growing income gap between the developed industrial countries, the "North," and the less developed countries, the "South." This problem has recently been dramatized by the report of a prestigious "independent commission on development issues" under the chairmanship of Willy Brandt, former chancellor of the Federal Republic of Germany. The title of the report is: "North-South: A Program for Survival." [50] The subtitle, "A Program for Survival," indicates the alarmist tone of the report. No one can fail to be appalled by the stark poverty in some less developed countries. Still, the Brandt commission's statement that poverty in less developed countries and the great inequality between the North and the South are responsible for wars, violence, and tensions in the world cannot be taken seriously. None of the recent wars had anything whatsoever to do with the North-South income gap—not the two world wars, nor any of the many local postwar conflicts—the wars in Korea and Vietnam, the Israel-Arab wars, the Persian Gulf war between Iran and Iraq, or the conflicts between Greece and Turkey or Ethiopia and Somalia. The *East-West* tensions and confrontations are a real global threat compared with which the *North-South* skirmishes are of minor importance. [51] The so-called South, or third world, is a very heterogeneous group. It comprises many countries (Argentina, Brazil, Taiwan, and so forth) that are well on the way to joining the industrial North. The really poor countries, sometimes called the fourth world, are but a fraction of the South.

[50] Cambridge, Mass.: MIT Press, 1980.

[51] For recent U.S. and other Western policy statements (especially but not only before the Russian invasion of Afghanistan) that take the opposite position, see the article by the great historian and Soviet expert Adam B. Ulam, "How to Restrain the Soviets," *Commentary*, vol. 70, no. 6 (December 1980), p. 99.

Here is not the place to discuss the commonly proposed policies to deal with that problem ("resource transfer" from the rich to the poor countries, foreign aid and international charity, commodity price stabilization, and so on).[52] I confine myself to saying that if the industrial countries put their economic houses in order, curb inflation, resume normal growth, and liberalize trade, they will make a great contribution to the development of the less developed countries, including the very poor, by providing markets for third world exports, thus enabling them to continue the remarkable progress that, according to World Bank statistics, the less developed countries as a group have made during the prosperous period after World War II.[53]

[52] The largely dubious policy proposals of the Brandt commission have been critically analyzed by P. T. Bauer and B. S. Yamey in "East-West/North-South: Peace and Prosperity?" *Commentary*, no. 4 (September 1970), and P. D. Henderson in "Survival, Development and the Report of the Brandt Commission," *The World Economy: A Quarterly Journal on International Economic Affairs*, vol. 3, no. 1 (June 1980). For a thorough discussion of the so-called New International Economic Order, see Ryan C. Amacher, Gottfried Haberler, and Thomas D. Willett, eds., *Challenges to a Liberal International Economic Order* (Washington, D.C.: American Enterprise Institute, 1979).

[53] On this point see Gottfried Haberler, "The Liberal International Economic Order in Historical Perspective," in *Challenges to a Liberal International Economic Order*, pp. 43-65 and 85-90.

Part Three

Demographic Problems

Some Economic Consequences of the New Patterns of Population Growth

Mark Perlman

Summary

Changes in population size and composition have obvious connections to productivity and related economic policy issues. The current low rates of birth, fertility, death, and immigration raise a number of economic problems such as the implications of the increasing size of the age group over sixty-five and the expected decreasing relative size of the labor force. In addition, questions are raised about the effects on population size of the trend toward increasing labor force participation of women and about future investment levels in education as the group under age twenty-five begins to shrink.

This essay first summarizes the opinions of demographic economists in 1960 about the likely course of development of the American economy and then, in the second section, reviews the factual picture of the demographic economic variables since 1960. By 1970, birth rates and fertility rates had both fallen, and by 1980 the rate of population growth had slowed to an average compounded rate of well under 1 percent. Meanwhile, the median age of the population rose from 27.9 years in 1970 to 30.2 years in 1980, and the "aging" of the population is expected to continue at least through 1990.

The third section of this article discusses some of the current ideas in American demographic economics. In conclusion, the discussion turns to a variety of explicit economic policy problems, including economic issues raised by pronatalist and antinatalist policies, some implications of employment and retirement policies, and possible economic effects of immigration policies.

Introduction

As a nation, we have been increasingly concerned with productivity. Linked with this concern are the emotionally charged issues of economic growth or no growth, consumption of nonrenewable resources, the possible goal of a stationary population, and the selection of priorities among nonmaterial values. The changes in population composition and changes in size and in labor force participation have obvious connections, direct and indirect, to productivity as well as to the aforementioned related issues.

Much of our population policy (as it emerges in fact) is shaped by religious and cultural mores, which, if they change, do so as a result of nongovernmental (that is, nonpolitical) decisions. In addition, there are surely a priori and empirical reasons for thinking that economic factors also influence demographic changes systematically as well as in irregular ways. Then, too, it is clear that our national demographic performance, usually perceived as a conglomerate of bits and pieces, has been affected by legislation and judicial decisions. Population policy deals with more than matters of sheer growth in the aggregate like gross size, rates of natural increase, and legal immigration. In practice, it also involves the economic effects of subsidized investment in education, provisions for retirement allowances, the survival rates and costs of care for those whose lives have been extended by Medicare and Medicaid, and the like.

To start at the beginning, total population growth itself reflects most clearly any increases associated with births and immigration and the decreases associated with deaths and emigration. But these statistical relations have a more subtle effect—immigration affects births, since the immigrants are usually of the childbearing ages. Furthermore, as already implied, if recent public policy has had a great deal to do with certain sources of added population, namely, births and immigration, it has had also a great deal to do with changes in the numbers who die, for example, the effects of Medicare and Medicaid. Changes in the compositional elements making up demographic growth are often hidden in the totals. What is strangely pertinent is not only that these compositional elements are changing in response to public policy shifts but that there is an old, as well as recent, history of laggardness in the public's perception of what is occurring. Implicitly this intellectual sluggishness is accompanied by an unwillingness to recognize the importance of the spectrum of incentives and disincentives affecting individual, independent decisions. The range is vast, but in this essay one can touch only a few topics and mention their interrelationships. Yet a first step is needed, and the following discussion is intended to be just that.

This essay initially summarizes demographic economic facts pertinent to our present situation, first identifying what demographic economists generally believed in 1960 to be true about the likely course of development of the American economy. The next section reviews some elements of actual trends since then in population size, birth rates, fertility rates, death rates, immigration, age composition of the population, labor force participation rates, labor force effectiveness, and investment in education. Thereafter we focus on some of the ideas making up the basis of current American theorizing in demographic economics. Finally, we turn to discussing a variety of explicit economic policy problems.

What the Consensus Was

In the long history of data collection and analysis, more frequently than not the failures have occurred with unwarranted extrapolations. For example, the great baby boom after the Second World War was completely unanticipated, and even after it had continued for several years, it was considered simply temporary—a "making up for lost time," or a consequence of the dearth of babies during the Great Depression and the war.

Systematic speculation or theorizing about the relationship of population growth to macroeconomic performance emerged as early as the sixteenth century with Giovanni Botero's *La grandezza della città*.[1] It was the publication of Malthus's first edition of his *Essay on Population*[2] that began modern theorizing. Much work since Malthus's time has stressed the strain on resources and on the ties binding groups together that would result if the rates of natural increase remained at the peaks apparent in the latter eighteenth century. In some significant senses, the alpha and omega of theorizing in classical economics were Ricardo's assertion of the Iron Law of Wages and John Stuart Mill's articulated belief in the attainability of the stationary state. This is not the place either to lay out the spectrum of theoretical views about what does happen, much less what ought to happen; but I do offer my own conclusion that the a priori reasoning used in fashioning both old and new models of demographic and economic relationships for all of their 400-year gestation, is not sufficiently sophisticated to make recent attempts look much better than the early ones—or very useful, for that matter. A recent article by Julian Simon on the "low-level equilibrium trap" (the key Mal-

---

[1] Giovanni Botero, *La grandezza della città* (1588); translated into English as *Greatness of Cities* (1606).

[2] Thomas Robert Malthus, *An Essay on the Principle of Population as It Affects the Future Improvement of Society* (London, 1798).

thusian concept) attacks the idea logically as well as empirically.[3] Nor have the demographers and demographic economists only recently come on measurements and attempts at prediction. The actual analysis of population data began in 1662 when John Graunt's *Observations upon the Bills of Mortality* was first published.[4] A regular systematic collection of census material necessary for scientific work appears with the first U.S. census in 1790; the first French and British censuses were in 1801; and census collecting intimated its future degree of sophistication with Adolphe Quételet's fine analysis of the Belgian-Dutch census of 1829.[5]

Although no professional discipline can be said to have a corner on the hubris market, fate seems to reserve some of its strongest reprimands for demographic economists. By the time demographers and economists have collected and examined their data, fate has mischievously changed the behavior of some critical variables. The consequence is that the theoretical speculations and predictions of the profession have repeatedly suffered the worst destiny, "simple theories being overtaken by contrary complicated events." Withal, by 1960 most American demographic economists generally believed most or all of the following seven points:

• The 150 or more years of declining fertility of American women had been significantly reversed, and although it was unlikely that the high fertility rates of the post–World War II baby-boom years would continue, reversion to the old downward course was probably also unlikely. Birth rates would increase as the baby-boom cohorts entered the years of high fertility, generally believed to be the early twenties for most women.

• The era of antibiotics had established new high plateaus of life expectancy, and it was unlikely that there would be marked changes in the future life expectancy rates except insofar as black rates might move upward to convergence with white rates.

[3] Cf. Julian L. Simon, "There Is No Low-Level Fertility and Development Trap," *Population Studies*, vol. 34 (November 1980), pp. 476-86, which is a recent effort at refuting Richard R. Nelson, "A Theory of the Low-Level Equilibrium Trap in Underdeveloped Countries," *American Economic Review*, vol. 46 (December 1956), pp. 894-908, and Harvey Leibenstein, *Economic Backwardness and Economic Growth* (Princeton, N.J.: Princeton University Press, 1957).

[4] John Graunt, *Natural and Political Observations . . . upon the Bills of Mortality* (1662).

[5] See Adolphe Quételet, *Sur l'homme et le développement de ses facultés: Physique sociale* (Brussels, 1835), translated as *A Treatise on Man and the Development of His Faculties* (1842), and particularly his "Sur l'appréciation des documents statistiques et en particulier sur l'appréciation des moyennes," *Bulletin de la Commission Centrale de Statistique* [Belgium], vol. 2 (1844), pp. 205-06.

• America was unlikely to have large scale immigration in the coming decades; at any rate, the pattern of low-level-skill migration, which had dominated the historical record prior to 1924, would not be seen again.

• The American labor force would grow, reflecting the impact of the baby-boom years, but the labor force participation rates of women, which had already shown some increase, would stabilize.

• Of all investments, investment in formal education was, and was likely to continue to be, among the wisest that the individual (on the "micro" basis) and society (on the "macro" basis) could make to improve individuals' income streams and the growth of gross national product.

• The growth of gross national product per capita might from time to time falter (growth cycles), but the secrets of controlling the business cycle had been pretty well discovered.

• The future of productivity growth lay in institutionalizing mechanization (particularly automation) and in research and development. Results were perceived as being limited by the extent of a willingness to allocate resources; few, if any, thought that there would be cutbacks in this vital area.

What Has Actually Happened since 1960?

Population Size. In 1960 the American population was 179.3 million; in 1980 the population was about 222.5 million. The American population has grown 24.1 percent since 1960. This growth is at an average compounded rate of much less than 1 percent, which is well below the average of the 1945–1960 compounded growth rate of nearly 2 percent. The numbers of babies born in the period since 1960 fell substantially below the large numbers of babies born during the great baby boom (1945–1960). The variables entering into population size are: birth rates (and fertility rates), death rates, and immigration.

Birth Rates. The birth rate is the ratio of babies born per 1,000 persons in the population times 100. During the past two centuries there has been a general decline in this ratio. Reasons offered are not mutually exclusive and affect both the denominator and the numerator. A longer-lived population obviously causes the denominator to grow. Fewer deaths among babies and children may result in a need for fewer "replacement births." There are other reasons affecting the numerator, some of which will be mentioned later. The American birth rate,

TABLE 1
Birth Rates, 1930–1980

Year	Birth Rate
1930	21.3
1933	18.4 (the first nadir)
1940	19.4
1950	24.1
1957	25.3 (the peak)
1960	23.7[a]
1970	18.4[a]
1975	14.8[a] (the second nadir)
1978	15.3[a]
1980	16.2[a,b]

[a] Includes Alaska and Hawaii.
[b] Estimated.
Source: See footnote 6.

however, leaped up just after World War II. In 1940 it was 19.4; by 1950 it was 24.1; by 1955 it was 25.0; and in 1957 it peaked at 25.3. By 1970 it had fallen to 18.4, and in 1980 it was estimated at around 16.2.

Normally when there has been a short-term rise in the birth rate (or a short-term decline), we anticipate a similar repeat fluctuation (called an "echo") about twenty to twenty-five years later, as the bumper (or unusually large) crop of girls reaches the usual reproduction ages. The post–World War II baby boom lasted from about 1945 until 1960. Thus we anticipated its "echo" about two decades later, that is, between 1964 until shortly after 1980. For reasons advanced by Easterlin and by Becker (as I will explain later), this echo has gone all but unheard. The numbers in table 1 tell the story, with the 1978 and 1980 figures (both somewhat tentatively) being the echo.[6]

Fertility Rates. Fertility rates are the ratio of the number of babies born in any year to the average number of women in the childbearing

[6] Data through 1970 come from *Historical Statistics of the United States, Colonial Times to 1970*, series B-5. Figures for the 1970s come from the *Statistical Abstract of the United States, 1979*, table 80. The 1980 figure comes from the National Center for Health Statistics, *Monthly Vital Statistics Report*, vol. 29, no. 12 (March 18, 1981), p. 1.

ages, usually fifteen through forty-four. In some senses this rate is a better indicator of propensity to bear children than the birth rate, since the denominator of the birth rate includes not only men but also many females not in the childbearing years. So much has been written about the precipitous decline in total fertility rates since 1957 that I am loath to add more. At present there are about 1.7 births per woman aged fifteen to forty-four, just about half of the rate in the late 1950s (3.7 births per such woman). This figure is an average; variations about this mean associated with race, educational achievement, and rurality not only are great but are changing. Future fertility rates will clearly be affected by the compositional impact of these variations. Natural replacement requires 2.1 such births. There has been much literature about the delaying of childbearing in the last decade, with the conclusion repeatedly offered that women would make up in their late twenties for the children the demographers had expected them to have in their early twenties. Women did not do so, and the expectation was then delayed for the early thirties. Hopes for this delayed activity have not been fulfilled. Fertility rates remain very low.

Death Rates. In 1940 the death rate was 10.8 per thousand. By 1950, mainly because of the appearance of large numbers of babies, it had fallen to 9.6 per thousand; and by 1975 it had fallen even farther, to 8.8 per thousand. Much of this latest change is a function of better life expectancy (the rest may be attributed to changes in the age composition of the population).

Examination of figure 1 and table 2 suggests three points:

• There is upward convergence in age-of-death expectation for all four groups (white male, white female, nonwhite male, nonwhite female). This change signifies that mortality rates of the younger groups have been, if not eliminated, greatly reduced. Such an observation is consistent not only with our realization of better pharmaceutical therapy for infectious diseases, more general access to preventive care, and a rising standard of living for virtually all groups in the American economy but also with recent scientific advances in immunology (particularly with regard to poliomyelitis), hematology (particularly with regard to electrolytic balance), and other areas.

• After 1960 black women have had longer life expectancies than white men at all age levels. However, they have enjoyed longer life expectancy at age sixty since the 1930s. All of which suggests that variables associated with sex differences may well be more important in prolonging life than average income levels are.

FIGURE 1
MEDIAN AGE OF DEATH OF SURVIVORS, 1900–1978

(a) Whites

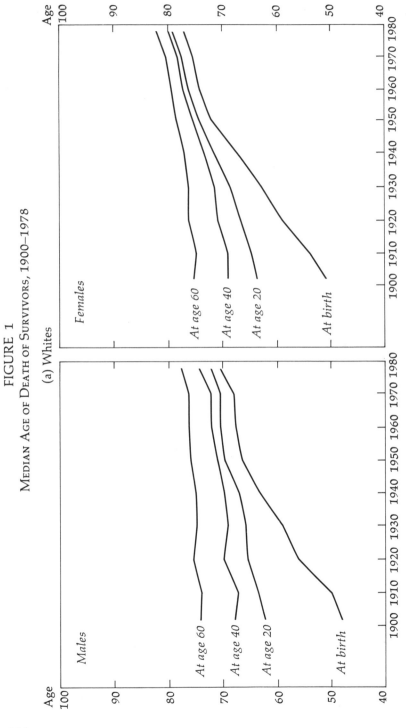

FIGURE 1 (continued)

(b) Blacks and other nonwhites

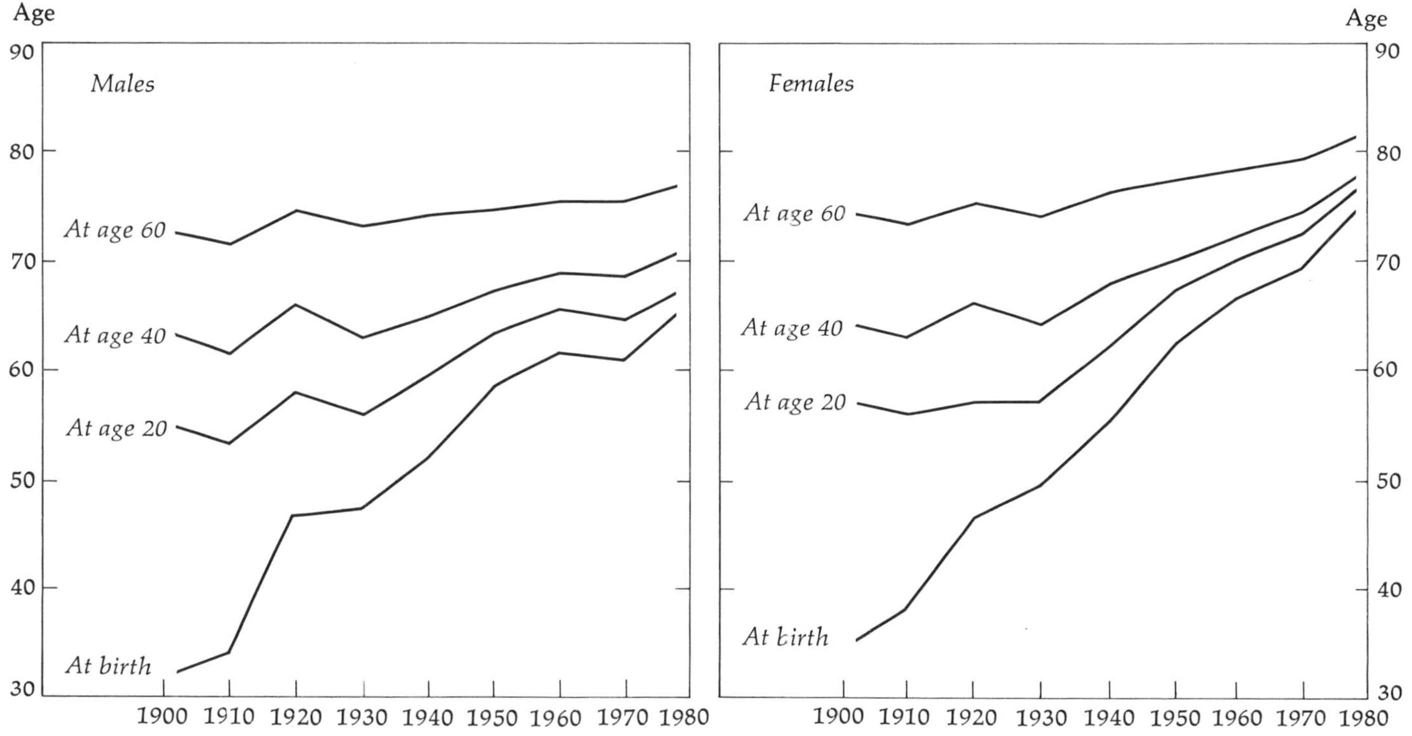

Males

At age 60

At age 40

At age 20

At birth

Females

At age 60

At age 40

At age 20

At birth

SOURCE: Table 1.

255

TABLE 2

LIFE TABLE VALUES BY AGE, COLOR, AND SEX, 1900–1978

Age	Color, Sex	Average Number of Years of Life Remaining ($\mathring{e}_x$)								
		1978 [a]	1969–1971 [a]	1959–1961	1949–1951	1939–1941	1929–1931	1919–1921	1909–1911	1900–07
	White, Male									
0		70.2	67.94	67.55	66.31	62.81	59.12	56.34	50.23	48.23
1		70.1	68.33	68.34	67.41	64.98	62.04	60.24	56.26	54.61
5		66.3	64.55	64.61	63.77	61.68	59.38	58.31	55.37	54.43
10		61.5	59.69	59.78	58.98	57.03	54.96	54.15	51.32	50.59
15		56.6	54.83	54.93	54.18	52.33	50.39	49.74	46.91	46.25
20		52.0	50.22	50.25	49.52	47.76	46.02	45.60	42.71	42.19
25		47.5	45.70	45.65	44.93	43.28	41.78	41.60	38.79	38.52
30		42.8	41.07	40.97	40.29	38.80	37.54	37.65	34.87	34.88
35		38.2	36.43	36.31	35.68	34.36	33.33	33.74	31.08	31.29
40		33.6	31.87	31.73	31.17	30.03	29.22	29.86	27.43	27.74
45		29.1	27.48	27.34	26.87	25.87	25.28	26.00	23.86	24.21
50		24.8	23.34	23.22	22.83	21.96	21.51	22.22	20.39	20.76
55		20.8	19.51	19.45	19.11	18.34	17.97	18.59	17.03	17.42
60		17.2	16.07	16.01	15.76	15.05	14.72	15.25	13.98	14.35
65		14.0	13.02	12.97	12.75	12.07	11.77	12.21	11.25	11.51
70		11.1	10.38	10.29	10.07	9.42	9.20	9.51	8.83	9.03
75		8.6	8.06	7.92	7.77	7.17	7.02	7.30	6.75	6.84
80		6.7	6.18	5.89	5.88	5.38	5.26	5.47	5.09	5.10
85		5.3	4.63	4.34	4.35	4.02	3.99	4.06	3.88	3.81

All Other, Male

Age								
0	65.0	60.98	61.48	58.91	52.33	47.55	47.14	34.05	32.54
1	65.5	62.13	63.50	61.06	56.05	51.08	51.63	42.53	42.46
5	61.8	58.48	59.98	57.69	53.13	48.69	50.18	44.25	45.06
10	57.0	53.67	55.19	52.96	48.54	44.27	45.99	40.65	41.90
15	52.1	48.84	50.39	48.23	43.95	39.83	41.75	36.77	38.26
20	47.4	44.37	45.78	43.73	39.74	35.95	38.36	33.46	35.11
25	43.1	40.29	41.38	39.49	35.94	32.67	35.54	30.44	32.21
30	38.8	36.20	37.05	35.31	32.25	29.45	32.51	27.33	29.25
35	34.5	32.16	32.81	31.21	28.67	26.39	29.54	24.42	26.16
40	30.4	28.29	28.72	27.29	25.23	23.36	26.53	21.57	23.12
45	26.5	24.64	24.89	23.59	22.02	20.59	23.55	18.85	20.09
50	22.8	21.24	21.28	20.25	19.18	17.92	20.47	16.21	17.34
55	19.5	18.14	18.11	17.36	16.67	15.46	17.50	13.82	14.69
60	16.5	15.35	15.29	14.91	14.38	13.15	14.74	11.67	12.62
65	14.1	12.87	12.84	12.75	12.18	10.87	12.07	9.74	10.38
70	11.6	10.68	10.81	10.74	10.06	8.78	9.58	8.00	8.33
75	9.8	8.99	8.93	8.83	8.09	6.99	7.61	6.58	6.60
80	8.8	7.57	6.87	7.07	6.46	5.42	5.83	5.53	5.12
85	7.8	6.04	5.08	5.38	5.08	4.30	4.53	4.48	4.04

White, Female

Age								
0	77.8	75.49	74.19	72.03	67.29	62.67	58.53	53.62	51.08
1	77.6	75.66	74.68	72.77	68.93	64.93	61.51	58.69	56.39
5	73.8	71.86	70.92	69.09	65.57	62.17	59.43	57.67	56.03
10	68.9	66.97	66.05	64.26	60.83	57.65	55.17	53.57	52.15
15	64.0	62.07	61.15	59.39	56.07	53.00	50.67	49.12	47.79

(Table continues)

TABLE 2 (continued)

Average Number of Years of Life Remaining ($\mathring{e}_x$)

Age	Color, Sex	1978[a]	1969–1971[a]	1959–1961	1949–1951	1939–1941	1929–1931	1919–1921	1909–1911	1900–07
20		59.1	57.24	56.29	54.56	51.38	48.52	46.46	44.88	43.77
25		54.3	52.42	51.45	49.77	46.78	44.25	42.55	40.88	40.05
30		49.5	47.60	46.63	45.00	42.21	39.99	38.72	36.96	36.42
35		44.6	42.82	41.84	40.28	37.70	35.73	34.86	33.09	32.82
40		39.9	38.12	37.13	35.64	33.25	31.52	30.94	29.26	29.17
45		35.2	33.54	32.53	31.12	28.90	27.39	26.98	25.45	25.51
50		30.7	29.11	28.08	26.76	24.72	23.41	23.12	21.74	21.89
55		26.4	24.85	23.81	22.58	20.73	19.60	19.40	18.18	18.43
60		22.3	20.79	19.69	18.64	17.00	16.05	15.93	14.92	15.23
65		18.4	16.93	15.88	15.00	13.56	12.81	12.75	11.97	12.23
70		14.8	13.37	12.38	11.68	10.50	9.98	9.94	9.38	9.59
75		11.5	10.21	9.28	8.87	7.92	7.56	7.62	7.20	7.33
80		8.8	7.59	6.67	6.59	5.88	5.63	5.70	5.35	5.50
85		6.7	5.54	4.66	4.83	4.34	4.24	4.24	4.06	4.10
	All Other, Female									
0		73.6	69.05	66.47	62.70	56.51	49.51	46.92	37.67	35.04
1		74.0	70.01	68.10	64.37	58.47	52.33	50.39	45.15	43.54
5		70.2	66.34	64.54	60.93	55.47	49.81	48.70	46.42	46.04
10		65.4	61.49	59.72	56.17	50.83	45.33	44.54	42.84	43.02
15		60.4	56.60	54.85	51.36	46.22	40.87	40.36	39.18	39.79
20		55.6	51.85	50.07	46.77	42.14	37.22	37.15	36.14	36.89

25	50.9	47.19	45.40	42.35	38.31	33.93	34.35	32.97	33.90
30	46.2	42.61	40.83	38.02	34.52	30.67	31.48	29.61	30.70
35	41.5	38.14	36.41	33.82	30.83	27.47	28.58	26.44	27.52
40	37.0	33.87	32.16	29.82	27.31	24.30	25.60	23.34	24.37
45	32.7	29.80	28.14	26.07	24.00	21.39	22.61	20.43	21.36
50	28.5	25.97	24.31	22.67	21.04	18.60	19.76	17.65	18.67
55	24.7	22.37	20.89	19.62	18.44	16.27	17.09	14.98	15.88
60	21.2	19.02	17.83	16.95	16.14	14.22	14.69	12.78	13.60
65	18.0	15.99	15.12	14.54	13.95	12.24	12.41	10.82	11.38
70	14.8	13.30	12.46	12.29	11.81	10.30	10.25	9.22	9.62
75	12.5	11.06	10.10	10.15	9.80	8.62	8.37	7.55	7.90
80	11.5	9.01	7.66	8.15	8.00	6.90	6.58	6.05	6.48
85	9.9	7.07	5.44	6.15	6.38	5.48	5.22	5.09	5.10

NOTE: Prior to 1960, excludes Alaska and Hawaii; data prior to 1929 are for states reporting death registration.

a Deaths of nonresidents of the United States were excluded beginning in 1970.

SOURCE: U.S. Department of Health and Human Services, National Center for Health Statistics, *Vital Statistics of the United States, 1978*, vol. 2, sect. 5, p. 15.

• Generally, we see that nonwhites still do not enjoy the life expectancies of whites if we adjust the data by sex. Such is particularly the case of the younger age groups. Still, there may well continue to be upward convergence by sex toward the white life-expectancy figures, since there is probably something to be said for the nurture side of the old "nurture versus nature" discussion.

Immigration. There has been a significant number of legal immigrants to the United States since 1950. These numbers are probably (no one really knows) dwarfed currently by those for illegal immigration. In 1950 there were 249,200 legal immigrants. By 1960 that number, at 265,400, had not materially changed. By the mid-1970s, the annual net legal immigration tended to run somewhat closer to 400,000 than to 300,000.

Several aspects of the data are very interesting. First, the percentage of immigrants aged sixteen to forty-four is very high. Second, there have been changes in point of origin. Until 1924 America was reasonably open, and immigrants were primarily European. Between 1924 and the 1950s, relatively little immigration was permitted, and the bulk came from northwestern Europe. In the 1960s, the immigration laws were changed. There had never been quotas for non-U.S. Americans (that is, for Western hemisphere residents) as such, although Eastern European families settled in Latin America (and Canada) had been required to obtain visas as though they came from their original country of origin. The congressional reforms of 1965 erased in large measure this distasteful atavism; in addition, not only were quotas set on a first-come, first-served basis, but special quotas for political refugees were established. In all, the numbers of Latin Americans and Orientals were greatly increased, particularly since our military failure in Vietnam, which led to the admitting of large numbers of Orientals. The American government has recently taken a far more tolerant view toward nonwhite immigration than it did prior to 1965, and the propinquity of the expanding southwestern economy to Mexico has also resulted in large flows of workers from Mexico seeking employment in the United States. All of this reflects legal immigration.

Illegal immigration is believed to have been largely Mexican. From 1 million to 6 million aliens are thought to be illegally in residence. The number grows very slowly, perhaps because many of the immigrants leave after they have been here long enough to save some money. Although the United States has traditionally furnished clear statistical information, this area remains very cloudy.

FIGURE 2
U.S. POPULATION AGE-SEX PYRAMIDS: 1960–1990

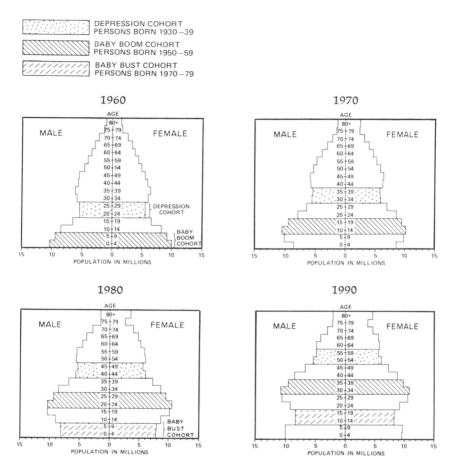

SOURCES: 1960-1970, U.S. Bureau of the Census; 1980-1990, unpublished tabulations prepared by Leon Bouvier for the Select Commission on Immigration and Refugee Policy, 1980. Based on a completed cohort fertility rate (after 1980) of 2.0, plus the annual admission of 750,000 aliens (legal and illegal). Illustration: Courtesy of the Population Reference Bureau, Inc., Washington, D.C.

Age Composition of the Population. The median age of the population in 1950 was 30.2 years; in 1960, 29.5; by 1970, it had fallen to 27.9 years; and by 1980, it had again moved up to 30.2 years. The change in the median age between 1950 and 1980 reflects the movement of the baby-boom-and-bust cohorts through the age structure. These changes and others are shown by the population pyramids in

261

figure 2. In 1950 only 10.8 percent of the American population was under the age of five; by 1960 that statistic had risen to 11.3 percent; but in 1978 it fell back far below the 1950 figure, to 7.0 percent. In other words, small children are a significantly lower percentage of the American population than they were as recently as thirty years ago. On the other hand, the size of the age groups of fourteen through twenty-four-year-olds has grown dramatically. In 1960 it was 15.1 percent of the population; and in 1978 it was an impressive 20.8 percent of the population.

By way of contrast, the portion of the population that has traditionally borne the burdens of livelihood winning and major social decision making has shrunk. In 1950, no less than 50.3 percent of the American population was between the ages of twenty-five and sixty-four; in 1960 that group had fallen to 46.1 percent; and by 1978 it was again starting to rise (46.8 percent).

Another way to view this change is to look at the growth in the size of the elderly cohorts (those over sixty-five years of age). In 1950 only 8.1 percent of the population was over the age of sixty-five; in 1960 it was 9.2 percent, and by 1978 better than a tenth (11.0 percent) was in this senior category; in 1990, depending upon how many babies are likely to be born, it will be 11.7 to 12.6 percent. The fourth pyramid shown in figure 2, that for 1990, offers a very interesting factual picture as well as inspiring speculation. We have every reason to believe that the upward end of the pyramid will be as fat or fatter than the one illustrated. These people are already in our midst, albeit now nine years younger than they will be in 1990. Our speculation is about the bottom end of the pyramid, however; as it is drawn, the pyramid suggests that we will in the aggregate be having more babies. The picture assumes that the completed cohort fertility rate will be around 2.0 and total immigration (legal or illegal) about 750,000.[7] As we know, however, it is assumptions or predictions like these that call down the wrath of fate.

Labor Force Participation Rates. Another great demographic surprise revealed in the 1960s and 1970s lay in the changes in certain labor force participation rates, particularly those for females; many of these changes are shown in figure 3 and table 3.

With regard to white males, what stands out is the impact of the draft during the Vietnam war, when a pattern emerged of lengthened formal education, which kept many men—more men than usual

---

[7] Unpublished information from Leon Bouvier for the Select Commission on Immigration and Refugee Policy, 1980.

under the age of twenty-five—out of the labor force. Also to be noted is the decline, since 1970, in labor force activity of males over the age of sixty.

The picture regarding black males is similar, although the Vietnam war did not have the same degree of impact that it did on white males with regard to postponement of entry into the labor force; most significant, however, for black males is the increased number remaining out of the labor force in the high school and college ages. Let it not be said that the educational effects of the forces creating civil rights legislation were without their influence. The other racial difference is that after age twenty-four the nonwhite rates generally have always tended to be lower than the white rates; after 1970 this generalization applies to all age groups.

Regardless of trends in male labor force participation rates, however, the great change has taken place on the distaff side. Among white women, not only has the movement been upward, but of recent years (since 1965) it has accelerated. Much the same is true of nonwhite (mostly black) women. Figure 3, providing a picture of the rate of increase, is particularly vivid with regard to women. If during World War II Vice-President Wallace argued that the postwar period in America was going to be the "age of the common man," he clearly lacked precision in his choice of words; it has been the "age of working women."

Labor Force Effectiveness. The 1979 volume of *Contemporary Economic Problems* had several essays on productivity. In mine I noted that the comparative youthfulness of the labor force in the 1970s,[8] compounded by the analogous "youthening" of the supervisory workers (the forepersons and the craftpersons), certainly seems to offer a prima facie reason for the decline in worker output.

The labor force will now become in the aggregate somewhat older because the baby-boom cohorts have now all but completed their entry.[9] But will that solve the productivity matter? On the demographic side, is the economy now permanently saddled with an inexperienced cadre of labor force supervisors, or will they (those who were promoted early and thus lacked the usual conditioning experi-

[8] Mark Perlman, "One Man's Baedeker to Productivity Growth Discussions," in William Fellner, ed., *Contemporary Economic Problems 1979* (Washington, D.C.: American Enterprise Institute, 1979), pp. 108-11.

[9] In a recent article in the *New York Review of Books* (Februry 5, 1981), pp. 12 ff., Emma Rothschild observes that the size of the absorption, 1960-1980, into the American labor force was as if all the labor force of Canada had moved into the United States.

264

FIGURE 3

U.S. Labor Force Participation, 1950–1980, by Sex and Race

(percent)

(a) Males

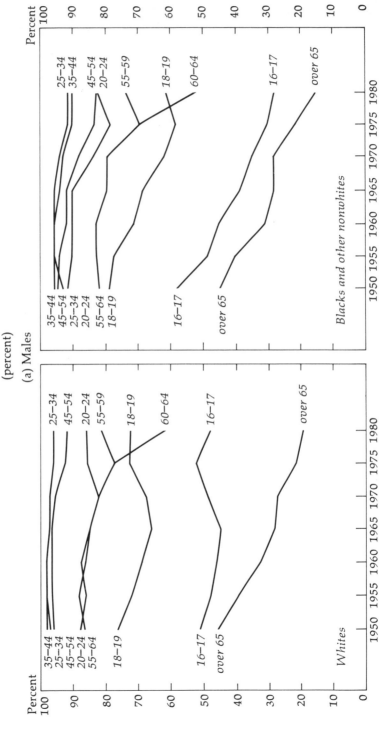

FIGURE 3 (continued)

(b) Females

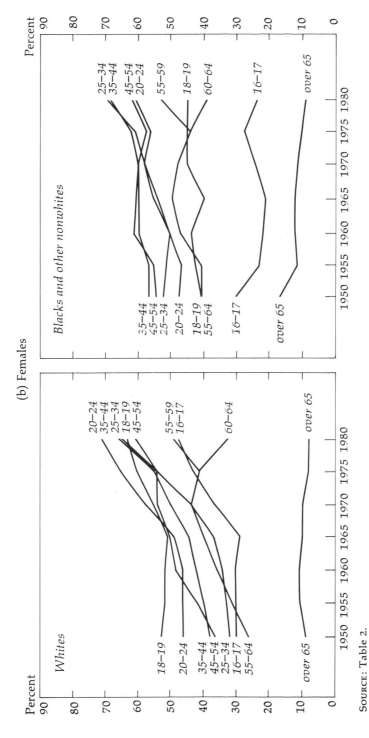

SOURCE: Table 2.

TABLE 3

Labor Force Paticipation Rates,
by Age, Color, and Sex, 1950–1980

Age	1950[a]	1955[a]	1960[a]	1965[a]	1970[a]	1975[b]	1980[c]
			White, Male				
16–17	50.5	48.0	46.0	44.6	48.9	51.8	48.4
18–19	75.6	71.7	69.0	65.8	67.4	72.8	72.0
20–24	87.5	85.6	87.8	85.3	83.3	85.5	86.4
25–34	96.4	97.8	97.7	97.4	96.7	95.8	96.2
35–44	97.7	98.3	97.9	97.7	97.3	96.4	96.5
45–54	95.9	96.7	96.1	95.9	94.9	92.9	92.2
55–59[d]	87.3	88.4	87.2	85.2	83.3	76.5	82.5
60–64[d]							61.6
65 and over	45.8	39.5	33.3	27.9	26.7	21.8	19.3
			Black and Other, Male				
16–17	57.4	48.2	45.6	39.3	34.8	30.1	27.7
18–19	78.2	75.7	71.2	66.7	61.8	57.5	60.9
20–24	91.4	89.7	90.4	89.8	83.5	78.4	82.3
25–34	92.6	95.8	96.2	95.7	93.7	91.4	91.3
35–44	96.2	96.2	95.5	94.2	93.2	90.0	90.4
45–54	95.1	94.2	92.3	92.0	88.2	84.6	83.2
55–59[d]	81.9	83.1	82.5	78.8	79.2	68.7	74.3
60–64[d]							52.5
65 and over	45.5	40.0	31.2	27.9	27.4	20.9	16.4
			White, Female				
16–17	30.1	29.9	30.0	28.7	36.6	42.7	45.8
18–19	52.6	52.0	51.9	50.6	55.0	60.4	63.2
20–24	45.9	45.8	45.7	49.2	57.7	65.4	71.0
25–34	32.1	32.8	34.1	36.3	43.2	53.5	65.1
35–44	37.2	39.9	41.5	44.3	49.9	54.9	65.6
45–54	36.3	42.7	48.6	49.9	53.7	54.3	60.7
55–59[d]	26.0	31.8	36.2	40.3	42.6	40.7	48.0
60–64[d]							33.2
65 and over	9.2	10.5	10.6	9.7	9.5	8.0	7.9
			Black and Other, Female				
16–17	30.2	22.7	22.1	20.5	24.3	26.5	22.5
18–19	40.6	43.2	44.3	40.0	44.7	45.1	45.0
20–24	46.9	46.7	48.8	55.2	57.7	56.2	61.2
25–34	51.6	51.3	49.7	54.0	57.6	61.4	68.9

TABLE 3 (continued)

Age	1950[a]	1955[a]	1960[a]	1965[a]	1970[a]	1975[b]	1980[c]
35–44	55.7	56.0	59.8	59.9	59.9	61.7	68.4
45–54	54.3	54.8	60.5	60.2	60.2	56.8	62.3
55–59	40.9	40.7	47.3	48.9	47.1	43.8	53.3
60–64							38.8
65 and over	16.5	12.1	12.8	12.9	12.2	10.5	9.5

[a] "Civilian Labor Force Participation Rates," in *1975 Manpower Report of the President*, p. 208, table A-4.

[b] "Civilian Labor Force Participation Rates," in *1976 Employment and Training Report of the President*, pp. 217-18, table A-4.

[c] Participation rates are those of total labor force.

[d] For the 1955, 1960, 1965, 1970, and 1975 data there is one 55-64 age group.

SOURCE: U.S. Department of Labor and Bureau of Labor Statistics, *Employment and Earnings*, table A-4, October, years shown.

ences) "learn" on their supervisory jobs and in the course of the next few years achieve the effectiveness associated with their counterparts two decades ago? I am not aware of any data or studies offering systematic answers to this query.

Investment in Education. Few economic issues are any more compli-cated than computing the advantages of investing in a college and/or university education.[10] At best the figures we use tend to be average costs of such training, and the rewards gained are not only average current salaries but income streams projected well into an uncertain future. Thus, investment in education by some specific individual may or may not be justified by the added income stream resulting— it all depends upon ex ante added costs and ex post returns, to be realized only years later. As such it may not be our question, insofar

[10] The analytical approaches for this topic were introduced by Professor Theodore Schultz in *The Economic Value of Education* (New York: Columbia University Press, 1963) and by Professor Gary Becker in his *Human Capital*, 1st and 2nd eds. (New York: Columbia University Press, 1964, 1975). I commissioned two essays in the *Journal of Economic Literature* giving a summary of the pros and cons of the approach: Jacob Mincer, "The Distribution of Labor Incomes: A Survey with Special Reference to the Human Capital Approach," vol. 8 (March 1970), pp. 1-26, and Mark Blaug, "The Empirical Status of Human Capital Theory: A Slightly Jaundiced Survey," vol. 14 (1976), pp. 827-55. More recently I have come across an interesting interoccupational study involving different kinds of vocational training for nurses and three other professions: Charles H. Belanger and Lise Lavallee, "Economic Returns to Schooling Decisions," *Research in Higher Educa-tion*, vol. 12 (1980), p. 23-35.

as we are concerned not with specific individuals but with the community generally. This point was similarly made by Frank Knight years ago when he observed that on the average, gold prospecting did not pay—but the lucky miner at the upper margin nonetheless could and did strike it rich.[11] Knight's point about social efficiency and individual gain should not be forgotten, even if we do choose to think in terms of aggregates, usually averages.

Early in the 1970s there began to be some evidence that average returns on collegiate education were no longer as large as they had been in the late 1940s, 1950s, and 1960s.[12] The GI Bill, enacted for World War II veterans, seems to have repeated itself several times over—a serendipity that has been generalized into a rule, "the more education you give everybody, the richer everybody will be." While several names could be cited, Richard Freeman's work serves as a fine representation of the revisionist view that the halcyon days of broad-front investment in collegiate education are probably over.[13] Freeman, using data for the federal census of population surveys (at times) and full censuses (at other times), reported in 1975 that average rates of return, although still positive, were falling.[14] There has been much discussion of the details relating to the precise conceptual apparatus in Freeman's work as well as his data, but common sense seems to indicate that for the present, at least, average costs of collegiate training are rising, and the resulting additional income streams are falling. Of course, there may be other reasons for going to college—individual cultural deepening, job security or priority in getting employment, or rewards in sheer consumption; but the hard-core conclusion is that collegiate education is not as great a deal as it was. This conclusion is even more probably believed about doctoral training, particularly in the humanities—although it is probably not true at all about

[11] Frank H. Knight, *Risk, Uncertainty and Profit* (New York: Harper, 1921).

[12] This point surfaced in Alice Rivlin's 1974 Ely paper for the American Economic Association but is not by any means established as canon; Rivlin, "Income Distribution—Can Economists Help?" *American Economic Review*, vol. 65 (May 1975), pp. 1-15.

[13] Richard B. Freeman, "Overinvestment in College Training?" *Journal of Human Resources*, vol. 10 (summer 1975), pp. 287-311; see also: Freeman, *The Overeducated American* (New York: Academic Press, 1976); "The Decline in the Economic Rewards to College Education," *Review of Economics and Statistics*, vol. 59 (February 1977), pp. 18-29; "The Facts about the Declining Economic Value of College," *Journal of Human Resources*, vol. 15 (winter 1980), pp. 124-42. Note also John R. Wish and William D. Hamilton, "Replicating Freeman's Recursive Adjustment Model of Demand for Higher Education," *Research in Higher Education*, vol. 12 (November 1980), pp. 83-95.

[14] Freeman, "Overinvestment in College Training?" pp. 287-311.

average returns on investment in certain kinds of business or possibly medical training.

The paucity of current data, to say nothing of the almost complete relative lack of widespread current analysis (particularly with respect to disaggregated units—Harvard with its costs and returns versus the University of Texas with its costs and returns) in light of the importance of the topic seems startling. The foregoing point, however, is not meant to suggest that no investment in education "pays off"; Finis Welch, for example, has suggested (not without criticism) that such investment is particularly beneficial to young blacks.[15] Perhaps university-employed academics fear the results of such research, and like the English (or the French) in the late seventeenth century who feared the weakness that they thought would be revealed by a census of population, they prefer not to know the truth. In any event, the intellectual situation in this area seems to be one of doubt—doubt not resolved by conscious and systematic broad-gauged efforts.

Current Ideas Relating to the 1980s

Richard A. Easterlin has for the past quarter of a century been developing a theory of fertility and economic opportunity cycles. If there is an attractive quality to the evolution of his theory, what should interest us most is its present form.[16]

Easterlin's theory, in large measure empirically derived, is that young people born in a numerous cohort must jostle their way through the educational process and scramble for jobs, and they generally feel the economic pinch throughout their working lives. They postpone normal household formation (marriage and children) and limit family size. But, as they produce fewer children, their children will not have to jostle their way through schools and will not have to scramble for jobs (unless an unusually large number of

[15] Cf., inter alia, Finis Welch, "Human Capital Theory: Education, Discrimination and Life Cycles," American Economic Review, vol. 65 (May 1975), pp. 63-73, but also see John S. Akin and Irwin Garfinkel, "School Expenditures and the Economic Returns to Schooling," Journal of Human Resources, vol. 12 (fall 1977), pp. 460-79, and Thomas J. Kniesner, Arthur H. Padilla, and Solomon H. Polachek, "The Rate of Return to Schooling and the Business Cycle," Journal of Human Resources, vol. 13 (spring 1978), pp. 264-77.

[16] Richard A. Easterlin, Birth and Fortune: The Impact of Numbers on Personal Welfare (New York: Basic Books, 1980); Easterlin, Victor R. Fuchs, and Simon Kuznets, "American Population since 1940," in Martin Feldstein, ed., The American Economy in Transition (Chicago: University of Chicago Press, 1980), pp. 275-347.

immigrants come in to share the relative prosperity), and they will organize normal households early and have larger numbers of children. The likelihood that this last phenomenon will occur depends, of course, on the possibility of immigration, an American pattern prior to 1924 but one not very important since then. Easterlin explains the post–World War II American baby boom by noting that the young people who were parents of that baby boom had been born in small cohorts and were not only beneficiaries of the many job opportunities after World War II but also felt rich and chose to marry young, have large families soon, and redesign society in the terms consistent with their self-perception. Easterlin explains the baby bust as the almost inevitable next step—the children of the baby-boom cohorts had to jostle each other and face competition.

According to Easterlin's view, a new American baby boom might start occurring sometime in the late 1980s, about twenty to twenty-five years after the period of low fertility commenced (in the early 1960s). It can be argued, particularly if one agrees with Easterlin, that the annual crop of youngsters will grow by the 1990s and that they will have a strong place in the allocative decisions faced by the community in that decade. Abandoned schools will have to be reopened or replaced; child-centered suburbs will again be the mode. One can easily expand the list of things that are likely to happen— but will they?

Women now have higher opportunity costs than ever before— they are well ensconced in the labor market, and what they have to forgo if they withdraw to bear *and raise* children would be substantial. This point, originally developed and stressed by Gary Becker[17] and such colleagues as Jacob Mincer and Marc Nerlove, has been called the New (Chicago/Morningside Heights) Home Economics. Their work suggests a barrier (but not necessarily an insurmountable one) to reversibility of fertility behavior. It also suggests grounds for fresh concern about quality of child-bearing, namely that women with high opportunity cost will bear few if any children and that those with low opportunity costs will be the large-scale reproducers. It does not follow automatically that women with well-paying alternative opportunities would not put a high enough value on childbearing

---

[17] Gary S. Becker, "An Economic Analysis of Fertility," in *Demographic and Economic Change in Developed Countries: A Conference of the Universities–National Bureau of Economic Research* (Princeton, N.J.: Princeton University Press for NBER, 1960), pp. 209-40; and also see Theodore W. Schultz, ed., "Fertility and Economic Values," in *Economics of the Family: Marriage, Children, and Human Capital* (Chicago and London: University of Chicago Press for NBER, 1974), pp. 3-22.

to be willing to become mothers; nonetheless, there is the implication that the more high-paying alternatives women have, the less likely they will be, ceteris paribus, to have large numbers of children. The dilemma thus suggested, namely that economic opportunity pulls the most educated from motherhood, does not have only one set of social conclusions because it has not been proven that work-place-oriented women are necessarily the brightest or the best mothers. A doctrine of specialization based on comparative costs had a short-run validity; the longer-haul implications are complicated.

Baby Booms and Such. Landon Jones in his attractive, if provocative, recent book[18] reports that when the Romanian authorities decided that that country's fertility rates had fallen too low and took steps in 1966 to restrict abortions severely, to outlaw contraceptives, and to enact such pronatalist measures as birth premiums and reduced taxes for couples with children, the number of births immediately tripled. "For the year of 1967, both the crude birth rate and the number of births was twice that of 1966."[19] Over the next decade Romania "doubled its rate of population increase and produced an estimated 39 percent more babies than might otherwise have been expected (compared with an 'excess' of 34 percent during America's baby boom)."[20] Jones's description of the possible working of this "baby boomlet" is startling: The boomlet "on a graph looks less like a pig in a python than a giraffe in a python."[21] Romania's kindergarten population doubled in one year. By the late 1980s, Romania, "will have twice as many people entering the labor force and marrying (and thereby, producing an 'echo' boom of their own)."[22] Thus, there is a possibility, even if seemingly a very small one, that the American public could emulate the experience, and the trend toward the aging of the population would be "unbalanced" (or more than balanced) by a new baby boom. Such a turn of events is not entirely impossible if a military draft is extended to young women and gives exemption preferences to couples with children and particularly to women with babies; all sorts of rapid reversals could occur. Nonetheless, the phenomenon is unlikely.

[18] Landon Y. Jones, *Great Expectations: America and the Baby Boom Generation* (New York: Coward, McCann & Geoghegan, 1980).

[19] Ibid., p. 289.

[20] Ibid., p. 290.

[21] Ibid.

[22] Ibid.

Some Present and Future Policy Implications

This final section of my essay focuses on economic impacts of some of the specific points that have emerged earlier. The relationship of population growth, economic growth, and economic welfare has received considerable attention in the past two decades. An important selection of professional economists' views may be found in volume 2 of the final report of the U.S. Commission on Population Growth and the American Future, *Economic Aspects of Population Change.*[23] The commission's efforts, themselves laid out in the initial volume of the report,[24] were largely educational and in that sense only a step toward policy formation. Still, what counts in the long run is how the Supreme Court decides to interpret the Constitution (vide the decision to permit voluntary abortion during the first trimester) and specific positive actions by Congress and the executive branch.

I withstand the temptation to discuss the commission's recommendations, which seem to me somewhat vague. There was some division among the commission members. Although the commission did in the end reflect in good measure the strong commitment to zero population growth of its chairman, John D. Rockefeller III, some caveats on this score seem to have been entertained by at least two of its members, including two leading economists, Professors D. Gale Johnson and John Meyer, who presumably were in part (at least) influenced by the papers in volume 2. Nonetheless, vagueness and qualifications included, the report (volume 1) favors no or very slow population growth. Volume 2 is another story.

There were in that volume eleven principal essays. Four particularly interesting expert papers were written by Allen C. Kelley, Harvey Leibenstein, Joseph J. Spengler, and Edmund S. Phelps. Kelley's paper held that no conclusive case could be made for desirable economic effects coming from a reduction in the growth and size of population. To put the matter explicitly, he concludes: "the impact of zero population growth over the foreseeable future on the average American's

---

[23] U.S. Commission on Population Growth and the American Future, *Population and the American Future*, vol. 2, *Economic Aspects of Population Change*, Elliott R. Morss and Ritchie H. Reed, eds. (1972), hereafter cited as U.S. Commission (1972).

[24] Like many such commission findings, this volume is replete with intentionally general or ambiguous declarations chosen because of a desire to diminish the number of dissenting views. Nonetheless, it is apparent that most of the commission thought there was a clear danger of overly rapid American population increase and that most of them believed that one *or more* techniques of reducing the number of births were desirable. The majority was also bearish about increasing legal immigration.

consumption level is uncertain. Moreover, a population policy justified noticeably by its favorable impact on pollution reduction may not only be unjustified, but also undesirable."[25] This is not to say that he was opposed to fertility control, particularly birth-control information, but that he was not certain of the economic consequences of it. Leibenstein argued that "the economies of scale and employment stimulation advantages of population growth more or less counterbalance the loss due to the dilution ... of natural resources. Another advantageous factor is that a younger population contains more 'human capital' per person."[26] Phelps in his essay argues that some "slowdown of the population growth by a percentage point will eventually raise the opportunities for consumption per head.... If fiscal policy maintains the capital intensity of the economy (the path of the capital-labor ratio), then there will result a definite rise in consumption per head, though the rate of growth of consumption per head will tend eventually to subside to the level of the technical progress rate. If, in contrast, a balanced-budget policy is followed, there will be a rise of capital intensity as well; this will probably increase consumption per head additionally. The opportunities of the representative family to increase its 'lifetime utility of consumption' will also be normally increased because of the consequent rise of wage rates."[27] Of course, Professor Phelps's argument presupposes a big "if," namely a successful fiscal policy.

Yet, Professor Spengler, whose faith in the social consequences of a stationary population is both old and undeterred, concludes that it is desirable to restrict natural fertility, since that will enable more women to work in the labor force and thus a larger fraction of the population will also be of working age.[28] Also, the ratio of *employed* members of the labor force to the population should be relatively high. Spengler goes on to argue that output per member of the labor force should be higher in a stationary population (or in a slowly growing population) because investment that would otherwise be devoted to educating the young could be devoted to increasing the capital-labor ratio. Finally (and most importantly), he believes that there will be an increasing need to retain in the labor force people above the

[25] Allen C. Kelley, "Demographic Changes and American Economic Development: Past, Present and Future," in U.S. Commission (1972), pp. 9-47, at p. 11.

[26] Harvey Leibenstein, "The Impact of Population Growth on the American Economy," in U.S. Commission (1972), pp. 49-65, at p. 51.

[27] Edmund S. Phelps, "Some Macroeconomics of Population Levelling," in U.S. Commission (1972), pp. 71-84, at p. 73.

[28] Joseph J. Spengler, "Declining Population Growth: Economic Effects," in U.S. Commission (1972), pp. 91-133.

TABLE 4

AGE COHORTS AS A PERCENTAGE OF THE TOTAL POPULATION, 1976–2025

	Year		
Age	1976	2000	2025
0–17	30.3	26.5[a]	24.5[a]
		23.1[b]	19.6[b]
65 and over	10.6	12.2[a]	17.2[a]
		12.9[b]	20.2[b]

[a] Assumes completed cohort fertility (of 2.1 births per woman) plus 400,000 annual immigration.

[b] Assumes extrapolation of current fertility trend (1.7 births [completed fertility] per woman) plus 400,000 annual immigration.

SOURCE: U.S. Commission on Population Growth and the American Future, *Population and the American Future*, vol. 2, *Economic Aspects of Population Change*, Elliott R. Morss and Ritchie H. Reed, eds., 1972.

age of sixty, a need perhaps induced by inflation but also brought about by a continuing reduction in the normal work week. Also implicit in this scenario, of course, is a need to reduce the dependency rates.

It is now clear that the low birth rate since the early 1960s, far from being a general social panacea, has had and is certain to continue to have some clearly established effects. The number of children to care for and educate will be a smaller portion of the total population (see table 4). In 1976 those between birth and seventeen years of age were 30.3 percent of the population. If we assume natural fertility at about the replacement rate plus immigration of 400,000 persons per annum, by the year 2000 the ratio falls to 26.5 percent. Further, if one extrapolates from current fertility patterns (as well as allowing for annual immigration of 400,000), that ratio falls farther, to 23.1 percent of the population. The two comparable figures for the year 2025 (which is about as far away as one should dare project) become somewhere between 24.5 percent and 19.6 percent.[29] The proportion of the "elderly" (that is, those sixty-five and over), which in 1976 was 10.6 percent, would become 12.2 percent and 12.9 percent by the year 2000, depending upon which of the two previously mentioned assumptions one chooses. The comparable figures for the elderly for

[29] U.S. Department of Commerce, Bureau of the Census, "Projections of the Population of the United States, 1977-2050," in *Current Population Reports*, series P-25, no. 704 (1977), tables 8-12, D-2.

the year 2025 are 17.2 percent or 20.2 percent. In brief, the relative decreases by the year 2000 among the young (ranging from close to 13 percent to 23 percent) are more than made up for by the increases (15.7 percent to 21.7 percent) among the elderly. The proportion of the population in the two age-dependency groups (zero to seventeen and sixty-five and over) in 1976 was approximately 40.9 percent of the population. By the year 2000 the total dependency rate will have slightly fallen to between 38.7 and 36.0 percent. But why is that in the net sense not social economic-cost saving?

Robert L. Clark estimates that the current cost of a program designed for a retiree is three times the cost of a program for youth.[30] If such an estimate maintains its validity, the aggregate cost of the dependent population will thus rise disproportionately, and the cost of youths and retirees will be a strong multiple of what we spent on both in 1976. Further, suggestions for reducing aggregate spending on education, in the name of efficiency, for the young have run into resistance not only from teachers who wish to maintain jobs but also from parents who wish to maintain schools near their homes. Together these groups prove to be quite a potent political force, so savings will likely not result.

The productively active population (ages eighteen to sixty-four) should increase in the 1980s and 1990s from its current 59 percent to 61.3 percent or 64.0 percent of the population. Assuming further that the labor force participation rate will not shrink by the year 2000, the American economy will still be able by steps to manage dependency, albeit the "savings" among the youth may be more than matched by the expected increase in costs for the elderly. However, looking even farther ahead—to the year 2025—one sees that the likely capacity to handle dependency is less rosy because these two dependent groups will be between 41.7 percent and 39.8 percent of the population. Their relative burden on the usual labor force age groups will be consequently much heavier.

What do these changes imply? First, the easy side; while labor inputs will still be increasing, they will do so at a lower or socially more manageable rate, and the need to tailor public policies to encourage creation of new jobs should diminish. In the recent past the effect on productivity of all of the efforts associated with some social emphasis on full employment has been socially detrimental (in the macroeconomic sense). In the last two decades the labor force expanded by 48 percent, and between 1968 and 1980 its annual growth

[30] Robert L. Clark, ed., *Retirement Policy in an Aging Society* (Durham, N.C.: Duke University Press, 1980).

275

rate was over 2 percent. However, projections for 1980–1985 are for an annual labor force growth of only 1.6 percent, and for a further 1.1 percent in 1985–1990.[31] Thus, it would seem clear that a reorientation in policy objectives toward productivity from employment expansion permitted by the reduction in the number of new entrants should work on both macro and micro levels. The existence of fewer inexperienced workers may require fewer supervisors; or to put the conclusion cheerfully, relatively more attention can be placed on increasing worker productivity. Yet, will this happen?

On the other, less pleasant side, there will be the great burden of the large number of elderly. How will the added cost of the increased number of elderly be met—by increasing social security (or general revenue) taxes? If so, will this added tax burden cause reduced savings, less capital investment, and greater personal reliance upon governmental aid for the superannuated, as well as decreased work incentives? This series of questions underlies Colin Campbell's essay in this volume. It also underlies the question of whether postponing retirement from sixty-five to sixty-eight or even to seventy years of age is a socially necessary, if not otherwise desirable, answer.

There is, however, a different but related side to the question— one that centers on the labor force's adaptability. Does a smaller group of young entrants into the labor force cut the number of new-type workers, when "new-type worker" means "trained in the newest technology?"—or, according to another view, is the educational system turning out too many workers slated to have their skill and wage expectations frustrated? In the recent period, emphasis has been on increasing formal investment in individual human resources. Yet, high private returns seem to be declining, and the next question is whether the mix of specialties conform to what the economy needs now or is likely to need in the future. Are we trying to produce too many white-collar specialists—particularly those either with the "wrong" specialities or oriented to the "wrong" (nonmarket) incentives? Where is labor force growth anticipated? The Bureau of Labor Statistics, for what its projections may be worth, expects that the annual rate of employment growth for 1977–1990 will range from as high as 7.1 percent in medical services and 3.5 percent in radio and television broadcasting to such low rates as −2.9 percent in the household domestic sector and −3.7 percent in chemical and fertilizer mining.[32] What about immigration, particularly of the unskilled?

[31] Valerie A. Personick, "Industry Output and Employment: BLS Projections to 1990," *Monthly Labor Review*, vol. 102 (April 1979), pp. 3-14, at p. 4.
[32] Ibid., pp. 11-13.

Such immigration supplies labor willing to work in physically unpleasant jobs (for example, stoop labor). It offers competitiveness for jobs, which should lower unit labor costs (and may result in lower average earnings, it must be admitted). What will our policies be? Can we effectively police entry, now that the source of immigrants is no longer over the seas? If so, at what cost? We could, for instance, provide a disincentive (for example, monetary fines and/or costs of repatriation transportation) for employers found to have hired illegal aliens. We could also spend more on the administration of welfare (where some illegal aliens have been getting government money). Brinley Thomas, one of the leading analysts of past and present immigration, has suggested in an as yet unpublished paper that the tide of Latin American immigration into the United States is not going to be stemmed without great and/or brutal political costs. He points out that the great socioeconomic advances of our black population came about during periods when immigration rates were low and that with higher rates "the substantial progress made by the blacks in recent decades will be halted."[33] In any event, these and other considerations are considered in Barry Chiswick's essay, also in this volume.

While on the one hand it may be desirable to improve the absolute lot of our own domestically-born unskilled by restricting immigration, that is not the only view involving charity, self-interest, or political considerations. The historic rationale, on the other hand, for our pre-1924 immigration policy was liberty for the individual and an almost boundless optimism that immigrant families could and would acculturate in two or three generations and in the process participate in the creation of new civilizations of increasingly high economic and innovative standards. In the last analysis the issue involves risk-taking propensities. Yet in the face of our low fertility and birth rates, immigration may be something to encourage.

Professor Simon Kuznets voiced the view more than twenty years ago that he knew of few, if any, periods of sustained economic growth that were not associated with population expansion, which he seems to have associated with expansion of the market.[34] His further argu-

[33] Brinley Thomas, "The Upsurge in Immigration to the United States" (Berkeley: University of California, Department of Economics, May 1980), paper presented to the Mont Pelerin Society, 1980 General Meeting, Hoover Institution, Stanford University, September 7-12, 1980.

[34] His point was put in a rather quizzical way, certainly one that did not preclude the current "Japanese miracle" or the other geographic miracles (that is, those of West Germany, Korea, Taiwan, etc.). Simon Kuznets, "Population Change and Aggregate Output," in Universities–National Bureau of Economic Research, *Demographic and Economic Change in Developed Countries* (Princeton, N.J.: Princeton University Press, 1960), pp. 324-51.

ments are that labor force expansion and greater output have been the traditional paths to social stability and individual happiness and that redistribution of relative shares is easiest to accomplish in an atmosphere of general economic expansion. Consciousness of economic scarcity, to put this matter the other way, brings out the worst, and the fears generated by it lead to self-fulfilling prophecies of relative doom. Population growth is *a* (if not *the*) key; it is one way to expand the market and thereby to offer the benefits of specialization. From this standpoint one policy solution may be to encourage population expansion (either by immigration, as indicated, or by extending the incentives for natural population increase) in order to rediscover economic expansion. The usual counterarguments have been that economic growth has used up too many resources, which are finite.

Certainly the earlier phase of the debate, which first surfaced in 1848 in John Stuart Mill's chapter on the stationary state in his *Principles of Political Economy* (elaborated by Hugh Dalton[35] and J. M. Keynes[36] in several articles in the 1920s and 1930s, reaching its apogee with the 1972 Club of Rome report [37]), is now beginning to be on the defensive. There are now increasingly scholars like Harold J. Barnett and Chandler Morse[38] and Julian Simon,[39] who have few if any worries about our running out of raw materials and who wonder ever more frequently in print whether in reality we can find in the stationary (population) state the necessary balance between the expectations of the young and the retired and the capacities of the economically productive.

Where do we come out? Any answer, it seems to me, has two elements—the rationale and the policy. Any changes with regard to both the rationale and the policy start with what we are currently thinking and doing. On the side of the rationale, I think that the pronatalist argument is emerging as the more interesting and relevant.

[35] Hugh Dalton, "The Theory of Population," *Economica*, n.s., vol. 8 (March 1928), pp. 28-50.

[36] John Maynard Keynes, "A Reply to Sir William Beveridge," *Economic Journal*, vol. 33 (December 1923), pp. 476-86; cf. also my essay, "Some Economic Growth Problems and the Part Population Policy Plays," *Quarterly Journal of Economics*, vol. 89 (May 1975), pp. 249-56.

[37] Donella H. Meadows, Dennis L. Meadows, Jørgen Randers, and William W. Behrens III, *The Limits to Growth: A Report for the Club of Rome's Project on the Predicament of Mankind* (New York: Universe; London: Earth Island, 1972).

[38] Harold J. Barnett and Chandler Morse, *Scarcity and Growth: The Economics of Natural Resource Availability* (Baltimore: Johns Hopkins University Press, 1963).

[39] Julian Simon, *The Ultimate Resource* (Princeton, N.J.: Princeton University Press, 1981).

I expect that future thinking will reflect this. And as for policy, the need to consider the community's future, as measured in terms of increasing output and expanding the ranks of well-educated youth, seems to me more important than worrying about increasing the equality of per capita consumption.

The Exploding Cost of Social Security

Colin D. Campbell

Summary

From 1970 to 1981, the payroll tax rate for social security, employer-employee combined, increased from 9.6 percent to 13.3 percent. By 1990, this rate is scheduled to rise to 15.3 percent. The taxable wage base of the payroll tax, now $29,700, more than tripled from 1970 to 1981 and will increase in line with average taxable wages in future years. In spite of these large increases, according to the intermediate forecast in the 1980 Annual Report *of the board of trustees of the OASDI trust funds, payroll tax rates scheduled for the next seventy-five years are 1.52 percentage points too low, not including the expected deficit for hospital insurance. It is hoped that the shortage expected in the early 1980s can be averted by shifting funds from the DI fund to the OASI fund. The financial problems of the entire system will become especially serious after the year 2030.*

As recently as 1972, benefits were raised 20 percent and the system was described as overfinanced. Because the system is financed pay-as-you-go (rather than by accumulating a reserve fund sufficiently large to meet its future financial obligations), the cost of the system is very sensitive to the actuarial assumptions used in assessing the balance between income and outgo. The demographic and economic assumptions relied on by the actuaries in the early 1970s were out-of-date. In recent decades, the birth rate, the real wage differential (the difference between the increase in wages and the increase in prices), and the mortality rate had dropped; also inflation and early retirement had increased. In addition, there was a flaw in the automatic indexing formula (corrected in 1977) that caused replacement ratios (the ratio of an individual's benefits to his preretire-

ment earnings) to be out of control during rapid inflation. The decline in the birth rate will reduce the funds available in the future to support the retired and disabled and their dependents. The increase in early retirement has both decreased the income of the system and increased the benefit load; the decrease in mortality has raised the benefit load. The decline in the real wage differential has caused an immediate shortfall of revenues relative to benefits.

Because of large increases in benefits in the early 1970s, average replacement ratios rose from under 35 percent in 1955–1971 to 43 percent in 1975 and to 46 percent in 1979. These higher ratios probably provide more than the floor of protection originally intended by the system. The benefits of those who are retired depend on the willingness of workers to pay the taxes required. The costs of social security must be kept within reasonable limits, and radical reform may be necessary.

The difficulties of the system are seen in this essay as a result of the nature of the system and the problems of long-range planning. Possible solutions to the exploding cost are to encourage people to work more years by extending the normal retirement age and by discouraging early retirement, to return replacement ratios to their pre-1970 levels by changing the method of indexing for inflation, or to substitute a flat rate grant that guarantees everyone a minimum of subsistence.

Introduction

The most important problem facing the social security system is its exploding cost. The exploding cost is significant because it raises questions about the system's viability and the possible need for radical reform. The objective of this essay is to show the way in which the social security system's financial problems developed and to inquire into the reasons for these problems.

As shown in table 1, from 1970 to 1981 the payroll tax rate (employer and employee combined) for old-age, survivors, and disability insurance (OASDI) was increased from 8.4 percent to 10.7 percent; including hospital insurance (HI), the tax rate was increased from 9.6 percent to 13.3 percent. Also from 1970 to 1981, the taxable wage base was increased from $7,800 to $29,700—over three times the original amount. Because of increases in the taxable wage base, the percentage of covered workers with their entire earnings taxed has risen from about 64 percent in 1965 to 85 percent in 1977 and will rise to more than 90 percent as a result of the increases in the

TABLE 1

SOCIAL SECURITY TAX RATES FOR OASDHI, EMPLOYEE AND
EMPLOYER COMBINED, 1969–1990

Year	Tax Rate[a] (excluding HI) (%)	Maximum Wage Base ($)	Tax Rate (including HI) (%)
1969–70	8.4	7,800	9.6
1971	9.2	7,800	10.4
1972	9.2	9,000	10.4
1973	9.7	10,800	11.7
1974	9.9	13,200	11.7
1975	9.9	14,100[b]	11.7
1976	9.9	15,300[b]	11.7
1977	9.9	16,500[b]	11.7
1978	10.1	17,700[b]	12.1
1979	10.16	22,900	12.26
1980	10.16	25,900	12.26
1981	10.7	29,700	13.3
1982–84[c]	10.8	[b]	13.4
1985[c]	11.4	[b]	14.1
1986–89[c]	11.4	[b]	14.3
1990[c]	12.4	[b]	15.3

NOTE: HI = hospital insurance.

[a] The OASDI payroll tax rate for the self-employed is approximately 75 percent of the combined employee-employer OASDI tax rate (or one and a half times the employee rate).

[b] From 1975 through 1978, automatic increases in the maximum wage base were made each January following automatic increases in benefits. The amount of the increase was determined by the rise in average taxable wages between the first quarters of the two previous years, rounded to the nearest multiple of $300. The substantial increases in the maximum wage base from 1979 through 1981 were legislated in 1977. After 1981 the maximum wage base will again be increased automatically in line with average wages.

[c] As scheduled in the law.

SOURCE: *Social Security Bulletin, Annual Statistical Supplement, 1977-79*, p. 34.

taxable wage base legislated in 1977.[1] The upward trend in payroll taxes will continue during the 1980s. The payroll tax rate for OASDI is scheduled to increase to 12.4 percent in 1990; the tax rate for OASDHI is scheduled to rise to 15.3 percent. The taxable wage base will increase with the rise in average wages.

[1] *Social Security Bulletin, Annual Statistical Supplement, 1977-79*, p. 88.

Despite the scheduled increases in payroll taxes, they are not expected to be large enough to cover either the short-run or the long-run needs of the system. In the *1980 Annual Report* of the board of trustees of the OASDI trust funds (which covers both the OASI trust fund and the separate DI trust fund), it was estimated that the OASI fund would be depleted in 1980 or 1982.[2] Although it is hoped that the depletion of the OASI trust fund can be avoided by shifting revenues to it from the DI trust fund, it is not certain that this will be enough. The social security system has been operating with a long-run (seventy-five-year) actuarial deficit ever since 1973 (see table 2). According to the intermediate forecast in the *1980 Annual Report,* payroll tax rates scheduled for OASDI over the next seventy-five years are 1.52 percentage points too low.[3] The financial problems of the system will become especially serious after the year 2030. Although it is estimated that there will be a surplus in the OASDI accounts of 1.19 percent of payroll from 1980 to 2004, and a small deficit of 1.17 percent from 2005 to 2029, there will be a deficit of 4.58 percent of payroll from 2030 to 2054.[4] If hospital insurance is included, the estimated deficit starting in the year 2030 is much larger—between 8 and 9 percent of payroll.[5]

The social security system is particularly vulnerable to rising costs because it is financed pay-as-you-go rather than by accumulating a reserve fund sufficiently large to meet its future financial obligations. The funds to pay current benefits come from the payroll taxes that are currently collected. In a pay-as-you-go system, funds are not set aside for a taxpayer's benefits when he retires but go to provide benefits for those who are currently retired. The benefits of

[2] The board of trustees is required by law to submit to Congress an annual report on the status of the OASDI trust funds. The members of the board are the secretary of the Treasury, the secretary of labor, and the secretary of health and human services. The commissioner of social security is the secretary of the board. The annual reports of the board include five-year estimates of income and outgo as well as estimates of OASDI expenditures as a percent of taxable payroll for the next seventy-five years. For the financing of the social security system to be in balance, the payroll tax rates scheduled in the future must be high enough to cover the future costs of the system.

[3] The board of trustees presents long-range cost estimates based on three alternative sets of demographic and economic assumptions. Alternative I is known as the optimistic set of assumptions; Alternative II, the intermediate set; and Alternative III, the pessimistic set.

[4] *1980 Annual Report of the Board of Trustees of the Federal Old-Age and Survivors Insurance and Disability Insurance Trust Funds,* p. 78. Hereafter OASDI annual reports will be cited simply as *Annual Report.*

[5] See A. Haeworth Robertson, *Social Security: Prospects for Change* (New York: William M. Mercer, 1978), p. 12.

TABLE 2

ESTIMATED AVERAGE EXPENDITURES, AVERAGE SCHEDULED
TAX RATE, AND ACTUARIAL BALANCE FOR THE NEXT
SEVENTY-FIVE YEARS, EXPRESSED AS A PERCENTAGE OF
TAXABLE PAYROLL, OASDI, 1972–1980

Year of Forecast	Estimated Average Expenditures	Average Scheduled Tax Rate	Actuarial Balance
1972	9.23	10.27	1.04
1973	10.95	10.63	−0.32
1974	13.89	10.91	−2.98
1975	16.26	10.94	−5.32
1976	18.93	10.97	−7.96
1977	19.19	10.99	−8.20
1978	13.55	12.16	−1.40
1979	13.38	12.19	−1.20
1980	13.74	12.22	−1.52

NOTE: These projections use the intermediate set of assumptions about future economic and demographic developments.
SOURCE: *Annual Report of the Board of Trustees of the Federal Old-Age and Survivors Insurance and Disability Insurance Trust Funds*, 1972 to 1980.

present workers are to be financed by the taxes paid by the working population as of some future date. The individual is viewed as having a right to benefits when he retires because he gave up part of his earnings during his working life to support the aged during their retirement. Still, because the benefits of those who are retired depend on the willingness of workers to pay the taxes required, the tax burden on workers must not become so heavy that workers are not willing to pay them.

The 20 Percent Increase in Benefits Legislated in 1972

An underlying cause of the system's financial difficulties during the 1970s was the 20 percent increase in benefits enacted by Congress in 1972. Benefits had also been increased 15 percent in 1970 and 10 percent in 1971.

An interesting aspect of the system's present difficulties is that in the early 1970s there was no awareness of any financial problems. In 1972, both the five-year and the seventy-five-year forecasts in the annual report of the board of trustees were very optimistic.[6] The trustees expected that over the next five years, payroll tax revenues would exceed expenditures by substantial amounts. Over the next seventy-five years, using dynamic assumptions of rising earnings and prices, the trustees predicted that an average payroll tax rate for OASDI of only 9.23 percent would be adequate and that the OASDI program was overfinanced by about 10 percent.

Looking back, the 20 percent increase in benefits in 1972 was a serious mistake. The year 1972 was an election year, and there were undoubtedly political pressures behind the increase. As a result of this increase in benefits, the ratio of benefits to preretirement earnings was raised sharply above the levels that had previously existed. From 1955 to 1970, the replacement ratio for a worker with average earnings varied from 31 to 34 percent; by 1975, this ratio had risen to 43 percent, and it rose further to 46 percent in 1979.[7] If replacement ratios had not been raised in the 1970s, tax revenues would probably have been large enough to cover the unanticipated rise in short-run cost.

The Indexation of Benefits. The 1972 amendments also provided for automatic increases in benefits whenever the consumer price index rises 3 percent or more. No action by Congress is necessary. The first automatic increase in benefits occurred in June 1975, and there have been increases in benefits in June of each year ever since.

Shortly after the enactment of indexed benefits, it was realized that the system's method of indexing benefits could lead to sharp and unpredictable increases in the long-range cost of the system. Although the method of adjusting benefits for inflation was changed in the 1977 amendments to the Social Security Act, there still are problems (discussed in the following section of this essay) with the method of indexing benefits whenever consumer prices rise rapidly as compared with the rise in wages.

Unexpected Demographic and Economic Trends

Starting in 1974, it became apparent that several unexpected demographic and economic trends were going to raise the cost of the system very sharply unless changes were made. These trends were (1) the decline in the birth rate, (2) the accelerated inflation and its

---

[6] *1972 Annual Report*, pp. 18-21, 32.

[7] U.S. Senate, Committee on Finance, *Staff Data and Materials Relating to Social Security Financing*, 95th Congress, 1st session, June 1977, p. 47.

effect on adjusting benefits for inflation, and (3) the decline in the real wage differential (the difference between the rate of increase in average wages in covered employment and the rate of increase in the consumer price index). The flaw in the method of adjusting benefits for inflation was corrected in the 1977 amendments. No changes have yet been made to adjust the system to the decline in the birth rate or the decline in the real wage differential. Two other developments that are adding to the system's financial difficulties are the decline in the mortality rate and the continuation of the trend toward earlier retirement. The following section discusses in more detail these unexpected problems.

The Decline in the Birth Rate. The *1974 Annual Report* of the board of trustees was the first to show that the trustees realized that future costs were going to be much higher than had been expected, even though the trustees were still unaware of how serious the problem was. As shown in table 2, the estimated long-run deficit for OASDI was raised from 0.32 percent to 2.98 percent of taxable payroll. A deficit of this size meant that payroll tax rates scheduled in the law for future years were about three percentage points too low.

The sharply higher long-range cost estimated in 1974 was the result primarily of changes in projections of population trends. Table 3 shows that the birth rate in the United States rose from 1940 to 1957 and then declined from 1957 to 1978. In 1972, the birth rate projections used to estimate long-range costs were still based on the high birth rates before the downturn.[8] If Congress had used lower birth-rate assumptions in that year, there would have been a seventy-five-year actuarial deficit rather than the reported surplus, and Congress might not have raised social security benefits 20 percent.[9] In 1974, the actuaries reduced their forecasts of fertility rates, and the predicted long-range actuarial deficit jumped several percentage points.

It is not surprising that the system's actuaries were slow to adjust their projections based on the birth rate. As shown in table 3, there had been a rise in the birth rate from 1940 to 1957. When the birth rate started to decline, the actuaries did not know that it would

[8] In 1972, the actual birth rate was 30 percent below the average of the high and low projected birth rates assumed by the social security actuaries. See Robert S. Kaplan, *Financial Crisis in the Social Security System* (Washington, D.C.: American Enterprise Institute, 1976), p. 5.

[9] Robert J. Myers warned in 1972 against relying on high birth-rate projections. See "Social Security's Hidden Hazards," *Wall Street Journal*, July 28, 1972. Myers was chief actuary of the Social Security Administration from 1947 to 1970.

TABLE 3
BIRTH RATE, UNITED STATES, 1940–1978

Year	Rate per 1,000 Population	Year	Rate per 1,000 Population
1940	19.4	1960	23.7
1941	20.3	1961	23.3
1942	22.2	1962	22.4
1943	22.7	1963	21.7
1944	21.2	1964	21.0
1945	20.4	1965	19.4
1946	24.1	1966	18.4
1947	26.6	1967	17.8
1948	24.9	1968	17.5
1949	24.5	1969	17.8
1950	24.1	1970	18.4
1951	24.9	1971	17.2
1952	25.1	1972	15.6
1953	25.0	1973	14.9
1954	25.3	1974	14.9
1955	25.0	1975	14.8
1956	25.2	1976	14.8
1957	25.3	1977	15.4
1958	24.5	1978	15.3
1959	24.0		

SOURCE: U.S. Bureau of the Census, *Historical Statistics of the United States, Colonial Times to 1970* (1975), p. 49; and *Statistical Abstract of the United States, 1979*, p. 60.

fall further. What is astonishing is that they did not begin to revise their birth-rate projections until seventeen years after the decline started. Of course, members of Congress would not have welcomed forecasts of higher costs based on lower birth-rate projections. Higher costs would have required higher payroll tax rates.

The decline in the birth rate since 1957 would not have increased estimated future costs if the social security system had been funded rather than financed pay-as-you-go. The costs of the pension systems of state and local governments and private institutions that are well funded are unaffected by the decline in the birth rate. In these systems, for each person a large enough fund is accumulated to cover the cost of his future benefits (assuming average life expectancy). One would not expect the architects of the social security system to have foreseen the financial difficulties caused by the sensitivity of costs in a pay-as-you-go system to changes in the birth rate, and there were some reasons to prefer pay-as-you-go financing.

In a pay-as-you-go system, a decline in the birth rate will raise the future cost of the system by increasing the number of beneficiaries relative to the number of workers paying taxes. The sensitivity of the payroll tax rate to the ratio of beneficiaries to workers may be illustrated by the formula for the payroll tax rate shown in equation 2. In a pay-as-you-go system:

Total payroll tax receipts = Total benefits
Total payroll tax receipts = The payroll tax rate (t) *times* the number of workers (N_w) *times* the average covered wage (W)
Total benefits = Number of beneficiaries (N_b) *times* the average benefit (B).

Therefore $t \cdot N_w \cdot W = N_b \cdot B$, and (1)

$$t = \frac{N_b}{N_w} \cdot \frac{B}{W} \qquad (2)$$

In equation 2, the payroll tax rate is equal to the ratio of the number of beneficiaries to the number of workers multiplied by the ratio of average benefits to average covered wages.

The decline in the birth rate since 1957 will eventually have a significant effect on the ratio of beneficiaries to workers. In 1980, there were approximately 35 million OASDI beneficiaries and 114 million persons paying social security taxes—a ratio of 30 percent.[10] Fifty years from now, according to the intermediate cost projections, this ratio is expected to rise to 52 percent. At that time, those persons born during the baby boom in the 1940s and 1950s will have retired, and the labor force will be relatively small because of the decline in the birth rate in the 1960s and 1970s.

As equation 2 shows, if the ratio of benefits to average covered wages is held constant, the payroll tax rate must rise if the ratio of beneficiaries to workers increases. Now, because the ratio of beneficiaries to workers is approximately 30 percent and the ratio of average benefits to average covered wages is 36 percent, a payroll tax rate of 10.8 percent (the OASDI rate scheduled for 1982) roughly balances receipts and expenditures. If the ratio of beneficiaries to workers rises, as predicted, to approximately 50 percent, and the ratio of average benefits to average wages is held the same (at 36 percent), a payroll tax rate of 18 percent would be necessary.

[10] *1980 Annual Report*, p. 85.

Problems with the Indexing of Benefits for Inflation. In the *1975 Annual Report* of the board of trustees, it was realized without any doubt that the system's financial problems were very serious. It was widely reported in the press that the system was "on the road to bankruptcy." As shown in table 2, in 1975 the seventy-five-year actuarial deficit was increased from 2.98 percentage points to 5.32 percentage points. A new problem had emerged—known as the flaw in the indexing system enacted in 1972.[11]

In 1976 and 1977, the estimated deficits over the next seventy-five years rose further. As shown in table 2, in 1977 long-range average expenditures as a percentage of payroll rose to 19.19 percent—more than double the rate estimated in 1972. When the flaw in the indexing system was corrected in 1977, long-range expenditures as a percentage of payroll fell from 19.19 percent to 13.55 percent, and the long-range actuarial deficit as a percentage of payroll fell from 8.2 percent to 1.4 percent.

The reason why the actuaries were not aware of the flaw in the indexing system in 1972 is that the defects in the traditional technique for adjusting benefits for inflation were not apparent as long as the actuarial projections of future cost were based on the assumption that future rates of increase in consumer prices would be only 1 or 2 percent a year. The overindexing problem became evident only after actuaries adjusted their long-range projections to the higher rates of inflation that started after 1965.[12]

The actuaries were again slow to change their projections. They viewed the more rapid inflation as temporary and expected the economy to return to the low rates of inflation that had prevailed before 1965.[13] If the actuaries had assumed higher rates of inflation in their seventy-five-year projections in 1972 when indexed benefits were legislated, they would undoubtedly have discovered at that time the flaw in the way benefits were being adjusted for inflation.

From 1975 to 1977, the large long-run actuarial deficits were considered less urgent than the need to raise additional payroll tax

[11] The overindexing problem was first publicized in 1973. See Geoffrey N. Calvert, "New Realistic Projections of Social Security Benefits and Taxes: Their Impact on the Economy and on Future Private Pensions" (Address delivered at the American Pension Conference, New York, December 4, 1973).

[12] For illustrations of the sensitivity of future social security expenditures as a percentage of taxable payroll to the rate of increase in the consumer price index, assuming a constant increase in real wages, see U.S. Senate, Panel on Social Security Financing, *Report to the Committee on Finance*, 94th Congress, 1st session, February 1975, pp. 15-18.

[13] Martha Derthick, *Policy-Making for Social Security* (Washington, D.C.: Brookings Institution, 1979), pp. 392-93.

revenues promptly. In the 1976 report, it was stated that the long-term deficits "should be interpreted with caution because they are based upon future benefit levels which are much higher, relative to preretirement earnings, than are currently prevailing benefit levels and which will not materialize if realistic legislation is enacted to redress the imbalance." [14]

The way in which overindexing increased the cost of the system is by increasing the ratio of average benefits to average covered wages in equation 2. Given the ratio of beneficiaries to workers, if the ratio of average benefits to average covered wages rises, the payroll tax rate necessary to cover the cost of the system will rise.

The old method of adjusting benefits for inflation was over-indexed because the promised benefits of workers *who had not yet retired* could rise not only because they were adjusted periodically for increases in the consumer price index but because at the same time inflation pushed up the average monthly wage on which a worker's benefits are based.[15] Table 4 shows the way in which social security benefits were adjusted for the increase in the consumer price index in 1978. The percentages allowed of a worker's average monthly wage were increased 5.9 percent. The amount of the increase was based on the increase in the consumer price index from the first quarter of 1976 to the first quarter of 1977. In this example, it is assumed that the worker retired at age sixty-five, had earnings equal to the maximum wage base throughout his averaging period, and was eligible for the maximum monthly benefit.

Table 5 shows the calculations of the average monthly wages of the same workers for whom benefits were calculated in table 4. The averaging period for estimating average monthly wages is based on all years of employment from 1951 to the year prior to that in which a person attains age sixty-two, excluding the five years of lowest earnings. If a person continues to work past age sixty-two up to age sixty-five, however, he is permitted to substitute these three years of earnings for three earlier years of lower earnings. The workers considered in table 5 are assumed to have done this. Table 5 shows that for a worker retiring at age sixty-five on January 1, 1977, the highest average monthly wage possible was $634; for a worker aged sixty-five retiring on January 1, 1978, the maximum average monthly wage was $688—8.5 percent higher than a year earlier.

[14] *1976 Annual Report*, p. 2.

[15] If benefits rose solely because of increases in consumer prices, inflation would not normally cause the ratio of average benefits to average wages to rise. Because wages usually rise faster than consumer prices, average benefits would rise less rapidly than average wages.

TABLE 4

ILLUSTRATION OF THE INDEXING OF SOCIAL SECURITY BENEFITS,
JANUARY 1, 1977, AND JANUARY 1, 1978

Benefit Formula[a]			Benefit Formula[b]		
Percentage allowed	Level of average monthly wage ($)	Primary insurance amount ($)	Percentage allowed	Level of average monthly wage ($)	Primary insurance amount ($)
137.77	First 110	151.55	145.90	First 110	160.49
50.10	Next 290	145.29	53.06	Next 290	153.87
46.82	Next 150	70.23	49.58	Next 150	74.37
55.05	Next 84	46.24	58.30	Next 100	58.30
			32.42	Next 38	12.32
Total	634	413.31	Total	688	459.35

[a] Worker retiring January 1, 1977, entitled to maximum benefit.
[b] Worker retiring January 1, 1978, entitled to maximum benefit.
SOURCE: U.S. Senate, Committee on Finance, *Staff Data and Materials Relating to Social Security Financing*, 95th Congress, 1st session, p. 5.

As shown in table 5, when there is inflation, a worker's average monthly wage will rise as the higher wages earned in more recent years are added to the lower wages earned in earlier years. In table 5, the increase in the average monthly wage was the result of substituting the new legislated maximum earnings base of $16,500 in 1978 for the low base of $4,200 in 1957. In both 1977 and 1978, nineteen years of covered wages were counted. This is unusual. In the future, the number of years counted will be increased by one each year until it reaches thirty-five years. Although the effect of inflation on a worker's average monthly wage is gradual, the effect can cause the future cost of social security to rise sharply.

Even with overindexing, the method of adjusting benefits for inflation illustrated in table 4 did not cause the benefit-wage ratio in equation 2 to rise if future rates of inflation were assumed to be low—1 percent or 2 percent a year. This is because at low rates of inflation the difference between the rate of expansion in prices and wages is very large. For example, if consumer prices are assumed to rise at 2 percent a year and wages at 4 percent (assuming a 2 percent increase in the productivity of labor), prices—and thus benefits—would rise only one-half as fast as wages. If consumer prices are assumed to rise at 6 percent a year, however, and wages at 8

TABLE 5

CALCULATION OF AVERAGE MONTHLY WAGE OF WORKER
ENTITLED TO MAXIMUM MONTHLY BENEFIT, RETIRING
IN 1977 AND 1978
(dollars)

Year or Period	Maximum Wage Base for Year	1977, Covered Wages for Period	1978, Covered Wages for Period
1958	4,200	4,200	—
1959–65	4,800	33,600	33,600
1966–67	6,600	13,200	13,200
1968–71	7,800	31,200	31,200
1972	9,000	9,000	9,000
1973	10,800	10,800	10,800
1974	13,200	13,200[a]	13,200
1975	14,100	14,100[a]	14,100[a]
1976	15,300	15,300[a]	15,300[a]
1977	16,500		16,500[a]
1958–76		144,600	
1959–77			156,900
Average yearly wage[b]		7,611	8,258
Average monthly wage		634	688

[a] Wages covered after reaching age sixty-two have been substituted for wages earned in earlier years.
[b] From 1976 to 1978, the total number of years in the averaging period for men was frozen at nineteen in order to eliminate the difference with the averaging period for women. Starting in 1979, the total number of years that must be counted for both men and women will be increased by one each year until it reaches thirty-five.
SOURCE: *Social Security Bulletin, Annual Statistical Supplement, 1975*, pp. 7, 32.

percent (assuming again a 2 percent increase in the productivity of labor), prices—and thus benefits—would rise three-fourths as fast as wages. As a result, at the higher rates of inflation it does not take much overindexing to raise the benefit-wage ratio. The effect of the higher average monthly wage of workers as a result of steadily increasing wages, combined with the rise in benefits as a result of the upward adjustment in the percentages allowed is enough to raise the benefit-wage ratio.

An example of the benefit formula that was designed to eliminate overindexing is shown in table 6. The formula shown may be

TABLE 6
New Social Security Benefit Formula for
Primary Insurance Amount, 1981

Percentage Allowed (1)	Average Indexed Monthly Wage ($) (2)
90	First 211
32	Next 1,063
15	Remainder above 1,274

Note: The amounts in column 2 are changed yearly to reflect changes in average wages of all workers. These amounts are for persons reaching age sixty-two in 1981. Until 1983, persons may use either the old formula or this formula.
Source: *Social Security Bulletin*, January 1981, p. 1.

used by persons reaching age sixty-two in 1981. This new formula enacted in 1977 radically changes the method of indexing benefits for inflation. For persons not yet retired, the principal change is that benefits are no longer increased by adjusting the percentages allowed as shown in table 4.

To calculate a worker's average indexed monthly wage on which benefits are now based, each prior year's wage is multiplied by the ratio of the average wage of all workers two years prior to that in which the worker reached age sixty-two to the average wage in the year the wage was earned. If the average wage doubled between 1967 and 1980, 1967 earnings of $7,000, for example, would be multiplied by two, and the resulting $14,000 would be the amount included in the 1980 calculation of a worker's average indexed monthly wage. The earnings for each year of a person's working history (1951 and later) would be indexed in the same way. Indexed annual wages are then averaged and converted to a monthly figure in the same way that unindexed wages formerly were.

Under the new benefit formula, the overindexing problem is eliminated. The benefit-wage ratio in equation 2 will not rise as a result of inflation because the benefits of those who are still employed will not rise any faster than the average wage of all workers. If, for example, the average wage of all workers rises 10 percent because of inflation, the average indexed monthly wages, and thus the promised benefits of those still employed, would go up the same percentage.

In the new formula, the average indexed monthly wage levels (also called wage brackets or "bend points") in column 2 of table 6 will be raised as the average wage of all workers rises. In 1981, for example, because the average wage of all workers had risen 8.75 percent, the lowest bracket was raised from $194 to $211; the middle bracket from $977 to $1,063; and the highest bracket from $1,171 and over to $1,274 and over. This adjustment is designed to keep rising wages from pushing persons up into higher brackets. Without this adjustment, inflation would cause replacement ratios to fall.

The Relatively Low Growth of Wages Compared with the Increase in Consumer Prices. The recent decline in the rate of growth of wages as compared with the increase in consumer prices is the third major change that has adversely affected the financial condition of the social security system. It has been an important cause of the system's short-range financial difficulties.

The first recognition of serious short-run financing problems was in the *1975 Annual Report.* In this report, the board of trustees predicted that additional revenues would be needed to prevent the exhaustion of both the OASI and DI trust funds soon after 1979.

The decline in the growth of wages relative to the growth of consumer prices in the 1970s is the result of both the slower increase in the productivity of labor and upward biases in the consumer price index. Table 7 shows the sharp drop in the average real wage differential from two percentage points in the 1960s to zero in the 1970s. If consumer prices rise faster than wages, the social security system is obviously in trouble. Because the benefits of those already retired are indexed to consumer prices, average benefits would rise faster than average covered wages. As is shown in equation 2, this would increase the cost of benefits as a percent of payroll and require higher payroll tax rates.

The decline in the growth of wages relative to the growth in consumer prices in the 1970s is unusual and is a type of change that one would not have expected the actuaries to have foreseen. Throughout most of the history of the United States, wages have risen faster than prices because of increases in productivity. The reasons for the decline in the growth of productivity during the 1970s are varied and are still not well understood.[16] It is also not known how long the decline in productivity growth will continue.

---

[16] See John W. Kendrick, "Productivity Trends and the Recent Slowdown: Historical Perspective, Causal Factors, and Policy Options," and Edward F. Denison, "Where Has Productivity Gone?" in William Fellner, ed., *Contemporary Economic Problems 1979* (Washington, D.C.: American Enterprise Institute, 1979), pp. 17-77.

TABLE 7

REAL WAGE DIFFERENTIAL, 1960–1979

(percent)

| Calendar Year | Average Annual Percentage Increase | | Real Wage Differential[a] |
	Average wages in covered employment	Consumer price index	
1960–64	3.4	1.3	2.1
1965–69	5.4	3.4	1.9
1970–74	6.3	6.1	0.2
1975	6.5	9.1	−2.5
1976	8.4	5.8	2.5
1977	6.9	6.5	0.4
1978	8.1	7.6	0.5
1979	8.3	11.5	−3.1

[a] The difference between the percentage increase in average annual wages in covered employment and the percentage increase in the average annual consumer price index.

SOURCE: *1980 Annual Report of the Board of Trustees of the Federal Old-Age and Survivors Insurance and Disability Insurance Trust Funds*, June 17, 1980, p. 41.

There are several causes of the upward bias in the consumer price index. When certain prices rise very rapidly, as did the price of oil in the 1970s, a fixed-weight index becomes overly affected by those items whose prices have risen rapidly, and the overall rate of inflation may be overstated. Also, in recent years of sharply rising prices of homes, the way the consumer price index treats newly purchased homes has been criticized. It is said that housing prices should be treated differently from the prices of consumer goods and services because houses are not consumed or used in the month they are purchased. Although revisions in the consumer price index to eliminate these upward biases could have a significant effect on the financing problems of the social security system, it is not known when or if such revisions will ever be made.

A major objective of the 1977 amendments to the Social Security Act was to avoid the depletion of the OASDI trust funds resulting from the decline in the real wage differential. The increases in payroll tax rates scheduled for the 1980s and the sharp increases in the taxable wage base from 1978 to 1981 shown in table 1 were enacted in 1977. In addition, in that year the portion of the payroll tax rate allocated to disability insurance was increased, and the portion allocated to hospital insurance was decreased. In the *1978 Annual Report*, the first following the 1977 amendments, the trustees state over-optimistically, "The Social Security Amendments of 1977 have restored the financial soundness of the cash benefit programs over the short-range and medium-range periods, beginning in 1981, and greatly improved the long-range actuarial status." [17]

By 1979 and 1980, the confidence of the board of trustees in the results of the 1977 amendments was fading rapidly. In 1980, it was estimated that in each of the next five years OASI expenditures would exceed income, and the assets in the OASI fund would become insufficient to pay benefits in late 1981 or early 1982. The reason for the unexpected shortfall in the OASI fund, estimated in 1980, is that the economic assumptions underlying the 1978 forecast turned out to be too optimistic. As shown in table 8, consumer prices rose more rapidly than expected, although wages in covered employment did not. As a result, the real wage differentials from 1977 to 1979 were much lower than those in even the pessimistic cost estimates made in 1978.

In the *1980 Annual Report* of the board of trustees, the real wage differential for the intermediate set of assumptions is assumed to rise from —4.6 percent in 1980 to 1.2 percent in 1984.[18] Whether or not the real wage differential rises as assumed will depend partly on whether the increases in the productivity of labor become larger than they have been in the 1970s. Unless the real wage differential rises as assumed, or unless Congress amends the law so that the benefits of those who are retired are no longer tied to the consumer price index, the short-run financial crises will continue. To change the system, it has been suggested that the pensions of those already retired be indexed either to the increase in wages or in consumer prices, whichever is lower. If social security benefits had been indexed in this way in the past decade, the short-run financial problems that have plagued the system would have been much less serious. It has also been suggested that because social security benefits are exempt from income taxes, the cost-of-living increases in social security benefits should be adjusted by 85 percent, instead of 100 percent, of the increases in the consumer price index. This indexing problem could also be eliminated by taxing social security benefits, although the revenues raised would go to general revenues rather

[17] *1978 Annual Report*, p. 53.

[18] *1980 Annual Report*, p. 41. For a critical analysis of the assumed rise in the real wage differential, see Roland E. King and Clifford K. Powell, "A Critical Analysis of the Assumptions in the 1980 Social Security Trustees' Reports," *Society of Actuaries, Transactions*, vol. 33 (1981), pp. 87-98.

TABLE 8
PESSIMISTIC ECONOMIC AND DEMOGRAPHIC ASSUMPTIONS IN THE 1978 ANNUAL REPORT OF THE BOARD OF TRUSTEES, COMPARED WITH ACTUAL CONDITIONS, 1977–1979

Calendar Year	Average Annual Percentage Increase			Real Wage Differential[a] (%)	Average Annual Unemployment (%)	Total Fertility Rate[b]
	Real GNP	Wages in covered employment	Consumer price index			
Pessimistic assumptions[c]						
1977	4.9	7.7	6.5	1.2	7.0	1,789
1978	4.7	7.2	6.1	1.1	6.3	1,745
1979	4.1	8.2	6.8	1.4	6.0	1,737
Actual conditions						
1977	5.3	6.9	6.5	0.4	7.0	1,795
1978	4.4	8.1	7.6	0.5	6.0	1,775
1979	2.3	8.3	11.5	−3.1	5.8	1,789

a The difference between the percentage increase in average annual wages in covered employment and the percentage increase in the average annual consumer price index.

b The number of children who would be born to 1,000 women in their lifetime if they were to experience the observed age-specific birth rates and were to survive the entire childbearing period.

c See footnote 3 of this chapter.

SOURCE: *1978 Annual Report of the Board of Trustees of the Federal Old-Age and Survivors Insurance and Disability Insurance Trust Funds,* May 16, 1978, p. 25; and *1980 Annual Report of the Board of Trustees of the Federal Old-Age and Survivors Insurance and Disability Insurance Trust Funds,* June 17, 1980, pp. 41 and 43.

than to the social security system.[19] A third suggestion is that the government tie benefits to some other type of index.

Other Causes of Increasing Cost. A new development that will raise the cost of social security is the decline in the mortality rate. The mortality rate has dropped sharply during the 1970s. The number of years that an average person at age sixty, for example, can expect to live increased more than one year between 1969–1971 and 1978 (for white males from 16.07 years to 17.2 years).[20] The improvement in life expectancy will add to the cost of social security by increasing the ratio of beneficiaries to covered workers.

During the past decade, the trend toward earlier retirement has also raised the cost of social security. The labor force participation rate of men aged fifty-five to sixty-four dropped from 83 percent in 1970 to 73 percent in 1979.[21] During the same period, the labor force participation rate of men aged forty-five to fifty-four dropped from 94 percent to 91 percent. Although the labor force participation rate of men sixty-five years of age and older has been declining over the past eighty years, for men before age sixty-five this is a new development. The trend toward earlier retirement is partially related to the increase in the number of persons receiving disability insurance.

The Significance of the Trends

Experts on social security have reacted very differently to the increasing cost of the system. Robert M. Ball, former commissioner of social security, opposes any major changes.[22] He suspects that the long-run projections of productivity and fertility are too low and that the forecasts of large deficits will turn out to be wrong. In his opinion, there will be adequate financing if the increases in payroll tax rates scheduled for the next ten years are implemented and if proposals to expand the program (such as eliminating the retirement test and giving married women workers larger benefits) are avoided. He is not concerned about the effect of the decline in the birth rate,

[19] On the taxing of social security benefits, see Mickey D. Levy, *The Tax Treatment of Social Security: Should the Exclusion of Benefits Be Eliminated?* (Washington, D.C.: American Enterprise Institute, 1980).

[20] *Vital Statistics of the United States, 1978*, vol. 2, sect. 5. See Mark Perlman, "Some Economic Consequences of the New Patterns of Population Growth," in this volume.

[21] Robert L. Clark and David T. Barker, *Reversing the Trend toward Early Retirement* (Washington, D.C.: American Enterprise Institute, 1981), tables 8 and 9.

[22] Robert M. Ball, *Social Security: Today and Tomorrow* (New York: Columbia University Press, 1978), pp. 74-76.

because he believes the increasing burden of providing benefits for the retired will be offset by the lower cost of caring for children. He advocates looking at the dependency ratio rather than at the ratio of retired persons to the working population.

In contrast, A. Haeworth Robertson, former chief actuary of the Social Security Administration, recommends major changes in the system.[23] He would (1) replace earnings-related benefits with a uniform retirement benefit for everyone set close to the poverty level, (2) raise the eligibility age (now sixty-two to sixty-five) to higher levels as people get healthier, and (3) eliminate the retirement test. He believes that major changes in the system are necessary to ensure that the rising costs are brought to a halt. In his opinion, the system should provide minimum benefits for people who can no longer work; he believes that it should not attempt to provide retirement benefits high enough to enable people to maintain a standard of living close to the level they were accustomed to before retirement.

Rising Tax Burdens. An important consequence of the financial crisis in the social security system is its effect on the overall tax burden. In the 1970s, the rise in the cost of social security was a major factor contributing to the increase in federal taxes as a percentage of net national product.[24] Because of the size of the social security system, when the cost of the system rises, the federal tax burden also tends to rise. In fiscal 1979, payroll tax collections for old-age, survivors, disability, and hospital insurance amounted to $119 billion, 25 percent of total federal tax revenues.

The scheduled increases in payroll tax rates during the 1980s will make it difficult to bring an end to the upward trend in the federal tax burden. The lower income tax rates proposed in the Reagan economic program will be offset to some extent by increased payroll tax rates. In addition, the large expansion in defense expenditures expected in the 1980s will add to the difficulty of reducing tax burdens.

Whenever additional revenues were needed in the past, they were obtained by raising either payroll tax rates or the taxable wage base; nevertheless, tax rates are now so high that further increases may be counterproductive. The higher tax rates may erode the tax base. The high income and payroll tax rates that now prevail already

[23] Robertson, *Social Security: Prospects for Change*, pp. 30-37.

[24] For an analysis of the rise in the federal tax burden, see Rudolph G. Penner, "The Future Growth of Government Budgets," in William Fellner, ed., *Contemporary Economic Problems 1980* (Washington, D.C.: American Enterprise Institute, 1980), pp. 103-33.

appear to be causing people to work fewer hours a week, take longer vacations, retire at an early age, take jobs where the conditions of employment are pleasant, or move to attractive areas of the country where the climate is mild. Also, recent studies of the underground economy indicate that high tax rates are encouraging widespread tax evasion.

The system's financial difficulties during the 1970s were caused in part by the decline in the increase in the productivity of labor. The supply-side effects of high tax rates on saving and investment may be one of the many factors that has contributed to the slower increase of the productivity of labor.[25] If so, raising payroll tax rates further would not be an effective way of correcting the system's financial imbalance.

It is often suggested that if old dependents merely replace young dependents, the increasing ratio of social security beneficiaries to workers as a result of the decline in the birth rate is not as serious a problem as is sometimes claimed. An increase in the tax burden caused by a rise in the ratio of social security beneficiaries to workers might be offset by a decrease in the tax burden because of a reduction in the ratio of children to workers. The dependency ratio including both old and young dependents is usually measured quite rigidly by counting all persons under eighteen years of age and all persons aged sixty-five and over as dependents (with those aged eighteen to sixty-five classed as nondependents). Projections of the dependency ratio measured in this way (assuming total fertility at the replacement level and net immigration at 400,000 a year) show little change in the dependency ratio from 1975 to 2050—41 percent in 1975, 39 percent in 1990 and 2000, and 41 percent in 2025 and 2050.[26]

Despite the relative constancy of the overall dependency ratio, changes in the composition of dependents may have significant effects on the tax burden. According to estimates by Robert L. Clark and Joseph J. Spengler, the per recipient public cost of transfers to the elderly is about three times as great as per recipient public expenditures for youths.[27] The changing composition of the depend-

25 See William Fellner, "The Declining Growth of American Productivity: An Introductory Note," and John W. Kendrick, "Productivity Trends and the Recent Slowdown: Historical Perspective, Causal Factors, and Policy Options," in William Fellner, ed., *Contemporary Economic Problems 1979* (Washington, D.C.: American Enterprise Institute, 1979), pp. 3-12, 17-69.

26 Robert L. Clark and Joseph J. Spengler, "Changing Demography and Dependency Costs: The Implications of Future Dependency Ratios and Their Composition," in Barbara Herzog, ed., *Aging and Income: Programs and Prospects for the Elderly* (New York: Human Science Press, 1978), pp. 55-89.

27 Clark and Spengler, in Herzog, *Aging and Income*, pp. 62 and 71.

ent population will also affect the levels of government differently because state and local governments administer the bulk of the public expenditures on children, and the federal government pays for most expenditures on the elderly population. In addition, there is a difference in attitude toward children as dependents and the elderly as dependents. Public expenditures on children (mostly for education) are usually viewed as an investment in the future citizens of the country, whereas social security benefits are regarded as transfer payments. Also, the popular acceptance of social security is based on its analogy with insurance, and on the way tax payments made by individuals are related to the amount of the benefits a worker receives when he retires.[28]

Distributing the Burden between Taxpayers and Beneficiaries. The way in which the rising cost of the social security system is going to be distributed between taxpayers and beneficiaries has yet to be determined. If the expected increase in cost is paid for by raising payroll taxes, the burden would be on wage earners and the self-employed. They currently number more than 114 million persons.[29] For most workers, coverage is compulsory. The only important groups still not taxed are approximately 2.4 million federal government civilian employees who have their own federal retirement system, plus approximately 3.5 million state and local government employees and 0.9 million employees of nonprofit institutions who have chosen not to participate.[30]

If, on the other hand, increases in payroll taxes are avoided by reducing benefits, the burden would be on the retired and other beneficiaries. There are currently more than 35 million OASDI beneficiaries.[31] With a total population of 225 million, this means that one in every six persons is receiving OASDI benefits. Only about 23 million of the persons receiving benefits are sixty-five years of age and over (but this is 92 percent of the total population in this age group).[32]

[28] William C. Mitchell, *The Popularity of Social Security: A Paradox in Public Choice* (Washington, D.C.: American Enterprise Institute, 1977).

[29] *1980 Annual Report*, p. 4.

[30] U.S. Department of Health, Education, and Welfare, *The Desirability and Feasibility of Social Security Coverage for Employees of Federal, State, and Local Governments and Private Nonprofit Organizations*, Report of the Universal Social Security Coverage Study Group, March 1980, pp. 137, 162, and 256.

[31] *Social Security Bulletin*, September 1980, p. 1.

[32] The 11.9 million under sixty-five include the disabled, survivors (children and dependent widows), dependents between the ages of eighteen and twenty-two who are attending school, and persons who chose to retire between ages sixty-two and sixty-five.

Although some beneficiaries work part time and pay some pay-roll taxes, in general if the higher cost of social security benefits were paid for by higher payroll taxes, there would be very little burden on beneficiaries. Because of the earnings test, social security beneficiaries may have only very limited earnings.[33]

Whether or not the long-run financial problem should be solved by reducing benefits depends partly on the general level of benefits. If the benefit level were very low, many persons would prefer raising payroll tax rates. Social security benefits have become larger than most people realize. In 1980, the *average* old-age benefit received by retired workers (men and women) was more than $4,000 a year.[34] An average retired worker with a spouse also age sixty-two or over would receive $6,000 a year. These benefits are tax-free and since 1975 have been indexed to consumer prices. In early 1981, the maximum benefit possible was approximately $8,000 per year for a retired worker age sixty-five and $12,000 for an elderly married couple. At the bottom end of the range, there are two minimum benefits. In 1980, the regular minimum benefit was $1,836 a year ($153 a month) for a worker who retires at sixty-five, and $2,754 for a couple. In the 1977 amendments, the minimum benefit was frozen at $121 a month ($1,452 a year), but for persons retiring at age sixty-five it amounts to more because of the way it is adjusted for cost-of-living increases. An alternative special minimum benefit is payable to workers who have been employed for many years at low wages. It is based on the number of years in covered employment rather than on a worker's average earnings. In 1980, the highest special minimum benefit was $3,468 a year ($298 a month).[35]

The official targets for social security replacement ratios for 1985 and subsequent years in table 9 show that social security bene-

---

[33] If a retired person aged sixty-five to seventy-one earns more than $5,500 in 1981, for example, his benefit is reduced one dollar for every two dollars earned, and if his earnings were sufficiently high, he would not be entitled to any benefit. For persons aged sixty-two to sixty-four, the earnings limit in 1981 was $4,080.

[34] *Social Security Bulletin*, November 1980, pp. 30-31.

[35] Ibid., p. 33. Many persons have recommended that the minimum benefits be eliminated. See U.S. General Accounting Office, *Minimum Social Security Benefit: A Windfall That Should be Eliminated*, Report to the Congress of the United States by the Comptroller General, HRD-80-29, December 10, 1979. The regular minimum benefit has enabled persons whose principal job is not covered by social security—primarily federal government and state and local government employees—to qualify for social security benefits even though they have paid only a small amount in payroll taxes. Also, because the Supplemental Security Income (SSI) program now assures a minimum income to all persons over sixty-five, minimum OASDI benefits are no longer necessary for this purpose.

TABLE 9

TARGETS FOR SOCIAL SECURITY REPLACEMENT RATIOS FOR
1985 AND SUBSEQUENT YEARS
(percent)

| | Replacement Ratio[a] | |
Level of Earnings	Single	Couple
Low[b]	53–56	79–84
Average[c]	40–42	60–64
Maximum[d]	23–29	34–43

[a] For each level of earnings and category of beneficiary, replacement ratios vary within the ranges indicated because of different years of retirement and different economic and demographic assumptions.

[b] $4,600 in 1977 with the values for other years adjusted to the trend in the average wage in covered employment.

[c] Average wage in covered employment.

[d] Maximum taxable earnings in covered employment ($16,500 in 1977).

SOURCE: *1978 Annual Report of the Board of Trustees of the Federal Old-Age and Survivors Insurance and Disability Insurance Trust Funds*, p. 51.

fits are now large enough to enable most workers to maintain their preretirement standard of living quite easily. These replacement ratios are the ratio of the benefit amount payable to a worker in his first year of retirement to his earnings in the year before retirement. Replacement ratios decline as the level of earnings increases because of the progressive tilt in the percentages allowed in the benefit formula. According to most estimates, retirees with incomes of $15,000 a year or less can maintain their preretirement living standards with social security benefits ranging from 80 percent down to 65 percent of preretirement earnings, depending on their level of earnings.[36] To persons with incomes as high as $50,000 a year, preretirement living standards can be maintained with replacement ratios of only 50 to 55 percent. This is primarily because (1) preretirement incomes are taxed heavily both by social security taxes and by federal, state, and local government income taxes, whereas social security benefits are excluded from both of these taxes; and (2) retirees do not have to pay work-related expenses. Estimates of

[36] See Alicia H. Munnell, "The Future of the U.S. Pension System," in Colin D. Campbell, ed., *Financing Social Security* (Washington, D.C.: American Enterprise Institute, 1979), pp. 254-61; and *An Interim Report: President's Commission on Pension Policy*, May 1980, pp. 12-18.

work-related expenses vary from 6 percent to over 13 percent of disposable income. Although social security benefits amount to less than 65 percent of preretirement income for many persons, most of these families had relatively high incomes and could be expected to own homes and to have at least some financial assets. Social security replacement ratios are least adequate for single persons.

Reducing the Cost of Social Security

An increase in payroll tax rates in future years could be avoided if social security replacement ratios were gradually reduced over the next three or four decades to the levels that existed before 1972. A proposal of this type was recommended to Congress by Professor William C. Hsiao in 1976. Professor Hsiao was the chairman of two important committees appointed by Congress to investigate the financial problems of the social security system.[37] His proposal, known as the Hsiao plan, was designed to solve both the overindexing problem and the problem resulting from the decline in the birth rate.[38] As has been explained, an alternative plan that solved the overindexing problem, but not the demographic problem, was adopted by Congress in the 1977 amendments. The Hsiao plan would have indexed a worker's past wages to consumer prices rather than to wages. As shown by the projections made by Hsiao in table 10, indexing past wages to prices would have made it possible to avoid the increase in expenditures as a percentage of taxable payroll caused by the decline in the birth rate. Despite this advantage of the Hsiao plan, Congress rejected it primarily because it resulted in a decline in social security replacement ratios to the same levels that existed before 1972, and in years after 2020 to lower levels. An estimate of the decline in replacement ratios under price indexing for single workers with average earnings is shown in table 11.

The principal argument against holding replacement ratios fixed despite contingencies such as the decline in the birth rate is that such a policy places the entire burden on the taxpayer (the wage

[37] The two reports prepared by these committees were U.S. Senate, Panel on Social Security Financing, *Report to the Committee on Finance*, 94th Congress, 1st session, February 1975; and Consultant Panel on Social Security, *Reports to the Congressional Research Service, Prepared for the Use of the Committee on Finance of the U.S. Senate and the Committee on Ways and Means of the U.S. House of Representatives*, Joint Committee Print, 94th Congress, 2d session, August 1976.

[38] See William C. Hsiao, "An Optimal Indexing Method for Social Security," in Colin D. Campbell, ed., *Financing Social Security*, pp. 19-40.

TABLE 10

Comparison of OASDI Long-Range Costs under Wage Indexing and Price Indexing, 1979–2050

(percent)

Year	Expenditures as a Percentage of Taxable Payroll[a]	
	Wage indexing	Price indexing
1979	10.9	10.9
1990	11.6	11.0
2000	12.2	10.5
2010	13.5	10.6
2020	16.4	12.0
2030	18.7	12.8
2040	18.1	11.8
2050	17.5	10.9

[a] Prices are assumed to increase 4 percent a year, and real wages are assumed to increase 1.75 percent a year.

Source: William C. Hsiao, "An Optimal Indexing Method for Social Security," in Colin D. Campbell, ed., *Financing Social Security* (Washington, D.C.: American Enterprise Institute, 1979), p. 32. Estimates are based on data from U.S. Senate, Committee on Finance, *Staff Data and Materials Relating to Social Security Financing*, 95th Congress, 1st session, June 1977, pp. 50-53.

earners and the self-employed).[39] The inequity of holding replacement ratios constant becomes clear if one considers the other extreme—a policy of holding payroll tax rates constant. As shown by equation 2, if payroll tax rates were held constant while the ratio of beneficiaries to workers increased because of a decline in the birth rate, the entire burden would be on the beneficiaries. Having both taxpayers and beneficiaries share the higher cost resulting from unexpected demographic and economic changes would appear to be more equitable than placing the entire burden on either the taxpayers or the beneficiaries.

A second argument for lowering replacement ratios as in the Hsiao plan is that it would reduce the size of the social security program.[40] Both benefits and taxes are higher under the present

[39] Richard A. Musgrave, *Financing Social Security: A Reappraisal*, Discussion Paper No. 753 (Cambridge, Mass.: Institute of Economic Research, Harvard University, April 1980).

[40] See Robert S. Kaplan, "A Comparison of Rates of Return to Social Security Retirees under Wage and Price Indexing," in Colin D. Campbell, ed., *Financing Social Security*, pp. 141-44.

TABLE 11

ESTIMATES OF ANNUAL BENEFIT IN 1977 PRICES, AND REPLACEMENT
RATES FOR SINGLE WORKERS WITH AVERAGE EARNINGS UNDER
WAGE INDEXING AND PRICE INDEXING, 1979–2050

	Wage Indexing		Price Indexing	
Year	Annual benefit in 1977 prices[a] ($)	Replacement rate (%)	Annual benefit in 1977 prices[a] ($)	Replacement rate (%)
1979	4,326	45	4,369	45
1990	5,169	44	4,515	38
2000	6,098	44	4,820	34
2010	7,206	44	5,263	32
2020	8,514	44	5,855	30
2030	10,061	44	6,546	28
2040	11,888	44	7,361	27
2050	14,047	44	8,325	26

[a] Real wages are assumed to increase 1.75 percent a year.
SOURCE: U.S. Senate, Committee on Finance, *Staff Data and Materials Relating to Social Security Financing*, 95th Congress, 1st session, June 1977, pp. 51, 53.

program than under the Hsiao plan. Even though real benefits would not increase as fast as the growth of the economy if wages were indexed to prices, the real level of social security benefits would still continuously increase. By cutting back on the expansion of the real level of social security benefits, individuals would have a greater opportunity to decide for themselves how they wished to save for the future.

The future stability of the social security system may depend on the way in which Congress decides to distribute the increasing cost of the system between taxpayers and beneficiaries. Because of the greater political power of beneficiaries than of taxpayers, one would predict that Congress will have taxpayers bear the cost. Over the years, this could result in steadily rising tax burdens on the working population. Just how far this can go depends on how large a burden future generations are willing to bear. Still, as tax burdens increase, so will the possibility that the system will be radically altered by Congress or that people will increasingly evade paying payroll taxes. In either case, the retired generation will not get the benefits they expected. The future success of the social security system will not be assured unless this kind of instability is avoided.

Conclusion

A basic problem in all types of long-range plans (including those made by social security systems) is adjusting to unexpected developments. The current period is such a time for the social security system. The very slow adjustment thus far to the important changes that have occurred—the decline in the birth rate, the higher rate of inflation, the decline in the real wage differential, the decline in the mortality rate, and the continued trend toward early retirement—is not reassuring.

F. A. Hayek has written that he would expect social security systems to have greater difficulty adjusting to unexpected changes than most other institutions.[41] He gives two principal reasons for this inflexibility. Because social security systems are typically national institutions in which membership is compulsory, Hayek believes they can be viewed as "sheltered monopolies" and would be expected to suffer like most monopolistic organizations from an inability to adjust to changed conditions. In addition, he believes that social security systems are inflexible because they are political institutions in which benefits have been based partly on need as determined by the political process rather than on what persons have paid for them. Because of this, it is very difficult to reduce benefits even though such reductions might be necessary, and there is a tendency for social security systems to overexpand, creating excessive burdens on the working population.

An important study by Martha Derthick has attributed the system's difficulties primarily to the historical evolution of its political organization—the domination of the system by a dedicated group of leaders, the political support of the labor unions, and the passive approval of Congress and other governmental groups involved.[42] Derthick concludes that the social security system may be able to evolve more successfully if the political organization changes so as to be more open and responsive to a wider range of interest groups. Although such a change in political orientation would help, Hayek's criticism of the basic organization of the system suggests that more drastic reforms may be necessary. What may be required is a system with less ambitious goals or a benefit policy guided primarily by the payments persons have made rather than by welfare objectives.

---

[41] See F. A. Hayek, *The Constitution of Liberty* (Chicago: University of Chicago Press, 1960), pp. 285-305.

[42] Derthick, *Policy-Making for Social Security*, pp. 17-210, 412-28.

Guidelines for the Reform of Immigration Policy

Barry R. Chiswick

Summary

This study is concerned with the optimal immigration criteria for the United States. As the focus is on the economic consequences of immigration, it is concerned with the labor-market productivity of the immigrants and their impacts on the native population.

The study begins with a discussion of current immigration law, the enforcement of this law, and the magnitude of immigration under the various categories. It shows that the law places a very heavy emphasis on kinship with a U.S. citizen or resident alien as the criterion for rationing immigration visas. Little weight is given to the skills or likely labor-market adjustment of visa applicants. The small occupational-preference categories are burdened with an arbitrary and cumbersome administrative procedure. The enforcement of immigration law appears to be minimal and has declined in both real resources and effectiveness in recent years. The result of the emphasis on both kinship and the limited enforcement is a relatively large proportion of low-skilled immigrants.

Immigrants are shown to vary in their productivity as measured by their earnings and employment. Productivity is higher among those immigrants with more schooling, with more skills acquired on the job or in vocational training programs, and with skills that are more transferable. Productivity is greater among economic migrants than among either refugees or tied (kinship) movers. Immigrants from less developed countries, particularly Mexico, earn less than other immigrants, both overall and if other factors are constant.

The impact of a cohort of immigrants depends on its characteristics. A cohort of low-skilled immigrants depresses the earnings of low-skilled American workers but raises the earnings of high-skilled workers and the owners of capital. A cohort of high-skilled immigrants depresses the earnings of high-skilled American workers but raises the earnings of low-skilled workers. In either instance, in the absence of income transfers, natives as a whole are better off. Low-skilled immigration, however, widens income inequality, and if income transfers are used to mitigate the losses of low-skilled natives, and immigrants participate in the transfer system, the native population as a whole can be made worse off. In the case of immigrants with high levels of skill, inequality among natives declines, income transfers decrease, and all native groups can, in principle, be made better off. The commonly held view that immigration causes unemployment is shown to be groundless.

A skill-based rationing system for visas is proposed as an alternative to current policy. Under this proposal the applicant's level of skill would be the primary determinant as to whether a visa is issued. Except for the immediate relatives of U.S. citizens, kinship would play a minor role. A point system would be used to combine the multidimensional aspects of skill. This policy, combined with more stringent enforcement of immigration law, would raise the skill level and hence also the favorable economic impact of immigrants. In contrast, the recommendations of the Select Commission on Immigration and Refugee Policy are shown to favor low-skilled immigrants and would shift much of the economic burden of enforcing immigration law from the appropriate government authorities to employers, who would be forced to screen all workers for their legal status.

Introduction

Immigration to the United States, and hence U.S. immigration policy, can have a substantial long-term impact on the economic well-being of the country as a whole and on the various demographic groups that compose the population. It is, however, an issue on which there is much public confusion primarily because people approach it in an emotional rather than a rational, systematic manner.

The purpose of this paper is to provide a framework or a set of guidelines for the analysis of immigration policy, that is, policy regarding the granting of permanent resident-alien status. The framework will focus on both the overall economic impacts of immigration and the distribution of these impacts. With this approach the economic benefits and costs of alternative immigration policies can be evaluated.

Immigration policy includes the laws and administrative regulations regarding who may enter the United States, for what period of time, and for what purposes (such as work, study, travel). Equally important is the enforcement of immigration laws and regulations. A policy of stringent criteria for entry combined with lax enforcement would be a policy of relatively easy entry for persons willing to violate the law. The focus of this study is on permanent resident aliens or immigrants and not on foreign students, visitors, or temporary workers.

As with most of our other social regulations, the original intent of immigration restrictions was to protect the health and safety of the resident population. The earliest restrictions (made in the nineteenth century) were intended to bar persons with contagious diseases, criminals, and the indigent, as well as other "social misfits." Quantitative restrictions were then introduced, first against East Asians, and then against eastern and southern Europeans, in part because of racial and religious prejudice and xenophobia and in part to protect the wages of low-skilled native workers from the competition of unskilled immigrants. Most of the racism and ethnocentrism implicit in U.S. immigration policy was eliminated by the 1965 amendments to the Immigration and Nationality Act. These amendments, along with the 1977 amendments regarding the Western Hemisphere, substituted kinship (with a U.S. citizen or a resident alien) for country of origin as the primary criterion for obtaining immigration visas.

Because of its direct and indirect impacts on the labor market and hence on the entire economy, and because a much larger number of persons would like to immigrate than the United States is willing to accept, immigration restrictions have widespread implications. After a decade of experience with the new policy there is substantial dissatisfaction. A policy based on kinship is superficially appealing on humanitarian grounds, and in 1965, a time of seemingly unlimited prosperity, adopting this policy may have been essential for eliminating the pernicious quota system based on national origins. In the current era of slower increases in productivity, it is even more appropriate to ask who bears the burden of the immigration policy and whether alternative equally nonracist policies can have a more favorable economic impact.

In a policy-related discussion of the economic consequences of immigration, or of any issue, it is important to distinguish between those concerns that are legitimate and those that are based on a faulty understanding of the issues. A recognition of legitimate concerns can result in the identification and development of policies to ameliorate these concerns. The identification of false issues that impede progress toward the development of sound policy is equally important.

The labor-market adjustment of immigrants in the United States and their impacts on the income and employment of the native population are issues of particular importance. The labor-market impacts of immigrants are *not* unidimensional, in part because immigrants are not homogeneous with respect to skills and other characteristics related to the labor market. Even if immigrants were homogeneous, their impacts on the native population would not be uniform because of the heterogeneity of the native population. Insights regarding the productivity of immigrants add a whole new dimension to the policy debate. They suggest that it is not just the number of immigrants that is relevant but also the characteristics of these immigrants. The characteristics of an annual stream of immigrants are not exogenous, as they can be largely determined by immigration policy.

This study begins with a review of current immigration policy. Attention is given to the extent to which this policy selects immigrants on the basis of their productivity. The economic adjustment of immigrants in the United States is then considered with an emphasis on the determinants of differences in economic success, as measured by immigrants' earnings and employment. The economic effects of immigration are analyzed in terms of the impact on the unemployment and income of the native population. The effects on the native population of immigrant cohorts that differ in productivity characteristics are considered.

Two alternatives to current policy are presented and discussed. One is a skill-based rationing system in which productivity characteristics are the primary criteria for rationing visas. The other is the set of recommendations from the Select Commission on Immigration and Refugee Policy that would increase the role of kinship in the issuance of immigration visas and grant amnesty to illegal aliens. The study concludes that a skill-based rationing system better satisfies the objectives of promoting economic growth and reducing the relative size of income transfers in the economy.

Current Immigration: Policy and Flows

Current immigration law has its basis in the 1965 amendments to the 1952 Immigration and Nationality Act.[1] The 1965 amendments abolished the pernicious national-origins quota system instituted in the 1920s, as well as the emphasis (introduced in 1952) on skill or productivity for rationing visas among applicants from within a country. In their place, the amendments created a system of "preferences" with a very heavy emphasis on kinship with a U.S. citizen or resident alien as the rationing mechanism. Skill and refugee status were given relatively minor roles.

[1] The 1952 act was primarily a recodification of existing law.

312

The basic features of current immigration law, including the changes introduced by the Refugee Act of 1980, are outlined in table 1.[2] The number of immigrants "admitted" to the United States under various categories is shown for two years in table 2.[3] The worldwide, country, and preference category quotas indicated in table 1 refer to ceilings on the number of visas issued in a year. The data on immigration refer to the number of persons entering the United States with an immigrant visa or receiving a change in status to permanent resident alien. Immigrant visas need not be used in the fiscal year they are issued, and some are never used.

A person can receive immigrant status (permanent resident-alien status) under one of four general categories—as an immediate relative of a U.S. citizen, by other kinship criteria, by occupation (skill), and through refugee status.[4] In addition, refugees can be given asylum or parole status by the attorney general, which enables them to enter and work in the United States indefinitely, although most eventually obtain an adjustment of status and become permanent resident aliens.[5] Obtaining permanent resident-alien status is, of course, the first step toward acquiring U.S. citizenship.

Kinship Criteria. The immediate relatives of U.S. citizens, that is, the spouse, unmarried minor children, and parents of adult citizens, can enter the United States without numerical limitation. Although the number of persons entering the United States in this manner had

[2] For a brief review of the history of U.S. immigration law and trends, see Barry R. Chiswick, "Immigrants and Immigration Policy," in William Fellner, ed., *Contemporary Economic Problems 1978* (Washington, D.C.: American Enterprise Institute, 1978), pp. 285-325. The major legislative development since 1978 is the Refugee Act of 1980, which is described below.

[3] Of the 601,000 immigrants "admitted" in 1978, 230,000 were already in the United States and received an "adjustment of status." Of these, 122,000 were Cuban and Indochinese refugees (28,000 and 94,000, respectively) whose adjustment of status outside the numerical limitations was made possible by legislation in 1976 and 1977. Of the 101,000 adjustments made under section 245 of the Immigration and Nationality Act, the official status at entry of nearly 60 percent was "temporary visitors for pleasure"; another 18 percent were students. An immigrant visa is often easier to obtain from inside the United States than from outside. (Source of data: *1978 Statistical Yearbook, Immigration and Naturalization Service,* U.S. Department of Justice, 1980, tables 4, 6B, and 6C.)

[4] "Private bills" are enacted in a small number of cases (138 in the Ninety-fifth Congress) to grant immigrant status to individuals who would not otherwise qualify. The Federal Bureau of Investigation used bogus bribes to congressmen for introducing private immigration bills in its ABSCAM investigation of congressional corruption.

[5] In 1978, for example, 122,000 Cuban and Indochinese refugees were made permanent resident aliens outside the preference and quota system under legislation enacted in 1976 and 1977.

TABLE 1

Summary of the Immigration Preference System
under the 1965 Amendments to the Immigration and
Nationality Act and Subsequent Amendments

Immigrants Not Subject to Numerical Limitation
Spouse and minor children of U.S. citizens and the parents of U.S.
citizens over age 21

Immigrants Subject to Numerical Limitation in the Preference System

Quotas (visas per year)

	1965–1978	*1979–1980*	*1981–present*
Eastern Hemisphere[a]	170,000 ⎫	290,000	270,000
Western Hemisphere[a]	120,000 ⎬		
Country ceiling[b]	20,000	20,000	20,000

Preference System[c]

Preference	*Characteristic*	*Maximum proportion of visas*
First	Unmarried adult children of U.S. citizens	20 percent
Second[d]	Spouse and unmarried children of permanent resident aliens	20 percent plus any not required for first preference[d]
Third	Professionals, scientists, and artists of exceptional ability	10 percent
Fourth	Married children of U.S. citizens	10 percent plus any not required for first three preferences
Fifth	Siblings of U.S. citizens	24 percent plus any not required for first four preferences

314

TABLE 1 (continued)

Sixth	Workers in occupations for which labor is scarce in the U.S.	10 percent
Seventh[e]	Refugees[e]	6 percent[e]
Nonpreference	Any applicant not entitled to a preference	Numbers not required for preference applicants
—	Spouse and minor children of any preference applicant can be classified with the same preference if a visa is not otherwise available	Charged to appropriate preference

[a] The hemisphere quotas were converted to a combined world ceiling of 290,000 visas by the 1978 amendments and reduced to 270,000 visas per year when the Refugee Act of 1980 removed refugees from the preference system.

[b] Country ceiling applicable to the Eastern Hemisphere under the 1965 amendments and the Western Hemisphere since the 1977 amendments.

[c] Preference system applicable to the Eastern Hemisphere under the 1965 amendments and the Western Hemisphere under the 1977 amendments. Prior to 1977, Western Hemisphere visas issued on a first-come, first-served basis.

[d] Increased to 26 percent of the 270,000 visas with the passage of the Refugee Act of 1980.

[e] The Refugee Act of 1980 established a quota of 50,000 visas for refugees outside of the preference system and gave the president authority to admit additional refugees. The act changed the definition of "refugee" to a person with a well-founded fear of religious, political, or racial persecution regardless of country of origin, whereas refugee status was previously applicable only to persons fleeing a Communist country or the general area of the Middle East.

SOURCE: Immigration and Naturalization Service.

fluctuated around 100,000 per year since 1965, recently it has increased to about 125,000 per year, primarily because of increased immigration of spouses of citizens and secondarily because of the increased immigration of parents.

Among the immigration visas subject to numerical limitation, at least 74 percent (prior to the 1980 Refugee Act) were reserved for other relatives of U.S. citizens and resident aliens (see table 1).[6] In

[6] The 6 percent quota for refugees was given to the second preference (a kinship preference) when the Refugee Act of 1980 removed refugees from the preference system.

TABLE 2
IMMIGRANTS ADMITTED TO THE UNITED STATES, FISCAL YEARS
1975 AND 1978

Immigrant Category	1975	1978
Total immigrants	386,194	601,442
Immigrants exempt from numerical limitation	104,633	260,338
Immediate relatives	91,504	125,819
Immigrants Act of October 12, 1976, and October 30, 1977[a]	—	122,442
Other	13,129	12,077
Immigrants subject to limitation[b]		
Eastern Hemisphere	160,460	165,743
Relative preferences	95,945	123,501
First preference	871	1,120
Second preference	43,077	44,116
Fourth preference	3,623	5,954
Fifth preference	48,374	72,311
Occupational preferences	29,334	26,295
Third preference (professionals)	8,363	4,822
Sixth preference (other workers)	6,724	7,705
Their spouses and children	14,247	13,768
Refugees—seventh preference	9,129	9,724
Nonpreference, private bills, and others	26,052	6,223
Western Hemisphere	121,101	175,361
Relative preferences	—	66,796
First preference	—	2,572
Second preference	—	33,631
Fourth preference	—	5,450
Fifth preference	—	25,143
Occupational preferences	—	4,582
Third preference (professionals)	—	465
Sixth preference (other workers)	—	1,183
Their spouses and children	—	2,934

TABLE 2   (continued)

Western Hemisphere (continued)		
Refugees—seventh preference	—	585
Nonpreference, private bills, and others	—	47,987
Natives of Western Hemisphere and Immigrants Act of 1966 [c]	121,101	55,411

NOTE: Dashes indicate category is not applicable.

[a] These acts provide for Cuban and Indochinese refugees adjusting to resident alien status in the United States.

[b] Except for the occupational preferences, spouses and minor children are included in the totals for the preference category of the immigrants.

[c] Refers to immigrants who obtained visas prior to the extension of the preference system to the Western Hemisphere.

SOURCE: *1978 Statistical Yearbook, Immigration and Naturalization Service*, U.S. Department of Justice, 1980, table 4.

1978, of the 165,743 immigrants from the Eastern Hemisphere subject to numerical limitation, 75 percent entered under the kinship preferences (see table 2). Little use was made of the first preference (unmarried adult children of U.S. citizens and their children) or the fourth preference (married children of U.S. citizens and their spouses and children), but to the extent that these preferences were undersubscribed, additional persons entered under the second preference (spouses and unmarried children of resident aliens and their children) and the fifth preference (siblings of U.S. citizens and their spouses and children). During the 1960s and early 1970s the kinship preferences were not fully subscribed, and "nonpreference" visa applicants could immigrate. The rapid increase in the use of the fifth preference, however, has eliminated this alternative.[7]

For the Western Hemisphere, until 1977, visas were issued on a first-come, first-served basis; and as of 1978, new visas were issued under the preference system. In 1978 over 55,000 Western Hemisphere immigrants entered with first-come, first-served visas. Of the nearly 120,000 immigrants who entered in that year with preference system visas, 56 percent immigrated under the kinship preferences. Of these, immigration under the first and fourth preferences was small, whereas immigration under the second and fifth preferences

[7] "Nonpreference" applicants have to obtain a labor certificate (that is, demonstrate they have a "needed" skill and a job waiting for them), invest money in a business in the United States, or satisfy some other criterion to demonstrate their economic value to the United States.

317

was large. The very large proportion of immigrants in the nonpreference category in 1978 is a transitional phenomenon as the preference system was too recently introduced for the kinship categories to be filled.

Occupational Criteria. The 1965 amendments reserved up to 20 percent of the visas in the preference system for rationing on the basis of occupation. The third preference provides for the immigration of professionals and persons of exceptional ability in the arts and sciences. The sixth preference refers to skilled workers whose services are needed in occcupations for which U.S. workers are in short supply. For both occupational preferences a cumbersome application procedure administered by the Department of Labor's Office of Labor Certification is required of both the immigrant and a U.S. employer.[8] In general, the U.S. employer must demonstrate that appropriate workers are not available in the U.S. at the prevailing wage for that job. This requirement is meaningless, since for a sufficiently high wage—a new prevailing wage—fewer workers would be demanded, and more workers already in the United States would be available to the occupation or employer.

For some jobs the Office of Labor Certification had "predetermined" that a shortage exists. These jobs, referred to as Schedule A, currently include physicians in areas where the Department of Health and Human Services determines that there is a shortage, nurses who are already registered in the state of intended residence or who have passed the examination administered by the Commission on Graduates of Foreign Nursing Schools, and physical therapists qualified to take the state licensing exam; persons in the sciences and (nonperforming) arts with exceptional ability, including college and university teachers of exceptional ability; religious practitioners; and managers in multinational corporations.[9] The Labor Certification Office has "determined" that other occupations are not to be used as a basis for labor certification, although labor certifications are given on occasion to applicants in these occupations. These Schedule B occupations include many that provide employment for immigrants who enter the

---

[8] For the current regulations see "Labor Certification Process for the Permanent Employment of Aliens in the United States: Final Rule," *Federal Register*, part 9, Department of Labor, Employment and Training Administration, vol. 45, no. 246, December 19, 1980, pp. 83, 926-83, 949.

[9] Physicians and nurses were added to Schedule A in 1980, having been removed from the list in 1976. Dieticians were removed from the list in 1980 apparently because the national association asserted that there was no shortage. There is apparently no research basis for the Office of Labor Certification's determinations.

United States under other criteria, including personal service attendants, cleaners (hotel, motel, household), kitchen workers, laborers, nurses' aides, taxicab drivers, and gardeners.

Although up to 20 percent of the visas subject to the preference system are reserved for occupational preferences, the system's impact on the skill distribution of immigrants is smaller than might appear. First, the spouse and minor unmarried children of workers receiving an occupational-preference visa are generally charged to that preference. Of the 26,295 persons from the Eastern Hemisphere who entered under an occupational preference in 1978, 52 percent were spouses and children, many of whom subsequently will enter the labor force.[10] Of the 4,582 persons from the Western Hemisphere, 64 percent were spouses and children. Second, when a worker obtains a visa through a labor certification, there is no legal obligation to work for the employer or in the occupation. The extent of this "leakage" is not known. Third, there is a tendency for the occupational preferences to be used by persons already in the United States with nonimmigrant visas who seek an adjustment of their status. Of the 14,175 occupational-preference visas in 1978, 65 percent received an adjustment of status. That is, they were in the United States under a student, tourist, or other visa, or were in the United States illegally, but were able to obtain a labor certification. The cumbersome certification process, which generally requires considerable employer cooperation, gives decided advantage to persons who are already working in the United States.

In spite of these limitations on the size and scope of the number of immigrants who may enter under the occupational preferences, they are an important source of professional workers in the immigration stream. Among immigrants in 1978 who reported an occupation on their visa application, nearly one-fifth of the professionals were beneficiaries of an occupational preference (see table 3). More than one-quarter of the engineers, nurses, physicians, research scientists, and college and university teachers who immigrated did so under an occupational preference. As would be expected, only a very small proportion of immigrants in other occupations received an occupational preference, with the notable exception of cooks, including chefs (14 percent).

In summary, there are many features of the current occupational preferences that have the effect of substantially reducing the program's ability to facilitate the immigration of high-productivity work-

---

[10] The data in this paragraph are from *1978 Statistical Yearbook*, tables 7A and 8A.

TABLE 3

Beneficiaries of Occupational Preferences, by Immigrant Status and Occupation, Fiscal Year 1978

Occupation	Third Preference		Sixth Preference		Total	Percentage[a]
	Admissions	Adjustments of status	Admissions	Adjustments of status		
Professional, technical, and kindred	2,091	3,181	736	2,968	8,976	18.4
Engineers	356	454	197	646	1,653	24.7
Nurses	731	238	45	479	1,493	30.2
Physicians	146	743	23	159	1,071	24.1
Research workers (not specified)	21	369	8	179	577	43.4
Scientists (life and physical)	108	237	45	144	534	29.5
Teachers (college and university)	47	195	47	180	469	25.3
Writers, artists, and entertainers	43	99	112	211	465	9.4

Managers (except farm)	10	3	466	1,285	1,764	8.4
Sales, clerical, and kindred	2	0	145	299	446	1.3
Craftsmen and kindred	0	0	519	399	918	3.3
Operatives (including transport)	0	0	119	139	258	0.5
Laborers (except farm)	0	0	51	61	112	0.5
Farm (laborers, foremen, and managers)	0	0	27	90	117	1.0
Service (except private household)	0	0	504	501	1,005	4.0
Cooks	0	0	399	364	763	14.3
Private household workers	0	0	263	316	579	5.5
Total	2,103	3,184	2,830	6,058	14,175	5.7[b]

NOTE: All detailed occupations with 450 or more beneficiaries of an occupational preference are listed separately.

[b] Percentage of immigrants reporting a labor-market occupation.

[b] Percentage of immigrants reporting a labor-market occupation. The figure is 2.4 percent if expressed as a percentage of all immigrants, including housewives, youths, students, the aged, and others.

SOURCE: *1978 Statistical Yearbook, Immigration and Naturalization Service*, U.S. Department of Justice, 1980, table 8A.

321

ers. In spite of these features, the preferences are an important source of high-level manpower. That there are queues for obtaining an occupational-preference visa suggests that even more high-productivity immigrants would be forthcoming if the preference quotas were increased, country ceilings on these categories were removed, and the requirements of prearranged employment and the burdensome application procedure were eased.

Refugees. The 1965 amendments and the Refugee Act of 1980 have attempted to regularize the flow of refugees. Events have proved that this is difficult. The 1965 amendments allocated 6 percent of the visas within the preference system to refugees and retained the requirement that a refugee had to be fleeing a Communist country or from the general area of the Middle East. The 1980 Refugee Act increased the annual quota of refugees from 17,400 to 50,000 visas.[11] In addition the act stipulated that a refugee was any person subject to or with a well-founded fear of political, religious, ethnic, or racial persecution (whether from a Communist country or otherwise) and was already in a country of first asylum.

The 1980 Refugee Act was based on the desire to be evenhanded in the treatment of persons fleeing Communist and non-Communist government persecution; it was also based on the experiences of the Vietnamese boat people. It was immediately found deficient. The definition of a refugee is not so clear, and the first asylum provision penalizes refugees from countries in close proximity to the United States. The Haitians seeking asylum in Florida claimed they were refugees from poverty and, having fled, could not return without being persecuted by an authoritarian regime. The Cuban boat people, the more than 120,000 persons who entered the United States in 1980, were technically not eligible for admission under the Refugee Act, as the United States was the country of first asylum. Whereas the Cubans were admitted under the attorney general's ad hoc authority to parole persons into the United States, the status of the Haitians is still ambiguous.

Illegal Immigration and Enforcement Resources. The enforcement of immigration law is minimal, in terms of both the magnitude of the resources and possibly also the deterrent effect of the deployment of these resources. The limited, but not negligible, enforcement of immigration law tends to attract low-skilled illegal aliens.

---

[11] The president was also given the authority to admit additional refugees if the situation warranted.

The number of violations of immigration law is, of course, unknown.[12] The stock of illegal immigrants in the United States has been variously estimated at 2 million to 12 million persons, but a recent review of these estimates by the U.S. Bureau of the Census suggests a range of 3.5 million to 6 million persons of whom about half are Mexican nationals.[13] Data exist, however, on the number of apprehensions of illegal aliens. The number of deportable aliens located increased from 70,000 in 1960 to over 1 million per year since 1977 (see table 4).[14] Of the more than 1 million deportable aliens located in fiscal year 1978, nearly 950,000 were Mexican nationals who entered without inspection (see table 5), nearly 28,000 were Mexican nationals who entered the United States under other statuses, and just over 81,000 were persons of other nationalities.

The increase in apprehensions is believed to reflect a large increase in illegal immigration. The end of the bracero program (for temporary farm workers) in 1964, the introduction of numerical limits on Western Hemisphere immigration in 1965 and subsequent tightening of restrictions on Western Hemisphere immigration, the prospect of amnesty as proposed by the Carter administration in early 1977, as well as improved transportation and information networks, and increased competition for jobs among low-skilled workers in the major sending countries have all served to increase illegal immigration.

The data on apprehensions reflect, in part, administrative decisions on the allocation of enforcement resources. More apprehensions per dollar of enforcement expenditure occur if there is a relative concentration along the Mexican border. This may not, however, be the maximum deterrent for a given enforcement budget. Apprehensions along the border may have a minimal deterrent effect if, as is believed to be the situation, most illegal aliens who are apprehended and deported while entering without inspection simply try again a few nights later. An apprehension and deportation may have a greater long-term

[12] A person may violate immigration law and become an illegal alien by violating the condition of a legally obtained visa (such as unauthorized employment, with a student or visitor visa, or remaining in the United States beyond the date specified in the visa), entering the United States with a fraudulent visa, or making surreptitious entry.

[13] See Jacob S. Siegel, Jeffrey S. Passel, and J. Gregory Robinson, "Preliminary Review of Existing Studies of the Number of Illegal Residents in the United States," mimeographed, U.S. Bureau of the Census, January 1980.

[14] The decline in apprehensions in fiscal year 1980 (see table 4) has been attributed to the three-month moratorium on interior enforcement, which was intended to increase compliance with the 1980 census, and to the diversion of INS resources for the registration of Iranian students and the Cuban boat people. There are no data on the extent to which the same individual is apprehended more than once in a year.

TABLE 4

IMMIGRATION AND NATURALIZATION SERVICE PERSONNEL, IMMIGRANTS,
NONIMMIGRANTS, AND DEPORTABLE ALIENS LOCATED,
FISCAL YEARS 1960–1980

	INS Personnel			Workload		
Year	Perma- nent positions	Average paid employ- ment[a]	Total compen- sable work years[a,b]	Immi- grants	Nonimmi- grants admitted	Deport- able aliens located
1960	6,895	6,522	—	265,398	1,140,736	70,684
1965	7,043	6,747	—	296,697	2,075,967	110,371
1970	6,920	6,672	—	373,326	4,431,880	345,353
1975	8,020	7,992	—	386,194	7,083,937	766,600
1976	8,832	—	9,227	398,615	7,654,491	875,915
1977	9,473	—	9,705	462,315	8,036,916	1,042,215
1978	10,071	—	9,804	601,442	9,343,710	1,057,977
1979	10,997	—	11,655	460,348	—	1,076,418
1980	10,943	—	9,885	—	—	910,361

NOTE: INS = Immigration and Naturalization Service. Since 1977, the fiscal year runs from October 1 to September 30; prior to 1977, it was from July 1 to June 30. Dashes under INS Personnel indicate data not included in the source. Dashes under Workload indicate data not available.

[a] The data include the full-time equivalent of nonpermanent positions.

[b] Includes the full-time equivalent of overtime and holiday hours worked. This accounted for the equivalent of 1,484 compensable work years in 1979 and 1,771 compensable work years in 1980.

SOURCE: Columns 1-3: *Budget of the United States Government: Appendix,* various years; columns 4-6: *1978 Statistical Yearbook, Immigration and Naturalization Service,* U.S. Department of Justice, 1980, table 23, and the Immigration and Naturalization Service.

deterrent effect if it occurs after an illegal alien has penetrated the border and incurred costs in locating a job and residence. Even though the cost per apprehension away from the border is higher, it is not obvious that it is less cost effective in deterring illegal immigration.[15]

[15] David North estimates that the 1979 cost per apprehension by the border patrol (for border enforcement, interior enforcement, and antismuggling activities) was $108 compared with $156 for the investigations unit (interior enforcement). The cost per apprehension for just border-control activities is even less than for overall border-patrol activities. See David North, "Enforcing the Immigration Law: A Review of the Options," mimeographed, New Transcentury Foundation, September 1980, p. 17. North's study includes several interesting ideas for increasing the efficiency of the enforcement of immigration law at the border and in the interior.

TABLE 5

DEPORTABLE ALIENS LOCATED, BY STATUS AT ENTRY AND NATIONALITY,
FISCAL YEAR 1978

Nation-ality	Status at Entry					
	EWI	Visitor	Student	Crewman	Other	Total
Europe	295	5,521	585	6,317	1,263	13,981
Aisa	138	5,008	2,969	4,940	1,720	14,775
North America	968,219	33,498	944	828	9,234	1,012,719
Mexico	948,891	21,484	349	40	5,903	976,667
South America	2,708	5,557	655	919	962	10,801
Africa	28	998	1,135	507	242	2,910
Other	68	1,699	525	281	218	2,791
Total	971,456	52,281	6,813	13,788	13,639	1,057,977

NOTE: EWI=entry without inspection.
SOURCE: *1978 Statistical Yearbook, Immigration and Naturalization Service*, U.S.
Department of Justice, 1980, table 30.

That there is such a large and increasing number of apprehensions along the Mexican border suggests that the border is porous and that the cost of being apprehended is low for the illegal alien. If the probability of apprehension were very high and the cost of apprehension were high, few persons would attempt illegal entry, and the number of apprehensions would be small.

Little is known about the characteristics of illegal aliens. There are reasons to believe, however, that they are not a random sample of persons desirous of but unable to obtain a legal immigrant visa but rather a group consisting disproportionately of low-skilled workers. There is a probability greater than zero of being apprehended at the border or in the interior. The probability of detection in the interior is greater for those who come into contact with the authorities—the police, an occupational licensing board, or the personnel department of a government agency or a large firm. Persons with high levels of skill, particularly professionals who require a certification of one sort or another, may be particularly likely to be detected. In addition, the cost of deportation is greater for persons with higher levels of skill. Unskilled workers (and workers with skills that are readily transferable internationally) do not lose the value of U.S. investments in training if deportation occurs. Country-specific investment in training tends to rise with the skill level, and a deported skilled illegal alien finds that investments in U.S.-specific training are not relevant when he returns to the home country and that some of the skills specific to the country of origin acquired prior to the illegal migration have subsequently depreciated.

The resources devoted to the enforcement of immigration law are relatively small, and it would appear that they have not kept pace with the workload.[16] The number of permanent positions in the Immigration and Naturalization Service increased by nearly 60 percent from 1960 to 1979 (see table 4).[17] During the same period the annual number of immigrants more than doubled, nonimmigrant admissions of aliens increased eightfold, and the number of apprehensions of illegal aliens increased fourteenfold. Not all of the increase in permanent positions reflects more resources devoted to direct enforcement activities, particularly in recent years. For example, from fiscal year 1977 to 1979 the INS operating budget increased 11 percent in real dollars, and the real resources devoted to service to the public, support operations, and program direction increased 47 percent, but border enforcement resources increased 1 percent, detention and deportation resources decreased by 4 percent, and interior enforcement resources decreased by 15 percent.[18] This reallocation of resources within the Immigration and Naturalization Service away from enforcement activities, particularly interior enforcement, appears to be reflecting a decision by the Carter administration to grant de facto amnesty for

[16] In addition to screening persons entering through legal gateways (a function shared with the customs service) and other enforcement of immigration law through patrols along the border and interior enforcement, the INS administers the annual registration of aliens and administers naturalization applications and proceedings. Visa applications are administered by the State Deparment's Visa Service and labor certifications are issued by the Labor Department's Office of Labor Certification. David North estimated that in fiscal year 1980 there were 11,869 "immigration law enforcement positions." Of these, 8,433 were in the INS (including 2,694 in the border patrol and 1,019 in interior enforcement), 2,287 in the customs service, 907 in the State Department, and 242 in the Labor Department's Employment Standards Administration (enforcement of minimum-wage and farm-worker regulations). North, "Enforcing the Immigration Law," p. 13.

[17] The INS publishes detailed tables on immigrants, nonimmigrants, apprehensions, naturalizations, and so forth in its annual reports and in its 105-page *1978 Statistical Yearbook*. Still, data on the INS budget, number of personnel, or number of personnel in enforcement units are not to be found in the annual reports, the *1978 Statistical Yearbook*, or the *INS Reporter*, a house organ. Apparently the only published materials are in the *Budget of the United States: Appendix*.

[18] The percentage increase in nominal expenditures was adjusted by the deflator for federal nondefense purchases of goods and services, which increased 14 percent during the period.

illegal aliens already in the United States. Congress had shown no interest in the administration's 1977 legislative proposal for amnesty.[19]

Conclusion. Taken as a whole, U.S. immigration policy is best characterized as focusing on kinship as the primary criterion for rationing immigration visas. Few visas are issued on the basis of skill or likely productivity in the United States, and for these few a cumbersome application procedure is required that gives decided advantages to persons already in the United States in some other status. Policies toward illegal immigration are characterized by minimal effective enforcement, particularly in recent years. There has been a reduction in interior enforcement, and there are no penalties other than deportation against apprehended illegal aliens. The resources devoted to border control, particularly along the Mexican border, may be operating a revolving door rather than having a substantial deterrent effect. As a system, these policies result in the immigration of a larger number and proportion of lower-skilled workers than the alternative to be discussed below, a skill-based rationing system.

Heterogeneity among Immigrants

Much of the popular discussion tends to view immigrants either as unskilled and poorly motivated workers or as highly successful and aggressive achievers. These characterizations focus on the extremes. The average immigrant is at neither pole but is apparently closer to the latter than the former. More striking, however, is the heterogeneity among immigrants. Immigrants differ almost as much as natives in their earnings, occupational distribution, schooling, and on-the-job training. They also vary widely in country of origin. There is, however, a tendency for most to be young adults (in their twenties) when they immigrate, but this is more the case for economic migrants than for refugees.

Analytically, the productivity of immigrants is most fruitfully considered within the context of two models, the transferability of skills and the self-selection of migrants. Immigrants from English-speaking countries at a similar level of economic development as the United States are more likely to have readily transferable skills than

[19] The Carter administration's proposed 1982 budget included a further decline in real resources for the INS. "Mr. Crosland (Acting Commissioner) said that the new budget would maintain the strength of the border patrol but cut the number of investigators who look for illegal aliens inside the country and trim the number of inspectors who screen travelers at ports of entry." "Immigration Agency's Staff to be Reduced in Fiscal 1982 Budget," *Wall Street Journal*, January 9, 1981, p. 8.

immigrants from other countries. This implies that the former have higher earnings at arrival and a smaller rise in earnings with duration of residence. Because of the greater economic incentive for migration among the most able and ambitious, if other factors are the same, immigrants tend to be favorably self-selected for labor market success. Because labor market considerations are less relevant for the decision to move among refugees and tied movers (those who move primarily as a consequence of the immigration decision of a family member) in comparison with economic migrants, the latter would tend to have more readily transferable skills and are more favorably self-selected for labor market success.

The productivity of immigrants, as measured by their labor-market earnings, varies systematically with several readily measurable variables.[20] Earnings are higher for immigrants with more schooling, and it does not appear to matter whether the schooling was acquired in the United States or in the country of origin. The effect of schooling on earnings is greater for immigrants with highly transferable skills, such as economic migrants from English-speaking countries, and is least for refugees, such as the Cubans. Earnings are also positively related to the number of years of labor-market experience in the country of origin prior to immigration. Again, this effect is greatest for economic migrants from English-speaking countries and least for refugees.

Most striking is the generally positive effect of duration of residence in the United States on the earnings of immigrants. The effect is curvilinear, as earnings generally rise very sharply during the first few years and continue to rise, but at a decreasing rate with the duration of residence. The magnitude of the rise in earnings with duration of residence is greater for those who must undergo the greatest economic adjustment on arrival (refugees) and is weakest for those with the smallest economic adjustment (English-speaking economic migrants). Although on arrival male economic migrants have lower earnings than their native-born counterparts, if other factors are the same, economic migrants reach earnings parity after eleven to fifteen years, and thereafter the immigrants have higher earnings.

Earnings are also related to the cause of the migration. Earnings are greater for economic migrants than for political refugees, presumably because noneconomic factors influenced the migration decision

---

[20] Much of the discussion on earnings in this section is based on Barry R. Chiswick, *An Analysis of the Economic Progress and Impact of Immigrants*, Report Submitted to the Employment and Training Administration, U.S. Department of Labor, June 1980, NTIS No. PB80-200454. The data are from the 1970 Census of Population.

of the latter, and they have fewer transferable skills. Earnings on arrival are very low for refugees (again, other variables the same), and although the gap narrows with a longer residence, it is not closed. The data also suggest that those who base their decision to migrate primarily on the migration decision of a family member (referred to as "tied movers") have lower earnings than the primary economic migrant. Using data from the 1970 Census of Population, I found that, if other forces are the same, women who married prior to immigration had consistently lower hourly earnings than those who married after immigration.[21] Using data on internal migrants, Mincer found that tied movers had lower earnings and higher unemployment rates at their destination than similarly situated internal migrants who were not tied movers.[22] It has also been found that, ceteris paribus, after seven years in the United States, persons admitted under the kinship immigration criteria have lower earnings than occupational-preference and nonpreference immigrants.[23] The superior performance of primary economic migrants in comparison with those whose migration is influenced by kinship ties, even when other measured variables are the same, is presumably related to the transferability of skill, ability, motivation for personal labor-market advancement, and continuity of attachment to the labor market.

There tends to be a substantial difference in earnings between immigrants from advanced industrialized societies and those from less developed countries. Some of this difference is attributable to the smaller number of years of formal schooling of the latter. Even so, however, some substantial and significant differences remain. For example, when other factors remain constant, including area of residence in the United States and marital status, immigrants from Mexico earn about 20 percent less than European immigrants. Perhaps this arises because the earnings gain from migration from Mexico is so substantial that it is worthwhile even if earnings are lower than average in the United States, whereas immigration from the higher-income countries is profitable only if higher than average earnings can be obtained in the United States.[24]

[21] Chiswick, *An Analysis of the Economic Progress*, chapter 9.

[22] Jacob Mincer, "Family Migration Decisions," *Journal of Political Economy*, October 1978, pp. 749-774.

[23] Although David North reports that in his relatively small sample (211 observations) the coefficient of the kinship variable is insignificant, the *t*-ratio is 1.64, which is statistically significant at a 5 percent level, one-tailed test. See David North, "Seven Years Later: The Experiences of the 1970 Cohort of Immigrants in the U.S. Labor Market," mimeographed (Washington, D.C.: Linton, June 15, 1978), pp. 102-104 and appendix B, page B-9.

[24] For reasons that are as yet unclear, other variables the same, the earnings

In summary, the productivity of immigrants in U.S. labor markets tends to be greater for those with higher levels of schooling; for those with more skills acquired on the job or in vocational training programs; for those with the more transferable skills; and for economic migrants rather than refugees or kinship migrants. Immigrants from less developed countries, particularly Mexico, tend to earn less than others even after variables that determine earnings are held constant.

Economic Impact

The formation of immigration policy, as with much other public policy, would be simpler if the native population were homogeneous. Then the average effect of immigrants on the native population would be the effect on each and every native person. The heterogeneity among natives in the ownership of both human and nonhuman assets means that in policy debates the distribution of the impacts can be as important as, if not more important than, the overall impact. This section will first consider the impact of immigrants on unemployment, a topic of considerable interest to policy makers. It will argue that much of the conventional wisdom is based on myths. The discussion will then focus on the more important impact—the impact on the overall level and distribution of earnings and income.

Unemployment Myths and Realities. Much of the public debate regarding immigrants is expressed in terms of unemployment. In recent years there has been bipartisan political support for the immigrant-unemployment connection as the secretary of labor in the Carter administration and the commissioner of the Immigration and Naturalization Service in the Ford administration attributed the unemployment of at least 2 million to 3 million Americans to illegal aliens.[25] The economic fear is that immigrants take jobs that natives would otherwise have, thereby creating unemployment.

---

differential of about 20 percent between Mexican-Americans and Anglos also exists among second generation Americans (native-born but with at least one foreign-born parent) and higher-generation Americans (both parents born in the United States).

[25] See "Illegal Aliens Cost U.S. Jobs—Marshall," *Los Angeles Times*, December 2, 1979, part 1, p. 1, and " 'Silent Invasion' That Takes Millions of American Jobs," *U.S. News and World Report*, December 9, 1974, pp. 77-78. This view is not confined to the United States. "One and a half million unemployed is one and a half million immigrants too many" is also the slogan of antiimmigrant elements in France. "Immigrants in France are the Target of Resentment From the Left and Right," *New York Times*, September 30, 1980, p. 3.

It is important to distinguish between taking a particular job "slot" and depriving a native worker of a job. Clearly, if an immigrant takes a particular job washing dishes in the Sears Tower restaurant, that job slot is not being filled by a native-born worker. This is the visible effect that generates resentment.

It is, however, the availability of jobs that attracts workers into the U.S. labor market, both from the household sector (outside the labor force) and from other countries. The absolute growth in employment has consistently exceeded the growth in the numbers unemployed. There is no fixed number of jobs in the economy, and the extent of employment generally increases with increased immigration, although, as will be discussed below, relative wages may change.

Suppose a new immigrant takes a job that would otherwise have been occupied by a native worker. The immigrant may either hoard his earnings or spend it all, or do something in between. If the immigrant hoards the earnings, natives gain the benefit of his production, giving nothing in return but green pieces of paper that are inexpensive to produce. The effect is deflationary—it is as if the Federal Reserve System reduced the money supply by the amount hoarded.[26] Natives as a whole have greater income, native workers allocate themselves among jobs in the labor market, and the rate of increase in the price level is lower than otherwise. As long as there is some flexibility in wages and workers can change jobs, no permanent unemployment is created.

The more likely case is that the immigrant spends the earnings either in the United States or via emigrant remittances in the home country. There is no deflationary effect, as the extra output produced by the immigrant is matched by the increase in the aggregate demand for goods and services. Employment is generated as workers produce the goods and services purchased by the immigrants.

In either instance, immigration per se does not result in a permanent net loss in jobs to natives even if immigrants take particular job slots that native workers would otherwise occupy. There are, however, three circumstances in which immigration could result in increased measured unemployment, although they are not what the proponents of the immigrant-unemployment connection appear to be discussing. The first is the unemployment of immigrants per se. The second is frictional unemployment among the native population, whereas the third is structural unemployment arising from wage rigidities.

[26] The deflationary effect could, of course, be offset by appropriate adjustments in monetary policy.

Recent entrants to the labor force, whether they are youths leaving school, women entering or reentering the labor market after a period of child rearing, or new immigrants, engage in a job search. It takes time to find a job, and one way of learning about occupations and employers is to experience a variety of jobs. Higher than average voluntary job turnover is therefore a characteristic of recent labor force entrants. Recent immigrants in particular experience substantial upward occupational mobility, presumably often accompanied by periods of voluntary unemployment, as their skills adjust to the U.S. labor market. Recent labor-market entrants may also experience greater involuntary separations from employment, as employers had less information about them when they were hired and they have less seniority and training specific to the firm.

Data from the 1970 Census of Population and the 1976 Survey of Income and Education (SIE) suggest that, if other factors remain the same, for adult white men the number of weeks worked in a year was lower among recent immigrants (mainly those in the United States less than three years) than among the native-born and long-term immigrants.[27] In the 1970 census, in which year of immigration is reported in five-year intervals, the foreign-born in the United States less than five years worked three weeks less than the native-born, immigrants in the United States five to nine years worked one week less, and for those in the United States ten or more years there was no difference from the native-born. Among the foreign-born, those in the United States for less than five years worked about three weeks fewer than others, with no significant differences among the six year-of-immigration cohorts in the United States for five or more years. Although the sample sizes in the 1976 Survey of Income and Education are smaller than in the one-in-a-hundred sample from the census, the greater detail on specific year of immigration for those in the United States five or fewer years is illuminating. The SIE data suggest that most of the smaller number of weeks worked among those in the United States five or fewer years is concentrated among the very

---

[27] The analyses reported here using the 1970 Census of Population and the 1976 Survey of Income and Education were done for weeks worked in the prior year and unemployment in the reference week. Similar patterns emerged in the two data sets and in the weeks-worked and unemployment analyses. The explanatory power is much greater in the weeks-worked analyses, as the dependent variable is based on fifty-two weekly observations, thereby reducing the influence of random variations. Similar patterns also emerged in analyses for Hispanic and nonwhite men. The empirical analyses reported in this paragraph and the next are based on Barry R. Chiswick, "Estimating the Impact of Immigrants on Earnings and Employment," mimeographed (Chicago: University of Illinois at Chicago Circle, 1981), part A.

recent arrivals; in addition the difference in weeks worked narrows rapidly and virtually disappears by the end of three years.

As is true among the native-born, the number of weeks worked is greater the higher the level of schooling and the greater the extent of labor-market experience (both before and after immigration) for the foreign-born. The number of weeks worked is also greater for those whose skills are more readily transferred to the U.S. labor market. Compared with immigrants from the British Isles, other things the same, immigrants from Cuba, southern Europe, and the Balkans worked one fewer week, and those from Mexico worked two weeks fewer, whereas those from other Latin American countries worked 1.5 fewer weeks.

An influx of workers due to immigration will generate frictional unemployment among native-born workers. Frictional unemployment will arise whenever there is a change in the demand for or supply of labor that affects relative wage opportunities. Some workers will quit their current jobs in search of now higher-paying new jobs. Employers in sectors where workers' marginal productivity has fallen below the wage will lay off some workers. Given the change in labor market opportunities, both workers and employers invest more in information regarding the labor market, and one consequence is frictional unemployment. Note that given the immigration, the frictional unemployment represents an efficient process through which workers identify and gravitate to what is now their best employment opportunity and through which employers adjust their work force to the new economic conditions.

Only a small proportion of native-born workers will experience frictional unemployment arising from immigration, and this unemployment will be short-lived—it will dampen as workers find their best employment opportunities in the new environment. The extent of frictional unemployment will be less the greater the extent to which the immigrants are attracted to the United States, and particular occupations or geographic areas, by expanding job opportunities. Frictional unemployment will be greater if immigrants are entering stagnant occupations or economically stagnant regions. Thus, for a given size of a cohort of immigrants, frictional unemployment among the native population will tend to be smaller if the immigration is predominantly economic in nature rather than based on kinship or other criteria.

Wage rigidities, whether instituted by a legal minimum wage, a union wage, or social convention, can result in unemployment among the native-born if immigration would depress the market wage below the wage floor.[28] If the wage floor exceeds the market wage, more workers offer their labor services than there are job slots. One solution is, of course, to eliminate the wage floor. A "second best" solution to avoid this unemployment is to have an immigration policy that is not likely to result in pressures against the wage floor. The second best solution is a policy favoring the immigration of high-skilled workers, thereby raising the productivity of low-skilled native workers and reducing the pressures against the federal minimum wage. This would have particularly favorable impacts on the employment opportunities of native-born youths and disadvantaged minorities. It would, however, place downward pressure on the wages of high-skilled workers.

Impact on Income. For simplicity of exposition regarding the impact of immigrants on the level and distribution of income, let us assume that there are two types of workers, low-skilled and high-skilled, that within each type all workers are homogeneous, and that the only other factor of production is physical capital.[29] This is a world in which the three factors of production are substitutes for each other and the production function approximates one with constant elasticity of substitution. Even in such a simplified world, the answer to the question "What is the impact of immigrants?" can be complex because of the potential for immigrant cohorts with quite different productivity characteristics. Although partially determined by external forces, such as a recession in one country or a revolution in another, under current circumstances and immigration quota ceilings, the characteristics of immigrant cohorts are largely determined by U.S. immigration policy over a period of years. Again, for purposes

---

[28] Some of the high unemployment or low number of weeks worked among immigrants during their first few years may be a consequence of such wage rigidities. On arrival immigrants tend to have low productivity, but with the passage of time, including job experience, they acquire skills relevant for higher-paying jobs in the United States. By reducing the option of working in very low wage jobs that provide substantial training, the minimum wage may be impeding the upward economic mobility of immigrants.

As of January 1981 the basic federal minimum wage was raised to $3.35 per hour. The minimum employment cost exceeds the minimum wage because of several payroll taxes (social security, unemployment compensation, and worker's compensation) and mandated employer fringe benefits.

[29] The discussion in this section is based on a theoretical analysis developed in detail in Barry R. Chiswick, "The Effect of Immigrants on the Level and Distribution of Economic Well-Being," in Barry R. Chiswick, ed., *The Gateway: U.S. Immigration Issues and Policies* (Washington, D.C.: American Enterprise Institute, 1981).

of exposition, let us consider the implications of two polar cases—a cohort of low-skilled workers and a cohort of high-skilled workers.

The immigration of low-skilled workers reduces the marginal product of low-skilled native workers but raises the marginal product of high-skilled workers and capital. The former effect arises from the greater labor supply of low-skilled workers who are good substitutes in production for native low-skilled workers. The latter arises from the principle of complementarity, that the marginal product of a factor increases, the greater the quantity of other factors of production with which it works. Although one native factor loses and the other native factors gain, the overall income of the native population increases. That is, the losses to native low-skilled labor are more than offset by the gains to native high-skilled labor and capital. Thus, average income among the native population increases, but the distribution of this income becomes more unequal.

The increase in the aggregate and hence also the average income of the native population is in contrast to the decline in the average income of the total population (natives augmented by immigrants). This decline in the average income arises from the assumption that the low-skilled immigrants have lower incomes than the average of the native population. Thus, if the average income of the native population is a variable of primary interest for determining the appropriate immigration policy, changes in the average income of the total population (natives and immigrants) may be a misleading indicator.

The decline in the earnings of low-skilled native workers as a result of low-skilled immigration is partially mitigated by the income tax and the mix of income transfers. Many of the recipients of income-contingent transfers, particularly recipients of Aid to Families with Dependent Children (AFDC) and Supplemental Security Income (SSI), have little or no attachment to the labor market and hence do not suffer a direct adverse impact. Those who suffer a direct impact, the working poor, may be eligible for food stamps and Medicaid and, in single-parent families, AFDC, and if they become unemployed, for state unemployment compensation or AFDC-UP (unemployed parents' component of AFDC). Because the aggregate income of the native population has increased, at least in principle sufficient income can be transferred from the gainers (high-skilled workers and owners of capital) to the losers (native low-skilled workers), so that all groups among the native population are at least as well off as before the immigration.

A dilemma soon arises. By tradition as well as by law, legal immigrants (resident aliens) are eligible for the same income-transfer benefits as similarly situated natives.[30] The theoretical model indicates that if the low-skilled immigrants are to receive transfers that bring their incomes up to the preimmigration income of native low-skilled workers, the aggregate transfers will exceed the increase in income of high-skilled workers and capital. Thus, the native population as a whole can be made worse off.

Let us next consider the immigration of a cohort of high-skilled workers. The wages of native high-skilled workers decline, whereas the wages of native low-skilled workers and the returns to capital increase. The aggregate income, and hence the average income of the native population, increases. The change in the average income of the total population is ambiguous unless it is determined whether the high-skilled immigrants have a higher or lower average income than the income (earnings and return to capital) of the native population. The narrowing of skill differentials would appeal to those who favor smaller inequality in labor-market outcomes.

The rise in the wages of native low-skilled workers increases their tax payments and lowers their receipt of income-contingent transfers. By using these resources, as well as the higher taxes paid by capital, and the positive taxes paid by high-skilled immigrants, the marginal tax rates on the earnings of native high-skilled workers can be lowered. Thus, net of the tax-transfer system, high-skilled workers can be made at least as well off as before the immigration, without eliminating all of the gains of native low-skilled workers and capital. With high-skilled immigrants, equal treatment of immigrants and natives can be maintained in the income-transfer system, and all native groups can be made at least as well off as before the immigration.

Recent empirical research has examined the relation between the characteristics of immigrants and the earnings of the native-born.[31] The analysis has been done for adult white non-Hispanic native-born men, using the 1970 Census of Population. Holding constant the native-born person's human capital and demographic characteristics, weekly earnings among the native-born are higher the greater the level of schooling and labor-market experience of the foreign-born. In addition, using immigrants from the English-speaking developed countries as the benchmark, earnings among the native-born are affected the same way as by immigrants from Mexico, but are higher

---

[30] A recent exception (1980 amendments to the Social Security Act) limits the receipt of Supplemental Security Income benefits during the first three years in the United States unless an unanticipated disability arises after immigration. SSI provides cash benefits for low-income aged and disabled persons.

[31] Chiswick, "Estimating the Impact," part B.

the greater the proportion of immigrants from Europe and the smaller the proportion from Cuba and other countries. Thus, more highly skilled or more productive immigrants are associated with greater earnings among the native-born.

One concern that is often expressed is that immigrants can take advantage of society's investment in public capital. Immigrants use roads, schools, dams, and parks constructed prior to their immigration and "dilute" the public capital available to the native population, thereby decreasing the income of the native population. That is, even high-skilled immigrants would be substantial beneficiaries of income transfers broadly defined to include the consumption of public capital.[32] This point, however, confuses the timing of the construction of public capital with the financing of this capital. The construction of most public capital is financed not out of current tax receipts but rather out of bonds that are retired with revenues raised from user-fees (for example, highways, bridges) or taxes (for example, schools, parks) as the capital is consumed. To the extent that the public capital is paid for as it is consumed, immigrants do not gain, and there is no dilution of the natives' public capital even if it is constructed prior to the immigration.

Alternative Immigration Policies

The review of current U.S. policy showed that kinship is the primary criterion for rationing immigration visas and that the skills or productivity characteristics of visa applicants play a relatively minor role. The discussions of occupational distributions and earnings indicated that there is a considerable difference in the skill levels and earnings of immigrants admitted under kinship and under productivity criteria. The analysis of their impact showed that more favorable impacts on the level and distribution of income of the native population arise from higher-skilled immigrants than from lower-skilled immigrants.

This section reviews two very different approaches to the reform of immigration policy.[33] The first is a skill-based rationing system in which an applicant's skill level, and hence likely economic success in the United States, is the primary determinant of whether a visa is issued. A point system is proposed as the mechanism for administering the program. The second approach is the set of

---

[32] This is one of the arguments in Dan Usher, "Public Property and the Effects of Migration upon Other Residents of the Migrant's Countries of Origin and Destination," *Journal of Political Economy*, October 1977, pp. 1001-20.

[33] Policies regarding refugees and temporary (guest) workers are beyond the scope of this section.

recommendations from the Select Commission on Immigration and Refugee Policy for modifications of the current system. The commission's recommendations would apparently reduce the already small role of productivity characteristics in issuing immigration visas, would grant amnesty for illegal aliens, and would increase the relative and absolute number of low-skilled workers in future cohorts of immigrants.

A Skill-Based Rationing System. As an alternative to the current system, the focus of immigration policy could be radically shifted from kinship criteria to productivity characteristics. Under a productivity or skill-based policy, the primary criterion for rationing admissions would be the person's likely productivity in the United States.[34] Although additional research would be beneficial, research to date indicates that an immigrant's productivity, as measured by earnings and employment, appears to be related to the level and transferability of preimmigration skills, including level of schooling, vocational and on-the-job training, occupation, and knowledge of English. Prearranged employment may also be a favorable characteristic.

One temptation in a productivity-based immigration policy is to grant visas to applicants in narrowly defined occupations in which there are "shortages" and deny visas to applicants in "crowded" occupations. Indeed, in the occupational preferences in current immigration law, this approach has been adopted with absurd consequences. Physicians, nurses, physical therapists, and dieticians, among others, are added or withdrawn from the list of the most favored (Schedule A occupations) on the basis not of labor-market studies but of political pressures of interested parties. Studies are not done to determine whether other occupations, such as engineering, are in equally "short supply." The economic aspects of the issues, including the subsequent occupational adjustments of the immigrants and the change in the occupational structure of the native-born labor force as a consequence of immigration, appear to play no role in the rule-making process.

Visas granted on the basis of narrowly defined occupations invite efforts to subvert the system. How can we avoid the manipulation of a skill-based rationing system by narrow occupational interests? The more broadly defined the occupational categories, the more diffused the adverse impact from a cohort of immigrants and the smaller the incentive for any one occupation to attempt to close that category. Equally relevant, it is difficult for planners to know where

[34] Productivity or skill characteristics and a point system form the basis for rationing visas by Canada, Australia, and New Zealand.

there will be labor "shortages" and where there will be labor "surpluses" in the coming years. Even with this information, occupational adjustments occur not only through the immigration of persons in the occupation but also through the substantial occupational change of immigrants after they arrive in the United States, as well as through the occupational change of natives. The focus in a skill-based rationing system should be on skill level rather than on the applicant's narrowly defined occupation.

To combine the multidimensional aspects of skills into rationing criteria may necessitate the adoption of a point system rather than a preference system. Under a preference system, as formulated in current law, a person must meet a minimum standard under any one of several categories to be eligible for a visa. There is no possibility for combining equities under each of two or more categories to raise one's rank in the queue. On the other hand, under a point system it is the sum of points obtainable from several categories, rather than crossing a threshold in any one category, that is relevant.

A certain number of points could be earned for various productivity traits, and a visa would be issued to persons who satisfied a minimum number of points.[35] Each year of schooling completed may be worth, for example, two points. Apprenticeship training, vocational training, and relevant on-the-job training would also earn points for the candidate. Points could be earned, say on a scale of 0 to 5, for fluency in English, and other points could be received for prearranged employment. To preserve the nonracist character of immigration policy, points should not be granted on the basis of race, ethnicity, religion, or country of origin.[36]

[35] Persons exempt from the point system would be the immediate relatives (spouse and minor children) of U.S. citizens, refugees and their immediate relatives, and the immediate relatives of persons given an immigrant visa if they accompany the immigrant or come within, say, a year.

[36] Canada uses a point system similar to the one suggested here for persons who are not the immediate relatives of citizens. In addition to the criteria indicated in this section Canada gives points for the intention to settle in a geographic area the Canadian government wishes to populate. This policy is of limited effectiveness, as internal geographic mobility after immigration is not restricted. As specific residential location would also not be enforceable in the United States and as the United States does not have a clearly defined regional policy, this would appear to be an inappropriate criterion for U.S. policy. Indeed, efforts by the U.S. government to disperse the Indochinese refugees geographically have been ineffective; there has been substantial internal migration from the community of first settlement to California, their preferred state of residence. See Linda W. Gordon, "Settlement Patterns of Indochinese Refugees in the United States," *INS Reporter*, spring 1980, pp. 6-10.

For a description of the Canadian point system, see *New Directions: A Look at Canada's Immigration Act and Regulations*, Ottawa, Canada, Employment and Immigration, April 1978.

The evaluating of skills and the awarding of points should be the responsibility of a single agency, the immigration service. To have this function performed in either the Department of Labor or the Department of Commerce is to invite efforts by interest groups entrenched in either agency to subvert the system for their own purposes. As an independent agency the immigration service would be subject to influences from many sources and might be better able to steer a middle course.[37]

To reduce variations in the annual number of immigrants, a worldwide annual quota could be retained, with visas issued to those with the largest number of points among those who satisfy the threshold. To reduce some of the uncertainty as to when immigration will occur among those in the queue, additional points (that do not count toward the minimum threshold) might be given for waiting in the queue. Of course, if the queue gets too long, either the minimum-threshold number of points or the annual quota should be increased.

The point system can be flexible to provide greater immigration opportunities for persons with relatives in the United States. This should be done without violating the rationing system's concern for the economic impact of immigrants. Thus, a small number of points may be awarded, for example, to applicants with relatives in the United States who will guarantee their financial support for, say, a five-year period. In this manner persons who do not satisfy the general productivity criterion but whose presence is of "consumption value" to their relatives in this country would be more able to immigrate legally.

There is some historical experience for the implications of the change in immigration policy considered here for the occupational distribution of immigrants. In 1962 Canada shifted from a kinship-based immigration policy, not unlike current U.S. policy, to a system with kinship criteria for immediate relatives of Canadians and a primarily skill-based point system for others. The proportion of professional and technical workers among the immigrants increased from an annual average of 12 percent in 1956–1960 to an annual average of 26 percent in 1962–1971. The annual average proportion

---

[37] There is no compelling reason for immigration matters to be part of the Department of Justice. The immigration and naturalization functions are separable, and the latter may be an appropriate function for the Justice Department. As an independent agency the new immigration service would be less constrained by Justice Department interests in making its case for more resources for enforcement and would be in a better position to institute regulations and recommend policy changes based on overall economic considerations. The agency should not have cabinet status.

of unskilled workers declined from 36 percent in 1956–1960 to 16 percent in 1962–1971.[38]

It may be argued by some that the productivity criterion outlined above is antifamily, that is, that such a dramatic change from the current system would end the humanitarian goal of family reunification. This is not the situation. Foreigners with more kinsmen in the United States would still be more likely to apply for an immigrant visa, as coming to the United States is more attractive to them than to others in their home country. The immediate relatives of U.S. citizens would still be eligible for admission without numerical restrictions. For other applicants, those who have sufficient points to immigrate can do so and be "reunited" with family members. Those with kinsmen in the United States would have two advantages. Their relatives could help them prearrange employment, and they could guarantee the immigrant's financial support for the first five years. Willingness to engage in these activities is one test of the U.S. relative's interest in the immigration of kinsmen.[39]

There will be many who could immigrate under the current kinship criteria but not under the productivity criteria. The immigration of these persons is at the expense of the U.S. population, which accepts a less productive worker instead of a more productive worker without relatives already here. The largest adverse impact is experienced by native-born low-skilled workers who face greater competition in the labor market and in the allocation of income-contingent transfers from a larger number of low-skilled immigrants. The current system provides the largest benefits to the U.S. relatives of immigrants entering under kinship criteria, many of whom are themselves recent citizens and resident aliens.[40] This inequity would be removed under the productivity criteria.

[38] Louis Parai, "Canada's Immigration Policy: 1962-74," *International Migration Review* (winter 1975), pp. 469-472.

[39] Voluntary family dislocations that arise from economic migration are a less compelling reason for special "family reunification" visas than are the involuntary separations and dislocations often arising from situations that create refugees.

[40] The supporters of kinship preferences do not disagree with this interpretation. In an address before the American Committee on Italian Migration, Sen. Dennis DeConcini, a SCIRP commissioner, said: "Proposals have been offered to eliminate the 5th preference. It is felt by some to be too generous, as it refers to a horizontal rather than a vertical family concept. . . . But to deny that brothers and sisters are an integral part of the family is to impose upon many ethnic groups a narrow concept of family and one that especially discriminates against the Italian-Americans. We also should stress the rights of U.S. citizens by allowing them to bring their families to America. This view should precede the technical notion that we need certain types of specialists and skilled workers." Reported in American Committte on Italian Migration, *Immigration Update 1980—National Symposium* (New York, 1980).

There would be more broadly based political support for admitting a larger number of immigrants each year under a skill-based rationing system than under the current kinship system. This would arise from the more favorable impact of immigration on both the level and distribution of income. The extent to which the optimal number of immigrants would increase as a consequence of the change in criteria is an empirical question that warrants further study.

The SCIRP Recommendations. The Select Commission on Immigration and Refugee Policy (SCIRP), created by an act of Congress in 1978, released its recommendations in February 1981.[41] The commission's recommendations focused on a modification of the preference system for legal immigrants, amnesty for illegal aliens in the United States, and policies to control future illegal immigration. The apparent thrust of the commission's recommendations is to increase the role of kinship and decrease the already small role of skill or productivity in rationing immigration visas, to increase immigration of low-productivity workers, and to shift much of the burden of the enforcement of immigration law to employers through a requirement that they screen all workers for their legal status.

SCIRP recommended retaining the current policy of allowing immigration without numerical limit for the spouses, minor unmarried children, and parents of adult citizens. It recommended adding adult unmarried children (currently the first preference) and grandparents of adult citizens to the exempt list. Under current regulations there is little binding constraint on first-preference visa applicants from most countries, with Mexico being the main exception.[42]

The commission endorsed a worldwide numerical limit and country quotas for other relatives and "independent immigrants." The recommended worldwide limit is 350,000 visas per year, with an additional 100,000 visas per year for five years to reduce the number of "active immigrant visa applications," that is, the visa backlog.[43]

---

[41] Select Commission on Immigration and Refugee Policy, *U.S. Immigration Policy and the National Interest*, March 1, 1981 (hereafter designated "SCIRP").

[42] As of January 1, 1980, Mexican nationals were 38 percent of the first-preference visa backlog (SCIRP, table 9).

[43] As of January 1, 1980, there was a backlog of 1.1 million visa applications, an increase of 100,000 over the previous year (SCIRP, table 9, p. 146). The commissioners called for reducing the visa backlog as quickly as possible. Although no formal vote was taken, the report notes that "many commissioners are of the view that per-country and preference ceilings—although applied to new applicants under the proposed system—should not apply to those in the backlogs" (SCIRP, p. 150). Much of the backlog is concentrated in a small number of countries—Mexico, 25 percent; Philippines, 23 percent; Korea, 7 percent. The backlog exists

The categories for other relatives would consist of the current second, fourth, and fifth preferences (see table 1), as well as a new category, the unmarried adult children of resident aliens. It further recommended that a "substantial" number of visas be set aside for the spouses and unmarried (minor or adult) children of resident aliens, that there be no country ceilings for the spouses and minor children of resident aliens, and that these visas should be issued on a first-come, first-served basis. The second-preference country ceiling is severely binding only for Mexico. As of November 1980, second-preference applications by Mexican nationals filed in October 1974 were at the top of the queue.[44] The recommendations regarding the current second preference are related to the commission's proposal of amnesty.

The independent immigrant category, which would replace current occupational and nonpreference categories, is viewed by SCIRP as a means of creating new kinship immigration streams ("new seed" immigrants) rather than as a mechanism for selecting workers with the greatest productivity in the United States: "It is the Commission's hope that this category will provide immigration opportunities for those persons who come from countries where immigration to the United States has not been recent or from countries that have no immigration base here."[45] The independent category includes a numerically limited number of persons with "exceptional merit and ability in their professions." Still, SCIRP writes: "The Commission's intent is not to provide a separate category for highly trained or needed professionals (for example, nurses, doctors, engineers), artists or other persons of merit unless they are exceptional and qualify under specific established guidelines. . . . (T)he Commission further cautions against the creation of a significant channel which could deprive other nations of the highly skilled persons they need."[46] A

primarily in the kinship preferences and nonpreference categories (5 percent in the second preference, 50 percent in the fifth preference, 26 percent in the nonpreference category), with only 7 percent in the occupational preferences, primarily Philippines, China, India, Korea (SCIRP, table 9).

[44] The second-preference visas were current (no backlog) overall and for all other independent countries, with the exception of China (April 1980) and the Philippines (October 1978). *Immigrant Numbers for December 1980*, Visa Service, U.S. Department of State, vol. 5, no. 3.

[45] SCIRP, p. 16.

[46] SCIRP, p. 130. The commission's view regarding the immigration of professionals is exemplified by its statement on nurses: "The Commission concludes that the continuing shortage of practicing nurses in the United States justifies the admission of foreign nurses while the shortage continues, but urges that efforts be intensified to make nursing a more attractive career to induce more inactive U.S. nurses to return to that profession" (SCIRP, p. 223).

presumably somewhat larger category of other independent migrants is also proposed to "allow the entry of persons without family ties in the United States and of persons whose family ties are distant. . . . One *possible* benefit will be the increased proportion of immigrants screened for labor market impact which will both protect U.S. workers and enhance economic growth."[47]

SCIRP recommended amnesty for illegal aliens in the United States as of January 1, 1981. Once given an adjustment of status, these persons could serve as sponsors for their relatives. Amnesty would increase the number of low-skilled workers in the United States in three ways. First, the prospect of amnesty would encourage the illegal migration of other low-skilled workers with the expectation that, once granted, amnesty would be offered repeatedly; indeed, illegal immigration increased sharply when President Carter made his proposal for amnesty in 1977. Second, amnesty would substantially increase the demand for immigration visas by the spouses and children of those given amnesty, and many of these would soon enter the labor market. The recommendations mentioned above for more favorable treatment of this category of immigrant, especially for Mexican nationals, would allow the system to satisfy much of this increased demand for visas. Third, many illegal aliens who return home during periods of seasonal and cyclical slack in employment would remain in the United States, as their families would be with them and they could legally receive income transfers.

SCIRP proposes to control future illegal immigration through increased resources for border enforcement and employer sanctions. The commission favors border enforcement over interior enforcement by the immigration authorities; "It is both more humane and cost-effective to deter people from entering the United States than it is to locate and remove them from the interior."[48] As noted above, however, border enforcement may be more cost effective per apprehension, but it is not necessarily more cost effective per deterred alien. A recommendation is made for a "substantial increase" in funding and personnel for the border patrol, but no parallel recommendation exists for interior enforcement. There are no recommendations for penalties other than deportation against apprehended illegal aliens, even for those who engage in flagrant and frequent violations of the law. SCIRP also endorsed the ruling by the attorney general that "state and local law enforcement officers should be prohibited from apprehending persons on immigration charges, except in alien

[47] SCIRP, p. 135, italics added.
[48] SCIRP, p. 47.

344

smuggling cases."[49] This ruling limits the scope for effective interior enforcement.

In spite of this hands-off policy for official law enforcement agents, the commission endorsed civil penalties against employers who knowingly employ illegal aliens and criminal penalties against those employers who engage in "flagrant and extended violations of the law following the imposition of civil penalties."[50] The commission was vague as to the mechanism through which employers could verify a worker's legal status; they "support a means of verifying employee eligibility that will allow employers to confidently and easily hire those persons who may legally accept employment."[51] The report does not indicate the magnitude of these costs of employee verification, their effects on the employment opportunities of high-turnover, low-skilled American workers, or whether such verification is feasible without a national identity card. Employer sanctions are not likely to reduce employment opportunities for illegal aliens without both a reasonably fool-proof means of checking a person's legal right to work and vigorous internal enforcement.

Although there is much public concern about the use of welfare and subsidized medical care by illegal aliens, the commission did not offer any recommendations on this issue. It did not, for example, endorse or even vote on proposals that have been made to alter current regulations of the Department of Health and Human Services that bar welfare and other public aid agencies from reporting suspected illegal aliens to the immigration authorities. Indeed, it is curious that SCIRP endorsed extending the burden of enforcement to employers while favoring the current restrictions on referrals by state and local law enforcement authorities and welfare agencies.

The overall thrust of SCIRP's policy recommendations is to increase both the number and proportion of low-skilled immigrants while decreasing the number of high-skilled immigrants. This emphasis presumably arises from the commission's concern for "global inequities"[52] and what appears to be a desire to increase immigration from Mexico substantially. In nearly every instance recommended modifications of current policy would favor Mexican immigrants over immigrants from other countries. These policies would deprive the United States of many highly productive foreign workers, depress the earnings of low-skilled American workers, and result in increased

[49] SCIRP, pp. 256-257.
[50] SCIRP, pp. 63-64.
[51] SCIRP, p. 67.
[52] SCIRP, p. 20.

taxes to pay for an expanded income-transfer system. The economic impacts of its recommendations on the United States appear to have been of minor concern to the commission.[53]

Conclusion

Immigration will continue to play an important role in American economic life. The public policy issue is not simply whether immigration per se is beneficial but rather whether increased benefits to the United States can be obtained from changes in the number of immigrants and the rationing criteria. In an era (such as the nineteenth century) when public policy showed little regard for the income-distribution impacts of immigration and when there were no public income-transfer systems to mitigate the losses to groups for whom the impact was adverse, an open-door or laissez-faire immigration policy was politically acceptable. These conditions no longer prevail, and an open-door immigration policy is not a politically viable alternative. If there are to be limits on immigration, there must be a rationing mechanism. A rationing mechanism that would provide a more rapid growth in the income of the native population and a relatively smaller income-transfer system is generally to be preferred to one that offers opposite effects.

Current immigration policy is characterized by a rationing system that is based on kinship and by lax enforcement of immigration law. This policy has resulted in a relatively larger number of low-skilled immigrants than would have been here if the rationing criteria had focused on the level of skill. The Select Commission on Immigration and Refugee Policy would apparently further increase the role of kinship and decrease the already small role for the productivity characteristics or skills of the visa applicants. Rather than endorsing a major strengthening of the enforcement of current immigration law, the select commission proposes legalizing the status of illegal aliens in the United States and shifting much of the enforcement responsibilities to employers through sanctions on those who employ illegal aliens. The commissioners equivocated, however, on the crucial issue of how employer sanctions were to be administered. Also, they did not address the adverse impact of the additional cost of employer screening of workers on employment opportunities for native workers in low-wage, high-turnover jobs.

[53] This was perhaps foreshadowed by the commission's research agenda, which virtually ignored research on illegal aliens and the labor-market impacts of immigrants. See SCIRP, appendix G, pp. 432-437.

As an alternative, a two-pronged policy approach could be adopted. One prong would be the more stringent enforcement of current immigration law, not only at the border but also in the interior. Under this approach there would be no blanket amnesty for illegal aliens, and the responsibility for enforcing immigration law would not be shifted to employers. The second prong would involve shifting the focus in rationing visas from kinship to the applicant's level of skill. As skill is not unidimensional, a point system should be adopted to combine the diverse elements into a single number. With the exception of the immediate relatives of adult U.S. citizens, whose entry would not be subject to numerical limitations, visas would be issued to those with the greatest number of points, that is, to those with the greatest likely productivity in the United States. Points could also be given for less immediate kinship relationships, but this should not be allowed to overwhelm the productivity criteria. These proposals would better satisfy the twin objectives of increasing the productive potential of the economy and reducing the relative size of the income transfer system than would either the current system or the select commission's recommendations.

CONTRIBUTORS

William Fellner—*Project Director*

Sterling Professor of Economics emeritus at Yale University, former member of the Council of Economic Advisers, and past president of the American Economic Association. Resident scholar with the American Enterprise Institute.

Phillip Cagan

Professor of economics at Columbia University and former senior staff economist for the Council of Economic Advisers. Adjunct and visiting scholar with the American Enterprise Institute.

Colin D. Campbell

Loren M. Berry Professor of Economics at Dartmouth College. Director of social security and retirement policy studies and adjunct scholar with the American Enterprise Institute.

Barry R. Chiswick

Research professor, Department of Economics and Survey Research Laboratory, University of Illinois at Chicago Circle, and former senior staff economist for the Council of Economic Advisers. Adjunct scholar with the American Enterprise Institute.

Gottfried Haberler

Galen L. Stone Professor of International Trade emeritus at Harvard University, and past president of the American Economic Association and International Economic Association. Resident scholar with the American Enterprise Institute.

D. Gale Johnson

Eliakim Hastings Moore Distinguished Service Professor of Economics at the University of Chicago, and past president of the American Farm Economics Association. Member of the Council of Academic Advisers and adjunct scholar with the American Enterprise Institute.

John W. Kendrick

Professor of economics at The George Washington University. Former chief economist, U.S. Department of Commerce, and vice-president for economic research, the Conference Board. Director of the special project on productivity and adjunct scholar with the American Enterprise Institute.

Geoffrey H. Moore

Director of the Center for International Business Cycle Research on the Newark Campus of Rutgers University, research associate emeritus of the National Bureau of Economic Research, and former U.S. commissioner of labor statistics. Adjunct scholar with the American Enterprise Institute.

Mark Perlman

University professor of economics at the University of Pittsburgh and adjunct scholar with the American Enterprise Institute.

Herbert Stein

A. Willis Robertson Professor of Economics at the University of Virginia, former chairman of the Council of Economic Advisers, and former vice-president and chief economist of the Committee for Economic Development. Member of the Council of Academic Advisers and senior fellow with the American Enterprise Institute.

A NOTE ON THE BOOK

*The typeface used for the text of this book is
Palatino, designed by Hermann Zapf.
The type was set by
Hendricks-Miller Typographic Company, of Washington.
Everybodys Press of Hanover, Pennsylvania, printed
and bound the book, using Warren's Olde Style paper.
The cover and format were designed by Pat Taylor,
and the figures were drawn by Hördur Karlsson.
The manuscript was edited by
Marcia Brubeck and others and
by Margaret Seawell of the AEI Publications staff.*

SELECTED AEI PUBLICATIONS

Contemporary Economic Problems 1980
William Fellner, project director. $9.25
Studies by Fellner, Phillip Cagan, Herbert Stein, Rudolph G. Penner, Gott-
fried Haberler, Geoffrey H. Moore, Jack A. Meyer, Mark Perlman, Barry R.
Chiswick, and D. Gale Johnson.

Contemporary Economic Problems 1979
William Fellner, project director. $9.25
Studies by Fellner, Herbert Stein, John W. Kendrick, Edward F. Denison,
Mark Perlman, Phillip Cagan, Marvin H. Kosters, Gottfried Haberler,
D. Gale Johnson, Walter J. Mead, Barry R. Chiswick, Geoffrey H. Moore.

The AEI Economist
Herbert Stein, editor. $1 per issue; one year $10
A monthly newsletter on issues of economic policy.

Regulation: The AEI Journal on Government and Society
Antonin Scalia, editor; Anne Brunsdale, managing editor. $2.50 per issue;
one year, $12; two years, $22
A bimonthly magazine devoted to examining the policy implications of
regulation in all its manifestations, in a readable style.

AEI ASSOCIATES PROGRAM

The American Enterprise Institute invites your participation in the competition of ideas through its AEI Associates Program. This program has
two objectives:

The first is to broaden the distribution of AEI studies, conferences, forums,
and reviews, and thereby to extend public familiarity with the issues. AEI
Associates receive regular information on AEI research and programs, and
they can order publications and cassettes at a savings.

The second objective is to increase the research activity of the American
Enterprise Institute and the dissemination of its published materials to
policy makers, the academic community, journalists, and others who help
shape public attitudes. Your contribution, which in most cases is partly tax
deductible, will help ensure that decision makers have the benefit of
scholarly research on the practical options to be considered before programs
are formulated. The issues studied by AEI include:

- Defense Policy
- Economic Policy
- Energy Policy
- Foreign Policy
- Government Regulation

- Health Policy
- Legal Policy
- Political and Social Processes
- Social Security and Retirement Policy
- Tax Policy

For more information, write to: **American Enterprise Institute**
1150 Seventeenth Street, N.W., Washington, D.C. 20036